MONTICELLO

Dominion of Memories

ALSO BY SUSAN DUNN

Something That Will Surprise the World:
The Essential Writings of the Founding Fathers (ed., 2006)

Jefferson's Second Revolution:
The Election Crisis of 1800 and the Triumph of Republicanism (2004)

George Washington (with James MacGregor Burns, 2004)

The Social Contract and *The First and Second Discourses,*
by Jean-Jacques Rousseau (ed., 2002)

The Three Roosevelts: Patrician Leaders Who Transformed America
(with James MacGregor Burns, 2001)

Sister Revolutions: French Lightning, American Light (1999)

Diversity and Citizenship: New Challenges for American Nationhood
(ed., with Gary J. Jacobsohn, 1996)

The Deaths of Louis XVI:
Regicide and the French Political Imagination (1994)

Dominion of Memories

Jefferson, Madison, and
the Decline of Virginia

SUSAN DUNN

A Member of the Perseus Books
New York

Monticello photo courtesy of the Manuscript Print Collection Department, University of Virginia.

Published by Basic Books,
A Member of the Perseus Books Group

Books published by Basic Books are available at special discounts for bulk purchases in the United States by corporations, institutions, and other organizations. For more information, please contact the Special Markets Department at the Perseus Books Group, 11 Cambridge Center, Cambridge, MA 02142, or call (617) 252-5298 or (800) 255-1514, or e-mail special.markets@perseusbooks.com.

Designed by Brent Wilcox

Library of Congress Cataloging-in-Publication Data
Dunn, Susan, 1945-
    Dominion of memories : Jefferson, Madison, and the decline of Virginia /
Susan Dunn.
        p.   cm.
    Includes bibliographical references and index.
    ISBN-13: 978-0-465-01743-0 (alk. paper)
    ISBN-10: 0-465-01743-6 (alk. paper)
    1. Virginia—History—1775-1865.   2. Virginia—Politics and government—
1775-1865.   3. Virginia—Social conditions.   4. Elite (Social sciences)—Virginia—
History—18th century.   5. Elite (Social sciences)—Virginia—History—
19th century.   6. Regionalism—Virginia—History—18th century.   7. Regionalism—
Virginia—History—19th century.   8. Virginia—Economic conditions.   9. Jefferson,
Thomas, 1743-1826—Political and social views.   10. Madison, James, 1751-1836—
Political and social views.   I. Title.
    F230.D86 2007
    975.5'03—dc22
                                                                    2007001452

10 9 8 7 6 5 4 3 2 1

For Jim

CONTENTS

Prologue   1

1   The Cult of the Soil   15

2   The Cankers of Indolence and Slavery   31

3   "Let Us Have Our Own Schools"   61

4   Roads, Canals, Railroads: Moving in Place   85

5   Deluded Citizens Clamoring for Banks   113

6   The Case of *Virginia v. John Marshall*   133

7   Another Constitutional Convention   149

8   Tariff Wars   171

9   Abolitionists and Other Enemies   191

Epilogue: Jefferson and Virginia, a Hundred Years Later   213

Notes   225

Acknowledgments   289

Index   291

Prologue

In the late autumn of 1824, Thomas Jefferson made his way slowly down the steps of his home, quickening his pace as he approached his friend, the Marquis de Lafayette. The two men had not seen each other for more than three decades. "Let me once more have the happiness of talking over with you," Jefferson had expectantly written to Lafayette a few months earlier, "your first labors here, those I witnessed in your own country, its past & present afflictions and future hopes."

On the steps of Monticello, the two old friends embraced and wept as American dignitaries and Lafayette's official entourage of cavalry looked on. The "Nation's Guest," Lafayette had recently begun an official, ceremonial tour of all twenty-four states, enthralling all who saw him. He found the eighty-one-year-old Jefferson "much aged" but "marvelously well" and "in full possession of all the vigor of his mind and heart." At sunset, just as they were finishing dessert, James Madison, now seventy-four years old, joined them. Madison later commented that Lafayette appeared in fine health and spirits but so much increased in bulk and changed in aspect that he hardly recognized him.

Jefferson seemed happiest discussing the new university he had founded only a few miles away and the banquet to be held there to celebrate the opening of the Rotunda, the majestic building housing the library. At that banquet, Lafayette sat between Madison and Jefferson; Madison charmed the guests with his affectionate toast to Lafayette. Afterward, they all toured the campus. Jefferson showed them the Rotunda and the classical pavilions he had designed and shared his hope of

1

attracting eminent professors from Europe to the school. Before leaving the new University of Virginia, Lafayette's son, George Washington Lafayette, was delighted to receive an unusual gift from a professor: a Virginia rattlesnake.

Lafayette lingered for ten more days at Jefferson's gracious estate. As they strolled around the grounds, rode their horses side by side, and dined together, sipping Jefferson's excellent French wines, they reminisced about the astonishing revolutions they had helped lead. "What a history have we to run over," Jefferson said. They revived memories of the evenings they had spent together in Paris in 1789, when Jefferson was the American minister to France and Lafayette one of the early leaders of the French Revolution. Jefferson mentioned the American presidential election—among five candidates, all from the same party—taking place that autumn, but declined to express his feelings about the candidates.

The conversation took a sociological turn as Lafayette pondered the differences he already perceived between North and South. Having just visited the "delightfully situated" New Haven, the "beautiful village" of Cambridge in Massachusetts, and the bustling, dynamic city of New York, Lafayette and his secretary, Auguste Levasseur, could not but notice, "at every step," the relative backwardness and poverty of Virginia. It had taken them six hours to travel the 25 miles from Richmond to Petersburg. Along the way, they saw isolated towns, sleepy villages, and signs of depleted soil. The cause seemed only too clear to them, as did the remedy. Only when Virginia comprehended "her true interests better" and abolished slavery, Levasseur believed, would it catch up to the Northeast.

Slavery: the inescapable subject to which Jefferson and Lafayette returned again and again. Lafayette "never missed an opportunity to defend the right which *all men without exception* have to liberty," Levasseur commented, and Jefferson himself could not condone the indefinite perpetuation of slavery. One of Jefferson's slaves, Israel Jefferson, overhearing Lafayette and his master discuss the condition of the "colored" people, later wrote that the conversation was "gratifying to me and I treasured it up in my heart." Indeed, Jefferson found it difficult to grasp how an American patriot could "inflict on his fellow men a bondage, one hour of which is fraught with more misery than ages of that which he rose in rebellion to oppose."

And yet, the Virginian had neither freed his slaves nor recognized the children he had fathered with one of them, Sally Hemings. Nor had he played an active public role in opposing slavery. He had penned the very words—about the "unalienable rights" of the individual to life, liberty, and the pursuit of happiness—that had become the foundation of American civic morality, but he did not extend those rights and that dignity to slaves. Indeed, to the extent that Jefferson gave serious thought to solutions to the wrenching problem of slavery, he was more concerned with rescuing white people from the moral degeneration of slaveholding than with securing freedom for blacks.

Lafayette did not hide his impatience. While politely praising Jefferson's plan for the deportation of blacks to colonies in the Caribbean and on the African coast, he implored his friend to go further than wishful thinking, reminding him of "the importance and urgency" of emancipation. "I would like, before I die," Lafayette had written Jefferson two years earlier, "to be assured that progressive and earnest measures have been adopted to attain in due time, so desirable, so necessary an object. Prudence as well as honor seems to me to require it."

In August 1825, Lafayette returned to bid a final farewell to Jefferson, Madison, and James Monroe. This time, Jefferson was too weak to attend another banquet at the university. "These partings and many others are very painful," Lafayette wrote in his memoirs, sensing that it was the sunset of his friend's life.

It was also the sunset of the Virginia Dynasty. Four of the first five American presidents had been Virginians; but after Monroe, only one other Virginian—John Tyler—would occupy the presidency. Tyler would ascend to the presidency in 1841; when he died two decades later, it was as a member of the Confederate Provisional Congress and as a citizen of the Confederate States of America.

Virginia's eclipse was visible on the United States Supreme Court, too. Four Virginians, led by the great Chief Justice John Marshall, served on the high court during the first decades of the young republic. But between 1841 and 1971, when Lewis Powell was appointed, only one Virginian would occupy a seat on the Court: Peter Daniel, who voted with the majority in the Dred Scott case that helped precipitate the Civil War.

By that time, the days when intrepid, daring Virginians had led thirteen backwater colonies in a war against the mightiest power on the planet had become a distant memory, and their fiery patriotism a dying ember.

The delegates streaming into Philadelphia in September 1774 for the First Continental Congress were eager to meet the gentlemen from Virginia. They were "the most spirited" of all the delegates, John Adams noted in his diary. "We all look up to Virginia for examples." Next to the Virginians, said one Pennsylvanian, in a comment Adams might not have appreciated, "the Bostonians are mere Milksops." In truth, it was the delegates from Massachusetts who formed the avant-garde of the revolutionary movement. But recognizing that the participation of Virginia, the most populous colony, was indispensable, they showed appropriate and sincere deference to the leaders from the Old Dominion. "I look back with rapture to those golden days," wrote John Adams to Jefferson a year before they both died, "when Virginia and Massachusetts lived and acted together like a band of brothers."

Indeed, the Virginians did not disappoint. Passionately demanding independence, penning unforgettable words, demonstrating their courage, they helped make the revolutionary movement a national one. At the Constitutional Convention in 1787, their ideas would dominate the agenda. No other state played as prominent a role in shaping the young republic. No other state produced such a galaxy of brilliant, forward-looking, transforming leaders: not just George Washington, Thomas Jefferson, James Madison, James Monroe, and John Marshall, but also George Mason, who framed the Virginia Bill of Rights; Patrick Henry, who issued the call in 1774 for a continental congress; George Wythe, jurist, teacher, and signer of the Declaration of Independence; Peyton Randolph, president of the First Continental Congress; Edmund Pendleton, president of the state convention of 1776 that drew up a constitution for the Old Dominion as well as president of the Virginia Ratifying Convention of 1788; Edmund Randolph, governor of Virginia, delegate to the Philadelphia Convention, and Washington's attorney general. The Virginians, wrote Henry Adams, were "equal to any standard of excellence known to history." They created a nation.

The other states, surpassed by Virginia in wealth and influence as well as size and population (a fifth of the people in the colonies lived there), almost took it for granted that Virginia would be their leader. During thirty-two of the first thirty-six years of constitutional government, the Old Dominion had a monopoly on the executive branch of government. Of course, in the presidential election of 1796, Virginians George Washington and especially John Marshall had opposed Thomas Jefferson, disagreeing with his philosophy of limited government and his agrarian vision for the nation's future. Instead they supported their fellow Federalist John Adams. But after Adams's one term in office and Jefferson's ascension to the presidency in 1800, Virginians returned to the executive mansion. By 1816, some people wondered if Virginians would forever occupy the presidency. Was Virginia unstoppable?

Virginians seemed to have hatched, as one disquieted politician asserted, "a systematic design of perpetually governing the country." Indeed, many Americans were convinced that it was the unstated policy of the Virginia presidents to block the political rise of any potential rival who might threaten their dynasty. Conspiracy theories circulated from North Carolina to New York. Some suspected that Jefferson chose New York governor George Clinton, already advanced in age, as his vice president in 1804 so that Secretary of State James Madison would be his unchallenged successor in 1808. And when President Madison appointed the talented young John Quincy Adams to serve as minister to Russia in 1809, shipping him off to the other side of the world, people surmised that it was a maneuver to assure the continued dominance of the Virginians. Wouldn't Americans balk at electing James Monroe, Lord Liverpool asked John Quincy Adams at a London dinner party in 1816, "on account of his being a Virginian?"

By then, people in the North and South, Republicans no less than Federalists, were demanding a change. Anti-Virginia Republicans, including Albert Gallatin, treasury secretary to both Jefferson and Madison, rallied around other candidates in 1816—New York Governor Daniel Tompkins and Secretary of War William Crawford of Georgia. Some politicians even called for a constitutional amendment to "wrest the sovereignty of the union out of the hands" of the Old Dominion and prevent any one state from dominating the presidency. But neither caucuses, nor political maneuvers, nor backroom machinations could block Monroe's nomination and election in 1816 and again in 1820. "That nothing less than a Virginian will satisfy Virginia is to me perfectly demonstrated," wrote John Quincy Adams in his diary in 1818.

Still, the real danger, according to Supreme Court Justice Joseph Story of Massachusetts, lay not in Monroe's election, or even in Virginia's hold on the presidency, but rather in the contagion of its doctrine of states' rights. Virginians, including Thomas Jefferson, had recently denounced several Supreme Court decisions, claiming that the federal judiciary had no constitutional authority to overturn state statutes or the judgments of state courts. Their insistence on the sovereignty of their state, on states' rights, and on strict limits on the powers of the federal government terrified Justice Story. "As a republican & a lover of the Union," Story wrote in 1821 to John Marshall, who shared his nationalist views, "I look with alarm upon [Virginia's] opinions & conduct. I would rather allow her the *exclusive possession of the Executive power for a half century* than witness the prevalence in other States of any of her new constitutional dogmas. If they prevail, in my judgment there is a practical end of the Union."

George Washington would surely have agreed with Story and Marshall. More than half a century earlier, Washington had already criticized the provincialism of his fellow Virginians. "Our Views [are] too confined," he had written in 1770. The first president always encouraged Americans to adopt a national perspective, to see that "our interest, however diversified in local & smaller matters, is the same in all the great & essential concerns of the Nation." Especially in the late 1780s and 1790s, he was disappointed to find among Virginians "the most malignant (and if one may be allowed the expression, the most unwarrantable) disposition toward the new government." His own people, Washington lamented, identified only with their own state; cool to his great vision of a unified nation and an energetic, dynamic government, they refused to follow his lead.

Joseph Story did not exaggerate the dangers of Virginia's doubts about the national government and its retreat into the domain of states' rights. In fact, James Madison himself would later forcefully and unequivocally condemn the growing states' rights movement. Though he had toyed with states' rights in 1798, toward the end of his life Madison came to view Virginia's determination to defend its sovereignty against the national government not only as a real threat to the Union but, just as important, also as a convenient pretext for refusing to face and address the state's escalating economic and moral woes. Madison had named Story to the U.S. Supreme Court in 1811 even though Jefferson had warned him against the appointment, branding Story a "tory." Now, echoing Justice Story, Madison predicted that the states' rights doctrine would ultimately poison and divide the nation. What he did not predict was that violence would become the only mediator between North and South.

But as for northerners' apprehension about Virginia's hold on the presidency, the growing anti-Virginia contingents need not have worried. After Monroe, the Virginia Dynasty—as well as the state itself—would reach an abrupt dead-end.

Virginia had been one of the few states to prosper during the early 1780s under the Articles of Confederation. But forty years later, signs of that prosperity had disappeared. Crops had failed, and Virginia planters could not pay their debts, for there were no buyers to purchase their depleted land.

"The times are hard indeed," wrote James Madison to a young friend in 1820. The former president had been excited to return home to Montpelier in 1817, relieved to give up the cares and responsibilities of public life. James Paulding, who accompanied him part way home on a steamboat on the Potomac, later wrote that "during the voyage he was as playful as a child; talked and joked with everybody on board, and reminded me of a schoolboy on a long vacation." Jefferson, too, congratulated Madison on his return to his books and farm, to tranquility and independence. "A day of these," Jefferson said, was "worth ages" of public life.

But Madison found little tranquility back at Montpelier, his vast 5,000-acre estate. By 1826, he had suffered a succession of crop failures and was falling deeply into debt. A turnpike company he had invested in went bankrupt. He desperately needed the enjoyment and relaxation he found in discussing philosophy and in recounting anecdotes about children's sayings and doings. Still, another friend remarked that during his retirement, Madison looked "as if he never had been young, so thoughtful was his brow."

In 1827, Virginia Congressman James Mercer Garnett lamented the dramatic decline of his state. "Virginia—poor Virginia furnishes a spectacle at present, which is enough to make the heart of her real friends sick to the very core." With the state's agriculture nearly gone to ruin, the situation could not have been more destructive, he grieved, "if destruction had been its sole objective."

Over the next decades, the desolation of much of the Virginia countryside would sadden visitors to the Old Dominion. Even the grand homes of Washington and Jefferson would fall into disrepair. At Monticello, all was "dilapidation and ruin," wrote the visiting William Barry, the nation's postmaster general, in 1832. Newspaper editor Horace Greeley reported in 1856 that all of Mount Vernon had "an aspect of forlorn neediness which no description can adequately paint." Had Mount Vernon been situated in Massachusetts, wrote a shocked reporter from Boston, "how the spot would be treasured in our hearts, and beautified by our hands!"

Dispiriting scenes of poverty and cruelty disheartened William Seward, the soon-to-be governor of New York, and his wife when they visited Virginia with their young son in 1835. Frances Seward described ten naked little boys being led to a slave auction, "tied together, two and two, by their wrists, all fastened to a long rope, and followed by a tall, gaunt white man, who, with his long lash, whipped up the sad and weary little procession." Sick of slavery and the South, the Sewards cut short their tour and returned home.

A decade later, Frederick Law Olmsted, the writer, landscape architect, and sociologist of the South, left his farm in New York State to visit eastern Virginia. He described the poverty and dejection he observed. "The mass of the citizen class of Virginia earn very little and are very poor," he wrote, "immeasurably poorer than the mass of the people of the adjoining Free States." Peering into houses and inspecting farms, Olmsted found that everything was "slovenly and dirty," with swine, dogs, and black and white children "lying very promiscuously together on the ground about the doors." There were few signs of industry—one tannery and two or three sawmills in one 75-mile stretch; never had he seen so little evidence of an active and prosperous people.

As he traveled from the Alleghenies to the banks of the James River, Olmsted almost never saw a volume of Shakespeare, a piano, a sheet of music, a reading lamp, an engraving, or a copy of a work of art. "I am not speaking of what are commonly called 'poor whites,'" he explained. "A large majority of all these houses were the residences of slaveholders."

Methodically, Olmsted set about compiling and comparing statistics about life in the North and South. Whereas there was a post office to every 14 square miles in New York, in Virginia there was only one to 47 square miles; he counted more than 500 publishers and booksellers in New York, but only 40 in Virginia; 800,000 volumes in public libraries in New York, but 30,000 in Virginia. Land in Virginia, he noted, produced less than one-eighth as much per acre as in the Northeast.

The Old Dominion had fallen from the first to the fifth most populous state, as a steady stream of Virginians—whites searching for better lives, slaves accompanying their masters or sold out of state—abandoned the state. During the 1830s, while the nation's population increased by 33 percent, Virginia's population increased a meager 2 percent.

Voting statistics revealed a population of slumbering citizens, demoralized and passive. In the election of 1800, when native son Thomas Jefferson challenged Federalist John Adams, only 25 percent of eligible voters in Virginia cast ballots. In 1804, when Jefferson ran for reelection, 11 percent voted. By 1820, when Monroe ran for reelection, only the smallest fraction—a mere 3 percent—of eligible voters bothered to go to the polls.

Nor did Virginia keep up with other states in the field of education. Illiteracy among whites was four times higher in the Old Dominion than in New England and the mid-Atlantic states. Wealthy Virginians, historically averse to taxation, refused to support public schools.

Economic indicators were also ominous. The value of farm land in Virginia was less than one-third of what it was in adjoining Pennsylvania. In areas of Virginia where there were few slaves, with a white-to-black ratio of 15 to 1, the value of land was over $7 an acre, but where the white-to-black ratio was only 2.2 to 1, the value was $4.50 an acre.

Trade, too, was in decline. In 1800, while the exports of a relatively small state like Massachusetts were valued at $11 million, Virginia's were worth $4.5 million. By 1853, Massachusetts' exports totaled $16 million, and Virginia's had sunk to $3 million—less than half that of Maryland, one of the smallest exporters in the nation. Meanwhile, in the 1850s, the cotton exports of the Deep South accounted for almost half of the nation's foreign shipments, creating "flush times" in Alabama and Mississippi.

"We slight the warnings of dull statistics and drive lazily along the field of ancient customs," commented one Virginian in 1852, adding that other states "glide past us on the road to wealth and empire." Bewildered Virginians could see their power ebbing, their influence almost extinct, their cherished way of life vanishing. "Nothing can be more melancholy," congressman John Randolph of Roanoke wailed, "than the aspect of the whole country in Tidewater—dismantled country seats, ruinous churches, fields forsaken."

Even Virginia's aristocracy seemed to be deteriorating morally as well as economically. John Randolph's own brother Richard, deeply in debt, obliged to sell the family plantation, was accused of murdering the infant child he was said to have fathered with his sister-in-law. Though John Marshall successfully defended him, Richard Randolph died prematurely in 1796, unable to preserve and pass on his family's traditional, privileged way of life. Another illustrious family would meet a more violent end when, a few years later, the famous jurist George Wythe, with whom Thomas Jefferson had studied law, was murdered by a depraved grand-nephew who was impatient for his inheritance.

Dejected novelists of the 1820s and 1830s, like John Pendleton Kennedy, John Randolph's half-brother Nathaniel Beverley Tucker, George Tucker, and James Kirke Paulding, described the dilapidated estates of incompetent plantation owners and portrayed the offspring of "ancient cavaliers" anxious to leave the Old Dominion and begin their lives anew in the West.

"Whither has the Genius of Virginia fled?" cried United States Senator Benjamin Watkins Leigh. "Virginia has declined, and is declining—she was once the first State in the Union—now she has sunk to be the third, and will soon sink lower in the scale." Virginia's House of Delegates no longer bore any resemblance to the House in which Jefferson, Pendleton, Henry, Wythe, and others were members, wrote Virginian William Wirt, the attorney general under James Monroe and John Quincy Adams. "I am a disappointed man," Wirt sighed.

"Where are our men of abilities? Why do they not come forth to save their Country?" George Washington had impatiently demanded in 1779. In the nineteenth century, Virginians of ability would indeed come forth, wielding considerable power and influence in Virginia as well as in Washington—men like John Randolph, Spencer Roane, Philip Barbour, James Barbour, William Branch Giles, John Tyler, John Floyd, and others. And yet, although they admired and were influenced by the great men of Washington's generation, they shared virtually none of their boldness, their creativity, or their optimism. They possessed neither Washington's inclusive continental vision, nor Jefferson's passion for democracy and equality, nor Madison's nationalism, nor John Marshall's faith in the Constitution.

In truth, despite their disappointment, frustration, and lamentations, the members of Virginia's social and political elite would not have wished for the return of those founders, the transformational, adventurous, forward-looking revolutionary leaders who had so courageously and imaginatively embraced change. On the contrary, Virginia's leaders in the nineteenth century prized social and political stability, having grown disenchanted with a revolutionary experiment that had given them far more than they had bargained for. They prized independence and liberty but took a dim view of democracy, a vociferous, insubordinate people who might challenge their authority, and an intrusive national government. Bereft of an inspiring, compelling vision of the future, they were comfortable with the status quo.

In 1810, the young Henry St. George Tucker remarked that the greatness of the American patriots "was their *aversion to change*." His strange reinterpretation of the American revolutionary past would have baffled both Jefferson, who had the bracing perception that the "earth belongs to the living," and Madison, who extolled the Framers for charting a path with "no parallel in the annals of human society." But unlike the men of the founding generation, the eminent Virginians who inherited the Revolution looked backwards, clinging to the aristocratic idyll of a leisurely, gracious life of family, hospitality, books, and slaves on lovely Tidewater plantations, loyal to the agrarian myth of yeoman farmers leading independent, virtuous lives on the sacred soil. This generation of nostalgic Virginia leaders located the future in the past—and in the South. They rejected the northern faith in economic growth and industrialization as the guarantors of happiness. In the industrializing trend sweeping the North, they perceived not the potential for development and prosperity, but only the deadening prospect of dehumanization and anomie. And if those material, commercial values of the North were coloring—even defining—the very idea of America, as the visiting Alexis de Tocqueville perceived in the 1830s, then Virginians would have no choice but to proclaim and defend their collective difference and unique identity.

Even if Virginia's arts, literature, manufactures, commerce, and agriculture were all in a state of decline, Benjamin Watkins Leigh said defiantly, "is Virginia inferior to any of her sister States in social peace and happiness, in intelligence, in the virtues of private life, in political purity, in national character? No, sir—I say, proudly and confidently, no. I shall not vaunt of her superiority—but I acknowledge no inferiority."

Withdrawing into the murky shadows of domesticity, frustration, and nostalgia, failing to grasp that happiness, like life itself, cannot survive without energy, these Virginians looked inward instead of outward. And, in doing so, they shortsightedly and tragically shut the doors to improvement and to the future.

"My dearest grandfather," Ellen Randolph Coolidge wrote in 1825 to Thomas Jefferson, upon arriving in Boston with her new husband, "it is certainly a pleasing sight, this flourishing state of things: the country is covered with a multitude of beautiful villages; the fields are cultivated and forced into fertility; the roads kept in the most exact order; the inns numerous, affording good accommodations; and travelling facilitated by the ease with which post carriages and horses are always to be obtained." Wishing to show his bride the beauty and prosperity of the New England states, Joseph Coolidge had decided not to take the direct route from New York to Boston but instead to journey up the Hudson to Albany, and then to lakes George and Champlain, north to Burlington, Vermont, and then on to the towns of the Connecticut Valley before finally reaching Boston.

Ellen happily described for her grandfather the densely populated villages, with their "air of neatness and comfort that is delightful"; the churches, with their tall white spires; the many schoolhouses; and the groups of "little urchins returning from school with their books in their hands," who courteously greeted travelers. Citizens of each town and city paid taxes to maintain their schools, she reported, adding that "there is no tax paid with less reluctance." Children of both the rich and poor attended these schools and were educated gratis.

She and her husband also visited one of the huge textile factories that had recently begun to spring up in New England. "Although it was a flourishing establishment, and excited my astonishment by its powers of machinery and the immense saving of time and labor," she wrote, "I could not get reconciled to it." She hated the hot and crowded factory rooms, which smelled from sour and greasy chemicals; her head ached from the constant whirl and deafening roar of machinery. Instinctively she preferred "the pure air of heaven and the liberty of the fields in summer" to the domain of the rich manufacturer, and she thought that the farmers she had glimpsed looked more cheerful and healthy than the men and women employed in the factories.

It had been a fatiguing voyage, but Ellen did not regret having taken it: "It has given me an idea of prosperity and improvement, such as I fear our Southern States cannot hope for, while the *canker of slavery* eats into their hearts, and diseases the whole body by this ulcer at the core."

Replying to his granddaughter, Jefferson acknowledged that slavery was indeed destroying the South. "One *fatal stain*," he wrote, "deforms what nature had bestowed on us of her fairest gifts." Still, he did not dwell on the subject, or on his granddaughter's penetrating observations about New England. He was content instead to resurrect memories of his own trip through New England thirty-four years earlier. Ellen's itinerary, he wrote, was "almost exactly that which Mr. Madison and myself pursued in May and June 1791," when the two friends had traveled up the Hudson to Lake Champlain.

While the problems of Virginia had become too complex even for Jefferson to ponder and address, his astute young granddaughter had pointed to virtually all the ingredients for a vital and prosperous society: fertile soil and farmers who are knowledgeable about agriculture; citizens who are willing to pay taxes to support good roads and free public schools; numerous densely populated areas; churches; factories; a diversified labor force—and the ideals of freedom and equality.

The reluctance of Virginians in the early nineteenth century to dismantle slavery and launch practical plans to improve their state and enrich the lives of ordinary Virginians would condemn the Old Dominion to irrelevance and poverty. But loath to give up memories of slow-moving, honey-colored days and the long shadows of soft Tidewater evenings, the members of the Old Dominion's small ruling class believed they were right to take a principled, courageous, and rational stand in defense of a way of life—and a civilization—that they cherished. And might they have been right in their skepticism about laissez-faire capitalism, materialism, urbanization, commercialization, and even about the inflated promise of progress itself? That skepticism would linger for a century. "It all comes down to the most practical of all points—what is the end of living?" wrote one southerner, Stark Young, in 1930. It may be that success, competition, speed, and progress are the goals of life, he remarked. And yet his southern instincts told him that the true meaning of life could be found in "more fleeting and eternal things . . . more grace, sweetness and time."

Were the early nineteenth-century Virginians who desired those "fleeting and eternal things" hardy optimists who believed it possible to retrieve an idyllic past? Or were they moody dreamers determined to wage an impossible battle—a battle against time itself? "I linger still in the haunted domain of my memory," wrote Virginia novelist John Esten Cooke before the Civil War, "a company of ghosts which I gaze at, fading away into mist. A glimmer—a murmur—they are gone!"

1

The Cult of the Soil

"Let me then describe to you," wrote the visiting Marquis de Chastellux after meeting Jefferson at Monticello in 1782, "a man, not yet forty, tall, and with a mild and pleasing countenance, but whose mind and attainments could serve in lieu of all outward graces; an American, who, without ever having quitted his own country, is Musician, Draftsman, Surveyor, Astronomer, Natural Philosopher, Jurist, and Statesman."

At first, Chastellux, a major general in the French army, found Jefferson's manner grave—even cold. But after two hours of conversation, he felt as if they had spent their whole lives together. The two new friends took long walks in the afternoon and conversed late into the night, sharing their feelings about poetry, discussing natural philosophy and the arts, debating politics. "No object has escaped Mr. Jefferson," Chastellux marveled. "It seems indeed as though, ever since his youth, he had placed his mind, like his house, on a lofty height, whence he might contemplate the whole universe." Chastellux's four days at Monticello sped by "like four minutes."

Other visitors to Monticello also commented on Jefferson's exquisite hospitality, his easy and natural manners and casual attire, his wide-ranging interests and love of conversation, his daily horseback rides, the long hours he spent alone in his study.

At Monticello, Jefferson produced, directed, and starred in the life he most wanted to lead, surrounded by his daughters, their husbands and children, and his slaves. He reveled in his own private utopia. "There is no quarter of the globe so desireable as America," Jefferson wrote in 1795, "no state in America so desireable as Virginia, no county in Virginia equal to Albemarle, and no spot in Albemarle to compare to Monticello." He had it all.

His sophisticated refuge was Virginia at its best. At Monticello, he had brought to life his own trinity of supreme values: life, liberty, and the pursuit of happiness. By life, Jefferson had meant security and order, without which nothing else is possible. He had made Monticello a secure and sheltered realm, insulating it from strife and bitterness. It was the one place, he wrote, "where all is love and peace." The key to its serenity? Good humor and courtly manners. They were, Jefferson believed, the "preservatives of our peace & tranquillity." He prided himself on having mastered the art of "giving a pleasing and flattering turn to our expressions," and he was convinced that his happiness depended on earning the goodwill of others. Prizing above all harmony and conciliation in his private life, Jefferson advised his friends to "take things always by their smooth handle," and he cautioned his grandson to "never enter into dispute or argument with another."

As for liberty, Jefferson had worked to ensure that the kind of freedom most precious to him—freedom of conscience—would flourish in Virginia. His 1777 draft of Virginia's Statute for Religious Freedom had engaged him in the "severest of . . . intellectual labors," James Madison later recalled. In Jefferson's Virginia, reason would be left free, and neither the government nor the church would attempt to dominate or inhibit the human mind. Secure and free on his mountaintop, Jefferson could pursue and practice his personal happiness.

This art of pursuing happiness, he once wrote, lay in "the art of avoiding pain." Though sometimes tempted by life's more intense and dangerous pleasures, Jefferson concluded that the most effective way to protect oneself against pain "is to retire within ourselves, & to suffice for our own happiness." A life of books, reflection, and ideas would never disappoint. Intellectual pleasures, he wrote, are "ever in our power, always leading us to something new, never cloying." Such an existence would permit him to "ride serene & sublime above the concerns of this mortal world." While a perfect host to the endless stream of guests at Monticello, Jefferson valued, above all, his family and his books and was content to devote himself to the people and to the intellectual pursuits he most cherished.

Jefferson's carefully arranged plantation offered its inhabitants not only life, liberty, and the practice of happiness, but also equality—or at least its illusion. Although magnificent plantation houses like Monticello symbolized the social domination and political power of the planter class, sophisticated, aristocratic, patriarchal, slaveowning Virginians like Jefferson could nevertheless convince themselves that they were living in an egalitarian democracy.

In their eyes, all whites were equal—that is, equal because they were free and not slaves. Since most Virginians were engaged in the cultivation of the soil, they shared the same rhythms of life—planting, harvesting— and the same concerns about the weather. As for the slaves in Jefferson's home, many of his ingenious inventions—self-opening doors, dumbwaiters and pivoting windows to deliver food—deftly camouflaged them. One could imagine Monticello inhabited by self-reliant whites.

Still, Jefferson would dutifully descend from his paradise and embark on long sojourns in Williamsburg, Philadelphia, Richmond, Paris, New York, and Washington, playing leading roles in the political life of colonial Virginia, revolutionary America, and finally, the United States. Like other men of his social class in the 1770s, 1780s, and 1790s, he accepted the privileges and responsibilities of his social rank, taking it for granted that he would play a key role in public life. His goal, however, never changed: It was always to fulfill his political mission and then return, as quickly as possible, to his Eden—permanently, he claimed to hope. "My first wish is a restoration of our just rights," he wrote to a friend in 1775, when he served as a delegate to the Continental Congress. "My second," he continued, "a return to the happy period, when, consistently with duty, I may withdraw myself totally from the public stage, and pass the rest of my days in domestic ease and tranquility, banishing every desire of ever hearing what passes in the world." In 1781, at the end of his governorship of Virginia, he sounded a similar note: "I have taken my final leave of everything of that nature, have retired to my farm, my family and books from which I think nothing will ever more separate me."

In reality, Jefferson craved public life and was rarely satisfied in a world without politics and newspapers. He needed more than books and trees: Until the end of his presidency in 1809, he always sought an extroverted public life—not for the esteem or the glory, but for the stimulation, the impact, the power. And despite his professed desire for the "love and peace" of Monticello, he thrived on the conflict of the political arena. In 1782, a year after he had taken "final leave" of politics, his wife died. He could hardly wait to escape from Monticello and from unbearably sad memories, from a "stupor of mind" that had rendered him, he wrote, "dead to the world." When Congress offered him the appointment of minister to France, he jumped at the chance to flee. "My only object now," he wrote, "is to hasten over those obstacles which would retard my departure."

Nor was he entirely eager to return to Monticello in 1793, after resigning from Washington's cabinet. He claimed to long for a quiet life of farming and reflection, but he was really more concerned about his deteriorating finances. Soil depletion, plummeting land values, and his increasing debts weighed on him. "The ravages of overseers," he wrote, had "brought upon [the land] a degree of degradation far beyond what I had expected."

The years he spent at home between 1793 and 1797 would take their toll on Jefferson. In 1802, he would look back at the psychological cost of his isolation from public life. It had rendered him "unfit for society" and had given him a "misanthropic state of mind." "Happiness," he counseled his daughter, "requires that we should continue to mix with the world . . . and every person who retires from free communication with it is severely punished afterwards by the state of mind into which they get." When James Monroe hinted at his own early retirement from politics, Jefferson suspected that the pastoral life would not satisfy his friend. "I do expect that your farm will not sufficiently employ your time to shield you from ennui," he wrote in 1798. "Your mind is active, & would suffer if unemployed."

And yet, despite Jefferson's deep desire to participate in the political life of the nation, he created for himself the myth that he had selflessly sacrificed what was most precious to him—his secluded life at Monticello—for his community and his nation. "Domestic life and literary pur-suits, were my first and my latest inclinations," he would confide to his friend Margaret Bayard Smith in 1809. "The circumstances of our coun-try at my entrance into life, were such that every honest man felt himself compelled to take a part, and to act up to the best of his abilities."

The myth of a return from the strife and sacrifices of public life to happi-ness and fulfillment at home exerted a magnetic pull on many Virginians. At the height of the struggle for independence, in 1776, George Mason, one of Virginia's premier revolutionary statesmen, prayed for "a return of those halcyon Days when every Man may sit down at his Ease under the Shade of his own Vine, & his own fig-tree, & enjoy the Sweets of home." And in 1784, George Washington, after leading his country to indepen-dence, wrote contentedly that "I am become a private citizen on the banks of the Potomac . . . not only retired from all public employments, but I am retiring within myself."

In part, the fixation on a return to vines and fig trees was a yearning for an unchanging, unthreatening world, a childlike, wistful dream of un-troubled security in the bosom of one's family. Jefferson's granddaughter, Ellen Randolph Coolidge, who had married and moved to Boston, would always yearn for the safety of her lost Virginia childhood. "When I dream," she wrote many years after her grandfather's death, "it is mostly of long past time. Night after night I have been surrounded by the friends of childhood and early youth—my grandfather, mother, brothers, sisters, those whom I dearly loved and who dearly loved me, and who I hope in god's own time to rejoin."

But nostalgia for one's Virginia home meant more than emotional se-curity. Above all, Virginia meant a life on the soil. "Those who labour in the earth are the chosen people of God," Jefferson had memorably written in his *Notes on the State of Virginia.* The only truly virtuous, free, ethical, and republican way of life, he believed, was that of independent, self-sufficient, literate, self-governing farmers. Living and laboring on the land, they could enjoy great personal autonomy as well as a socially

stable community. There could be no "corruption of morals," Jefferson asserted, "among people who work their own soil." The proportion of
yeomen to all other classes of citizens in any state, Jefferson held, is the
proportion of its "healthy parts" to its "unsound" ones. Although Virginia
was politically dominated by large plantation owners and slaveholders, a
new cult hero—the small farmer—was born. In the 1770s and 1780s, Jefferson would do everything in his power to make the myth a reality.

Because morality, self-sufficiency, attachment to the community, good
citizenship, and the right to vote all derived from ownership of the soil,
Jefferson would strive to make land more accessible to average Americans. In the constitution that he drafted for Virginia in 1776, he had included a provision that gave to every adult white male 50 acres of land.
That same year, he introduced a bill in the Virginia House of Delegates
abolishing entails, a feudal relic that imposed a specified succession of
heirs and served to maintain the undiluted wealth of patrician families.
Ten years later, as a result of the movement Jefferson had helped initiate,
primogeniture, the right of the eldest child to inherit the entire estate of
his parents, was also abolished in Virginia.

A "political metamorphosis" had taken place, Jefferson rejoiced, very
prematurely, pitying the "half dozen aristocratical gentlemen agonizing
under the loss of preeminence." In truth, his efforts did not destroy the
economic or political power of the Virginia Tidewater planters and pa-
tricians; nor did they prevent speculators and large land companies from
making off with immense tracts of land. One economist estimated that
the top 10 percent of Virginia property owners held about 70 percent of
the value of the state's real estate in the late 1790s. And yet, Jefferson's
suggested reforms did help create more property owners, and hence
more citizens with the right to vote. Later, as president, Jefferson pro-
moted his agrarian vision for the entire nation, especially through the
Louisiana Purchase, which added vast and unsettled lands to the nation's territory. Fearing that the old northeastern states would eventually become "degenerate," corrupted by commerce and industry, he
expected the new territories to provide almost endless opportunities for
healthy, independent lives on the land; he saw the West as a potential
nursery for republican virtue.

Land was a badge of independence and citizenship, but it offered something else, too: the promise of *permanence*. Only land could assure rootedness, stability, security—the antithesis of the flux, corruption, materialism, and anomie of cities. "I cherish a narrow attachment for the spot of earth where I was born," said Senator Benjamin Watkins Leigh, who lived in the Tidewater, "and where sleep in peace the ashes of my parents, and of all the dead whom I have loved and honoured in my youth." So precious and prestigious was life on the land that some Virginians incorporated proprietary titles into their names, calling themselves, for example, John Randolph of Roanoke or John Taylor of Caroline.

The only *real* property was land. The superiority of *real* estate over other forms of estate, especially the transportable, ephemeral paper wealth of predatory northern capitalists, seemed obvious to Virginians, who anchored their lives, their traditions, and their fortunes in the soil. "Never part with your land," John Randolph's mother taught her son. "Keep your land and your land will keep you." Mere money "will melt like Snow before a hot Sun," wrote Washington in 1778, but "lands are permanent." Jefferson shared Washington's desire for the security of landed wealth. "We are now taught to believe that legerdemain tricks upon paper," he wrote, "can produce as solid wealth as hard labor in the earth."

Virginians had fashioned their own faith. On the Great Seal adopted by the Virginia commonwealth in 1776, there appeared four goddesses: On one side of the seal stood Virtus, trampling upon Tyranny; on the reverse side appeared the goddess Libertas flanked by Ceres, the goddess of agriculture, and Aeternitas, the goddess of permanence. There was no goddess of commerce or industry.

Despite the mantra of the land's permanence, the value of land in Virginia was anything but permanent. It was steadily falling. The price of land in Pennsylvania, a dismayed Washington commented in 1796, had increased "beyond all calculation," even though it was not superior in quality to land in Virginia. Washington looked for explanations and discovered that in Pennsylvania, the availability of smaller, more accessible parcels of land, as well as the demand for land created by floods of immigrants, served to increase the value of property.

But Washington was willing to probe even deeper for the truth: He perceived that whereas many talented and energetic Virginians were leaving the state, fleeing the moral stain of bondage and injustice, anxious to live in places where white men's work was prized and rewarded, Pennsylvania had wisely enacted laws in 1780 for the gradual abolition of slavery. And indeed, by 1804, all states north of Pennsylvania would take steps toward abolishing slavery. Unprofitable as well as morally corrosive, slavery, Washington perceived, was eating away at Virginians' wealth as well as their work ethic, ravaging their economic future. He understood that Virginia would not prosper economically unless it abandoned slavery.

More than thirty years later, the problem had grown even worse. Poor crops, a glut of land put on the market by desperate debtors, and the attraction of cheap, fertile land in the West all conspired to bring land values in Virginia even further down. Impoverished landowners, James Madison wrote in 1828, "have no resource but in the sale of property which none are able to purchase." In a bewildering reversal, paper had become more valuable than land. Only "paper property," Madison sadly remarked, "can find a tolerable and certain market."

Not only was the value of land unstable, its very ownership was temporarily in jeopardy. In 1792, Congress considered new federal bankruptcy laws that would give creditors the right to seize and sell land. The consequences for Virginia seemed dire, for freehold land in the Old Dominion had traditionally been beyond the reach of creditors. Fiercely objecting to the proposed bill, Jefferson wrote to his son-in-law, Thomas Mann Randolph, that it could "render almost all the landholders of this state liable to be declared bankrupts." Wasn't the nation almost completely agricultural? he asked. "Should not all laws be made with a view essentially to the poor husbandman?" Always in debt, in 1795 Jefferson himself feared that his own land would be seized for nonpayment of taxes.

When the House finally passed the bill in 1800, by a vote of 49 to 48, virtually all the southerners voted against it. "Many planters had been swindled out of their property by this ruinous law," John Randolph grieved, railing against the new economic culture of "paper"—mortgages, bonds, and bank notes. After only three years, the bankruptcy bill was repealed, defeated in part by men of landed wealth and financial debts like Jefferson and Randolph. Virginians would keep a national bankruptcy act at bay for another thirty-eight years.

But, above all, undermining the worth of the land was the soil itself.

One visitor from France in 1795, the Duke de la Rochefoucauld-Liancourt, was shocked by the farming methods he witnessed in Virginia. For six or seven years, he remarked, farmers would continuously plant wheat until the soil produced no more. Then that land would be abandoned, and another field would be cleared, planted, exhausted, and abandoned in its turn. By 1800, Albemarle County had become a "scene of desolation that baffles description," one Virginian wrote. Farms were "worn out, washed and gullied, so that scarcely an acre could be found in a place fit for cultivation." Unsightly woods of a stunted growth covered the exhausted land.

So deficient was Virginians' understanding of the cultivation of crops that, as George Washington complained, no real system of agriculture could be said to exist in the Old Dominion. "There is perhaps scarcely any part of America where farming has been less attended to than in this state," he wrote to the eminent English agriculturist Arthur Young. He was quite right in his diagnosis of the problem: Farmers raised their crops until they exhausted and ruined the soil, then abandoned it, turning to another plot until they ruined that too.

It was not surprising that wealthy, educated Virginians—like Jefferson, Madison, John Taylor of Caroline, and agronomist Edmund Ruffin—immersed themselves in agricultural research. They correctly understood that, first and foremost, Virginia had to shift away from a reliance on single-crop farming—the cultivation of tobacco. Tobacco had traditionally been Virginians' all-important cash crop, almost a substitute for currency. They shipped tobacco to England in exchange for luxury manufactured goods. But by the 1790s, most realized that tobacco was the principal culprit and cause of the depletion of the soil and that it required more manure and fertilizer than they could produce. Planters like Washington and Jefferson indeed tried to cut down—if not completely eliminate—their tobacco production, at least until debt made them fall back on it again.

Indeed, in 1799, with his debts mounting, Jefferson decided to return to the exclusive cultivation of tobacco, come what may.

Washington imported new iron plows from England, optimistic that deeper plowing would help regenerate the soil. He advised his friends to invest in movable threshing machines—"nothing is more wanting," he wrote—and he experimented with fertilizers. He tried new crops and grasses and different methods of crop rotation. Of the 900 volumes in Washington's library, 57 were devoted to agriculture.

Even city-dweller John Marshall, president of the Richmond Society for Promoting Agriculture, walked around the state capital with experimental seed in his pockets. Jefferson, too, conducted experiments, reporting to Washington in 1794 that one pint of "essence of dung" might be enough to fertilize an acre. He hoped that different grasses—lucerne, chicory, succory, sainfoin, clover—might improve crop rotation and also provide feed that, in turn, would increase the supply of animal manure. Work done by John Alexander Binns of Loudon County on replenishing soil with plaster of paris and gypsum also impressed Jefferson. Madison, too, took an interest in agriculture. Addressing the Agricultural Society of Albemarle County in 1818, he recommended deep and horizontal plowing, fertilization of the soil, irrigation, and an end to the excessive destruction of timber. Speaking to the society again several years later, he proposed the creation of an agricultural college in Virginia.

John Taylor of Caroline wrote articles and treatises on agriculture, among them his famous 1818 *Arator* (Latin for "Farmer"), in which he argued for crop rotation, raising and applying manure, and resting the land. In minute detail, he examined where barns should be placed, what hogs should be fed, how Indian corn compared to other crops, how "live fences" of cedar hedge could be grown, and how furrows for manure should be dug ("details, unentertaining," Taylor noted, "may not be useless").

But Taylor's goal was not merely agricultural reform: Fertile soil was the garden path that led to a larger, more idealistic and political end, the preservation of the virtuous republican way of life. By constantly replenishing his land, the farmer, instead of forever searching for new fields to plant, could root himself in his land and his community, where he could develop the virtues of the independent, self-sufficient republican citizen.

Agriculture, Taylor explained, "becomes the best architect of a complete man," for it exercises the body and mind and invites people to practice morality. Taylor's own well-run estate, Hazelwood, brought to life his agricultural and republican theories.

Edmund Ruffin's later experiments with manure, however, made him question Taylor's ideas. Ruffin's study of chemistry led him to believe that the problem lay in the acidity of the soil; he proposed regenerating the soil with marl, a calcareous matter derived from marine deposits. Marl neutralized the acidity of the soil and added potassium and phosphates. Indeed, crops doubled and even quadrupled in soil treated with marl, gypsum, and manure.

The ideas of Taylor, Ruffin, and others spawned periodicals in the 1820s and 1830s like *The American Farmer* and the *Farmer's Register* that taught sound theories of land management. In the 1810s, the Virginia Society for Promoting Agriculture, the Albemarle Agricultural Society, and other farmers' and planters' associations sprang up. At their meetings, agricultural research papers were presented, experiments described, and farm machinery demonstrated. Bringing together isolated farmers, the associations sponsored exhibitions and awarded prizes for the best grains, animals, and plows. In January 1836, at a statewide agricultural convention held in Richmond, attendees proposed establishing an agricultural professorship, model farms, and a state department of agriculture. The state legislature debated the proposals and then decided to do—nothing. One man who pleaded the case of farmers complained that, though it was deemed essential to educate lawyers, physicians, and ministers, farmers were left completely ignorant of the theory and practice of agriculture.

Some Virginia farmers embraced rational farming, but many others remained skeptical of new-fangled ideas. New plows sent to one region remained untouched and unused for almost a year as wary farmers eyed them with suspicion. Short-sighted, desperate for quick, if meager, profits, they persisted in overworking the soil, finding it more expedient to abandon exhausted land and purchase new parcels at low prices than to invest in improving the land they already owned. Indeed, Jefferson's decision in 1799 to return to the production of tobacco was emblematic of the Virginia farmer's distress.

Ironically, wealthy landowners like Washington, Jefferson, and Madison, try as they might to improve agricultural techniques, were hampered by their wealth—that is, by their large estates and their slaves. Small parcels of land might have been successfully cultivated, given the limited supply of manure and other fertilizers. But their hundreds of acres of land, along with a surplus of slaves, made efficient agricultural practices and the development of labor-saving methods and machinery all the more difficult to pursue. There was no doubt, Madison wrote in 1820, that "slavery and farming are incompatible." After selling three of his farms, Madison brought the slaves who had worked on those farms to his estate, Montpelier, where they were, of course, too numerous for the cultivation of his land; in addition, two-thirds of them were too young or too old to work. His slaves were impoverishing him, he confessed to his friend Edward Coles in 1832. Four years later, just a month before his death, he expressed admiration for Richard Rush's 10-acre farm near Philadelphia, certain that it was more profitable than his own huge estate.

Absentee plantation owners and incompetent, corrupt overseers and managers compounded the problems on large estates. Washington despaired that his overseers refused to follow his instructions for crop rotation. "In spite of all I can say, if there is the smallest discretionary power allowed them," he wrote to Jefferson during his second term as president, "they will fill the land with Indian Corn, altho' even to themselves there are the most obvious traces of its baneful effects." Back at Mount Vernon after his retirement, Washington was appalled by the exhausted state of his fields. Jefferson's experience was similar. Virginia estates were so unprofitable, he wrote to his daughter in 1798, that it seemed next to impossible for a planter to avoid ruin. What had to be done, he wondered, to "save us and our children from beggary"? Was the essence of the Virginia idyll—the large plantation attended to by slaves—proving to be a delusion?

Despite advances in soil management—especially between 1830 and 1860—the situation was slow to improve. Although John Taylor's writings on agriculture had inspired the hope that "all Virginia would soon be a perfect garden," one Virginian later recalled, only those planters whose soil was already rich ultimately profited from his system. New methods of plowing proved ineffective; highly touted but misunderstood fertilizers like gypsum seemed only to impoverish the soil.

A far-sighted willingness to confront and solve the problems of Virginia agriculture—to experiment, spend, and persevere—was sadly lacking, even in the state that had given birth to Jefferson's powerful and enduring agricultural vision. Ruffin's final diagnosis of the predicament was entirely correct: The problem of soil exhaustion, he concluded, began not in the earth but in the minds of lethargic Virginians, in their complacency and insularity. "The great evils which serve to prevent agriculture from being prosperous in Virginia," he wrote, "may be summed up in the single word, *ignorance*." So wretched was the land that "all wished to sell, none to buy." In 1843, giving up on Virginians, whose grandiose plans, he believed, never led to any innovation and change, he leaped at the chance to direct an agricultural survey of South Carolina and perhaps arrest that state's economic decline.

Even Thomas Jefferson's grandson, Francis Eppes, took his family to Florida. With Virginia's soil exhausted, "what inducement is there to remain?" he asked in 1828. "We will never witness better times here." The land itself, Jefferson's foundation of liberty and virtue, seemed to totter.

One Virginian expressed his gloom in verse:

No smiling pastures spread inviting here,
But dry hot fields on ev'ry side appear.
A sultry scene, a dismal waste, alas!
Where man's great object is to kill the grass.

And yet, the myth of splendor and permanence of the land still held sway. Tobacco had ruined the soil, weevils and rust had attacked the wheat, and the value of their estates had declined, but Virginians continued to idealize the pastoral life. Even though slave labor proved unprofitable and human property became more valuable than land, the mystique of the soil held Virginians spellbound.

Prisoners of their own plantations, many of Virginia's first families found themselves close to ruin. With debts mounting to over $100,000, Jefferson sold his cherished library to Congress in 1814 for a mere $23,950, and then, in his last years, contrived the odd scheme of a lottery as the most profitable way to sell some of his land. Because agriculture was in a state of "abject depression," he explained in 1826, "property has lost its character of being a resource for debts." Madison, admitting that he had "no resources but in the earth I cultivate," suffered nine crop failures in ten years. In 1825, unable to secure a loan for $6,000 from the Bank of the United States to cover his losses, he was obliged to ask his friend Nicholas Biddle for one. Monroe, virtually penniless at the end of his life, was forced to sell all his land in Albemarle County along with his home at Oak Hill in 1826. And yet, the powerful notion of the sublime, imperishable land still enthralled Virginians. Indeed, even as the old gentry foundered, the ideal of genteel plantation life seemed all the more alluring.

Jefferson had never been blind to Virginia's shortcomings. In 1785, in his *Notes on the State of Virginia*, he had been willing to cast a cold, judgmental eye on the Old Dominion, frowning at the poor state of its agriculture and the putrid effects of raising tobacco, and condemning the disastrous impact of slavery on both whites and blacks.

Even so, an optimistic Jefferson believed that Virginia would remain a republic of virtue and that, more than any other state, it would stay faithful to the fresh, bold, idealistic spirit of 1776 and steadfast in its tradition of love of the soil. He intended to do everything in his power to defend "the Southern interest," he had written to Madison in the 1790s, though after penning the word "Southern" he prudently crossed it out and wrote in "Republican." Yet it was clear that the values of the agrarian South were central to his hopes for the nation's—and Virginia's—future, and that he wanted to prevent the corrupt, commercializing, industrializing, urbanizing trends of the northern states from contaminating the rest of the country.

As the gap between the mentalities of North and South widened, as he saw northern greed and corruption advancing on the southern states, and as he saw the United States entangled in war in 1813 because of the "sordid avarice" of Great Britain, Jefferson came to believe that republican virtue and the principles of free government were retiring "to the *agricultural states* of the south and west as their last asylum and bulwark."

Three years later, in 1816, he expressed disgust that much of the United States had become a commercial appendage of the city of London. Convinced that agricultural pursuits—and not "the mimicry of an Amsterdam, a Hamburgh, or a city of London"—would make Americans a happy people, he took the extraordinary step of proposing, quite casually, that the modernizing, industrializing states of the Northeast, "which are for unlimited commerce and war," simply withdraw from the Union, leaving the states "which are for peace and agriculture" to form a new confederation. He envisaged not civil war, but a pacific parting of the ways. "I have *no hesitation* in saying," Jefferson blithely wrote, "'let us separate.'" It was not the first time that an "s" word had been pronounced: Northern politicians, stung by President Madison's trade policies and dismayed by his conduct of the war with Great Britain, had discussed separation at the Hartford Convention the previous year. But it *was* the first time that separation had been proposed by a former president.

Jefferson envisioned the South, and especially Virginia, as a land of peace, security, and restricted commerce, a domain devoid of "pseudo-citizens . . . infected with the mania of rambling and gambling," and devoid, too, of a wretched urban working class toiling sixteen hours a day and "still unable to afford themselves bread." Though his call for secession was impulsive and rash, the offspring of his penchant for abstract, novel, and revolutionary ideas that had, more than once, gotten him in trouble, it nevertheless served well to reveal his nightmare—a Virginia polluted by banking, capitalism, industry, and urban corruption—and to highlight his dream, the idyll of a harmonious, agrarian state, peopled by free and independent citizens cultivating the soil. And yet this anachronistic cult of the land, while denoting republican virtue, peace, and security, offered little hope of prosperity to average Virginians. Instead it only masked a dark reality of impoverishment, slavery, isolation—and stagnation.

2

The Cankers of
Indolence and Slavery

"For god's sake, what is the *deus nobis haec otia fecit?*" exploded Thomas Jefferson in 1776 upon hearing that Virginia had just adopted an incomprehensibly lame motto—"God bestowed upon us this leisure"—for its state seal. "It puzzles everybody here," he wrote. "If my country really enjoys that otium [leisure], it is singular, as every other colony seems to be hard struggling." At the threshold of an epoch of uncertainty, sacrifice, and violence, with "an enemy within our bowels," why would Virginia's ruling elite seek to portray the inhabitants of the state as living at ease? "If it puzzles now," Jefferson tartly concluded, "it will be absolutely insoluble fifty years hence." The foolish motto was dropped in favor of "Perseverando."

A decade later, Jefferson's indignation would fade, replaced by a glum recognition that his beloved Virginia, in truth, did not value labor. Compared to Pennsylvanians, whom he recognized as having an "enterprising temper," Virginians, he judged, were indeed "indolent." One day, to amuse and enlighten his friend the Marquis de Chastellux, Jefferson sketched two parallel lists encapsulating the differences between northern and southern mentalities. In the North, he wrote, people were sober, in the South voluptuary; in the North they were laborious, in the South indolent; in the North, persevering, in the South unsteady. Chastellux agreed; the power that masters held over slaves, he wrote, nourished "vanity and sloth."

But Jefferson did not conceive Monticello as a place of leisure. It was, rather, a locus of purposeful activity and the fruitful use of time. Dominating every important room was a chiming clock; even at the foot of his bed, a clock, mounted on the wall, rang out the hour and the half hour. The great virtue was activity; the sin was indolence. The "wretched" of the earth, he wrote in 1787, were the idle.

Scolding a languid friend, he cautioned that a love of repose and leisure leads to "a suspension of healthy exercise, a relaxation of mind, an indifference to everything around you, and finally to a debility of body, and hebetude of mind." He always recommended two hours of physical exercise a day. Although study—that is, the mind's exercise in the purposeful acquisition of knowledge and culture—was a major part of the Jeffersonian regimen, he was adamant that health not be sacrificed for books and learning. Physical exercise—and the indispensable flow of blood to the brain—came first. "A strong body makes the mind strong," he wrote. The best exercise? Walking. "Habituate yourself to walk very far," he advised a young relative. "There is no habit you will value so much as that of walking far without fatigue." And the best companion for that walk? A gun: "It gives boldness, enterprise, and independence to the mind," he wrote. When, in his later years, he could walk only with difficulty, Jefferson would boast that he rode 6 or 8 miles a day—and sometimes up to 30 or 40—without fatigue.

"Of all the cankers of human happiness," Jefferson counseled his daughter Martha, "none corrodes it with so silent yet so baneful a tooth as indolence." And if indolence of mind and body was the premier vice, the premier virtue was the productive use of time. His advice to young people was never to be idle, never to waste time, never to lose time.

George Washington, like Jefferson, valued time and work. Insisting that labor on his estate be organized and efficient, he carefully constructed schedules and work plans; he demanded regularity and punctuality. Otherwise, "the business becomes a mere chaos," he wrote in 1799. Nothing was worse than a "*waste of time* or idleness." Decades before pocket watches and clocks became consumer items, symbolizing the efficient and rational organization of time, Jefferson and Washington had adopted, if not a modern clock consciousness, a keen awareness of the value of time. But they were the exceptions in Virginia, where many still clung to the ideal of leisure, the otiosity the state had sought to celebrate in 1776.

———

At a small dinner party in Boston in 1831, Alexis de Tocqueville, researching what would become his book *Democracy in America,* found himself seated next to the former president, John Quincy Adams. "He speaks French with facility and elegance," Tocqueville later wrote. Did Mr. Adams regard slavery as a great wound on American society? Tocqueville asked. Adams's answer surprised Tocqueville, for he spoke not about the moral stain of slavery but rather about the damage it inflicted on the work ethic and economic future of the South. "We can't conceive how far the idea that *work is dishonourable* has entered the spirit of the Americans of the south," Adams said. "No enterprise in which negroes cannot serve as the inferior agents can succeed in that part of the Union. . . . I remember that a representative from the south being at my table in Washington could not keep from expressing his astonishment at seeing white domestics occupied in serving us. He said to Mrs. Adams, 'I find it a degradation of the human race to use whites for domestics. When one of them comes to change my plate, I am always tempted to offer him my place at table.'"

Anxious to hear firsthand the point of view in the slave states, Tocqueville ventured into the South. "Do you personally find that there is a great difference between the state of society in the North and in the South?" he asked an Alabama lawyer. "Immense," was the reply. "We men of the south, we have perhaps more natural ability than the Northerners, but we are very *much less active and above all less persevering.* . . . You don't see . . . the same forethought for the future."

Did the South have any ships to carry its produce? Tocqueville asked when he visited South Carolina. "Not one," replied Joel Roberts Poinsett, a member of the South Carolina legislature and future secretary of war under Martin Van Buren. "It's the North that comes to pick up the products of the South and carry them all over the world." He explained that there were no southern vessels because there were no southern sailors—

that is, no white working class from which to draw them. But couldn't black sailors be employed? Poinsett replied that they would simply desert. Fathoming the dire economic consequences of the South's dependency on the North, Tocqueville sought to understand the different mentalities of the two regions. The words he chose to describe the character of the North were plain: "strong, regular, durable." But he found the southern mentality more elusive; in the South, he felt there was "something feverish, disorderly, revolutionary, passionate"—traits alien to the methodical, shrewd, and calculating intelligence of northern entrepreneurs.

Life in Virginia seemed to take place in slow motion. Simple tasks took far longer to accomplish than in the North; more workers, more hands, and more aggregate wages were required to get things done. When Frederick Law Olmsted visited Virginia in the 1850s, he described lackadaisical workers miming exertion. He was not surprised that slaveowners themselves performed little visible work, but he remarked that white southerners who owned no slaves did not appear to work either. On the contrary, Olmsted said, they seemed "unambitious, indolent, degraded and illiterate . . . a dead peasantry so far as they affect the industrial position of the South."

But was Olmsted a skilled observer? Perhaps he did not grasp something deeper, something more subtle, that is, the rhythm of southern life. In the South, time had a different meaning—as did life itself. The ideal good life, for a Virginian, meant not work or the maximization of time but rather leisure and enjoyment. Almost a century later, in 1930, the writer Andrew Nelson Lytle took Olmsted to task for his superficial analysis of a civilization that prided itself on its very difference from the North. When Olmsted traveled in the South, wrote Lytle, "he called to a young ploughman to inquire the way, and when not one, but several ambled over and seemed willing to talk as long as he cared to linger, [Olmsted's] time-ordered attitude was shocked at their lazy indifference to their work." Lytle purported to understand what Olmsted did not: that "the farmer knows that he cannot control time." In industrial production, time has value; but in an agrarian society, the most the farmer can do is "wrestle with space." A colleague of Lytle, John Crowe Ransom, agreed that the privileged agrarian life and the cultivation of the soil transcended the notion of labor, for they entailed, he believed, a form of work that is pursued with intelligence and leisure. Labor itself, Ransom underscored, should be performed in a leisurely manner.

Apparently, neither Lytle nor Ransom—unlike Olmsted—had actually ever risen at dawn and worked in the fields alongside farmers. For if they had, they would have known that farmers indeed wrestle mightily with time—with weather, with daylight, with seasons, with growth—even if they cannot control it. Their dreamy, fanciful notions of southern culture served not to refute Olmsted's deep understanding of efficient, scientific farming but only to shed light on the self-defeating myth of "leisurely work" that doomed much of Virginia and the South to poverty before the Civil War.

The business of America might be business, but the business of Virginia, in the minds of its most distinguished citizens in the early nineteenth century, was to fashion the good life, one consisting of the pleasures of family, reflection, and leisure along with the responsibilities of hospitality to friends and strangers.

Perhaps Virginians were naive in comparison to hard-nosed northern businessmen, John Randolph acknowledged, but he would defend that well-bred naïveté. His people, he wrote in 1824, were "respectable, and kind-hearted, and hospitable, and polished." They were also guileless and backward in financial matters, even to the point of losing their estates. But material gain and profit were not their goals. On the contrary, as long as they had some financial means, even if it required selling their last acre or their slaves, they would remain faithful to the ethos of their civilization and their class, eager to "give a hearty welcome to whomsoever should drop in to eat, friend or stranger, bidden or unbidden." No existence offered greater pleasures, discovered the narrator of John Pendleton Kennedy's 1832 novel *Swallow Barn*, than the elegant, calm, dignified, and book-filled life of a Virginia planter. "I only want a thousand acres of good land," the narrator tells us, "an old manor-house, on a pleasant site, a hundred negroes, a large library, and a host of friends."

How could the drive to maximize profits and acquire material possessions compete with the sheer enjoyment of life? Although southern planters were becoming more sensitive to questions of time and efficiency, and although they recognized that economically they were falling far behind the North, many Virginians nevertheless remained scornful of the economic hyperactivity in the North and sought only to hold on to their dreams, their land—and their slaves. Indeed, slaves made possible, Virginia Governor Henry Wise would stress on the eve of the Civil War, "a class of masters who have leisure for the cultivation of morals, manners, philosophy, and politics."

That ideal Virginia existence depended on the institution of slavery. But which came first? Did Virginians' enjoyment of leisure produce a slave-holding society? Or was the opposite true? Did slavery generate a society that valorized leisure?

Southern mores—the taste for the unhurried life—came first, maintained historian David Bertelson. Slavery, he contended, did not cause southern sloth, though it did intensify it. But historian C. Vann Woodward responded that slavery could not be relegated to "the category of consequences," arguing that it played an essential role in the evolution of the southern ethos. The influence of slavery, Woodward underscored, was "all-pervasive." Tocqueville, for one, would have agreed. "Almost all the differences which may be noticed between the Americans in the southern and in the northern states," he wrote, "have originated in slavery."

But looking at their own civilization, many Virginians found that a penchant for slow, gracious living came first. Some pointed to the Virginia climate, noting that it inspired a carefree but also a slothful attitude toward life and work. The "pleasantness of the weather and the goodness of the fruit" had spoiled the inhabitants of the Old Dominion, wrote Robert Beverley in his 1705 *History and Present State of Virginia*. Scolding Virginians for their lethargy, he blamed them for depending "altogether upon the liberality of nature without endeavoring to improve its gifts by art or industry. They sponge upon the blessings of a warm sun and fruitful soil and almost grudge the pains of gathering in the bounties of the earth." But William Byrd, writing in 1728, far from denigrating a work-free life, hoped that reports about the mild air and fruitful soil would entice many of his foreign friends to emigrate to Virginia, where they would find "provisions of every kind which may be produced with little labor in the greatest plenty."

In other words, it was not slavery that gave rise to the Virginia planter intent on leisure; rather, leisure-inclined gentlemen settled in Virginia and found it convenient to use slaves to satisfy their desire for a life of pleasure and ease. Indeed, many of the early settlers in Virginia were a breed apart from the typical New Englanders who had fled England and Scotland for political and religious freedom and who located the overriding purpose of life in work. Unlike those "Yankees," Virginians were "cavaliers," that is, English gentlemen, many of whom were wealthy and who had crossed the Atlantic seeking peaceful, agrarian lives of pleasure, family, and books rather than of work and self-denial; they wanted only to enjoy—rather than add to—their fortunes.

Whether the taste for leisure or the institution of slavery came first, many prominent and self-critical Virginians in the late eighteenth and early nineteenth centuries had no doubt that slavery had destroyed the work ethic in Virginia. "No man will labour for himself," Jefferson wrote in his *Notes on the State of Virginia*, "who can make another labour for him. This is so true, that of the proprietors of slaves a very small proportion indeed are ever seen to labour." A few years later, at the Constitutional Convention, George Mason insightfully remarked that poor southern whites were disinclined to work because they were loath to associate themselves with the labor performed by slaves. Whites regarded labor as disgraceful, concurred Virginia legislator Charles J. Faulkner in 1832. Slavery crushes any "incentive to enterprise [and] converts the energy of a community into indolence," he commented, adding that the impoverished Virginia countryside displayed all the marks of a wasteful, idle, and reckless population.

Even the yeoman farmer—the independent, landholding republican figure par excellence, vaunted, admittedly, for his political and public qualities rather than for an adherence to a work ethic—would fall victim to slavery. "Slavery," said Thomas Marshall, the son of the chief justice of the Supreme Court, "retards improvements—roots out an industrious population—banishes the yeomanry of the population." Slavery, he was forced to conclude, was ruinous to whites. So many young white men, explained Samuel Moore of Rockbridge County, might be encouraged to lead honest and honorable lives cultivating the soil, and yet, because they saw black slaves working in the fields, they regarded such labor as a degrading mark of servitude.

"Where there is Negro slavery there will be laziness, carelessness, and wastefulness," asserted Virginian Francis Corbin. "Nor is it possible to prevent them." Virginia society was becoming so decadent, Corbin unflinchingly told James Madison in 1818, that "our intelligent Negroes are far superior in mind, morals and manners to those who are placed in authority over them."

Nor was the elite planter class contributing to the productivity of Virginia or setting itself up as a model for the community. The owner of a plantation, commented one visitor to Virginia in 1810, though proud of the "the stately name of planter," attended to nothing but his pleasures. A visiting Frenchman remarked two decades later that the typical Virginia gentleman was surrounded from infancy by his slaves who relieved him from all personal exertion. There was apparently no escaping indolence, noted Charles Ball, a freed slave: "Every kind of labour is strictly prohibited to the sons and daughters of the planters, by universal custom, as if a law of the land made it punishable by fine and imprisonment." How different from the work ethic of a disciplined New Yorker like Alexander Hamilton, who always emphasized that habits of labor were essential to healthy minds and bodies as well as to the welfare of the state.

The taboo on work applied especially to women. The role of a mistress of a plantation required that she maintain the appearance of leisure even though her household duties entailed much hard work. Indeed, it was fortunate that such upper-class women were excellent managers, remarked a visiting Englishmen in 1785, for, with few exceptions, he found their husbands to be dissipated gamesters. With their husbands frequently absent, these women confronted multiple challenges. Two of the women in the Randolph-Tucker clan managed farms, dealt with unhappy slaves, and raised children. "My life has been one uninterrupted series of suffering," wrote the beleaguered Judith Randolph. While northern women could look outside the home to voluntary associations for stimulation, the southern wives of plantation owners, struggling to conform to the stereotype of the ornamental woman, turned to female friends and relatives for support.

Many white Virginians—the elite dedicated to leisure as well as poor folks inclined toward laziness—convinced themselves that freedom from the demands of work was meant for whites, while hard labor was meant for blacks. One southern woman, writing in 1711, simply stated that the name of the game was to "get a few slaves and . . . beat them well to make them work hard." But most defenses of slavery were far less crude. More than a hundred years later, Abel Upshur, the Virginia judge who would serve as secretary of state under President John Tyler, approved the idleness of whites, finding it appropriate and just that "one portion of mankind shall live upon the labors of another portion." The menial work that whites performed in other societies, argued George Fitzhugh, a Virginia lawyer who wrote pro-slavery tracts in the 1850s, was simply not meant for whites in the South.

And yet, these men would have vehemently denied that their defense of slavery was selfish or self-serving. On the contrary, they would have insisted on the benevolence of slavery, pointing out that forced labor actually benefited blacks by rescuing them from their natural state of sloth. The patrician Virginia judge St. George Tucker had wanted to free his slaves and had even come up with different schemes for doing so, but he agonized about their becoming idle and dissipated. People must be "bound to labour," he wrote, "if they do not voluntarily engage therein." Virginian William Grayson held that the Negro naturally preferred a careless life of indolence, but that slavery brought him a more civilized form of existence. "Slavery makes all work, and it ensures homes, food and clothing to all. It permits no idleness, and it provides for sickness, infancy and old age." James Madison, too, fretted that not even emancipation could overcome blacks' "natural and habitual repugnance to labour."

Of course, as Jefferson noted, enslaved human beings possessed no moral necessity to labor for the benefit of their masters. One opponent of slavery, Virginian George Summers, ridiculed the idea that slavery bestowed a salutary work ethic on blacks. He argued instead that it was "natural" for slaves to perform their work in the worst possible manner, inasmuch as they could have no possible interest in the product of their labor. Indeed, in the anomalous political economy of the South, slaves had their own "work ethic." Laziness for a slave was a "virtue" and a means of resistance; like breaking tools, it was a way to make demands and set limits on what slaveowners could require of them. The problem of inefficient, unmotivated slave labor was compounded, Washington had remarked, by corrupt, lazy overseers who permitted the slaves "to be idle, to bribe them against a discovery of [the overseers'] own idleness."

Was it possible to employ white workers instead of enslaving blacks? Some southerners did indeed believe that free labor was more productive and moral than slave labor, but many others simply rejected the use of free labor out of hand. They contended, first of all, that Virginia was without a white laboring class. And second, they feared that even if that had not been the case, an economy in which one class of white men worked for another would dispel the illusion that all whites were equal despite their differences in wealth and power. And perhaps even more important, a class of white proletarians who could organize and make demands for a variety of reforms would disrupt the southern social system. The die had been cast. "Our bodies, as well as our minds have been molded under the influence of the principle of labor among us," wrote one pro-slavery advocate to the *Richmond Enquirer*.

No subject preoccupied Virginians—and even visitors to Virginia—more than slavery. Spending a long rainy afternoon in a Petersburg tavern in 1815, English tourist Morris Birkbeck commented that the prevailing topic of conversation among the men was slavery: "an evil uppermost in every man's thoughts; which all deplore, many were anxious to flee, but for which no man can devise a remedy."

As blacks worked and whites watched, some Virginians who grasped the true economic and moral cost of slavery fled. Talented, energetic people— including Quakers anxious to quit the land of slavery and its "Egyptian darkness"—were leaving behind deteriorated soil, a countryside strewn with worn-out plantations, a tenaciously stagnant society, and especially the abject culture of slavery.

Some, like Henry St. George Tucker, left the Tidewater for more opportunity in western Virginia. The eastern part of the state was no place for a young man starting out on his own, his father, St. George Tucker, impressed upon him. The West offered opportunity: An agricultural revival was taking place west of the Blue Ridge, where market towns and even fashionable spas were springing up. The epoch when merely owning land and slaves could secure a family's prosperity was over. Some people ventured even further west. Many poor whites, seeking greater economic opportunity, fled Virginia, where slavery devalued free labor. In the Old Dominion, poor whites were taught, said one Virginian whose parents left for Ohio, "how poor a thing a poor white man who labors for a living is usually considered, both by slaves and slaveowners in a slaveholding State."

Even James Madison had once considered leaving Virginia. One of his wishes, he wrote in 1785, was "to depend as little as possible on the labor of slaves." Captivated by the Mohawk Valley of upper New York State, he bought 900 acres of prime land. By speculating in New York land, he may have hoped to achieve financial independence and liberation from the ownership of slaves. Or perhaps his land deal revealed, even more, a desire to move north and completely abandon plantation life and the degrading domain of slavery. "No *local partialities*," he wrote at the time of his land purchase, would "keep me from any place which promises the greatest real advantages." Madison, of course, did not join the exodus from Virginia; he would be tied to his plantation for the rest of his life, watching enviously as others fled. In the West, Virginians could purchase vast tracts of fertile land for "125 Cents per acre," Madison wrote in 1833. Meanwhile, the depleted land in Virginia was rapidly losing its value.

Edward Coles, Madison's private secretary, made the decision in 1814 to move to a free state or territory where he planned to emancipate his slaves and give each head of family 160 acres. Jefferson—and not Madison—tried to dissuade him, urging him not to abandon the state to slaveholders but rather to remain in Virginia and work "softly but steadily" to extinguish slavery in the Old Dominion. But, pessimistic about the prospects for change in Virginia, in 1819 Coles moved with his slaves to Illinois, informing them, on board the barges that carried them up the Ohio River, that they would soon be free. "The effect on them was electrical," Coles later wrote. "In breathless silence they stood before me, unable to answer a word, but with countenances beaming with an expression . . . which no language can describe." In Illinois, Coles would go on to

become the governor of the state in 1822, where he would help defeat
pro-slavery forces and become a Free-Soil Party stalwart.

Lost to Virginia were the intelligence, energy, and ambition of people
who might have invested their talents—as well as their labor and money—
in Virginia's future. About 230 men born in Virginia before 1810 were
elected to Congress from other states. One Virginia expatriate was Henry
Clay. Raised in Hanover County, Clay studied law in Richmond but left
the state for Kentucky, depriving the Old Dominion of a progressive-
minded politician whose beliefs in union and the abolition of slavery
would inspire Abraham Lincoln. Another émigré, William Henry Harrison, who moved to the Northwest territories, would be elected president;
and still another, Edward Bates, would serve as attorney general under Lincoln. The "surplus talent" of Virginia, wrote Joseph Glover Baldwin in
1853, "has colonized the other States."

"Emigration to the West and South is going on beyond anything imagin-
able," Jefferson lamented in 1818. Ten years later the exodus was continuing—his own granddaughter, Ellen Randolph Coolidge, had recently
moved to Boston. Ellen's sister Mary had approved her decision to move
up North, leaving the wretched domain of slavery behind. It would be
preferable "to submit to any personal inconveniences however numerous
and annoying," Mary wrote in 1827, after witnessing a slave auction at
Monticello, "than to live in a state of society where such things as this are
of daily occurrence." Their mother, Jefferson's daughter Martha, was also
happy that Ellen had left Virginia. "How much trouble and distress you
have been spared, my beloved Ellen, by your removal, for nothing can
prosper under such a system of injustice."

Thomas Jefferson had long desired nothing more than the abolition of
slavery. In 1774, he had condemned King George III for vetoing legislation to end the slave trade. Ten years later, in the Northwest Ordinance
he proposed in 1784, he sought to exclude slavery from the western territory that Virginia was ceding to the United States—and limit slavery to
the original thirteen states. Slavery, he had no doubt, was irremediably
corrupting white society. "The whole commerce between master and
slave," he wrote in his *Notes on the State of Virginia* in 1785, consisted of

"the most unremitting despotism on the one part, and degrading submission on the other." Since human liberties were the gift of God, how could Americans dare to violate them without incurring his wrath? "Indeed, I tremble for my country," Jefferson wrote, "when I reflect that God is just: that his justice cannot sleep forever."

There was no doubt that slavery was an evil, and yet Jefferson, at once a starry-eyed idealist and a steely, cautious pragmatist, sought above all to accommodate his slaveowning Virginia neighbors. "The habits of the governed," he wrote, "determine in a great degree what is practicable."

The problem of slavery—and the search for solutions to it—became even more complicated in the wake of the Missouri Compromise of 1820. The Compromise was a nimble response to the potentially explosive issue of whether slavery should be entirely barred from all new western states, or whether new states should be allowed to make their own decisions on slavery. Its solution was to prohibit the spread of slavery in states carved out of northern portions of the Louisiana Territory. Though President Monroe and Virginia's two senators supported it, many Virginians, including eighteen of Virginia's twenty-two congressmen, did not.

Neither Jefferson nor Madison approved of the Compromise. It would do nothing to decrease the slave population, Jefferson contended. And worse, it would be counterproductive: By prohibiting slavery in certain states, the Compromise released the people of those states from the burden of helping to find a solution to the issue of slavery. Slavery, after all, was not just the predicament of one region; it was a national problem, and it required a national solution. Jefferson must have hoped that the diffusion of slavery would help Virginia rid itself of much of its slave population, but he also believed that the spread of slavery to new states would make it incumbent upon the North to join in the search for a permanent solution to the agonizing problem.

Madison, too, feared that if slaves were confined to Virginia while the white exodus to the West continued, the state would soon resemble a black ghetto, provoking unrest as well as repression. Thus both races would suffer in the South from restrictions on the movement of slaves to other parts of the country. "An *uncontrouled* dispersion of the slaves now in the U.S.," Madison advised Monroe, "was not only best for the nation, but most favorable for the slaves."

But while Madison's objections to the Compromise were primarily sociological, Jefferson's most bitter objections went beyond the sociological to the political. For Jefferson it was not just a question of the racial predicament that would result from restricting slavery to the South; even more important, it was a question of the ominous new power that the Compromise accorded to the national government. He resentfully denounced the Compromise for allowing the federal government to infringe upon the rights that had been reserved to the states. Surely it should continue to be left to the people of each new state, Jefferson reasoned, to decide for themselves whether they wished to enter the Union as a free or a slave state. Congress's next dictatorial move, he worried, might be to "declare that the condition of all men within the U.S. shall be that of freedom," an intolerable imposition, he believed, on the rights of states to govern their affairs. New York Senator Rufus King's startling demand that any laws upholding slavery be considered "absolutely void" vastly increased his anxiety. For Jefferson, the only way to end slavery was for North and South to join together in finding a formula for emancipation without the right "of third persons" (read the federal government) to interfere in the discussions. That is, unless the federal government was *invited* to intervene, perhaps invited to pay for the deportation of slaves, as Jefferson went on to propose in 1824.

Jefferson had no desire to perpetuate slavery, but he grasped the tragedy inherent in two alternatives that he viewed as irreconcilable. "Justice is in one scale," he wrote, "and self-preservation in the other." Justice, of course, meant life, liberty, and the pursuit of happiness. But what did Jefferson mean by "self-preservation"? First of all, it meant bodily security for whites; and that could best be ensured by separating the races and deporting all blacks. If the slaves were simply freed, their wrath and violence, he feared, would descend on white Americans, and those who lived south of the Potomac and Ohio would have no choice but to evacuate their states en masse.

But self-preservation also meant small and limited national government. It meant preserving the leverage the South enjoyed in the House of

Representatives and the Electoral College, accorded to it by the three-fifths rule, which counted three-fifths of the slave population in a state census.

But above all, self-preservation meant security for one's private wealth. Indeed, an economic angle colored Jefferson's stance on slavery. In 1805, he had written optimistically that "the value of the slave is every day lessening," suggesting that slavery was becoming economically unprofitable as well as morally untenable. "Interest is really going over to the side of morality," he added. But as land values declined, and as the one valuable asset of the planter class became human property, "self-interest" and "morality" once again drifted apart. Although some planters considered slavery so repugnant that they simply emancipated their slaves, most Virginia planters put economic self-interest ahead of human rights. They understood that emancipation would cost Virginia more than half its wealth.

In the 1830s, Virginia, the state that had once exported luminous revolutionary ideas, exported human property instead. After the United States closed its ports to the foreign slave trade in 1808, the Old Dominion became the leading exporter of slaves in America. The Louisiana Purchase, Thomas Jefferson's signature achievement as president, provided a vast new market for Virginia slave breeders. The value of Virginia's slaves increased significantly, and the trade in slaves became the Old Dominion's chief entrepreneurial activity. A young male slave in 1795 was worth $300; by 1860, a slave's worth would increase to $1,250. Virginia would reap millions of dollars selling tens of thousands of slaves to work on cotton and sugar plantations in the gulf states of Louisiana and Mississippi. The South and West, Virginia Governor William Branch Giles had uncritically remarked, provided "an almost boundless reservoir for the reception of slaves."

The equation was straightforward: more slaves, more money—and Thomas Jefferson understood this math. When he heard about the high mortality rate of infant slaves on his Poplar Forest plantation, Jefferson scolded his overseers for overworking the mothers of young children, for he knew that the breeding of slaves brought more profit than their labor in the fields. "The loss of 5 little ones in 4 years induces me to fear," he wrote in 1819, "that the overseers do not permit the women to devote as much time as is necessary to the care of their children." The overseers were focusing only on the productivity in the fields of a female slave, but Jefferson calculated that the capacity of a "breeding woman" to produce a child every two years was far more lucrative than her toil—and more valuable than the labor of even the hardest-working male slave. Thus it served both interest and morality to look after female slaves in their reproductive years. "Providence," Jefferson concluded, "has made our interest and our duties coincide perfectly." Usually a mild and considerate master, Jefferson considered it satisfying as well as providential that the kindly care of "breeding" slaves and their offspring might bestow a moral dimension on the cold business of slavery.

Still, despite the high profitability of owning and breeding slaves, he recognized that ultimately a plan for emancipation would have to be devised. Virginia's survival as a dominion of republican virtue and honor depended, he believed, upon the abolition of slavery. For him, this meant the deportation of blacks, since it was inconceivable to him that the two races could live alongside each other in peace, freedom, and harmony.

Though Jefferson had inspired the world with the ringing words that "all men are created equal," he imperiously pronounced blacks "inferior to the whites in the endowments both of body and mind." Any mixing of the races, he feared, would produce "a degradation" of the white race in America "to which no lover of his country, no lover of excellence in the human character can innocently consent." A corollary of degradation was inextricable entanglement: The presence of children of mixed race, he fretted, would make it hard, if not impossible, to eventually separate the two races. As for his own children of mixed race, not surprisingly, he refrained from condemning slaveholders like himself who produced offspring with female slaves. Indeed, he "recoiled more from the children of mixed-race unions," historian Peter Onuf acutely remarked, "than from the sexual practices of slaveholders."

"My proposition would be," Jefferson wrote in 1820, reviving a plan for emancipation that he had suggested in his *Notes on the State of Virginia*, "that the holders should give up all born after a certain day . . . that these should be placed under the guardianship of the State, and sent at a proper age to S. Domingo." His idea was that slaveowners would be required to give up ownership of newborn slave children and raise them, at the state's expense, until they could be deported to the Caribbean.

Four years later, he decided to calculate the cost of a more ambitious scheme, that of freeing the 1.5 million slaves in the United States over the course of twenty-five years. He figured that the slaves represented $600 million in personal wealth that would be lost. To that sum he added the cost of their expatriation, another $300 million. Confronted with this astronomical figure, he concluded that "it is impossible to look at the question a second time." The only practical plan, he judged, was the one he had proposed in 1820, that is, freeing newborn infants.

Though only several years earlier, the idea of breeding and selling more slaves had whetted his appetite for profit, in 1824, in a strange reversal, he surmised that the monetary value of those infants would be so minimal "that it would probably be yielded by the owner gratis." The slave children, he reasoned, could work just long enough for their owners to compensate for their "maintenance" before reaching the age at which they would be freed and deported. But, willing to recognize slaveowners' property rights, he calculated that $37 million—and not $600 million—would ultimately be needed to compensate them for their slaves. These expenses, along with the costs of food and transportation, could come from the sale of public lands. After all, Virginia had generously ceded its immense western territory to Congress for the common good, and it would only be just for the money from the sale of those lands to go toward the deportation and colonization effort.

According to his scheme, the rights of both slave states and slaveowners would be recognized, and North and South would together agree on and subsidize emancipation and colonization under a fair formula. This collective acceptance of responsibility for slavery, Jefferson understood, was probably the only *realistic* way to assure the abolition of slavery. As for the humanitarian question of the separation of children from their mothers, Jefferson acknowledged that this might produce "some scruples of humanity." But his calculations quickly overcame any concern for the feelings of the mothers and fathers of the children who would be deported. Nothing less than mass deportation, in Jefferson's mind, could redeem the nation—and especially Virginia. And yet, the idea of transporting more

than a million people from the United States was anything but realistic—
or morally adequate. But, unable to imagine a just, biracial society, Jefferson could think of no better plan.

Slavery meanwhile was casting a foreboding shadow on the demographic profile of Virginia. In 1820, east of the Blue Ridge mountains, slaves outnumbered whites by more than 60,000. James Madison's Orange County was typical: In 1820, black slaves made up 60 percent of the population. Complaining about the likely effects of the Missouri Compromise that confined slavery to the South, Spencer Roane, the chief justice of the Virginia Court of Appeals, wrote that he would rather see secession than be "dammed up in a land of slaves by the Eastern people." Roane understood population statistics and fertility rates: Virginia was rapidly becoming blacker, poorer, and more isolated than much of the rest of the nation.

By 1830, the situation had worsened. While the region west of the Blue Ridge had only a small black population, east of the Blue Ridge blacks now outnumbered whites by 81,000. Slaves made up more than half the population of Tidewater and Piedmont. Stark fear—the fear that the eastern regions of the Old Dominion were blackening—gripped many whites, who saw the frightening specter of servile insurrection.

They did not have long to wait. The siege took place in August 1831 in Southampton County, where the slave preacher and prophet Nat Turner, believing that God had chosen him to lead slaves to freedom, secretly raised an "army" of seventy recruits. After killing Turner's owner, Joseph Travis, along with his wife and child, they moved out through the countryside; over the course of two days, they murdered and decapitated fifty-five white people, mostly women and children. The governor, John Floyd, sent out four state militia companies, who were joined by three companies of federal troops from Fortress Monroe as well as by sailors stationed nearby. On the second day, the insurgency was put down; a hundred slaves were killed. Those not shot on sight were put on trial. Two months later, Turner himself was caught, tried, and executed.

Could more violent slave insurrections be expected? Might more slaves revolt and cut their masters' throats? In the wake of Turner's revolt, Georgia and Louisiana passed laws banning the importation of slaves from other states. The closing down of markets for the ever-growing population of Virginia slaves ratcheted up the anxiety level of white Virginians, who were distressed at the prospect of inhabiting an increasingly black state. The American Colonization Society offered a hint of relief late in 1831, when it chartered a ship to take 200 free blacks from Southampton County to Liberia.

The subject of slavery was a tinderbox, James Madison had told his abolitionist friend Lafayette in 1830. Any mention of it in public, he worried, might be "a spark to a mass of gunpowder." And yet, in the wake of Nat Turner's insurrection, the Virginia legislature made the startling and courageous decision to hold a free and open debate on slavery in the winter of 1831–1832.

In late December 1831, 134 members of the Virginia House of Delegates gathered in the statehouse in Richmond. Well-dressed ladies and gentlemen, eager to listen to the historic speeches, crowded into every seat in the galleries. "Our wisest men cannot give too much of their attention to this subject," editorialized the Richmond Enquirer, "nor can they give it too soon." Surely Virginians could find means that were "gradual, systematic but discreet," the Enquirer wrote, to reduce the "evil" of slavery.

"I wish from my soul that the Legislature of this State could see the policy of a gradual Abolition of Slavery," George Washington had fervently written in 1797, adding that such action "would prevent much future mischief." Thirty-four years later, the subject that was on the minds of all Virginians was finally open for frank discussion—perhaps even for action. About sixty delegates were willing to consider proposals for abolition; another sixty believed that emancipation was not yet possible or practical; and, holding the balance of power, a dozen delegates were disposed to some form of compromise.

A heady atmosphere of hope filled the air. Many of the delegates were young, representing a new generation of Virginians: John Marshall's oldest son, Thomas Marshall; Jefferson's grandson, Thomas Jefferson Randolph; Patrick Henry's grandson, William Henry Roane; and Governor Floyd's two nephews, James McDowell and James Preston. Perhaps these energetic young men could succeed where their fathers had not. "This is the act to which after time people will trace the origin of American abolition," said one optimistic delegate, George Summers, as the debate began.

James Madison, too, was hopeful. He despised slavery, even though he had long accommodated himself to the Old Dominion's way of life. Although he believed that his state had made moral progress over the years, and that Virginia's slaves were "better fed, better clad, better lodged, and better treated in every respect" than they had been in the past, Madison had not given up on finding a solution to the problem of slavery. Indeed, he was optimistic that the debate in the Virginia legislature might lead to an end to the "dreadful calamity which has so long afflicted our Country." Just like white Virginians, slaves, too, he remarked, coveted "that liberty for which we have paid the price of so much blood, and have proclaimed so often to be the right . . . of every human being." And yet, although blacks had an equal right to liberty, they would have to enjoy it in some area outside of the United States, for the idea of a biracial society was as inconceivable to Madison as it was to Jefferson. He termed it "universally obnoxious." Since the prejudices of whites were "unalterable," and the objections to mixing the two races "insuperable," blacks, he held, would have to be permanently removed beyond the region occupied by a white population.

Thus, as the moment for the debate on slavery in Richmond approached, the key problem for Madison was not emancipation, but rather the question of where to deport the growing black population, for he worried that there was a dearth of acceptable places. Still, if enough "outlets" and places of asylum for their expatriation could be found, either in Africa or in the "vacant" uninhabited western territories of America, all obstacles, he cheerfully surmised, "would yield to the emancipating disposition." But was the deportation scheme realistic? Madison himself acknowledged that his slaves had a "horror of going to Liberia"—one more of the contradictions that even well-intentioned slaveowners were forced to live with.

Governor Floyd opened the conference on December 5. A few weeks before, he had expressed, in private, his hope for an end to slavery. "I will not rest until slavery is abolished in Virginia," he had written in his diary, mentioning his idea of the gradual purchase and expulsion of all slaves and the prohibition of slavery west of the Blue Ridge. But his official opening remarks gave no inkling of such views; instead he evoked dark memories of Nat Turner's rebellion and called for tougher restrictions on blacks and appropriations for the expulsion of free blacks from the state.

The first step was the formation of committees, followed by the introduction of motions, proposals, and petitions. The select committee of the House of Delegates introduced its proposal—that it was "not expedient to legislate" on the subject of emancipation. Then some delegates presented their own motions. William Preston countered with a motion that it *was* expedient to legislate on slavery. Patrick Henry's grandson, William Roane, introduced two motions, one calling for the immediate expulsion of all blacks from Virginia, free as well as slaves; the other, a petition from the Society of Friends calling for the gradual emancipation of slaves and their removal from Virginia. Thomas Jefferson Randolph offered his late grandfather's plan for the buy-out and removal from the United States of slaves born after July 4, 1840.

On January 11, the debate began.

Their voices filled with righteous indignation, their words sincere and idealistic, young delegates rose to speak for emancipation. They harkened back to the Declaration of Independence, to the pleas for abolition made by Jefferson, George Mason, St. George Tucker, and George Wythe. But whereas Wythe had proposed simple abolition, convinced that the objection to "color" was founded solely in prejudice, all of the proposals for emancipation made during the debate called for the expulsion of emancipated blacks from the soil of Virginia. Indeed, the slavery debate of 1831–1832 could rightly be called the Deportation Debate, as historian William Freehling remarked.

On the emancipation side of the debate, the speeches were honorable and passionate. Liberty belonged not only to the white man but to the black man, too, declared delegate Samuel McDowell Moore. "The right to the enjoyment of liberty is one of those perfect, inherent and inalienable rights, which pertain to the whole human race," he said. "The poorest, tattered negro," concurred delegate George Williams, "feels within that spark which emanates from the deity—the innate longing for liberty." James McDowell followed suit. The idea that man was born free is "a torch lit up in his soul by the hand of the Deity and never meant to be extinguished by the hand of man," he said. The slaveowners' focus on private property was a canard, McDowell added, contending that slaves were a form of property that jeopardized the security and well-being of the entire community. McDowell's rousing speech, Madison said to Robert Winthrop, gave him for the first time the hope that slavery would yield to a system of gradual emancipation.

Knowing well that his grandfather had been in the business of breeding slaves, Thomas Jefferson Randolph denounced such practices, exclaiming that the illustrious Old Dominion, once peopled by great patriots who served the cause of liberty, had been converted into "*one grand menagerie where men are to be reared for market like oxen for the shambles.*" Other delegates railed against the policy of keeping slaves illiterate. "It is in vain," remarked delegate Henry Berry, "unless you can extinguish that spark of intellect which God has given them." And while blacks remained uneducated, whites were schooled in tyranny. Mimicking the abusive language of their parents, young children easily became the "embryo tyrants" of their little domains, said delegate George Summers.

Delegates also addressed the devastating impact of slavery on the economy as well as on the social fabric of Virginia. Must Virginia "languish, droop, die, that the slave-holder may flourish?" asked the twenty-five-year-old Charles Faulkner of Berkeley County. "Shall all interests be subservient to one?" Slavery was a cancer consuming the health of the Old Dominion, contended Samuel Garland. All the natural gifts that had been lavished upon Virginia, all the energy and talents of its citizens, he declared, had "been lost and paralyzed by this national calamity. Like a pestilence, it has swept over our land, withering and blighting whatever it breathed upon."

But pro-slavery delegates cast aside all the arguments and heartfelt pleas made by the foes of slavery. They dismissed their moral principles, denied their economic insights, mocked their revolutionary ideals. Not even Christ rebuked slavery, declared delegate John Thompson Brown of

Petersburg. "On the contrary, He gave it his implied approbation by exhorting masters to be kind to their servants—and enjoining it on servants to be faithful and obedient to their masters. Shall we, sir, affect a morality more pure and exalted than . . . the blessed author of our faith?" Happy and relieved to locate themselves in the mainstream of the history of civilization—well, at least ancient civilization—defenders of slavery denounced "new-light" politicians whose radical calls for equal rights for all threatened to destroy the organic nature of Virginia society. "The bands which bind society together," asserted James Gholson, "would at once dissolve," undermining relations of husband and wife, parent and child, master and apprentice, master and servant.

Though a fully formulated, militant pro-slavery ideology would not appear for several years, virtually all of its elements—moral, social, political, and economic—were already surfacing. John Brown rose to defend the principle of states' rights, explaining that any plan to free slaves by using federal funds to compensate slaveowners for their slaves simply empowered the federal government at the expense of the autonomy of the states.

James Gholson made the economic argument, reminding his colleagues that "private property is sacred" and that slaves were a principal source of wealth in Virginia. Others denied that slavery impoverished Virginia or detracted from a determination to improve the state. Virginia was "in a state of improvement," contended a cheerful William Goode. "A better system of agriculture has been introduced. We do better ploughing. We attend more to the rotation of crops. We attend more to the raising of manure. . . . Sir, the agricultural product of our State is greater now than it ever was at any previous period." The problem of slavery, he promised the delegates, would solve itself, for slaves would be sold to the gulf states. Since planters in the Old Dominion were already abandoning the cultivation of tobacco and turning instead to farming, the necessity for slave labor would diminish over time. Another delegate addressed the issue of the population decline, denying that people were leaving Virginia to escape the domain of slavery. "The emigrant, so far as my observation extends," said John Shell, "almost invariably settles again among a slave population." Gholson conceded that much of

Virginia was not prosperous. But, he added, "poverty, though a heavy misfortune, is no crime."

The debate was a historic occasion: Politicians had gathered, in good faith, to try to resolve the problem of slavery together. Throughout the nation, people intently followed the discussions in Richmond. Newspapers reprinted articles from the *Richmond Enquirer* and the *Constitutional Whig*. Even the visiting Alexis de Tocqueville heard that Virginians were discussing the "utility and dangers" of slavery; he voiced optimism that the Old Dominion would "give up slavery and tobacco at the same time."

In late January, after both sides concluded their arguments, delegates cast their votes. The three key antislavery motions—William Preston's motion that legislation on slavery was "expedient," the Quaker proposal for gradual emancipation, and Thomas Jefferson Randolph's proposal for the buy-out and removal of slaves born after July 4, 1840—all failed. Instead, the delegates approved the select committee's motion stating that "it is *inexpedient* for the present legislature to make any legislative enactments for the abolition of slavery." A majority of the delegates, however, also favored a moderate "preamble," proposed by a western Piedmont representative, stating that the general "removal of slaves should await more definite development of public opinion." Though hardly a promise to eliminate slavery at some future time, the preamble was, the *Enquirer* editorialized, an "entering wedge" against slavery, a word of encouragement to sustain the hopes of Virginia abolitionists.

Had the historic debate on slavery accomplished so little? Was there no vision, no plan, no will to act? A majority of delegates passed one other proposal as well—one promising "an immediate effort" to remove free blacks from Virginia. Two weeks later, the Virginia legislature allocated $50,000 for the deportation of free blacks, most of whom declined to move to Africa or the Caribbean and remained in the Old Dominion.

Ironically, the debate on slavery had only made life worse for Virginia's black population. Before adjourning in March 1832, the Virginia Assembly tightened its regulations on blacks—placing more restrictions on them, stripping them of legal privileges such as trial by jury, and making it illegal to teach slaves or even free "negroes or mulattoes" to read and write. All blacks—both free and enslaved—were barred from preaching or attending religious meetings unless accompanied by whites.

The Virginia debate of 1831–1832 marked one of the last chances the nation had to reverse course before the tragedy of the Civil War. If Virginians had shown true leadership, if they had courageously and farsightedly voted on a plan to abolish slavery, perhaps American history would have flowed in a different channel. For the Confederacy might not have been sustainable without Virginia—without its prestige, wealth, and population, and without the leadership of its politicians and generals.

Still, the debate did mark a turning point. Before 1832, Virginians had often openly proclaimed their regret, if not their antipathy, for slavery. Jefferson had always stressed that slavery was evil. Patrick Henry had predicted the eventual extinction of "this lamentable evil" of slavery. Slavery was "an evil," insisted John Taylor in 1818, that the United States must look in the face. "To whine over it, is cowardly; to aggravate it, criminal; and to forbear to alleviate it, because it cannot be wholly cured, foolish."

But after 1832, those apologetic, embarrassed, ambivalent words largely disappeared, as did the old vague and evasive promises to end slavery at some future time. Instead, people began to bow to the inescapability of slavery. Over the next twenty-five years, a new mood of resignation replaced the old hopes for abolition, for there seemed to be few realistic other options. One member of the House of Delegates said that Virginia had "no alternative" in the matter of slavery. "We must submit to our destiny."

Jettisoning the long-term promise of emancipation that seemed so far beyond reach, some well-intentioned people expressed instead the modest hope that the condition of slaves could be slightly ameliorated. But even those good intentions became moot as a new cadre of aggressive, unflinching champions of slavery in the 1850s defended the status quo, emphasizing the prodigious benefits to society of bondage.

Indeed, the slavery debate had legitimized pro-slavery arguments, making it socially, intellectually, and morally acceptable to condone, defend, and even extol slavery. There appeared a new mood of defiance, a new willingness to protect and preserve slavery. "Be that property an evil, a curse, or what not, we intend to hold it," wrote one man to the *Constitutional Whig* in the spring of 1832. Citizens in Mecklenburg County announced their determination to defend their right to their human property *"unto death,"* adding that they would not tolerate being "wheedled by any insidious promise of compensation."

In statewide elections in the spring of 1832, pro-slavery delegates like William Goode and Alexander Knox were reelected. Some of the delegates who had spoken out against slavery were branded "Negro lovers" and defeated, though a few, like Thomas Jefferson Randolph—whose wife, Jane, longed to "quit at once and move North"—held onto their seats.

Other stories quickly replaced the debate over slavery in Virginia newspapers—opposition to tariffs, the states' rights movement in South Carolina, a bill to recharter the Second Bank of the United States, the Reform Bill in England—and slavery was relegated to the back pages. "Our political power is fast passing away," wrote one disappointed antislavery Virginian to the *Enquirer* in the spring of 1832. "Our relative influence in this union [is] rapidly decreasing." What future did Virginia have, he asked, when "one half of our population is taught to look on labor as degrading?"

Soon, the abolition of slavery would become a taboo subject in Virginia. "Arguments in favor of negro emancipation, once open and urgent, have been completely silenced," wrote George Tucker, a professor of political economy at the University of Virginia. Those who still favored abolition, he added, found it prudent to conceal their opinions; slaves, he predicted, would experience no changes in their condition for at least another half century. In 1836, the Virginia legislature passed a law making it illegal to deny the right of a master to property in his slave or to circulate literature of an "inflammatory and mischievous character." The debate on slavery that many hoped might herald a new era had run its course.

"We will never witness better times here," sighed a gloomy Francis Eppes, Thomas Jefferson's grandson, in late 1832. In 1833, only seven years after the death of her father, Jefferson's daughter Martha Randolph sadly admitted, "Virginia is no longer a home for the family of Thomas Jefferson." That same year, John Marshall, too, confessed that he felt like "an alien" in Virginia.

Before the end of the year 1832, Thomas Roderick Dew, a thirty-year-old professor at the College of William and Mary, published his widely read "Review of the Debate in the Virginia Legislature." A vindication of the pro-slavery position, Dew's "review" outlined all the essential arguments that had been made in favor of slavery and that would continue to be made in the decades leading up to the Civil War. Proponents of slavery would repeatedly turn to it as their primer.

Conceding that some good isolated points in favor of abolition may have been expressed during the debate, Dew claimed to be disappointed that "no enlarged, wise and practical plan of operations was proposed by the abolitionists." In fact, he continued, warming to the subject, virtually all of their proposals had been "of a wild and intemperate character" reflecting "misguided philanthropy." Especially the notion of the colonization of hundreds of thousands of slaves in Africa was "a *stupendous piece of folly*." With no practical alternative to slavery and no free laboring class to replace slave labor, southerners, Dew suggested, had little choice but to defend the way of life that had been imposed upon them.

Dew's first line of defense was to underscore the individual's sacred right to own property. Indeed, the primary object of government was the protection of private property, Dew reminded his readers, noting that abolitionist schemes subverted that right. Estimating the value of Virginia's slaves at about one-third of the wealth of the state, he warned that if that wealth were destroyed, Virginia would "be a desert."

Those economic points might have settled the issue, but Dew decided to summon both biblical and ancient history to demonstrate that slaves had always formed the largest portion of the human race. Not only were the glorious days of the republics of both Greece and Rome underwritten by slaves, but the children of Israel, too, had enslaved their prisoners. Even "the meek and humble Savior of the world" never meddled with the established institutions of mankind. It would be a rebuke to Jesus Christ, Dew asserted, to disturb the "deep foundations" and organic structure of society. In any case, the hands of Virginians were "unpolluted with the original sin" of slavery. The institution had almost been forced upon Virginia by Great Britain and other European nations that trafficked in slaves, a trade Virginians had taken the lead in barring from American ports. Virginia, in short, had "nothing to reproach herself with."

Consolidating and codifying the arguments that had been made to prove that, far from being an evil, slavery was a positive good, Dew taught that bondage played a key civilizing role. It encouraged productive labor, destroyed habits of indolence, and offered protection to the weak. Good for blacks, slavery, he marveled, was even better for whites, for it created a spirit of equality among them. The result was a classless white society that was "both the generator and preserver of the genuine spirit of liberty." Piling argument upon argument, Dew traced the roots of equality, freedom, and republican virtue to the institution of slavery.

And yet, Dew seemed to recognize that the perpetuation of slavery would ultimately depend on force. Turning to the painful question of slave rebellions, he suggested that whites could comfort themselves with the thought that in the previous 200 years, there had been only three attempts at insurrections. In the next 200 years, he predicted, far more whites would be murdered at the hands of robbers than of slaves. Even so, he seems to have recognized that slavery implied an ongoing state of war, and he realized that to meet any and all threats, Virginia would have to create enforcement agencies. "In 1929," he wrote, "our police [will] be much more efficient than now."

Still, how to discredit Thomas Jefferson's passionate condemnation of slavery? The great Sage of Monticello, the author of the Declaration of Independence who had given a nation its deepest moral values—life, liberty, and the pursuit of happiness—had abhorred slavery for the evil it inflicted upon the entire society, upon whites no less than blacks. Eager to refute Jefferson's humane, principled stand, Dew plunged boldly ahead, asserting that Jefferson had it backwards! Most masters were kind and indulgent to their slaves, often rewarding them with signs of cordial approbation. It was not true that white children were "nursed, educated, and daily exercised in tyranny," as Jefferson had written in his *Notes on the State of Virginia*. On the contrary, Dew contended that children learned benevolence, generosity, and even "elevation of soul" from the master-slave relationship. Eluding the question of the slaveowner's dread of slave revolts, Dew claimed that the slaves of a good master were his warmest, most constant, and most devoted friends. At best, Jefferson had been misguided, "too prone to judge of the happiness of others." He had seriously erred by setting himself up as the standard, attributing his own sophisticated, worldly desires, and ambitions to slaves.

Dew had written the foundational text for a powerful new pro-slavery movement, one that transformed slaveowners in the Old Dominion into blameless and moral citizens, cleansed of the stain of Jefferson's censure. Virginians could now preserve their myth of plantation life and safely and guiltlessly hold, breed, and sell slaves—especially if the police force continued to grow in efficiency and in numbers.

The proud author sent a copy of his book to James Madison. The former president was stunned by what he read. After politely acknowledging the gift, Madison icily distanced himself from Dew's position. "I am obliged to say," he wrote to Dew in February 1833, "that in not a few of the data from which you reason, and in the conclusion to which you are led, I cannot concur." Rejecting Dew's justification for the perpetuation of slavery, Madison believed that, as moral agents, Virginians could not forsake the struggle to end slavery. Even a "partial success will have its value," Madison emphasized, "and an entire failure will leave behind a consciousness of the laudable intentions with which relief from the greatest of our calamities was attempted." That same week, a hopeful Madison, refusing to abandon the only plan conceivable to him for emancipation, rededicated himself to the cause of deportation and colonization, accepting the presidency of the American Colonization Society, which sought to transport free blacks and emancipated slaves to Africa.

And yet, on the eve of his death in 1836, Madison recognized that the emancipation movement in the South had stalled and that Dew's reprehensible ideas were gaining popularity. Although in the past southerners had viewed slavery as a necessary evil, he feared that they would start to look upon it "as one of the greatest blessings they could enjoy."

Dew's book also reached the desk of John Quincy Adams, who, after his term as president, had won a seat in the House of Representatives. After intently poring over its pages, Adams pronounced Dew's work a "monument of intellectual perversion." Like Madison, Adams was terrified that

Dew had succeeded in making the pro-slavery stance intellectually and morally tenable for southerners.

As Madison and Adams both intuited, Dew's "Review of the Debate" would eventually become the foundational text of a radically new pro-slavery orthodoxy. Though most Virginians would remain moderate on the issue of slavery, some would turn during the next decades to Dew's panoply of arguments—historical evidence, biblical stories, axioms about sacred private property, moral-sounding principles, and a communitarian ethos—to aid them in defending their traditions.

But this new orthodoxy would do nothing to revitalize Virginia. Instead, it merely nailed shut the windows of the prison-house of slavery in which many Virginians had decided to live, banishing all rays of Enlightenment.

3

"Let Us Have Our Own Schools"

"Permit me to say that I do not think it would forward your design to send your son to this college," the president of Yale, Timothy Dwight, wrote dismissively to John Taylor in 1805. As far as Dwight was concerned, young Virginians inhabited another sphere, so unsuited were they for serious study in New Haven. "If I may judge from the Virginia youths who have been here during my presidency," he observed, "I cannot form a rational hope that youths from that country will at all acquire *here* any portion of the New England manners." Most of the southern students who had attended Yale, Dwight wrote, "despised and hated our manners, morals, industry, and religion. No part of our system or conduct was agreeable to them."

Whereas residents of Connecticut were "universally industrious," the youths of Virginia, Dwight maintained, "considered industry as the business of slaves and wretches only." An opponent of slavery, Dwight knew how to artfully turn the knife. "Your children," he told Taylor, "would regard their New England companions as plodding drudges, destitute of talents as well as of property. They would esteem their New England life as *slavery*, unreasonable and useless."

Given Dwight's stereotype of indolent, pleasure-loving southern youth and the widening cultural chasm between North and South, it was hardly surprising that some Virginians felt uncomfortable at Yale. "The faculty do not treat the Southerners as they should," wrote the seventeen-year-old Hugh Blair Grigsby of Norfolk to his stepfather, Dr. Nathan Whitehead, in 1825. "If a Southerner enters College, the bare fact of his coming from the South, makes him a suspicious character." Perhaps the students bore some responsibility for the faculty's mistrust, Grigsby conceded. "So many Southerners have been rather wild at Yale," he wrote, "that they set down every Southerner for a rogue until he can convince them to the contrary." The feelings seemed to be mutual, for Grigsby judged the faculty at Yale "a diminutive and low-minded set" who possessed not "a spark of nobleness of soul, not a glimmer of elegant literature." Dr. Whitehead declined to urge his stepson to give his instructors the benefit of the doubt. One tutor, Whitehead wrote, "can't be a Gentleman or he would not treat you as he does, and as he is not a Gentleman he is not worthy of notice."

Grigsby's closest friend was the only other Virginian at Yale. "We always call each other 'Virginian,'" he wrote to his stepfather. "We both slept together the other night on the only fine *Virginia* feather bed in College." The young Virginians could not adapt to the "dirty tea with dirty sugar" that was served at breakfast, to the dirty black molasses bread that "a Virginia dog would not eat" or to the sheets that were as hairy as blankets. But it was even more impossible for them to adapt to the Yale academic honesty and honor code, which required them to report other students' violations to the faculty. Young southern men who valued honor above all else should refuse to become "young Judases," Grigsby indignantly wrote, irate that Virginians were expected to conform to such alien cultural values. "If a young man so far violated the laws of propriety as to go and inform against a fellow student, the very fact would blast his every prospect of living, much less of distinction, in the South."

Hugh's sister Lelia hoped that her brother would remain at Yale long enough to find her a rich Yankee beau. But young Grigsby was not inclined to stay. Since the new University of Virginia was not yet "well recognized," any gentleman's library in Virginia would serve him as well as the New Haven faculty, decided his stepfather. After sixteen months at Yale, Hugh Grigsby returned to his books at home.

Virginians fared somewhat better at Harvard. Grigsby's friend John Tazewell of Norfolk went to Cambridge in 1822 with a more positive attitude. His father, Littleton Waller Tazewell, a Virginia lawyer and legislator, hoped that John would fit in with the other students and identify with the values and ethos of his new school. It was as much in his son's interest to "sustain and advance" the interests of Harvard "as it is theirs to support and assist you in your laudable efforts," Tazewell wrote to his son. "You and the college thus become assimilated," he added. But while the famous Harvard zoologist Louis Agassiz took a liking to his southern students, some Harvard men took a dim view of students from the South. They were so many "bladders of conceit," in the opinion of Harvard graduate Ralph Waldo Emerson. "The young Southerner comes here a spoiled child, with graceful manners, excellent self-command, very good to be spoiled here, but good for nothing else—a mere parader," he wrote. Moreover, northern and southern students seemed to have little in common, according to Emerson. "The Southerner asks concerning any man, 'How does he fight?' The Northerner asks, 'What can he do?'" It may be impossible to know whether the southerner or Emerson himself was the real "bladder of conceit."

Henry Adams, John Adams's great-grandson, would have disagreed with Emerson. When he was a student at Harvard in the 1850s, young Adams's closest friends were Virginians. "Roony" Lee, the son of Colonel Robert E. Lee, was hardly a gifted student. "No one knew enough to know how ignorant he was; how childlike; how helpless before the relative complexity of a school," Adams wrote. Roony "had no mind; he had temperament." And yet, although his friend had no intellectual training and could barely recognize, much less analyze, an idea, he had superb social instincts—and perhaps that was enough, mused Adams, to get along in life. Indeed, Adams felt a deep bond with Roony Lee, for neither man seemed suited to the modern age that was dawning. While he did not share Lee's acceptance of slavery, Adams, who grew up in Boston, considered himself "little more fit than the Virginians to deal with a future America which showed no fancy for the past."

"In one sentiment we agree," replied Taylor to Dwight's biting letter, "that it would be extremely injudicious in me to send my son in search of instruction to one who believes him to be a wretch destitute of morals, industry, and religion." But Taylor also took the high road, outlining for Dwight his own vision for American institutions of higher learning. Rather than exacerbating regional differences, shouldn't the nation's colleges promote understanding among the states and help obliterate those differences? "Consider, sir, the consequences of academical institutions, which teach local prejudices, State enmities, and individual hatred. What will become of the Union and national happiness, if errors calculated to arm State against State, with the most deadly moral weapons, are inculcated by zeal, rendered doubly dangerous by credulity?"

The creation of a national university that would bring students from all parts of the nation together in mutual understanding was George Washington's great hope and mission in the 1790s, during the last years of his life. What better symbol could there be of the new federal Union than a university sponsored by the republic itself? It was an imaginative and not impractical plan, and yet it remains unrealized more than two centuries later.

Washington himself never attended college. His years in the army instead provided him an education. Recalling the military experiences of his youth, he remembered especially the feelings of community and fraternity—the fraternity of men, from different sections of the nation and from different social classes, who sleep, dream, obey, fight, and die together. "A century in the ordinary intercourse, would not have accomplished what the Seven years association in Arms did," he wrote.

The university Washington envisioned would thus offer its students communion in learning. "Young men from different parts of the United States," he wrote, "would be assembled together, and would by degrees discover that here was not that cause for those jealousies and prejudices which one part of the Union had imbibed against another part." In his will, he donated land for the university, underscoring again his wish that it would "do away with local attachments." Instead of going abroad for their education, "where too often principles and habits not friendly to republican government are imbibed," students would remain in America and receive an education in republican values and principles.

Jefferson, too, often stressed the importance of an American education for American youths. "But why send an American youth to Europe for education?" Jefferson wrote in 1785 from Paris. "He acquires a fondness for European luxury and dissipation, and a contempt for the simplicity of his *own country*." The men Jefferson most respected had been educated in America, men "whose manners, morals and habits are perfectly homogeneous with those of the country." Twenty years later, President Jefferson returned to Washington's theme of a national university, proposing "a national establishment for education" in his annual message to Congress in 1806.

But that national perspective would not hold. By 1821, Jefferson had made a dramatic about-face. He still wanted students in Virginia to be educated in their "own country," but now "country" meant Virginia.

Too many Virginia boys, Jefferson complained, were going to Harvard, Yale, and Princeton for their education. Indeed, despite the cultural differences, sectional animosities, and the lonely experiences of students like Hugh Blair Grigsby, the steady stream of young Virginians into Cambridge, New Haven, and especially Princeton had not abated. Jefferson had heard—erroneously—that more than half the students at Princeton were Virginians! In northern colleges, he grumbled, students "imbibed opinions and principles in discord with those of their own *country*." Harvard sent students home to the South transformed into so many "fanatics & tories." Northern schools could no longer be considered "proper" for southern students. "The signs of the times," he sternly concluded, "admonish us to call them home."

Unlike Jefferson, George Washington never referred to Virginia as his "country." After the War of Independence, he disdained Virginia parochialism, always exhorting his fellow citizens to resist "every attempt to alienate any portion of our Country from the rest, or to enfeeble the sacred ties which now link together the various parts." And he was not intimidated by the excellence of the schools of New England. In 1795, he hoped that George Washington Lafayette, the visiting son of his dear friend, would attend Harvard. He wished, too, that his step-grandson,

George Washington Custis, had attended Harvard. That "inert" and undisciplined young man might have profited from the emphasis in Cambridge on "morals and a more regular course of life," he wrote. Harvard students, Washington sensed, were "less prone to dissipation and debauchery than they are at the Colleges South of it." Unfortunately, the young Custis had no interest in higher education north or south; he wanted only to lead the gracious, unhurried life of a Virginia cavalier.

Jefferson, on the other hand, would probably have been saddened to learn that his great-grandson, Thomas Jefferson Coolidge, studied at Harvard in 1850. He might have been even more dismayed to know that the young Coolidge, raised in Boston, regarded the many southern students in Cambridge as so many aliens. They "generally spent much money, drank freely, and considered themselves better than the Northern mudsills," Coolidge wrote. "They were overbearing and quarrelsome, but brave and full of honour, although they often did not pay their debts. In short, they had the vices and virtues which are generally found with slave owners."

In 1820, Thomas Jefferson had happily chosen to send a grandson, Francis Eppes, to the College of South Carolina "rather than anywhere northwardly." Later testifying to his grandfather's good judgment, Francis commented that, though the course of study in South Carolina was not as complete or comprehensive as that in Cambridge, he was relieved to attend a school where "the discipline is more lax and consequently better adapted to the feelings and habits of southern students." After one year, however, young Eppes's father ran out of money for tuition, and the young man had to return home.

Jefferson perceived a sharp cultural and political line of division slashing through the young nation. That line was the 36° 30' latitude of the Missouri Compromise, north of which slavery could not spread. His bitterness toward the northern enemies of states' rights who had voted for the Compromise in 1820 was deep and unappeasable. In 1821, Jefferson decided that it was no longer seasonable to furnish northern schools with Virginia "recruits." It would be absurd, he contended, to trust northerners, who opposed the bedrock southern principle of states' rights and who had so little appreciation for southern culture, with the "minds and affections" of young Virginia men. Southern students who studied in the North, he predicted, would return home deformed by the "sacred principles of our holy alliance of Restrictionists." The "canker" of the northern indoctrination of young Virginia men was eating away at the heart of Virginians' existence, Jefferson warned. If not arrested at once, the situation would "be beyond remedy."

And yet, there were no institutions in the South comparable to Harvard or Yale. The Old Dominion had severely neglected instruction on every level. "So miserable are the means of education in our state," Jefferson told his grandson Francis Eppes in 1821, "that it has been retarded and baffled to a most unfortunate degree." Like "beggars," Virginians asked other states to "bestow on us their miserable crumbs." Massachusetts was one-tenth the size of Virginia, Jefferson grumbled in 1820, and yet the Bay State had more influence in the nation than any other state. How to explain the ascendancy of Massachusetts? The answer was obvious: the attention that Massachusetts lavished on education at all levels. "If knowledge is power," Jefferson concluded, "we should look to it's advancement at home."

But what about Jefferson's own alma mater, the College of William and Mary? In 1787, he had considered it the best school in the nation. "I know of no place in the world," he wrote to a friend the following year, "while the present professors remain, where I would so soon place a son." But those professors would not remain: Jefferson's mentor George Wythe resigned in 1789; he was replaced by St. George Tucker, who left the school in 1803. Equally devastating to the college was the removal of the state capital from Williamsburg to Richmond in 1780. The move had been Governor Jefferson's idea; a capital, he believed, like the sun in the solar system, should be located in the center of a state, at the heart of activities. In the early nineteenth century, far from that sun, William and Mary languished.

"It is over with the college," Jefferson sighed in 1814. His private secretary, Isaac Coles, concurred that it was a "decaying institution"—decaying because of its dire financial condition, its dwindling enrollments, its location, its dilapidated buildings, and especially the resurgence of religious revivalism. Indeed, the college's new leadership was taking it in an evangelical direction, betraying the spirit and teachings of the Scottish Enlightenment that had served Jefferson's generation so well in the 1760s.

Disgusted with the "den of noise, of filth and fetid air" that William and Mary had become, Jefferson poured his attention, energy, and heart into the creation of a first-rate, entirely secular university for Virginia. "What service can we ever render her equal to this?" he asked his friend and collaborator Joseph Cabell in 1821. "What object of our lives can we propose, so important?" Too long the genius of the Old Dominion had slumbered, deprived of the prestige of excellent cultural and educational institutions, Jefferson wrote. But a distinguished university would help regenerate Virginia, permitting the Old Dominion once again to be the nation's premier state.

The new university in Charlottesville that opened its doors in 1825 was "more beautiful than anything architectural in New England," pronounced visiting Harvard professor George Ticknor. In 1818, Jefferson had meticulously designed the buildings and drawn the blueprints; several years later, he laid the stakes himself. At the head of the campus stood the majestic domed Rotunda, modeled after the Pantheon in Rome, that would serve as the university's library and planetarium. On either side, Jefferson had placed a row of classical "pavilions" connected to each other by colonnades. Each professor lived in his own pavilion, his residence upstairs and classroom downstairs. Jefferson's plan for education, modeled on Enlightenment principles, integrated professors' homes, classrooms, and student dormitories so that faculty and students could live together and participate, on an almost equal basis, in a familial community of learning. There would be no raised desks for professors, no physical or symbolic barriers separating them from their students. And there would be no prescribed course of study; students would be free to pursue the subjects that interested them. Nor did Jefferson want hierarchy in the university's administration: There would be no president, just a chairmanship that rotated among faculty members, along with a supervisory "Board of Visitors." As for religion, unlike the Episcopalian College of William and Mary, whose original mission had been, in part, to train priests, the University of Virginia would not hire a professor of divinity, and no compulsory religious services would be held. "By avoiding too much government, by requiring no useless observances," Jefferson explained, freedom and satisfaction would displace forlorn codes, rules, and discipline.

And the faculty? With only limited funds, Jefferson feared that "we shall be reduced to six professors, while Harvard will still prime it over us, with her twenty professors." But after securing more money from the state, he set out to compete with his northern rival, determined to assemble an eminent faculty. Though John Adams cautioned his friend against looking abroad for instructors, certain that there were enough qualified scholars in America to fill the professorships in Virginia, Jefferson sent a young Virginia lawyer named Francis Walker Gilmer off to England, France, and Germany to recruit the faculty. Gilmer hired professors to teach ancient and modern languages, mathematics, natural philosophy, and anatomy.

The ideological instruction of students, however, commanded more scrupulous attention than Latin and anatomy. "In the selection of our Law professor," Jefferson wrote to Madison, "we must be rigorously attentive to his *political principles*." Dismayed that many law professors and young lawyers had been indoctrinated into Federalist notions of expansive, energetic national government, forsaking the fundamental precepts of limited government and states' rights that he and Madison had always favored, Jefferson screened all candidates carefully. It was his duty, he wrote, to "lay down the principles which are to be taught." No professors would be hired, his collaborator Madison agreed, who favored an overbearing national government or an expansive interpretation of the Constitution. And yet, Madison allowed that "talents" and "amiableness of temper" might be almost as important as ideological "fitness" for a position.

In other words, Jefferson—and Madison to a lesser degree—wanted to impose a strict ideological conformity on the curriculum. Students would be instructed in the principles of the Republican Party—that is, principles of small, decentralized, passive government and states' rights, a philosophy of government far more attuned to southern agrarian values than to the nationalism of the industrializing North. Jefferson conceived the university as a "nursery of republican patriots as well as genuine scholars," but "republican" really meant "southern." Above all, he wanted to ensure that students at the University of Virginia would not become infected by the northern, Hamiltonian vision of the United States as a powerful, centralized, industrial and military state. Instead, they would absorb southern and Republican values and carry those "correct principles" not only to the statehouse in Richmond but back to other southern states as well. "If we are true and vigilant in our trust," Jefferson wrote to Madison in 1825, "within a dozen or twenty years a majority of our own legislature will be from one school, and many disciples will have carried its *doctrines* home with them to their several states."

Jefferson's first choice for the professor of law was his envoy Francis Gilmer. Gilmer, however, never recovered from the strain of his voyage abroad, and so Virginia lawyer John Tayloe Lomax was hired. To teach moral philosophy and political economy, Jefferson and Madison settled on Virginian George Tucker. Though he passed their ideological test, Tucker would turn out to be a surprise, displaying an independence of mind and a penchant for strong, centralized government that led some to believe that he was an enemy in their midst, a "Hamiltonian in Disguise." In 1845, disenchanted with the intellectual climate of the University of Virginia and with colleagues who used their talents to defend slavery, Tucker would leave for the "freer intellectual air" of Philadelphia.

Jefferson had undergone an astonishing transformation. He had once embodied, as few men in America, the critical, inquiring spirit of the Enlightenment. "I am never afraid of the issue," he had written in 1789, "where reason is left free to exert her force." Now, he backtracked. He became less interested in giving "a full scope to reason" than in imposing a new Virginian orthodoxy on generations of students. Jefferson had said that he wanted his "academical village" to be a "bulwark of the human mind in this hemisphere," an institution based on the "illimitable freedom of the human mind." But he really wanted it to be a "bulwark" to shield the southern mind against alien ideas from the North.

Indeed, Jefferson envisaged the University of Virginia as a "centre of ralliance" for the southern states that would keep alive the "Vestal flame" of the doctrine of states' rights. The cosmopolitan former minister to France, the sophisticated intellectual who had dabbled in political theory, the far-sighted former president of the republic who doubled the size of the nation became, in the years before his death, simply—and militantly—a *Virginian*.

After Jefferson's death, the university would become still more rooted in conservative southern principles. Especially after the contentious debate on slavery in the Virginia General Assembly in the winter of 1831–1832, faculty members tried to quell controversy by steering student debating clubs toward cooler subjects: Would it benefit the English government to separate church and state? Should the liberty of the press be restricted? Ought capital punishment to be abolished? After one student used the occasion of Jefferson's birthday in 1832 to deliver an oration calling for the abolition of slavery, the faculty eliminated political and partisan addresses. Six years later, the university's Board of Visitors went further, banning all public speeches. "We are forbidden to speak; the tongue falters, the lips are closed," editorialized the student magazine, *The Collegian*.

Politics—that is, southern politics—was taking over the University of Virginia. In 1860, the ban on the discussion of political subjects was lifted and students debated the question, "Has a State the right to secede?" The issue was decided in the affirmative. Nine months later, students debated another question: "In case of the election of Lincoln should the Southern States secede?" This, too, was decided in the affirmative. The vote: 33 to 6.

———

Even though Jefferson lavished his attention on the university in Charlottesville, he knew that primary and secondary education in Virginia were even more crucial to the well-being of the state than a university. "It is safer to have a whole people respectably enlightened," he wrote in 1823, "than a few in a high state of science, and the many in ignorance. This last is the most dangerous state in which a nation can be."

Already in 1779, in his "Bill for the More General Diffusion of Knowledge," an idealistic young Jefferson had envisaged an academic pyramid with elementary schools at the base, private grammar schools (or "colleges")—only for boys—at the next level, and the university at the pinnacle. So that citizens would be literate, all white children, girls as well as boys, would receive three years of elementary school education gratis. After those three years, education would no longer be free. At each level, however, a few potential *leaders* among the poor boys would be selected to continue their education at public expense. This plan would permit at least a fraction of the "mass of talents which lies buried in poverty" to blossom. Jefferson was convinced that his education bill would strike a blow against aristocracy and the powerful combination of wealth and birth. But, in truth, his meritocratic program provided only three years of elementary education for all children and only a few places at the college level for poor boys.

Even so, the idea of universal education always occupied a central place in Jefferson's conception of a society of virtuous citizens. For Madison, too, an educated electorate was essential in a democracy. "A popular government without popular information or the means of acquiring it," Madison wrote in 1822, "is but a prologue to a farce or tragedy, or perhaps to both." Like Jefferson, Madison understood that for self-government to work, men who intend to be their own governors "must arm themselves with the power which knowledge gives." Thus it was the government's obligation not only to protect citizens' rights but also to provide an education for them so that they could become conscientious, informed citizens.

And yet, Virginia's political and social elite hardly agreed with this vision of an educated populace. Education for the masses was not a priority for them.

To support a modest measure of public education, the state, instead of taxing its residents, like the New England states, had established the Literary Fund in 1810. With revenues from fines, forfeitures, confiscations, and other penalties, the fund grew to $1 million over the next few decades. And yet it represented a pitifully small amount for so crucial a cause as public education. "While you get millions to employ so usefully," Jefferson complained to Governor De Witt Clinton of New York in 1822, "I am laboring for a few thousands to save my fellow-citizens from the Gothic barbarism into which they are sinking for want of the means of education." Virginia's population was almost the same as that of New York, and yet New York had 6,000 common schools. In matters of education, Jefferson wrote, Virginia appeared a diminished "pigmy" next to the Empire State. Without more public schools, white Virginians, he said, would "fall into the ranks of our own negroes."

Ordinary Virginians were on their own as far as education was concerned. The young Mark Hopkins, the future president of Williams College, interrupted his education at Williams to spend a year teaching the children of two families—twenty barefooted boys and girls—in the early 1820s on a plantation near Mecklenburg, Virginia. "The fact is," he wrote to his parents, "the body of the people are very ignorant in this section of the country, and I am informed that not more than half of them can read and write." What most dismayed the young Hopkins in Virginia was the lack of books, which, he remarked, were "not generally diffused."

But for wealthy, cultivated Virginians, education was a different story. They collected large and choice libraries, hired tutors for their children, and sent them to the best private schools and colleges. In 1817, the young New Englander Bronson Alcott visited the homes of wealthy, well-educated Virginia planters. These patriarchs impressed him as "gentlemen in the best sense of the word." In their rich libraries, he happily discovered not the usual dry theological tracts typically found in New England, but works of literature, poetry, philosophy, and political theory.

Many of these gentlemen assumed that education and culture were a function of wealth. "Education can only be acquired by the fruits of property," wrote Hugh Blair Grigsby in his diary in 1828, reflecting the views of most wealthy Virginians. In other words, education was a privilege of the white male elite and therefore a private—not a public—responsibility.

Virginian John Randolph of Roanoke scoffed at the very concept of public education. How outrageous for propertyless men to expect "that all things must be done for them by the Government!" he exclaimed on the floor of the Virginia legislature in 1829. The "first and most obvious" duty of all parents, the one that only the most worthless people neglected, was the education of their children. If the government assumed the responsibility for educating citizens, Randolph said, it would only permit worthless fathers to spend more money on liquor.

From the 1780s until the Civil War, upper-class Virginians like Randolph stonily rejected Jefferson's desire to "throw on wealth the education of the poor." It was a violation of their property rights, they huffed, to force them to pay for the education of others. "I will put it in the power of no man or set of men," Randolph cried in 1829, "to tax me without my consent." What

Randolph left unsaid, of course, was that he and other slaveowners feared that taxation on their human property—whether for education, roads, or anything else that would improve the lives of average citizens—would make slavery economically unsustainable. And so education for young Virginians, like all the other vital signs of their society, fell victim to the protection of slavery. As one supporter of public education, William M. Rives of Campbell County, observed in 1832, "Let any plan be proposed, by which to facilitate and improve the education of the middle and poor classes of society, it [will be] met with the decided opposition of the large slave-holder."

But the objections of wealthy Virginians to funding public schools went beyond their arid, self-protective antipathy to taxation: It was also a question of power and class. Virginia's elite had no desire to spur the rise of a new class of men who might compete with them politically and economically. They knew well that universal, free education for whites, by disseminating knowledge and spurring upward mobility, would undermine the hierarchical social system that served their interests so well. And so they argued that there was no need to educate common laborers, and that in fact a few years of elementary education would be counterproductive. Public schools would create "half-made gentlemen" who were unfit to work as mechanics. The real problem, one Virginian wrote in a letter to the *Richmond Enquirer* in 1818, lay not in the lack of schools, but in Virginians' "indisposition to labor," which education would only aggravate.

Up until the Civil War, that mentality did not change. Men who engaged in bodily toil, wrote a defender of class distinctions in 1846, "have no leisure for mental culture." And the author of an article in *De Bow's Review* pointed out in 1856 that a society was under no obligation to educate its poorer citizens. On the contrary, the author argued, its sole responsibility was to "educate the wealthy in order to maintain their position as members of the white, privileged class of our society." And so, despite the myth of white equality, the result was an intentionally impoverished, uneducated, and disempowered white underclass.

Of course, some enlightened Virginians, such as James Madison, rejected social distinctions in the matter of education. A sound plan for schools, Madison insisted in 1822, should embrace every class of citizens and benefit all—advantaged as well as disadvantaged—equally. Scornful of the refusal of wealthy Virginians to contribute to the education of the poor, he observed that, given the well-known vicissitudes and reversals of fortune, rich men risked finding themselves one day at the bottom of the economic ladder. Thus, the wealthy man who contributes to the education of the poor, Madison wrote, "ought to reflect that he is providing for that of his own descendants."

Other Virginians joined Madison in urging the state legislature to provide more funds for education and, in the words of Virginia Senator James Barbour, to "perform the part expected of you by your best and most enlightened citizens." In the 1820s and 1830s, Virginians like John Marshall, James Barbour, William Rives, and especially Charles Fenton Mercer spearheaded a variety of plans for publicly funded elementary schools, southern textbooks, and teacher training. However important the new university might be, John Marshall wrote to Mercer in 1827, primary schools were "objects of deeper interest."

Unlike the wealthy planters who argued that working men had no need of schooling or "mental culture," these reformers understood that improved educational and work opportunities for average Virginians would increase the prosperity of all—and might also help stem the tide of westward emigration. "Let your common school system go hand in hand with the employment of your people," New England industrialist Abbott Lawrence advised Rives. In the western part of Virginia, men like E. W. Newton, the editor of the *Kanawha Republican*, demanded free public schools, a literate working force, and a better environment for business and economic development, hoping that educated citizens would eventually be able to loosen the grip of the eastern planter elite on Virginia society. Despite those pleas for more education and more economic opportunity, the state Literary Fund accomplished little. It did provide some subsidies for private schools and set up some charity schools that would be managed by the counties, but many counties did not even bother to claim their allotted funds. And when the state legislature authorized a county school tax, most counties comfortably ignored the directive.

In 1845, Governor James McDowell would implore the legislature to provide more funds for education and, above all, to agree to the principle that public education was the duty of the state. But no action was taken—

there would be no uniform plan for education and no push to increase the cultural resources of the state. Discouraged reformers dubbed Virginia "the banner state of ignorance."

If there was little interest in public education for boys and young men in Virginia, there was even less interest in educating young women. "A plan of female education has never been a subject of systematic contemplation with me," admitted an indifferent Thomas Jefferson in 1818, although he did hope that women would receive a "solid education" in order to be able to teach their own daughters and perhaps supervise the education of their sons, should the fathers be inattentive. The female mind merited an improved system of education, James Madison allowed, though it would have to comprise "a due reference to the condition and duties of female life, as distinguished from those of the other sex." In any case, the establishment of a college for young women, he wrote in 1821, "would require more consideration than is allowed by other demands on my time." Less than ten years later, a southern gentleman remarked that "the only chance a man has for a rational companion in his wife is to marry her when very young and cultivate her mind."

Still, some Virginians would persist in calling for a "thorough course of study for females." "The time has arrived when the general cultivation of the female intellect will be deemed (as it is) absolutely necessary for her happiness," the *Southern Literary Messenger* editorialized, lamenting that the term "Boarding School Miss" was used as a "term of contempt." Some short-lived private academies and seminaries for young women came and went, but in 1842, Mary Baldwin Seminary was founded in Staunton. A school that became Hollins College near Roanoke was also established.

Of course, there was absolutely no place in this deficient educational system for blacks. The planter elite had historically been opposed to education for slaves, enacting laws that imposed fines and prison sentences on whites who attempted to teach blacks to read. "The laws must be upheld," editorialized the *Norfolk Southern Argus* after the court sentenced Mrs. Martha Douglass to one month in jail for giving lessons to a black child. A special state law had to be passed in 1842 permitting a slave boy to be taught to read so that he could serve a young blind white man.

Free public schooling in the North was hardly in full bloom in the nineteenth century, and yet illiteracy among whites in Virginia was at least double what it was in the North. Few people in Connecticut were unable to read, commented Virginia legislator George Summers in 1832, adding, "I should blush to see the catalogue of my own State." Virginia would lag far behind New England; Massachusetts would introduce free— and compulsory—education in 1852, whereas Richmond and most other Virginia cities and counties would not begin to establish some free schools until a decade after the Civil War. The Commonwealth of Virginia would have no statewide public school system until the twentieth century. The process of educating poor whites and blacks in the South, wrote Robert Penn Warren in 1930, had "scarcely begun."

No, Virginia would not import "that peculiar system of free schools in the New England States," declared Senator James Mason of Virginia in 1859. Free schools, he said, would "destroy that peculiar character which I am happy to believe belongs to the great mass of the Southern people." On the eve of the Civil War, the attitude toward universal education had not changed from what it had been decades earlier. When a visitor from England in 1834 asked about public schools in Richmond, he discovered that there weren't any. "But then, there were capital races. The training that was denied to the children," he wrote, "was given to the horses."

In 1861, Hugh Blair Grigsby sent some of his publications to Cornelius Felton, the president of Harvard. After leaving Yale, Grigsby had edited a Norfolk newspaper, the *American Beacon*, and had written histories of the Virginia ratifying convention of 1788 and the Virginia constitutional convention of 1829–1830. "I could not help regretting," Felton sweetly responded, "that our country has not a common center where from time to time the men of letters, and leading professional gentleman may meet, and become personally acquainted with each other. Your books have taught me how little I know of the literary works of Virginia, and how much there is in them which I and all our northern men ought to know."

Southerners, on the other hand, felt they knew all too much about the literary works of the North. "I wish we had energy, capital and enterprise enough in the metropolises of the Old Dominion," complained James Heath in 1839, "to creep out of the vassalage that we are placed in, to New-York literature." But Virginia's miserly neglect of public education had infected and impoverished the intellectual life of the state, leaving the antebellum Old Dominion generally bereft of bookstores, libraries, and learned societies. Without a bolder commitment to education, it was unlikely that Virginia could end its vassalage, develop a vital intellectual culture of its own, and attract its talented young men back to its home institutions.

Some Virginians proposed that the state take the North as its model and guide. A variety of literary associations flourished in the North, James Mercer Garnett observed in 1834. "Why should not we profit by their meritorious example, instead of entertaining against them (as far too many of us do), dislikes and animosities which are much more disgraceful to ourselves than injurious to them?"

Virginians mobilized themselves to promote and defend their culture. A Literary and Philosophical Society, created to do "honor to the literature of the South," was established in 1824 at Hampden-Sydney College. In 1831, John Marshall, James Madison, and other prominent Virginians established the Virginia Historical and Philosophical Society. Myriad journals—the *Southern Magazine*, *Magnolia*, *Southern Quarterly Review*, *Southern Literary Messenger*, *De Bow's Review*—were founded in the 1820s, 1830s, and 1840s. Writing for them were Virginia's professors, intellectuals, and men of letters—including educator George Frederick Holmes; Nathaniel Beverley Tucker, a novelist who also taught at the College of William and Mary and was the half-brother of John Randolph of Roanoke; Professor Thomas Roderick Dew; and later, the master polemicist George Fitzhugh. Also communicating their thoughts and ideas were South Carolinians like the poet and writer William Gilmore Simms; James Henry Hammond, governor and United States senator; and the agricultural theorist Edmund Ruffin, who had moved to South Carolina from Virginia.

Convinced of their pivotal role in the regeneration of the Old Dominion and the South, Virginia's men of letters embarked on the mission of raising the region's intellectual stature and restoring its confidence in itself. How? By encouraging reform in some areas—in education and agriculture as well as in industry, transportation, and politics—but mostly by defending the status quo and explaining southern values and the southern way of life. Together they articulated an antimaterialist, paternalistic, spiritual vision that portrayed southern society as a high point in civilization.

The "first great object" of the *Southern Quarterly Review*, its editors explained, was "the calm, temperate, thorough discussion of the question of slavery." A more vital intellectual life in the South would emerge, Virginia's men of letters believed, from a disinterested, philosophical inquiry into slavery, one that seriously explored biblical history, world history, and ethnology, one that enabled southerners to adjust intellectually as well as emotionally to slavery. A clear comprehension of the benefits and universality of slavery, wrote Holmes, would stiffen southerners' spines once and for all, helping weak-minded men to overcome their "speculative doubts" about slavery, their "lukewarm, shilly-shally convictions" that only supplied more arms to their abolitionist enemies. Far from stifling intellectual creativity, the discussion of the slavery controversy, he insisted, would stimulate "the creation of a genuine southern literature."

In the 1830s and 1840s, writers and philosophers in the North—Ralph Waldo Emerson, Henry David Thoreau, Henry Wadsworth Longfellow, John Greenleaf Whittier, Oliver Wendell Holmes, and others—confronted an epoch of extraordinarily rapid and deep change and struggled to understand its nature, its direction, and how it might be shaped and led by human beings for the benefit of all. But during those same decades, southern intellectuals, as on a becalmed sea with the fixed stars for comfort, withdrew into their own dominion, philosophizing about slavery and about how to integrate it into traditional republican thought.

In a sense, their philosophy was not merely reactionary; it was also revolutionary, for it injected new ideas and new colors into the monochrome American intellectual landscape that was so dominated by the liberal creed of individualism and freedom. Political philosopher Louis Hartz even called the "reactionary Enlightenment" of southern thinkers a "great imaginative moment in American political thought." Those southern writers would have been pleased to receive kudos for originality and creativity, for they were eager to establish their superiority over the northerners, who continually ridiculed southern backwardness and moral decay. But, even more, they wanted to define and defend, with intelligence and subtlety, a civilization and a way of life that they cherished.

These southern writers developed a coherent, radical theory that wedded communitarianism, feudalism, and Christianity, portraying slavery as the antithesis of capitalist individualism, atomization, and exploitation. Slavery, they argued, guaranteed a gentle, moral world, one that permitted masters and slaves to participate in the same community of shared duties, responsibilities, and interests. Whereas a wild and chaotic clash of selfish interests raged in northern society, slavery, they claimed, created order, prosperity, and social and even spiritual harmony. So interdependent were masters and slaves, so united in their duties and affections, so aware that they were all bound to God, that slavery had become, in the words of George Frederick Holmes, "an affair of the heart." It made possible a good life for all, he wrote, one that assured a kind of equality in the pursuit of happiness. "It protects those that require protection," Holmes wrote in the 1840s, "the young, the aged, and the infirm. It resists the tendency to convert all life and all social action into a mechanism for the mere augmentation of gain, and directs the minds and hearts of men to other and more elevated objects."

If slavery was so benevolent and rational, why should it be limited to blacks or to the South? Shouldn't it be shared with others? The northern states as well as Western Europe, maintained George Fitzhugh in the 1850s, were unconsciously marching toward slavery, for slavery alone guaranteed a "safe, efficient and human community." And the truth of his thesis, he contended, was visible and measurable all over the nation and the world: Whereas poverty and labor unrest convulsed northern and European cities, in the slaveholding South "all is peace, quiet, plenty and contentment. We have no mobs, no trade unions, no strikes for higher wages, no armed resistance to the law, but little jealousy of the rich by the poor."

The members of this southern literary community also argued that the system of bondage had the additional merit of offering to some fortunate people the inestimable gift of elegant leisure, permitting a class of educated men—like these writers themselves—to live a life of the mind. Their goal was to create a vigorous southern intellectual culture, so critical to the future of the South, and ultimately to serve as their society's "moral stewards," whose mission was to explain to southerners the social benefits of bondage as well as the duties and burdens of the slaveowner.

These southern writers and thinkers congratulated themselves not just on producing ingenious essays on slavery, but, more important, on inspiring a revitalization of the culture and intellect of the South. And yet, in reality, the pro-slavery southern writers, strangers to the desire to change society, move it in new and better directions, and transform the conditions of human life, produced nothing like the searching, inquisitive literature of writers like Emerson and Thoreau. On the contrary, they simply converted their beliefs and prejudices into emphatic assertions and dogmatic maxims, some of which were so illogical that they required agile linguistic somersaults.

James Holcombe of the University of Virginia performed such verbal legerdemain when he described slavery as "consistent with the purest justice" and contended that bondage was sanctioned by "enlightened humanity." The only being who is a slave, asserted another writer seeking to prove the essential justice and harmony of southern society, is the one "who is forced into a position in society which is below the claim of his intellect and morals." Redefining the concept of freedom so that it could apply even to slaves, that writer claimed that freedom depended "upon the degree of *obedience* which we pay to the laws of creation."

George Fitzhugh's many readers in the South were similarly treated to new heights of verbal dexterity. They learned that "to protect the weak, we must first enslave them," and that slavery "is necessary as an educational institution, and is worth ten times all the common schools of the North." Little wonder that few people in the North were interested in entering into this discourse of the absurd. "Why the devil don't someone abuse me?" Fitzhugh muttered when he lectured on "The Failure of Free Society" to a silent, incredulous audience in New Haven, Connecticut, in 1855.

Even in the South, pro-slavery literature was a hard sell. Southerners continued to read northern periodicals. The editor of *De Bow's Review* in

1856 bemoaned that "periodicals, devoted mainly to the vindication of southern interests . . . continue to be neglected by many who should be their most prompt patrons and advocates." Why weren't southerners "trumpeting their own praise" instead of "crippl[ing] the efforts of home genius, and talent, and enterprize."

"Who of the North reads a Southern book, or attends a Southern college?" asked the *De Bow's* editor. Who indeed? No well-established publishing houses, like Harper and Brothers, established in New York in 1817, or Little, Brown, founded in Boston in 1837, existed in Virginia. Indeed, almost all of Virginia's authors—John Marshall, John Pendleton Kennedy, Beverley Tucker, George Tucker, and even Edgar Allan Poe—published their works in Philadelphia, Boston, and New York. There were no large public libraries, well-frequented book shops, or prominent learned societies like Benjamin Franklin's American Philosophical Society. The Virginia Society for the Promotion of Useful Knowledge, founded in Williamsburg in 1774, had disappeared by 1777. Though proud of their history, Virginians did not create the Virginia Historical Society until 1831, only to see it cease functioning by the end of the decade.

The efforts of southern writers and thinkers to propagate their ideas were handicapped by the absence of great cities and a large middle class accustomed to buying books and magazines. Already in 1821, James Madison had doubted that a new agricultural treatise would find readers in Virginia, "so difficult is a diffusion of literary production through its dispersed readers, and so universal is the present dearth of means, even for the minuter articles of cost." The *Southern Review*, founded in 1828, ceased publication five years later. The *Southern Literary Messenger*, despite talented editors like Poe and John Thompson, could not compare to some northern magazines; the circulation of the *Southern Quarterly Review* in the 1850s was only 3,000 copies; *Harper's*, by comparison, had a circulation of 93,000.

Southern thinkers had invested their energy and their intellectual capital in the defense, romanticization, and glorification of slavery. Mobilizing historical, communitarian, and spiritual arguments, theirs was not an unsophisticated enterprise, and yet it did not pay off. Indeed, it was a stunning and catastrophic failure. The fixation on slavery, far from strengthening the quality of the South's intellectual culture, rendered it more insular, shallow, and vulnerable, exiling southern men and women of letters to the unlit, irrelevant margins of Western intellectual life. George Fitzhugh admitted relishing arguments that were "odd, eccentric, extravagant and disorderly," but those arguments would never find a home in mainstream Western thought. "Is the Nineteenth Century to be a Contrast to the Eighteenth?" a disenchanted John Adams had asked Jefferson in 1815. "Is it to extinguish all the Lights of its Predecessor?" Some of the bright lights of the eighteenth century did indeed dim—in the South.

Jefferson's efforts in Charlottesville could not compensate for the degeneration of intellectual life in Virginia—nor could the successful establishment of the University of Virginia halt the migration of some young Virginia men to northern colleges and universities. "I never conversed with a cultivated Southerner," wrote Frederick Law Olmsted in the 1850s, "who did not express a wish or intention to have his own children educated where they should be free from demoralizing association with slaves." Southern mothers, too, Olmsted believed, preferred to send their sons to northern schools out of fear of miscegenation, recognizing that it was common for white southern men to have black concubines. "Under slavery we live surrounded by prostitutes," remarked one bitter southern woman. Before Madison died in 1836, he also expressed sympathy for the plight of white southern women, who he believed lived in a state of "perpetual suspicion" of the white men who had fathered the many mulatto children born to slaves.

In vain, southern newspaper editors in the 1840s and 1850s called for a halt to the student migration. "If Southern gentlemen would not be instrumental in the political prostitution of their sons," wrote the *Richmond Enquirer*, "they should not send them to Harvard for law or to Yale for science." A group of Virginians meeting in Richmond in 1854 issued the opinion that a "just self-respect" required Virginians to support southern literature and patronize southern schools. One southern group summed it up: "Southern men should have southern heads and hearts."

Only after John Brown's aborted attempt in 1859 to instigate a slave rebellion by attacking Harpers Ferry in western Virginia did southern students begin an exodus from the North. When 200 Virginians who had been studying medicine in Philadelphia arrived at the train station in Richmond in late December 1859, several hundred cheering people, including members of the Southern Rights Association of Richmond and the Richmond City Council, welcomed them home. At Capitol Square, the governor and 5,000 more people applauded them as a band played "Oh! Carry Me Back to Old Virginia."

"Virginia has contributed her blood and her intelligence to the country, and she now calls back her own," declared the governor, Henry Wise. "Let us have our own schools and our own centres of trade, our own manufactures and our own doctors, and then those people of the North . . . will learn to attend to their own business." But if they didn't, the governor warned, "let every man prepare, not only with the musket, for the crisis, but also prepare his soul to meet its demand."

Two years later, in 1861, after General Pierre Beauregard of South Carolina ordered the shore batteries in Charleston to fire on the small island of Fort Sumter, signaling the beginning of the Civil War, southern students left Princeton en masse. Almost 300 Harvard graduates would fight in the Confederate Army. The southern students in his class at Harvard, Thomas Jefferson Coolidge later wrote in his memoirs, had all been swept away by the Civil War.

4

Roads, Canals, Railroads: Moving in Place

"P.S. Have you considered all the consequences of your proposition respecting post roads?" wrote a dubious Jefferson to Congressman James Madison in 1796. Madison, in an expansive, nationalist mood, had just proposed a bill to survey a national post road from Maine to Georgia, calling his plan "the commencement of an extensive work." But Jefferson, having recently resigned from Washington's cabinet and relishing his farmer's life at Monticello, was happy for life to stay local.

Roads, Jefferson claimed, were best left to county governments or, better yet, to men "on the spot." Even a state legislature, he added, was too distant to supervise the building of roads. How then could the federal government possibly undertake such a task? "What will it be," he demanded, "when a member of N.H. is to mark out a road for Georgia?" Congress did have the power to establish post roads, he conceded, but did that mean it could "go to cutting down mountains and bridging of rivers"? Shouldn't states be masters of their own topography? Madison's proposal was defeated in Congress.

"Our country is too large to have all its affairs directed by a single government," Jefferson wrote in the summer of 1800, convinced that the states should be "independent as to everything within themselves." What tasks did he then wish to leave to the federal government? "Let the general government be reduced to foreign concerns only," he decided.

But the American landscape looked very different to him a few months later, after his election to the presidency, as he peered out the windows of the executive mansion in Washington. In the spring of 1801, he nervously awaited the arrival of his newly appointed secretary of state—James Madison. Roads were so poor in Virginia that Jefferson insisted on giving his friend detailed directions for finding a passable route up to the capital. "I tried the road by Ravensworth," Jefferson wrote, explaining that 2 miles of that road were so impassable that any carriage would surely overturn. The choice of roads was limited to bad and worse. "You must absolutely come by Fairfax courthouse, all that road being practicable till you come to Little's Lane." But two days of wind and sun, he predicted, would probably make the rest of the road passable for Madison.

As he began to grapple with the needs of his youthful nation, Jefferson would not seek to limit the national government's reach solely to "foreign concerns." In his second Inaugural Address in 1805 as well as in his sixth Annual Message two years later, he sketched out a proposal for surplus revenues to be applied—at least in peacetime—"to the great purposes of the public education, roads, rivers, canals." Not even the great national-ist Alexander Hamilton had dared go so far, conceding that there was in-deed doubt that the national government had the authority to supervise and fund a comprehensive plan for internal improvements. But Jefferson seemed undeterred, his vision sweeping. "New channels of communica-tion will be opened between the States. . . . The lines of separation will disappear, their interests will be identified, and their union cemented by new and indissoluble ties."

Congress asked Jefferson's Swiss-born secretary of the treasury, Albert Gallatin, to submit a comprehensive report on the nation's transportation needs. Gallatin consulted with engineers and other experts in all the states and, a year later, submitted his findings—a stunning blueprint for north-south canals extending from Massachusetts to North Carolina; east-west canals connecting the Atlantic coast and the Great Lakes; im-proved navigation on the Susquehanna, Potomac, James, and Savannah rivers; and roads to Detroit, St. Louis, and New Orleans. It would be a truly national system, reaching to the remotest points of the nation. Only the national government, Gallatin concluded, was competent to undertake such a vast project.

Hopes that Gallatin's plan might be adopted were dashed by the economic aftereffects of Jefferson's 1807 embargo—his attempt to avoid war with Europe by simply closing American ports to trade with European belligerents. The embargo had hurt American business and dried up surplus revenues. But Congress nevertheless did follow up on Gallatin's proposal for an interstate turnpike to run from Cumberland, Maryland, to the Ohio River. Jefferson approved and signed the Cumberland Road Act, even scolding the Pennsylvania localists who wanted to influence the road's route through their state.

But back in Virginia after his retirement, Jefferson's nationalist inclinations dissipated. He became once again a gentleman-planter, living, thinking, and feeling like a Virginian. He recorded the temperature when he awoke, wrote letters before breakfast, rode around his estate, enjoyed dinner at four in the afternoon with his family and guests, and retired to his bedroom in the early evening. There would be no more trips—either to Washington or to Europe. "I am held by the cords of love to my family and country," he wrote in 1809 to a friend in Paris, "or I should certainly join you."

Embracing the concerns of the old Republicans of the Tidewater, Jefferson returned to the narrow, cramped view of constitutional government he had held in the 1790s, before his presidency. And bolstering him as he increasingly assumed the mantle of advocate and defender of the interests of Virginia was the knowledge that he was not alone. He was surrounded, he wrote in 1824, by many "companions in sentiments, the Madisons, the Monroes, the Randolphs, the Macons, all good men and true, of primitive principles."

Not only did Jefferson choose only Virginians to be his "companions in sentiments," he also chose a Virginia newspaper, Thomas Ritchie's *Richmond Enquirer*, as his one source for news. The *Enquirer*, he wrote in 1823, was "the best that is published or ever has been published in America." Jefferson's mind continued to expand in his correspondence with his intellectual companion and sparring partner, John Adams of Massachusetts, but his political province shrank.

"He is now eighty-two years old, very little altered from what he was ten years ago," remarked a young Harvard professor who paid a visit to Jefferson at Monticello in 1825. The former president was still "very active, lively, and happy, riding from ten to fifteen miles every day, and talking without the least restraint, very pleasantly, upon all subjects"— well, pleasantly except when the topic was national roads and canals. Then he bristled and raged that the policies of the new president, John Quincy Adams, included a far-reaching national plan for internal improvements. "Under the authority to establish post roads," Jefferson railed, "*they* claim that of cutting down mountains for the construction of roads, of digging canals." And to justify this invasion of the jurisdictions that, he insisted, belonged "exclusively" to the states, the government deviously relied on powers it derived from the Constitution's ambiguous, overly vague "general welfare" clause, which gave to Congress the "Power . . . to provide for the common Defence and general Welfare of the United States."

Convinced that nothing less than a strong statement of principle and opposition was necessary to rescue the Constitution and the compact among the states, in 1825 he penned a "solemn Declaration and Protest of the Commonwealth of Virginia" lambasting the government's plan to violate the borders and sovereignty of the states. But Madison advised him to drop the matter; in the most prosperous and developing states, internal improvements were leaping ahead, and a protest coming from Virginia, already known for its "internal weakness," would not, Madison counseled, be seasonable.

Virginia's roads were "often knee-deep in mud, and many streams had to be forded," wrote Thomas Jefferson Coolidge, the president's great-grandson, when he visited Virginia in the mid-1800s. Frequently little more than trails or old bridlepaths, they meandered through the Virginia countryside and were dotted with tree stumps and all manner of holes and ruts. So-called "corduroy" roads, covered with saplings, although rough, were at least passable in winter. Only a drought made rivers and creeks fordable on horseback, wrote one Virginian, adding that "rainy spells" were a "grave annoyance." Indeed, few streams were bridged; wide rivers could be crossed only on ferries operated by boatmen with long poles. The construction of roads and bridges and the maintenance of ferries were all left to towns, counties, and private individuals. The few "turnpikes" in the Richmond area were really "mud pikes," quipped one visitor, adding that the only thing distinguishing them from other wretchedly neglected and dilapidated county roads was the toll.

"The embryo metropolis" of Washington on Virginia's border would set a better example for the young republic if it surrounded itself "with good roads and substantial bridges, in lieu of those inconvenient wooden structures and dangerous roads," wrote Englishman Morris Birkbeck when he visited the United States in 1817. Seventeen years later, it could still be a harrowing journey from Washington across the Potomac to Alexandria and Mount Vernon. "If you would see the last resting-place of the Father of his Country," wrote a visitor to Virginia in 1834, "you must consent to be jolted ten or twenty miles over the most execrable road that necks were ever broken upon." So poor were the roads that James Madison could only offer a horse and not a carriage to pick up a visiting friend at the Orange County Court House. "Such is the state of the roads," he apologized in 1832. They had not improved since 1769, when he first traveled along Virginia's harrowing byways to college in Princeton.

And yet, roads were a symbol not only of progress but of civilization itself. They were a moral as well as a physical sign of community and activity, observed Frederick Law Olmsted. To Olmsted, the appalling condition of Virginia roads bespoke an indifference to civic society and a retreat from activity into stagnation. Drawn in upon themselves, Virginians were simply unwilling to make exertions to maintain ties with neighboring communities or the broader world. "Bad roads meant bad morals," agreed Henry Adams, recalling a pilgrimage he had made as a little boy with his father to Mount Vernon over almost impassable roads. In New England, he commented, people associated roads as well as schools, clothes, and a clean face with order and morality. The abysmal roads in Virginia revealed to him the dispiriting decline of social morality in the Old Dominion.

In December 1811, De Witt Clinton, the young, handsome mayor of New York City, and Gouverneur Morris, a former United States senator and now chairman of New York State's board of canal commissioners, were quietly ushered into President Madison's office. Morris and Madison greeted each other politely, though not warmly; they no longer were political allies, although they could remember working together twenty-four years earlier, drafting the Constitution in Philadelphia. Now Morris had a request.

He had conceived the idea, he explained, of a 300-mile-long canal across upstate New York to connect the Hudson River (and thus New York City and the Atlantic Ocean) with Lake Erie and the Mississippi River. It would open extraordinary channels of communication, permitting unlimited development. "Hundreds of large ships will, at no distant period, bound on the billows of this inland sea," he said, seeking to arouse Madison's enthusiasm. Would the president help secure federal aid to build the canal? Madison was courteous but, Morris noted in his diary, mumbled that such funding might be unconstitutional. "We rely on your patriotism," Morris pointedly told the president.

Madison agreed to forward their request to Congress, along with his own recommendation that Congress take "whatever steps may be proper on their part" to give the nation the "signal advantages" of a system of canals and roads. Especially since the general security of the nation depended on such canals, Madison asked Congress to regard the merits of the plan "in the strongest lights." Treasury Secretary Albert Gallatin even found money to pay for the canal with revenues from a large land grant in northern Indiana. But the "microcosmic minds" in Congress, Morris sneered, rejected his scheme, telling New York to rely on its "own power."

And New York did. In 1817, work began. Eight years later, the Erie Canal—the world's longest canal and a masterpiece of engineering—was inaugurated. With its 18 aqueducts and 83 locks, and a rise of 568 feet from the Hudson River to Lake Erie, the 363-mile canal traversing New York State proved an immediate boon to the nation, an economic engine that opened the West to vast migration, trade, and development. The *New York Commercial Advertiser* exulted in the stupendous achievement, predicting—correctly, as it would turn out—the "incalculable benefits" to the state. The "meeting of the waters" would give farmers in the Great Lakes area access to the Atlantic coast; commerce and shipping would increase, sparking development and population growth in the West, augmenting the value of land traversed by the canal, and raising revenue from canal tolls for the government. The canal would not only boost the growth of upstate towns like Buffalo, Syracuse, and Rochester but would make New York City the busiest port and commercial hub in America. The canal would produce an explosion of prosperity for all.

Even Jefferson was impressed. Virginia had its own aspirations for western trade, but New York, he wrote to De Witt Clinton in 1822, seemed to have a "sounder calculating mind," able to amass capital "instead of useless consumption." In truth, it was more than just "sound calculations" that inspired New York. It was also creativity, vision, invention, an openness to experimentation, and a spirit of perseverance and state pride. Did Jefferson remember telling a New York assemblyman in 1808 that talk of a 350-mile-long canal was "little short of madness"?

On the same day that Clinton and Morris lobbied Madison for their canal—December 23, 1811—Madison also signed a reapportionment bill that gave the northern states a net increase of eighteen seats in the House of Representatives. New York itself gained ten seats, reflecting its new status as the most populous state in the Union. The only state to lose a seat? Virginia. But even worse was to come.

The "microcosmic minds" in Congress apparently did not recall that the Framers of the Constitution had come together in Philadelphia precisely to create a national government with the capacity to plan and support a system of roads and canals. From the very beginning, "internal improvements"—roads, canals, bridges—had been not only the new government's mission but its raison d'être.

"What a monument to your retirement it would be!" Jefferson had enthusiastically written to Washington after the War of Independence, encouraging the general to persist in his dream for a Potomac Canal. It could be a channel, Jefferson wrote in 1784, that would "pour into our lap the whole commerce of the Western world." There was no time to lose. "This is the moment in which the trade of the West will begin to get into motion and to take it's direction. It behooves us then to open our doors to it." Otherwise, he added, Virginia would lose out not only to the Hudson and Mississippi but also to the Susquehanna, for Pennsylvania's plan to improve that river and monopolize trade with the West was moving forward.

Jefferson himself was no newcomer to the importance of navigable rivers. The Rivanna River, the north branch of the James, passed through his own land, but it had never been used for navigation. Flooded in the winter, little more than a rivulet in the summer, "scarcely an empty canoe had ever passed down it," he wrote. One day the young Jefferson paddled along the Rivanna, mapping its obstructions. At the green age of twenty, he formed a "trusteeship" to raise money to clear the river. Four decades later, on the eve of his election to the presidency, in a contemplative moment, Jefferson soberly asked himself "whether my country is the better for my having lived at all." The first accomplishment that came to his mind was the Rivanna, for it could now "be used completely and fully for carrying down all our produce."

Jefferson's plea for a Potomac Canal buoyed Washington, animating his entrepreneurial imagination. The general plunged ahead, pouring his heart, energy, and managerial skill into the scheme. He lobbied Governor Benjamin Harrison and Virginia's legislature, touting the magnitude of the project. The Potomac would be a modern waterway "for the trade of a rising empire" and a wide door to the West. The fertile plains of the Ohio, he wrote to Lafayette, would then be opened "to the poor, the needy and the oppressed of the Earth"—as well as to Washington himself, who owned tens of thousands of acres that awaited development. But for Washington, the project was even more important politically than commercially, for unless the western regions were bound by trade to the Atlantic states, they would look elsewhere, to the Spanish southwest or to the British north, and would probably evolve into "quite a distinct People" or worse, become "very troublesome neighbours."

The plan was to broaden the Potomac at some points, at others to dig canals and install locks, ultimately linking the Mississippi and Ohio rivers with the Chesapeake Bay. Alexandria would most likely become a port and way station where cargo would be transferred from canal vessels to larger ships. "The earnestness with which [Washington] espouses the undertaking," marveled James Madison, "is hardly to be described, and shows that a mind like his, capable of great views . . . cannot bear a vacancy." Madison predicted that the project would double the value of land in Virginia and, even more important, create greater economic opportunity, thereby helping stem the steady flow of Virginians out of the state.

When the Potomac Canal Company received its charter from Virginia and Maryland, the two states bordering the river, the prestige of Washington's name quickly attracted members of the wealthy elite who, eager for a good investment, bought up twice the necessary number of shares. While James Rumsey, the inventor of mechanical boats that could sail upstream, attended to the engineering details, Washington busied himself with the governmental issues involved.

He was thinking not just as a profit-seeking investor and Tidewater Virginian but as an American. His was a national vision of improved transport and communication throughout the states. One of his first steps was to organize the Mount Vernon Conference, at which representatives from Virginia and Maryland would meet in March 1785 to work out commercial and legal issues. After Maryland invited Pennsylvania and Delaware to join the talks, Virginia proposed expanding the next meeting even more, so that representatives from all thirteen states could gather to consider a "uniform system" for regulating commerce and transportation across the nation. That conference, the Annapolis Convention, met in the fall of 1785 but proved a disappointment, with delegates from only five states in attendance. But they called for yet another convention, at which, they hoped, delegates would agree to authorize the federal government to initiate and orchestrate infrastructure projects. That convention would take place in Philadelphia in 1787. And so, a direct line of descent can be traced from the Constitutional Convention—at which Benjamin Franklin called for "a power to provide for cutting canals where deemed necessary"—back to George Washington's Potomac Canal.

"No circumstance, not even an earthquake," wrote an incredulous Speaker of the House, Henry Clay, could have excited more surprise than the announcement that President Madison, in his last official act in office in March 1817, had vetoed a bill he had previously supported and defended, the Bonus Bill.

Just months earlier, on December 3, 1816, Madison had enthusiastically urged Congress to approve a bill for "a comprehensive system of roads and canals" that would draw together every part of the country, promoting commerce, increasing prosperity, and enhancing the nation's security. And a year before that, he had even told the Congress that, although some individual states had begun road and canal projects "with laudable enterprise," he was convinced that only the federal government had the "national jurisdiction and national means" to complete so "estimable a work." Indeed, during the War of 1812, the difficulties that army and navy commanders encountered in getting crucial supplies to soldiers and sailors had brought home the lesson that better avenues of communication were needed between the Atlantic states and the West. No one doubted that Madison favored a strong federal role in infrastructure projects.

On December 6, 1816, on the floor of the Senate, James Barbour of Virginia called for the creation of a standing committee on roads and canals—only to see his proposal defeated. A week later, in the House, John Calhoun of South Carolina introduced a bill to funnel the dividends and "bonus" that the government would receive from its shares in the new Second Bank of the United States into a fund for improving the nation's road and canals. Calhoun argued that the political health of the republic demanded enlightened government with "enlarged views" and a willingness to act. The Bonus Bill passed in Congress, though in the end, watered down by amendments, it provided only for a national fund, not a national blueprint for roads and canals. The members of Congress expected that the fund would disintegrate into a trough for local spoilsmen and their pet projects, but its sponsors supported it anyway, willing to compromise with political reality and adapt to the new era of powerful local interest groups.

But when the bill arrived in Madison's office for his approval, he declined to sign it. "I am constrained by the insuperable difficulty I feel in reconciling the bill with the Constitution," he wrote. In his veto message, he explained stiffly that the power to construct roads and canals could not be deduced from the Constitution "without an inadmissible latitude of construction." Neither the government's power to regulate commerce nor its power to secure the "common defense" and the "general welfare," he said, were sufficient to justify the bill. "I have no option but to withhold my signature from it."

Before his veto, Madison had certainly seemed to endorse a government role in internal improvements. In two earlier messages to Congress, he had acknowledged that the states could not possibly manage the complex task of planning and constructing a system of interstate roads and canals. He had not asked for a constitutional amendment, though he said that a "defect" of constitutional authority "may" be encountered. Only two congressmen—Robert Wright of Maryland and Philip Barbour of Virginia—had raised the issue of constitutionality. Why, then, would the president decide to block legislation that he himself had favored? John Marshall's Supreme Court would not have objected to the Bonus Bill. Why then did Madison?

In words too understated for most mortals, Madison later explained to Monroe why he had not made it far clearer to Congress that he would absolutely not sign a bill for internal improvements unless and until there was a constitutional amendment. "I had not supposed that my view of the Constitution could have been unknown," he wrote with an excess of subtlety, "and I felt with great force the delicacy of giving intimations of it, to be used as a bar or a clog to a depending measure." When a young Virginia congressman ventured the opinion that perhaps a constitutional amendment was not really essential, Madison tartly reminded him where he had spent the summer of 1787. "I am not unaware that my belief, not to say knowledge, of the views of those who proposed the Constitution . . . may influence my interpretation of the instrument."

And yet, Madison had originally taken a very flexible approach to constitutional interpretation. "Wherever the end is required, the means are authorised," he had written in *Federalist* No. 44. "Wherever a general power to do a thing is given, every particular power necessary for doing it, is included." When a congressman in 1789 urged that all the powers of the federal government should be explicitly specified, and that the Tenth Amendment to the Constitution should read: "The powers not *expressly* delegated to the United States . . . are reserved to the States, or to the people," Madison sharply objected to the word "expressly." Unless people accepted that some powers were implied, he warned, the Constitution would have to descend "to recount every minutiae."

At the Constitutional Convention, Madison and George Mason had proposed a clause specifically authorizing the federal government to undertake internal improvements. At that time, Madison supported a government role in funding and overseeing infrastructure projects. And in *Federalist* No. 14, he had even sketched his own far-sighted blueprint for roads and canals. "Intercourse through the union will be daily facilitated by new improvements," he had written, envisioning well-kept, direct roads, interior navigation, and improved transportation between the western regions and the Atlantic.

Madison's approach to the constitutional powers of the government shifted back and forth over time, but those shifts were always in response to the changes he perceived in the balance of power between the federal government and the states and the balance among the branches of government. In 1787, he was eager to grant more power to the national government because it had proved too weak to govern effectively under the Articles of Confederation. But under Washington and Hamilton's energetic leadership, the balance had shifted too much, Madison believed, in the opposite direction: The national government was growing too powerful at the expense of the states, and the executive branch was growing too powerful at the expense of Congress.

Making Madison's approach even more complicated was the value he accorded historical precedent and public opinion; those factors could outweigh, in his mind, purely abstract constitutional arguments. Thus, in 1816, twenty-five years after opposing Hamilton's Bank of the United States, President Madison bowed to precedent and signed into law a bill chartering the Second Bank of the United States; and in 1824, seven years after vetoing the Bonus Bill, he would support the Survey Bill, a congressional proposal for a national system of roads and canals that was hardly different from the Bonus Bill itself. Madison reasoned that, since the majority of Americans considered canals and other internal improvements useful and of permanent benefit to the nation, it was not reasonable to resist "the great temptation of 'utility.'"

In all of these cases, the one constant was Madison's search for political stability. He was convinced that political balance could be achieved only through a careful weighing of constitutional imperatives, precedent, and the public interest.

In vetoing the Bonus Bill in 1817, it was unlikely that Madison was already anticipating his imminent return home and surrendering to Virginians' fears of unlimited government and to their distaste for economic development. Nor was he seduced, as was Jefferson in his later years, by the spirit of Virginia localism. On the contrary, Madison had made a meticulous and dispassionate examination of the Bonus Bill. And yet, he vetoed a farsighted and practical bill that might have launched Virginia along with the rest of the nation on a new dynamic course. Instead, the Old Dominion remained anchored in place, deprived of the impetus, funds, and expertise it would have needed to compete in the industrializing nineteenth century and complete the infrastructure projects that were crucial to its economic future.

Back home, Virginians applauded Madison's veto of the Bonus Bill. Fourteen of Virginia's eighteen representatives in the House, anxious to block what they viewed as a federal power grab, had cast their votes against the bill. Thomas Ritchie, the editor of the *Richmond Enquirer*, congratulated Madison for saving the country from "the gulph of consolidation" and the "waves of federal usurpation." The Tidewater planters, after all, already had easy access to water routes: Many of their homes— Mount Vernon, Shirley, Gunston Hall, Berkeley, and others—were situated on Virginia's navigable rivers, and oceangoing ships could sail to their wharves. Thus the Old Dominion at least appeared to have nothing to gain from a federal program.

Jefferson, too, rejoiced. Like the other members of Virginia's political elite, he considered the Bonus Bill a stark and dramatic case of federal overreaching hiding under the cloak of the Constitution's "general welfare" provision. It was not a mere "grammatical quibble," he wrote to Albert Gallatin, to read the Constitution correctly. The general welfare clause, he insisted, referred only to the federal government's power to lay taxes and pay debts. Madison's veto, he hoped, would "settle forever the meaning of this phrase."

Adding to Jefferson's negative feelings about internal improvements was a sense of betrayal by the western territories. Certain that republican virtue would flourish among those virtuous citizens who led self-sufficient lives cultivating the land, Jefferson had once hailed the West and its vast unspoiled territory as an "empire of liberty" that would ensure, for generations to come, the survival of the independent yeoman. But now, by asking for federal assistance to open up vital lifelines for trade and to provide desperately needed access to markets, westerners, Jefferson believed, had deserted the agricultural states and his concept of republican virtue. Instead they were allying themselves with—and helping to strengthen—the banking and industrial interests of the North, which wanted nothing more than a powerful, consolidated central government.

In 1822, another Virginian, President James Monroe, followed Madison's lead, vetoing a bill for the repair and extension of the national turnpike, the Cumberland Road. Construction had been authorized in 1806, and work had begun in 1811. By 1822, repairs were already needed, and many in Congress proposed to erect tollgates and use the proceeds to preserve the road. But Monroe vetoed the bill, explaining, in an interminable constitutional disquisition of 25,000 words, that—with some exceptions, such as for national defense or for the postal system—the government did not have the authority to create a national transportation system without a constitutional amendment. It was an "injudicious" decision, sighed John Quincy Adams, Monroe's disappointed secretary of state. But the following year, Congress passed appropriations for repairing the Cumberland Road and a bill for harbor improvements.

Three years later, Adams, now president himself, called once again for a national plan for internal improvements, bestowing special praise on the recently opened Erie Canal. Unlike Madison, he had not attended the Constitutional Convention, but he had no doubt that the Constitution allowed for such federal undertakings. If it had not, Adams mused, it could be said that the Founders "performed their work in a manner *so ineffably stupid* as to deny themselves the means of bettering their own condition."

"I ask gentlemen," declared Virginian John Randolph in the House of Representatives in 1824, "to look well to what they are now doing—to the colossal power with which they are now arming this Government." A Pennsylvania congressman had just proposed the Survey Bill, a national plan for roads and canals to assure the movement of the mail as well as the commercial and military viability of the nation. Randolph believed that the bill posed a great danger to Virginia, and he summoned all his rhetorical skill and ardor to tear the new proposal to shreds.

Strutting back and forth, booted and spurred, a whip often in hand, a favorite hound of his crouching beneath his desk, Randolph cut a strange, outlandish figure on the floor of the House. From one of the great families of Virginia, he had lived on an estate on the Appomattox aptly named Bizarre; but when he moved to Roanoke, he began calling himself John Randolph of Roanoke.

When he was not in Washington, Randolph led an eccentric, alcohol-saturated life on his run-down estate, surrounded by several hundred slaves. In Congress, he talked for hours on end in his high-pitched, squeaky voice. John Quincy Adams heard him orate in 1820. "His speech, as usual, had neither beginning, middle nor end," Adams wrote in his memoirs. "Egotism, Virginian aristocracy, slave-scourging liberty, religion, literature, science, wit, fancy, generous feelings, and malignant passions constitute a chaos in his mind, from which nothing orderly can ever flow."

Randolph's "rabid foam" notwithstanding, he was one of the most popular and powerful politicians in Virginia, a proud conservative and passionate anticapitalist ideologue. He saw his mission as representing the traditional elite of eastern Virginia. He was a new brand of Virginia leader who spurned national union, federal power, economic development, and public education.

Whereas George Washington had believed that national roads and canals, by facilitating travel, commerce, and the circulation of news and knowledge, would promote citizens' feelings of union and sense of connectedness, Randolph, for his part, cared not a whit about national connectedness. But he did care deeply about keeping the national government out of the affairs of Virginia. "No Government can be safe for Virginia," he declared, "that is not a Government of persons having a common feeling—a common interest—a common right with Virginia."

The Survey Bill, Randolph railed, was just one more example of the alarming and outrageous expansion of federal power that he believed was taking place in the country. "You are told that in making roads and digging canals, and spending millions upon them," he exclaimed on the floor of Congress, "you are promoting the honor, and interest, and grandeur of the country!" On the contrary, he cried, the bill only masked the real agenda of the national government: the expansion of federal power. If Congress could plan roads, it might also declare that commerce "shall be carried on only in a particular way, by a particular road, or through a particular canal." Fired up by his own words, he went further, claiming that the "vagrant power" to construct roads and canals was being subsumed under the power to defend the nation and make war. "And under this power to make war, sir, what may we not do?" Southerners, he darkly warned, had the most to lose: They would "perish like so many mice."

And then Randolph revealed his true hand—and the real reason for Virginians' opposition to federally funded internal improvements: If the national government could interfere in domestic policy, it could extend its reach to the abolition of slavery. Randolph clearly understood that the abolition of slavery, just like the construction of roads and canals, could be interpreted as promoting the "general welfare"—by an activist, empowered federal government. If Congress had the power to construct roads, Randolph shrieked, "they may emancipate *every slave in the United States.*"

The idea of a national plan to improve the nation's infrastructure had hit an acutely raw nerve, for many Virginians viewed any broadening of federal power as a threat to their slave property. Philip Barbour, Randolph's Virginia ally in Congress, cautioned that the Survey Bill was "like Aaron's serpent"; it would soon swallow up the state governments. Senator John Taylor of Caroline compared it to a Trojan horse and derided the idea that the states, "when they cease to be united by the Constitution, may be kept together by roads and canals." And Virginia governor John Tyler warned in 1826 that the government's assumed power over roads and canals, more than any other power, represented the greatest danger to the states.

The objections of Virginians notwithstanding, Congress passed the Survey Bill, and President Monroe signed it. Secretary of War John

Calhoun put together a Board of Engineers to conduct surveys and to design a national system of roads and canals, an updated version of Gallatin's 1808 blueprint. But within several years, as Jacksonian democracy dawned, the effort drowned in a sea of local jealousies, opportunism, and greed. Jacksonian Congresses allocated funds for internal improvements, but on a decentralized, ad hoc basis; a coherent, nationwide plan never materialized. When Jackson vetoed a bill in 1830 for a road from Maysville, Kentucky, to Lexington, the *Richmond Enquirer* cheered him for "arresting the rage of encroachment" on the jurisdiction of the states.

John Pendleton Kennedy's description of a Fourth of July celebration, in his gently satirical novel *Swallow Barn* of 1832, captured Virginians' skepticism about internal improvements, their dread of federal intrusion in their affairs, and their provincialism and insularity. On the Fourth, Virginians gathered at the "Landing" to hear speeches and toasts. Once an active trading port where tobacco was loaded onto foreign vessels, the Landing had become a sleepy dock for a few river craft, surrounded by a handful of dilapidated buildings and a swamp. And yet, Kennedy wrote, it was still a lovely scene of "that striking repose, which is peculiar to the tide-water views; soft, indolent and clear, as if nature had retreated into this drowsy nook, and fallen asleep over her own image."

At the celebration in Kennedy's novel, a group of thirty or forty people surround some speakers, who are debating an intricate point of constitutional law. "Can't Congress," asks a character named Sandy Walker, "supposing they were to pass a law to that effect, come and take a road of theirn any where they have a mind to, through any man's land? . . . What does Congress care about your state rights, so as they have got the money?" Things were getting worse and worse, says another character, railing that the government was coming into the state and cutting up orchards and meadows. Why, President Jackson behaved just like a dictator, like Napoleon! "What's the use of states if they are all to be cut up with canals and railroads and tariffs? No, no, gentlemen! you may depend, Old Virginny's not going to let Congress carry on in her day!"

Threatened by the idea of national interference in the infrastructure of their state, in 1816 the members of the Virginia Assembly created a Board of Public Works and established a fund for internal improvements. The Old Dominion could no longer afford to remain "stationary," the House of Delegates declared. It was no secret that, if Virginia possessed better means of transportation, its mineral wealth could be extracted and shipped to industrial sites and ports; new factories and foundries could be created. Lively, bustling cities would develop, and new markets would open for farmers. Land values would increase, emigration out of the state would slow, and a progressive spirit of innovation would take hold. But could the state manage to go it alone, asked the *Richmond Enquirer*, "without calling upon Hercules?"

In 1816, in the wake of the War of 1812, Virginians were optimistic. The country was prosperous and in a nationalistic mood, enjoying the period that was called the "era of good feelings." Tobacco prices had risen tenfold; wheat and corn prices had doubled. People were flush—and, until the Panic of 1819, hopeful about the future. The state was ready to make an investment in improving itself. Well, almost.

"Public works" were not to be truly public. The board would merely invest in private companies; if those companies and entrepreneurs furnished three-fifths of the capital, the board would then supply the rest. It was a "mixed-system" that tilted greatly toward profit-seeking private enterprise. The problem was that internal improvements were not an advantageous investment for capitalists eager for short-term profits. "Capitalists like no interregnum," wrote one disappointed Virginian nearly a quarter century after the board's creation, smarting from the lack of return on his investment.

In addition, the part of the state most in need of internal improvements was the relatively poor western section, whose residents did not engage in the kind of entrepreneurial activity that would have enabled them to raise three-fifths of the capital for road projects. And so the state funds were used almost entirely for improvements in the East. Moreover, it was not in the political or economic interest of the powerful Tidewater planters to further the economic development—and strength—of the western parts of the state. "What the Old Dominion required," wrote historian John Lauritz Larson, "was a transfer of wealth from the East to the

West in behalf of future development, and Virginia's approach effectively prevented exactly that result."

For many Virginians, the attempt to make improvements was a zero-sum game in which towns had to compete for limited funds; what one town gained, another town lost. Instead of statewide cooperation, there was fierce competition between cities, which thwarted a rational statewide plan. Sectional rivalries in Virginia even extended to the Congress in Washington. When representatives from the western part of the state pushed to be included in the route of a proposed Buffalo–New Orleans turnpike, representatives from eastern Virginia successfully led the fight to defeat the proposal in Congress.

The Board of Public Works, basically a lending organization, took no initiative in conceiving, planning, or even coordinating projects. It spread its resources so thinly—among eleven navigation companies, seven railroads, and thirty-eight turnpikes—that it accomplished little. The projects were unprofitable, the quality of work poor, and the competition among the different companies fierce. Within less than two decades, the board found itself reduced to the role of collecting data, making inspection tours, issuing annual reports, and administering a few of the infrastructure projects. Virginia's efforts lacked every ingredient for success: solidarity, urgency, will—and, of course, money.

"Internal improvements cannot be delayed much longer," the *Enquirer* desperately reminded readers in 1829. "Virginia has too much pride to sleep forever the sleep of death." "Cannot Virginia do what New York has done and Pennsylvania is doing?" the *Enquirer* editorialized a few months later. "Are we a beggared and exhausted people? Can we raise no money? Have we no credit?"

But while many citizens pleaded for development, the state government appeared unconcerned and unfazed, contenting itself with an indolent approach. "Government, rightly understood, is a passive, not an active machine," declared Governor William Branch Giles in 1827. "The less government has to do with the concerns of society, the better."

The Marquis de Chastellux found himself in a magical water world when he traveled through Virginia in the early 1780s. "The lowlands and the plains are watered by such large rivers and so intersected by creeks," he wrote, "the coasts are so frequently indented by gulfs and arms of the sea—which seem to carry the ocean into the very heart of the land and to the very foot of the mountains—that it is impossible not to be persuaded that all this part of the continent is of recent creation." Water held the key to trade, commerce, development.

Visionaries like Washington and Jefferson had seen that, by improving water transportation throughout the state, all parts of Virginia would profit and prosper. With improved navigation of rivers and with new canals, the fertile but lightly peopled land of western Virginia in the Ohio Valley could be opened up and settled. With new western markets, the eastern economy would also expand. But until the barrier of the mountains—the Blue Ridge and the more western Alleghenies—could somehow be breached and westerners could trade with the eastern part of the state, they would continue to practice nothing but subsistence farming. Western Virginia was rich in mineral resources, too, but heavier cargo, like coal or iron, could only be moved out on vessels and barges—not on wagons bumping along muddy roads.

Two canal projects in Virginia—one on the Potomac and the other on the James River—advanced slowly. The James River project, first incorporated in 1785, was even dearer to Virginians than the Potomac Canal, for the James flowed entirely within Virginia, from the Blue Ridge Mountains to Richmond and then to the deepwater harbor called Hampton Roads at the southern end of the Chesapeake Bay. The plan was, first, to clear the river and construct a 7-mile-long canal bypassing "The Falls" in Richmond, then to build a turnpike over the Alleghenies connecting the James with the Kanawha River in what is now West Virginia, and finally to improve the Kanawha down to the Ohio, assuring a minimum depth of 3 feet. It was a visionary plan. But it was so problematic that, after the state took it over in 1820, it would suck up more and more funds over the next decades. As it limped along, it monopolized the resources of the state, derailing most other plans for internal improvements.

While the financing and building of Virginia canals continued in fits and starts, the success of the Erie Canal touched off a fever of canal-building across the nation in the 1820s and 1830s. A canal cut across

New Jersey connecting New York harbor with the Lehigh River; the Pennsylvania Portage and Canal System wound its way across the state from Philadelphia to Pittsburgh. The Miami Canal extended from Cincinnati to Toledo on Lake Erie; northern Indiana was opened up by the Wabash and Erie Canal; and the Illinois and Michigan Canal, linking Lake Michigan with the Illinois River, spawned the growth of Chicago. In state after state, canals sliced through the countryside, quickening commerce in the cities and towns they touched. Could Virginia emulate those states? "We too of the Ancient Dominion," wealthy planter John Cocke wrote optimistically to De Witt Clinton of New York after the completion of the Erie Canal, "will follow the wake of your glorious example."

But in the end, Virginia's canal projects, after dragging on for more than half a century, were left unfinished; neither ever reached the Ohio River. The Potomac Canal got as far as Cumberland in northwestern Maryland; the James Canal extended to Buchanan in the Blue Ridge Mountains, tapping western Virginia's iron country but remaining more than 100 miles away from the Ohio. A more determined and purposeful legislature would have provided adequate funding to complete the turnpike over the mountainous terrain in order to connect the James and the Kanawha; a more imaginative legislature might have experimented with a combination of canal and railroad. By 1840, the United States had a canal system—but Virginia was not part of it.

"The dream of the great canals to the Ohio," wrote Virginian George Bagby, "must be abandoned along with other dreams."

Meanwhile, the construction of American railroads was under way. Twenty-three miles of railroad track in 1830 would increase a hundredfold over the next ten years. But as canals gave way to rail, Virginians wondered if the Old Dominion would fare any better in creating rail lines than it had in completing canals. "The canal, after a fair and costly trial," Bagby realized, "is to give place to the rail. Henceforth Virginia must prove her metal in front of steam, electricity, and possibly mightier forces still. If she can't hold her own in their presence, she must go under."

In the steam engines and locomotives that sought, through astonishing speed, to annihilate distance and space, Virginians perceived the symbols of a new, dynamic, accelerating nation peopled by aggressive, profit-hungry citizens on the make—and were stricken by a sense of profound dislocation. How would they find their place in the unrecognizable new world? "All local attachments will be at an end," one writer soberly cautioned. "Give me the old solemn, straight-forward regular canal—three miles an hour for express, with a yoke of oxen for heavy loads. I go for beasts of burden, it is more formative and scriptural, and suits a moral and religious people better—none of your hop, skip and jump whimsies for me!"

The investors in the James and Potomac canals, along with Tidewater planters, were among the first in the 1820s to oppose the development of railroads in Virginia, especially lines leading into the interior of the state that might have competed with the canals. Even into the 1850s, their influence held sway in the General Assembly, where legislators killed proposals for the expansion of railroads in some parts of Virginia.

The canal interests ultimately hampered the economic growth of the entire state. A vital rail line, only 15 miles long, from the Midlothian coal district to Richmond was delayed again and again. Even more counterproductive were restrictions the legislature imposed on the Baltimore and Ohio Railroad in the late 1820s. To eliminate rail competition with the James waterway, for example, the legislature insisted that the railroad take a route north of the Little Kanawha River in western Virginia, but once again its decision served only to isolate the western part of the state. The smoky, coal-rich town of Wheeling, the second fastest growing area in Virginia, found itself cut off from the rest of the state, with no water or rail routes to the Atlantic. To ship their rich loads of coal, copper, iron, and salt, westerners found themselves obliged to look to Pittsburgh and Maryland for lifelines.

When the state finally permitted railroads to develop in the 1830s, legislators did so without regulations and without a blueprint for a trunk line. Even though the state of Virginia owned 60 percent of each railroad and could appoint three of the five directors of each company, it made no effort to assert state power or to unify the rail system. On the contrary, competing groups of private investors, representing the interests of rival towns, successfully stymied a statewide plan. Railroads sprang up only where there was enough private capital to fund them. Although east-west lines were desperately needed, north-south lines were constructed instead. Those lines, located in the eastern part of the state, funneled raw materials up from the South to manufacturing centers in the Northeast. Virginia's railroads ignored potential markets and industrial centers in the Midwest, virtually forcing them to trade with the North, via the Erie Canal and the east-west trunk lines up North. Claudius Crozet, the state engineer, finally resigned in disgust when another of his plans for an east-west railroad that would connect Virginia with markets in the Midwest was rejected. The state would not begin work on an east-west line until the 1850s.

The want of internal improvements was "a reproach to our republican system," wrote James Madison in 1831. Fifteen years earlier, when he had vetoed the Bonus Bill, Madison had been wary of expanding federal power. But he had no such qualms when it came to the state improving its own infrastructure. Canals, railroads, and turnpikes were "the criteria of a wise policy," he wrote, convinced that internal improvements would guarantee prosperity. In the summer of 1828, he had chaired a convention on internal improvements in Charlottesville, learning firsthand how backward Virginia was in comparison to states like Pennsylvania and New York.

A chorus of Virginians joined him in urging development. Why was the Old Dominion in decline, asked a writer who called himself "Agricola" in the *Richmond Enquirer* in 1835. What was the "cause of Virginia remaining stationary while her sister states have advanced rapidly to wealth and political power?" "Agricola" proposed a complex answer, explaining that the lack of capital, the absence of public spirit and individual enterprise, and the "bad education" of pleasure-seeking young men all held Virginia back. But most of all, he ascribed Virginia's backwardness to the "want of facilities for developing and bringing into action the many hidden materials for wealth." In other words, "cheapness of transportation" was absolutely necessary to develop Virginia's mineral resources and stimulate new industry and prosperity. Virginians "have slept too long," editorialized the *Enquirer* in 1835, this time urging citizens to demand that the projected New Orleans and Nashville railroad pass through the lower part of the state. "Or shall we quietly rest, and permit ourselves to be cut out of the immense benefits?"

But once again, a lethargic state government proved more interested in denouncing tariffs and engaging in abstract ideological debates about the rights of the states to "nullify" federal laws than in diving into the nuts-and-bolts of the state's infrastructure. In his Annual Message in 1835, the governor of the state, Littleton Waller Tazewell, chose to condemn at length abolitionist agitation in the North. "The immense interests of Internal Improvements and Popular Education," fumed one angry reader in a letter to the *Enquirer*, "were not considered as worthy of one line in the whole Message." A few months later, the House of Delegates, ending its legislative session, attempted to sum up its accomplishments; but instead of lamenting the lack of progress that had been made in modernizing transportation in the state, it praised that very lack of progress, exulting that "the gigantic system of roads and canals is greatly reduced in its monstrous dimensions."

Two decades later, the situation had barely improved. The South had no time to lose, exhorted J. D. B. De Bow at the Southern Railroad Convention in 1851. "Every day increases the distance between ourselves and our enterprising neighbors and makes the contest between us a more hopeless one," he exclaimed. Some progress was being made, for example, on a remarkably well-engineered railroad bridge constructed in 1852 near Farmville, Virginia. But for impatient young Virginians, the pace was far too slow. Why had it taken twenty-five or thirty years to construct a railroad from one end of the state to the other? demanded a student at Hampden-Sydney College. "My native state seems to be doomed to the rule of enemies of progress," wrote Henry Clay Pate in 1852, excoriating Virginia's "old fogy" ruling class for its blindness to the importance of development. Where were the men who were ready to cut their ties to the past and lead Virginia into the future?

It was high time for action. John Calhoun, who had championed the original Bonus Bill of 1816 only to make an about-face and become the champion of states' rights in the 1830s, made another about-face in 1845. Seeing the South fall further and further behind the rest of the country, he returned to the idea of a federal program for internal improvements. Even conservative writers like Thomas Roderick Dew, Nathaniel Beverley Tucker, and George Fitzhugh joined the call. A modern transportation network, Dew predicted, would propel the Old Dominion "in wealth and numbers," while incidentally helping the state by providing an exit route for slaves to slave markets in other states. In 1855, Hugh Blair Grigsby urged the state to move forward and "connect in pleasant communion all the parts of our territory, all the children of one family."

In the 1840s and 1850s, people began to look less to the government than to commercial conventions—brainstorming sessions at which businessmen, bankers, entrepreneurs, and planters discussed how to compete with the North and how to inject momentum and diversity into the southern economy. But a hard-nosed determination was oddly absent. One convention ended with the self-defeating advice to southerners "not to freight Northern vessels when they can freight Southern, unless the Northern are the cheapest." A writer in Richmond commented that this reasoning resembled the oath Neptune had demanded of sailors: "never to eat brown bread when one could get white, unless he preferred brown." Few strong resolutions, initiatives, plans, or projects ever emerged from these conventions. The delegates, wrote one man in the *Southern Literary Messenger*, were willing only "to resolve and resolve to meet again."

By the 1850s, about 2,000 miles of track would vein Virginia, spurring prosperity in the places it reached. Towns bypassed by rail lines, like Scottsville in Albemarle County, slumbered, losing population and trade, while those touched by rail, such as Scottsville's rival, Charlottesville, prospered. In the railroad towns, population grew, property values rose, shops opened, farming techniques improved, and wealth increased.

And yet funding stalled and major rail lines remained uncompleted. As late as 1858, the *Lynchburg Daily Virginian* still opposed appropriations for the Covington and Ohio Railroad, arguing that the James River Canal should come first. That same year, a writer in the *Southern Planter* pointed out that the state was financing two competing—and unfinished—trunk lines.

Before the Civil War, nineteen different companies operated railroads in Virginia. Limited tracks, unconnected lines, and incompatible gauges made an integrated railroad system impossible. In Richmond, a city served by six different railroad lines, no central depot facilitated the transfer of freight. Transferring cargo and passengers was a troublesome problem during peacetime, but an almost fatal one in war. Indeed, half of the 12,000 troops traveling by rail from Virginia to Georgia to fight in the battle of Chickamauga arrived after the fighting was over. In addition, few rail lines connected Virginia to the other Confederate states; and the one line that united eastern and western Virginia—the Baltimore and Ohio—was owned by northerners. Virginia's inadequate and chaotic rail network would ultimately prove to be one of the causes of the Confederacy's defeat in the Civil War.

———

The point of constructing a transportation network is not merely to move people, goods, and mineral resources. Rather, it serves to develop those resources, to increase economic opportunity, to spread prosperity, and thus to strengthen and invigorate society. But Virginia managed to accomplish none of those ends. Although, by the late 1850s, the Old Dominion could boast almost 5,000 manufacturing establishments, it still lagged behind the North in industry and commerce.

Perhaps, if the state government had energetically supported a network of internal improvements, Virginia might have developed large, vital cities that could have attracted skilled labor, capital, and consumers. In 1840, the population of Richmond was only 20,000; Petersburg and Norfolk each had smaller populations than Utica, New York. Closer to the Cotton South than Massachusetts, Virginia could have become the epicenter of the textile industry in the United States. If the legislature had not cut off funding in 1842 for the state geological survey, developers might have discovered more of Virginia's deposits of coal, gold, iron, copper, lead, and even salt. William Barton Rogers, one of the members of the survey team, might not have left the University of Virginia for Boston, where he founded the Massachusetts Institute for Technology.

If the politically powerful men in eastern Virginia had permitted the development of railroads in the Kanawha Valley in the West, or had adequately funded the completion of the James-Kanawha route to the Ohio River, Virginia could have become a major salt- and coal-producing state. And if Virginia's coal, iron, copper, and gypsum could have been shipped east by water or rail, Richmond might have become a prime industrial center. Mineral-rich Virginia would have established itself as the iron center not just of the South but of the entire nation, supplying much-needed materials to the exploding railroad industry. Giant enterprises like the Tredegar Iron Works in Richmond would have been able to tap Virginia's raw materials without having to import pig iron from Pennsylvania and machinery and parts from the North.

Virginia's ports—Richmond, Norfolk, and Alexandria—might have rivaled Baltimore's, Philadelphia's, New York's, and Boston's. Instead, Yorktown, once the bustling "emporium of all Virginia," stagnated; one visitor to Norfolk, which in the 1820s had been a busy port for tobacco exports, found the place virtually uninhabited, with "grass grown streets and deserted wharfs." Years later, when Norfolk failed to receive funding from the state legislature for a rail connection, several local newspaper editors demanded that the sleepy port secede from Virginia.

The baneful consequences of Madison's short-sighted, fateful veto of the Bonus Bill in 1817 were still reverberating. They overshadowed George Washington's influence, especially his belief that roads and canals would promote national unity and connectedness; indeed, the "confined" views of insular, short-sighted Virginians that Washington had criticized still prevailed. It would take 100 years before the Federal Aid Road Act would finally be passed in 1916, a bill that, ironically, was inspired by a Virginian of a different generation, Logan Waller Page, the dynamic director of the federal Office of Public Roads.

Why did so many Virginians turn their backs on George Washington's conception of a powerful, dynamic nation, connected and fortified by a national system of roads and canals? Because, in the early nineteenth century, Thomas Jefferson's enduring agrarian vision was still compelling and attractive enough to drown out all the desperate calls for internal improvements, all the practical ideas for releasing mercantile and industrial vitality and energy, multiplying cities and factories, and creating wealth in the Old Dominion. Jefferson's gentle prescription for a healthy republican society—an agrarian population, a limited and largely passive national government, small-scale industry, towns instead of large cities with their unruly mobs—still held sway for many citizens in the Old Dominion. They remained ambivalent about modernization, fearful of the government in Washington, comfortable with the ways and the slow byways of the past, and content to inch unhurriedly along the impassable roads that literally grounded them, anchoring them in place, perhaps offering them, as Eudora Welty wrote, "the blessing of being located—contained."

"I don't deny that the steamboat is destined to produce valuable results," conceded Virginian Frank Meriwether, the hero of John Pendleton Kennedy's *Swallow Barn*. "But after all, I much question . . . if we are not better without it. I declare, I think, it strikes deeper at the supremacy of the states than most persons are willing to allow. This annihilation of space, sir, is not to be desired. Our protection against the evils of consolidation consists in the very obstacles to our intercourse. The home material of Virginia was never so good as when her roads were at their *worst*."

5

Deluded Citizens
Clamoring for Banks

"The soil is a gift of God to the living," Jefferson wrote to his son-in-law John Eppes in 1813. "We are an agricultural Nation. Such a one employs its *sparings* in the purchase or improvement of land or stocks." The prospect of economic diversification and industrialization in Virginia left Jefferson cold; he hoped that planters and farmers would pour their savings—their "sparings"—back into the land, improving the soil and investing in new crops and animals. But could Virginia survive and prosper if it continued to rely mostly on agriculture, shunning industrial development? During the first half of the nineteenth century, few questions were as urgent as this.

For Jefferson, it was essentially a moral choice. True progress, in his mind, meant *moral* progress: Self-sufficient farmer-citizens of an agrarian nation were more likely than anyone else to enjoy independence, equality, health, and life itself. Economic theorists like the English philosopher David Hume might call for an active commercial, industrial society, and thinkers like Dr. Benjamin Rush of Pennsylvania might urge Americans to "amass wealth . . . [and] to acquire as many of its conveniences as possible by industry and oeconomy," but Virginians like Jefferson preferred to turn to the ancient philosophers for wisdom. "The art of acquisition," Aristotle had taught, depends on nothing more than "self-sufficiency." To strive for greater wealth than that, the ancients—

and Jefferson—believed, was perverse and fundamentally at odds with the virtuous life of a citizen.

Jefferson had hardly been opposed to prosperity. "Our citizens have had too full a taste of the comforts furnished by the arts & manufactures," he wrote in 1784, "to be debarred the use of them." But he wanted those pleasures, like the ones he himself enjoyed—linens from Ireland and Scotland, wine from France, beer from Germany, fine clothing and furniture from England—to arrive by boat, not to be manufactured in America. "While we have land to labour," he wrote in his *Notes on the State of Virginia*, "let us never wish to see our citizens occupied at a work-bench. . . . *Let our work-shops remain in Europe. . . .* The mobs of great cities add just so much to the support of pure government, as sores do to the strength of the human body."

George Washington had been more awake than Jefferson to the advantages of economic diversification. At the time of the Stamp Act, in 1765, Washington had argued that Americans should simply import less from England; either Britain would repeal the Stamp Act, or Americans would be motivated to produce for themselves the "necessaries of Life." He even offered backhanded thanks to Britain for its unjust taxes, for they would ultimately provide "a necessary stimulation to Industry." Washington would soon discontinue the production and export of tobacco and introduce instead small-scale manufacturing at Mount Vernon. Delegates in Williamsburg in 1774 agreed with his strategy, calling on Virginians to turn away from agriculture and apply their energy to "manufactures of all sorts."

Of course, no American did more than Alexander Hamilton to push the young republic toward becoming a booming military-industrial giant rather than the self-contained, agricultural, backwater nation that Jefferson would have preferred. But Hamilton, a true economic visionary, was well aware of the importance of agriculture for southerners. He was even willing to concede that cultivation of the soil was the kind of labor "most favourable to the freedom and independence of the human mind." Eager to find grounds for compromise with southerners, he carefully addressed their qualms about manufacturing. There was no "contrariety of interests" between North and South, he stressed, or between manufacturing and agricultural interests. That idea was "the common error of the early periods of every country," he wrote in 1791 in his "Report on Manufactures." On the contrary, it was "a moral certainty" that a nation with a diversified economy would prosper. Thus it was in the interest of every state, he concluded, to divert "a part of its population from tillage to Manufactures."

According to Hamilton, industrialization would paradoxically improve the state of agriculture by increasing the domestic demand for agricultural products and opening up new domestic markets to offset the decline of markets abroad. Europe, he noted, liked to sell everything and buy nothing. This "want of reciprocity" made it economically untenable for the United States to remain a purely agrarian nation; an increase in American farm output would only glut European markets and depress prices. But if the United States industrialized, new manufacturing towns would spring up, creating greater American demand for agricultural products, while manufactured goods would become cheaper for farmers. The number of acres under tillage might decrease, but the productivity and value of land would increase.

But would Virginians adapt to Hamilton and Washington's progressive thinking? To some extent, they had unwittingly bought into the British crown's insidious strategy of discouraging American industry in order to keep its colonies dependent on the mother country. "Having no manufactories of their own," the British Board of Trade had informed the king in 1721, "their . . . situation will make them always dependent on Great Britain." But it was also true that Virginia planters like Jefferson simply preferred their agrarian way of life and the prestige of owning and investing in land and slaves.

Washington's pragmatism and Hamilton's visionary approach to industrialization and modernization were the road *not* taken in Virginia. The idea of a dynamic, growing nation whetted Washington's appetite, but it was a much more aesthetic and ethereal vision that attracted Jefferson. When President Washington toured New England in the fall of 1789, visiting towns, ports, and factories, he excitedly commented on ships, bridges, and roads as well as on spinning machines, crops and fish, gristmills and sawmills, and harbors and ports—everything that moved, grew, and made the country work. But when Jefferson and Madison toured New England in May 1791, it was the springtime beauty of the Hudson Valley and Lake

George that captured their attention. The two friends marveled at the beauty of the landscape, the astonishing varieties of trees and animals. "Not a sprig of grass shoots uninteresting to me," Jefferson wrote to his daughter.

Indeed, Jefferson's and Madison's principled, philosophical, economic—and even aesthetic—objections to Hamilton's vision of the young republic motivated them, in the wake of their tour of New England, to organize an opposition party. Whereas Hamilton's Federalist Party believed in an activist and expansionist national government and wanted to see the nation become a powerhouse of industrial development and thriving cities, Jefferson and Madison's Republican Party stood for small, frugal, limited government and respect for states' rights.

Jefferson had even objected to Hamilton's open immigration policies, which furthered his vision of industrialization. Hamilton wanted to encourage immigrants of all social classes to come to America where they might become innovators in industry and skilled workers in factories. But Jefferson was not ready to embrace a nation in which, as he saw it, factory workers labored sixteen out of twenty-four hours and still were "unable to afford themselves bread, or barely to earn as much oatmeal or potatoes as will keep soul and body together." Such "ephemeral and pseudo-citizens" should be excluded from our territory, he wrote, "as we do persons infected with disease." But at the same time, he was closing the doors to enterprise, opportunity, creativity, and a white working class, thereby immeasurably slowing the process of modernization in Virginia and diminishing the ability of the state to wean itself from slavery.

Ironically, Jefferson, the fervent anti-industrialist, was also an ingenious inventor and engineer who had always been fascinated with science and technical innovations. One of his overseers remembered that he spent no time at all behind a plow. What most intrigued him, according to the overseer, were new projects that demanded the mechanical or artisanal skills of his laborers. It was not just an intellectual interest in mechanics that motivated Jefferson to introduce some manufacturing to Monticello; crop failures and the vicissitudes of farming had also impressed upon him the need to diversify production.

"I found my farms so much deranged," he wrote in 1795, "that it was necessary for me to find some *other resource* in the meantime." His solution was to create a small nail factory, "drawing from it profit on which I can get along till I can put my farms into a course of yielding profit." In his nailery, Jefferson wrote, he employed "a dozen little boys from 10 to 16 years of age, overlooking all the details of their business myself." Jefferson immersed himself in every aspect of production, shipping, and merchandising. And yet, even as he played the part of an entrepreneurial industrialist and middleman, rather than a seigniorial gentleman planter, he considered his nailery an example of nothing more than a small-scale home factory created only to supplement a primarily agricultural economy.

If Jefferson countenanced the inclusion of some home industry in Virginia, it was out of a need for survival and a modicum of prosperity, not out of a Hamiltonian taste for grand-scale industrialization. He had visions, wrote historian Drew McCoy, "of literally domesticating the industrial revolution." It was a compromise, Jefferson believed, that would not fundamentally change Virginia: The traditional way of life would continue to hold sway. Some things would have to change—so that almost everything else could remain the same.

But after the War of 1812, Jefferson would change his thinking about industry. The British had imposed maritime blockades in Europe, both before and during that war, severely limiting American trade. So unstable had international commerce become that Jefferson realized that he would have to accept the inevitability of some accommodation with industrialism and capitalism. "We must now place the manufacturer by the side of the agriculturist," he conceded in 1816, acknowledging that industry could not be barred from Eden. "To be independent for the comforts of life we must fabricate them ourselves." Indeed, people who were against domestic manufacturing "must be for reducing us either to dependence on that foreign nation or to be clothed in skins and to live like wild beasts in dens and caverns. . . . Manufactures are now as necessary to our independence as to our comfort."

Even so, there were limits to Jefferson's tolerance for development and business. There was something "Satanic" in America's transformation from a "peaceable and agricultural nation" into a "military and manufacturing one," he had remarked in 1814, adding that the change was akin to the removal of "our first parents from Paradise." And while New York had become a sewer of all the depravities of human nature, he wrote in 1823, breaches of order were rare in Virginia; it was, in short, a rational, moral, and "affectionate" society. Economic opportunities and social mobility may have been more limited in the South than in the North, but Jefferson continued to see the future in Virginia's past.

Two-thirds of his own slaves were either too young or too old to work much, Madison said, and it took nearly all the money he made to feed, clothe, and care for them. Months before he died, Madison, an acquaintance later recalled, "spoke often and anxiously of slave property as the worst possible for profit, unless [slaves were] employed in manufactures."

Though Madison agreed with Jefferson about limited and frugal government, he had never shared Jefferson's mystical view of the soil. Nor was he convinced that a predominantly agricultural society—even one without slaves—could flourish. In 1786, analyzing the economic problems inherent in an agricultural society, Madison noted that a successful agrarian community would have to be founded on an equal distribution of land, simplicity of manners, and reduced consumption of manufactured goods. And yet, without domestic industry, he feared that an agrarian society would produce a surplus of food as well as a glut in farm labor. "No problem in political Economy has appeared to me more puzzling," he had confessed.

Over the next decades, Virginia's reliance on agriculture barely diminished, and by 1832, the economic situation in the Old Dominion had become critical. Nothing other than economic diversification could solve Virginia's dire economic problems, Madison concluded once again. Virginia's lands, he wrote that year, "have sunk most in their value, and the price of her exports most in foreign markets. The prices of her great staples, flour and tobacco, are, and have been for a considerable time, at a lower ebb than the more southern staples cotton and rice." For the first time, more tobacco was exported from New Orleans than from Virginia.

How could Virginia compete, he asked, with "the greater productiveness of capital" in the northern states? Northern capital, invested in a variety of enterprises, produced far greater profits, he wrote, than a Virginia estate consisting of land and slaves. The condition of Virginia planters was "worse than that of the merchant, the ship-owners, and the manufacturers, and the money-lenders." Calling for a "radical cure," Madison understood that the country simply had to become "a manufacturing as well as an agricultural one."

But how? Madison was not the ardent statist that Hamilton had been; on the contrary, he hoped to leave much of the impetus for development to the "sagacity of individuals, and to the impulse of private interest." And yet, he recognized that it was important for the state and federal government to encourage and support industrial enterprises, "though within certain limits," in a competitive marketplace. "Without public patronage," he observed, many costly and complicated projects "would either not be undertaken or come to a premature downfall."

While the planter aristocracy, along with many yeomen farmers, shared Jefferson's antipathy for cities and industry, many middle-class Virginians, heeding Madison's advice, began to diversify the economy. Flour mills, sawmills, and gristmills dotted the countryside. Forges and rolling mills produced pig iron and cast iron; mines in the Piedmont and in the Alleghenies produced bituminous coal. Richmond became the world's foremost tobacco-manufacturing center, and tobacco factories sprang up in other towns, too. After visiting Virginia in 1843, Daniel Webster, John Tyler's secretary of state, told of seeing cotton factories, blast furnaces, and foundries; he declared himself satisfied that "Virginia has every element and every advantage for manufacturing."

Still, the pace of industrialization in Virginia was slow. Even if Virginians could not reasonably have been expected to develop industry on a par with New Englanders, far more could have been accomplished by 1860. In much of the rest of the country, Jeffersonian egalitarianism and individualism—along with Jeffersonian opposition to the kind of centralized national government and planned economy that Hamilton had favored—were inspiring entrepreneurship and capitalism. Small businessmen and entrepreneurs could seek credit from many newly opened banks, not just for the grand-scale projects that the Bank of the United States continued to support, but for a variety of commercial, industrial, and agricultural ventures. Instead of the centralized, planned economic growth that

Hamilton had envisioned, unregulated private enterprise became the order of the day as the United States developed an expanding and diversified economy.

Why, then, the lag in Virginia? Was the problem a lack of capital to finance new enterprises? A dearth of inspired entrepreneurs? The absence of a white working class? Or did the entrenched ethos of the wealthy planter class, which had always prized the stability of land and slaves over the use of wealth to produce more wealth, inhibit the growth of industry?

Capital, a precondition for enterprise and industrial development, was less plentiful in Virginia than in northern states, and entrepreneurial Virginians in the 1830s hungered for more. Banks in the North exceeded Virginia in banking capital by three and a half times, the *Richmond Enquirer* pointed out in a series of fiery editorials from 1835 to 1837. The editorials demanded more banks and more assistance to business. "It appears incumbent on Virginia," the *Enquirer* remarked, "to free herself from the shackles imposed on her commercial spirit by the *want of adequate banking capital* which has made her tributary to our sister states." Abundant capital would permit Richmond to "soon lift up her head high among her sisters," the *Enquirer* wrote, adding, "Heaven speed her!" The following year, the *Enquirer* was still desperately shouting, "We want more Banking Capital in Virginia!" A group of citizens in one southwestern Virginia town, lamenting "our suicidal neglect of a due cultivation of our advantages," pleaded for more banks. Properly and judiciously managed, banks "tend much to the advancement of every enterprising and especially every mercantile community," they said.

The state had chartered four main banks with branches throughout the Old Dominion, and some private banks had also sprung up. But credit still did not meet the demand. "We must keep pace with the improvements of the age or we retrograde," wrote "A Consumer" to the *Enquirer* in late 1836. More capital, the writer recognized, "seems to be required to place our merchants upon a footing with those of the cities to which we are now tributary."

Although in 1836, the House of Delegates defeated a proposal to double the amount of bank credit in the state, it would eventually liberalize banking laws and allow more banks to open. And yet, capital remained scarcer in Virginia than in many other states, especially in the North. In 1840, Virginia banks held $7.34 per capita in deposits, whereas Massachusetts banks held $21.18 per capita in deposits. In 1840, bank loans per capita in Virginia were $12.58, compared to $63 in Massachusetts.

Virginia seemed to have been infected by Jefferson's famous antipathy for credit and banking. Although in 1784, Jefferson had devised a decimal currency system, even naming the ten-cent coin a "dime," he was slow to comprehend the new multiple meanings and uses of money, that is, money as credit as well as money as currency. Jefferson had written in 1787 that he looked "forward to the abolition of all credit," and yet the new spirit of entrepreneurship would be based almost entirely on credit. Perhaps Jefferson's antipathy for credit—and his lack of appreciation for capitalist finance—stemmed from his own distress at being in debt for most of his adult life. Perhaps, too, his opposition to Hamiltonian economics colored his aversion to credit. Hamilton had trumpeted a national debt as a national blessing because it established a nation's creditworthiness, thus securing its potential power. But Jefferson had no interest in increasing the nation's debt—or its power. As president, he was happy to reduce the national debt of $112 million, lower federal spending by a third, and eliminate almost all domestic taxes. Pay-as-you-go—not credit—was Jefferson's motto.

Over the years, his low opinion of banking did not improve. "Our deluded citizens are clamoring for more banks, more banks," he railed in 1816. Ironically, the following year, after a disastrous corn crop, Jefferson would ask his friend Wilson Cary Nicholas, the head of the Richmond branch of the Second Bank of the United States, for a loan. To return the favor, Jefferson later co-signed a loan for Nicholas—who defaulted, leaving Jefferson in his final years to fight off both his and Nicholas's creditors. After that, he loathed banks even more.

Many citizens of the Old Dominion, especially the Tidewater power elite, shared Jefferson's suspicions of banking and development. Claiming that the Bank of the United States was "not only unconstitutional, but a direct and fatal violation of State-rights," the House of Delegates in 1811 had instructed the state's two senators, William Branch Giles and Richard Brent, to vote against rechartering the bank—and censured them when they refused. Moreover, the "evils" ascribed to the national bank, commented John Tyler, one of the state's foremost politicians, were common to all banks; they were uniformly guilty, in his opinion, of promising prosperity while delivering grief.

"Our wise men flattered us into the adoption of the banking system under the idea that boundless wealth would result from the adoption," Tyler wrote in 1818. "Industry and enterprise were to be afforded new theatres of action, and the banks, like Midas, were to turn every thing into gold. The dream, however, is over,—instead of riches, penury walks the streets of our towns, and bankruptcy knocks at every man's door." Again and again Tyler lashed out—not just at banks but at money itself. "I believe the Bank [of the United States] to be the original sin against the Constitution," he wrote to Littleton Waller Tazewell. He informed another friend that "money is the great corrupter." "Let us expel the money-changers," he once declared in Congress, imagining a happy union of states liberated from banks, money, and corruption as well as from avarice and competition.

The suspicion of banks—federal, state, and private—had not dissipated by the 1830s. One member of the House of Delegates, opposing a bill in 1836 to establish a bank in the southwestern town of Buchanan, boasted that he "represented a people who had as little interest in Banks or Banking as any in the Commonwealth." Another delegate asserted that same year that "it would be better if we had no banks." "Just to be in fashion, it is proposed that our bank capital shall be nearly doubled," wrote one subscriber to the *Richmond Enquirer*. "What moral or physical necessities now exist for this flood of capital and galaxy of independent State banks?" Another citizen approved the saying that "it is always better to do too little than too much," noting that this wisdom applied with particular force to demands for more capital.

A series of thirteen essays published in the *Richmond Enquirer* fueled the antibanking movement. Published in 1829, the articles were written by a reader who used the pseudonym "George Clinton." The real George Clinton was the leader of the New York antifederalists who had cast the deciding vote against the bill to recharter the First Bank of the United States in 1811. An agrarian, the "neo-Clinton" viewed land as the foundation of every earthly blessing and the only source of true prosperity. Before Virginia had banks, he argued, Virginians were independent and their state prosperous. If a society had surplus wealth, "Clinton" maintained, it should be invested in "lands, slaves, and live stock of every kind." Entrepreneurs and speculators should be given no help by government or banking institutions. Warning that the "fangs" of banks had "deeply pierced the very vitals of society," "Clinton" foresaw a time "not far distant when, in Virginia, at least, Banks will cease to exist"—or else, he warned, "an explosion must take place and all our enterprizes must cease." One subscriber pointed out that no reader of the *Enquirer* had "offered a single syllable of argument in reply to G.C."

Not only was capital less available in Virginia than in the North, but Virginia bankers were also less proactive than their northern counterparts in promoting and financing industrial ventures. They seemed lackadaisical, contributing little to the mobilization of capital. In general, southern banks were not sources of industrial capital, as historian Eugene Genovese pointed out, but rather like clearinghouses of mercantile finance, serving, for the most part, to bolster the economic position of the planters.

Nor were there many southern investors tempted to invest in manufacturing rather than in land and slaves. Risk averse, refusing to believe the mounting evidence that manufacturing was more profitable than agriculture, they were quite comfortable putting their profits and capital back into their plantations, land, and slaves.

Their slaves, moreover, proved to be an excellent speculative risk, rising steadily in price. Southern slaveowners, who disdained investments in industry, were hardly economic masochists. On the contrary, in the entire South in 1860, the worth of the slaves owned by the planters alone was almost equal to all northern investments in railroads and manufacturing combined, as economic historian James Huston noted. And beyond that was the value of the planters' land. Prior to the surge in industry and railroads in the North in the 1840s, the imbalance of wealth in favor of the South was even more impressive. Thus, far from being irrational precapitalists whose money was frozen in land and slaves, southern planters and slaveowners fared well in their capitalist investments in land and human property.

Even so, in the early nineteenth century, some southerners felt that capitalism and slavery could not coexist. Slavery chained the South to a preindustrial, mostly agrarian economy, depriving it of an educated, free working class. Because of slavery, wrote Henry Clay in 1829, the South had fallen far to the "rear of our neighbors who are exempt from slavery in the state of agriculture, the progress of manufacturers, the advance of improvement, and the general prosperity of society." There was a "clog" in Virginia, a kind of social malaria, wrote Kentuckian Thomas Marshall, the nephew of the chief justice, in 1854. The clog "weighed down her enterprise, strangled her commerce, kept sealed her exhaustless fountain of mineral wealth, and paralyzed her arts and manufactures." The name of the clog was "negro slavery."

The South's staggering investment in human property, even if quite profitable, nevertheless starved the development of new industries, such as textile manufacturing and iron works. Over the long term, those industries not only could have been highly successful and profitable but, more important, would have diversified the economic base of the South while also permitting the rise of an upwardly mobile, educated working and middle class.

And yet, the lack of industrial development notwithstanding, neither Virginia nor Virginia slaveowners can be considered precapitalist. Even if Virginia banks were less aggressive than northern ones, and even if planters preferred to invest in slaves rather than in industry, capital *was* available to fund new enterprises. Banks did provide assistance to manufacturers and were not a cause of stagnation or retardation.

Why then the deplorable scarcity of industry? "Where enterprise leads finance follows," a leading economist, Joan Robinson, memorably wrote. More likely to thwart development than nonchalant bankers or a lack of capital was the dearth of entrepreneurs and ideas. In the South, there were simply not as many entrepreneurs interested in manufacturing as in the North. The deficit was not in capital, but in optimism. A backward-looking society, mired in the economics and culture of slavery, could not foster the kind of mentality that would have propelled Virginia forward.

Not only were bold, far-sighted entrepreneurs lacking, so were responsible, educated factory workers. Many contemporaries believed that slaves were an inappropriate work force in factories, that they made poor work-ers, that the depressed wages of slaves employed in southern factories dis-couraged whites from entering the work force, and that the mere presence of slave workers repelled many foreign immigrants.

Slavery, however, was not necessarily an inefficient or unproductive system of labor. Some slaves did work successfully in factories and iron mills, and many more were capable of such skilled labor. The Tredegar Iron Works in Richmond, as historian Charles Dew discovered, bought and trained slaves to work alongside whites in its rolling mills. But once slaves had mastered certain tasks, mill owners had little incentive to in-novate and introduce new techniques.

One writer in 1853 argued that blacks could become as skilled as white workers or even be trained—or compelled—to perform better than white workers. His point was that slaves were more efficient than whites because they could be raised from an early age to perform certain tasks throughout their lives, had no say about their working hours, and had no right to strike for higher wages or quit their jobs at their pleasure. Still, slaves' sta-tus as property limited their value as workers. When slaves helped dig the Blue Ridge Railroad tunnel in Virginia in the 1850s, their masters refused to let them work near blasting. Since a slave's life was worth as much as $1,800, Irish laborers were hired instead for the perilous work.

Ultimately, however, an enslaved labor force without purchasing power, even if able to work in factories and iron mills, could not provide a healthy home market for manufactured goods or contribute to the growth of the economy and the dynamism of industrial development.

If Virginians were hesitant entrepreneurs and reluctant industrialists, it was not because they were blind to the huge profits that could be made in manufacturing. Instead it was because the quest for profit and efficiency was not part of the value system and ethos of plantation society. The Virginia elite valued family, status, hospitality, and honor as well as the prestige that accompanied the ownership of land and slaves. And as Vir-ginians learned more about the social cost of industrial development in the Northeast—the grey, regimented lives of workers in mill towns like Low-ell, Massachusetts; the vast inequalities in economic and social conditions;

the potential for labor unrest—they would cling ever more tightly to their traditions and their civilization.

That civilization depended not only on an enslaved black work force but also on the absence of a class of poor white wage-workers, for such a class would have given the lie to the myth that equality reigned among whites in the Old Dominion. Virginia's aristocrats, in order to preserve their power and influence, needed the support of the "people"—their fellow whites; and to retain that support, it was necessary for them to dispel the idea that some white people were superior to others. It was far easier for them to spin the myth of white equality in a slave society than in a free one. In a slave society, white laborers, tenant farmers, and wealthy planters could all buy into the illusion that they were equal in not being slaves; and there were not enough discontented tenant farmers and white workers to destroy that illusion. But had an industrial working class existed, the claims and demands of workers might well have undermined the myth of equality, subverting the influence and prestige of the planter class.

The rise of industry in Virginia would have produced a host of other equally portentous changes: the transfer of slaves away from agriculture; more wealth—and thus more revenue to provide more public education for whites and perhaps also for blacks; more immigration and urbanization; more civic and cultural institutions; new markets for agricultural produce—along with agricultural reform in order to supply food to those markets; labor unionism and assertive workers with purchasing power; and increased demand for manufactured products. Such transformational changes in the social and economic fabric of Virginia would have profoundly undermined the slave-based economy as well as the ideological leadership, power, and prestige of the planter class.

Virginia's mythology of grace, leisure, republicanism, and equality could not have survived industrialization and the "constant whirl and deafening roar of machinery" that Ellen Coolidge had described to her grandfather. One dismayed Virginian who visited a textile mill in Connecticut saw 500 workers "trooping to their prisons." Never had he come across such a "degraded population." Indeed, many Virginians and other southerners believed that the corollary of industrialization was a new form of slavery; and the more they learned about mill towns in the Northeast, the more rational and moral black chattel slavery appeared to them.

Visitors to a mill town like Lowell, Massachusetts, saw the gentle face of industrialization, for Lowell offered a handsome landscape of graceful church spires, lending libraries, a savings bank, and attractive dormitories for women and child workers. The owners and investors in Lowell, who had established this textile manufacturing town around 1820, made sure that the girls were all well dressed and that the rooms in which they worked were orderly. Hundreds of cheering mill girls dressed in white, wearing silk stockings and carrying white parasols, lined the streets to greet President Andrew Jackson when he toured the town. Charles Dickens, visiting in 1842, noticed pianos in the dormitories and even green plants in the windows. Workers labored twelve hours a day, as was their "station" in life, but Dickens was impressed that they had recreational activities and even published their own periodical, the *Lowell Offering*.

"In all, there was as much fresh air, cleanliness and comfort, as the nature of the occupation would possibly admit of," a pleasantly surprised Dickens wrote. "I solemnly declare, that from all the crowd I saw in the different factories that day, I cannot recall or separate one young face that gave me a painful impression." There were schools, too, in Lowell, since state laws in Massachusetts prohibited children from working more than nine months of the year and required that they be educated during the other three. The difference between Lowell and English mill towns like Manchester, Dickens wrote, was like the contrast "between the good and Evil, the living light and deepest shadow."

Spires, banks, schools, libraries, and pianos—a lovely New England landscape. Or was it a theatrical set meticulously designed to disguise the hellish essence of an industrial town?

Lowell had been established by men acutely focused on maximum efficiency and maximum profits. In a single factory, raw wool and cotton were taken through various stages and made into finished cloth. Amid deafening, clattering machines in hot, humid, unventilated workrooms polluted by lint and by the fumes of whale-oil lamps, docile women and children labored long hours for low wages. They were driven to toil ever faster by tyrannical supervisors who received bonuses (called "premiums") for increased production. Inmates in Massachusetts prisons, commented Sarah Bagley, a Lowell worker and labor organizer, worked two hours a day less than the textile workers and had more time to use the library. Supervised twenty-four hours a day, workers led completely regimented lives—that is, if they survived the rampant typhoid, dysentery, and tuberculosis. As for the schools for child workers, they were established by the citizens of Lowell, not by mill owners, who predictably objected to paying higher property taxes to finance education.

A Lowell investor explained that the factories depended on "an industrious, sober, orderly, and *moral* class of operatives," brazenly defining the morality of the workers in terms of the self-interest of the mill owners. Moral meant docile submission to a highly sophisticated form of social coercion that crushed workers' sense of importance, independence, and creativity. Though mill workers were highly skilled at operating several looms simultaneously, they bowed to the demeaning definition of their jobs as "unskilled."

"UNION IS POWER," shouted 800 factory women as they rallied and marched on the mills in 1834. The mill's owners had cut wages by 15 percent in order to raise dividends for investors by the same percentage. "The oppressing hand of avarice would enslave us!" the women cried. But the strike failed; crushing the workers' last hopes, the Massachusetts legislature declined to pass a bill limiting the workday to ten hours.

The investors and owners of the mill towns simply bought themselves white female slaves, commented Ralph Waldo Emerson. These poor girls, wrote Dr. Josiah Curtis in a report to the American Medical Association, were kept "in a state little better than the machinery, which, when it gets out of repair, is taken to the repair shop and restored."

To many observers, there hardly seemed to be any difference between industrial wage-slavery and black chattel slavery. But if there *was* a difference between slavery in the North and South, white Virginians believed that the moral advantage was entirely theirs. Southern slavery included a safety net; slaveowners, typically living and working on their plantations, provided for their black laborers from cradle to grave. But northern industrialists and masters of capital, who produced nothing themselves and who had lost any sense of moral stewardship, forced workers into bondage while denying them dignity and security as well as the possibility of enjoying freedom. While slaveowners could use the lash, one southern newspaper editor wrote, capitalists had an even more potent whip: *fear of want.*

Years earlier, Jefferson had made a similar diagnosis. Because northern and European capitalists were afraid of the "brute force of the people," he wrote, they had devised a strategy for forcing workers into submission. They kept them down by hard labor, poverty, and ignorance while exploiting their labor, taking from them, "as from bees, so much of their earnings, as that unremitting labor shall be necessary to obtain a sufficient surplus barely to sustain a scanty and miserable life." Slaves had no reason to envy the lives of factory workers. Indeed, the condition of the slaves in Virginia was greatly improving, a hopeful Jefferson wrote in 1823, pleased to report that they lived as well as many free workers. Four years earlier, James Madison, too, had written that the "moral features of Virginia" had considerably improved and that slaves were better fed, better clad, better lodged and better treated "in every respect" than they had been in the past.

As Jefferson suspected, industrial "slavery" gave southerners a perfect foil for defending the morality of black slavery in the South. The radical abolitionists in the North, sneered Virginian John Taylor of Caroline, were merely hoping to use the spectacle of black slavery in the South as a "cunning device" to divert attention from the wretched conditions of industrial wage-workers. While abolitionists smugly railed against Negro slavery, it was industrial slavery, Taylor remarked, that was sapping the essential vitality of the republic.

Armed with their knowledge of the abject labor conditions in the Northeast, southerners could congratulate themselves for having used black slavery to avoid the social turmoil that accompanied industrialization. In 1839, Virginia judge Abel Upshur crowed that black slavery permitted a society without class conflict, while it prepared a class of educated gentleman for public service and citizenship by freeing them from labor. Slavery, Upshur underscored, kept industrialization, urbanization, and an industrial white working class at bay and assured the prosperity of an agrarian society.

Slavery to capital, George Fitzhugh would write in the 1850s, "is much more cruel and exacting than domestic slavery." In his cunningly entitled

book *Cannibals All!*, Fitzhugh denounced the cannibalistic "vampire capitalist class" and solemnly stated that he would "sooner subject his child
to Southern slavery than have him to be a free laborer of England."
Fitzhugh argued that, whereas slaves were part of the master's "family,"
sheltered and shielded by him, the capitalist employer simply used his
workers and then left them "to die in the highway," for it was "the only
home to which the poor in free counties are entitled."

Some outsiders, like the visiting Englishman Morris Birkbeck, laughed
at southern reasoning. "It has been confidently alleged," he had scoffed in
1817, "that the condition of slaves in Virginia, under the mild treatment
they are said to experience, is preferable to that of our English labourers."
It might be true, he wrote, that "the *most wretched* of our paupers might
envy the allotment of the *happy* negro," but it was unfair to compare two
such extreme cases. "The slave is punished for mere indolence, at the discretion of an overseer," while workers and peasants could "only be punished by the law when guilty of a crime."

It was easy, as Birkbeck proved, to dismiss the pro-slavery southern argument as preposterous, and yet not all northerners did. Some, in fact, supported Jefferson's warnings against wage labor and the "starved & rickety
paupers and dwarfs" of workshops and factories. James Kirke Paulding, a
New Yorker who defended slavery and who would become secretary of the
navy, denounced the hypocrisy of northern abolitionists who were obsessed
with southern slavery but blind or indifferent to the brutal and pitiless
industrial slavery in their midst. The "most distinguishing characteristic of
almost all the champions of the blacks," Paulding wrote, was "an utter dis-
regard to the rights of the white men."

But Bostonian Orestes Brownson would pen an even more convincing
denunciation of the bondage of industrial workers in the North. Because
Brownson, unlike Paulding, was a fierce opponent of slavery, his conclusion that the living conditions of white industrial workers were worse
than those of black slaves in the South jolted readers in the North while
reassuring those in the South. Though the slave had never experienced
freedom, Brownson wrote in the *Boston Quarterly Review* in 1840, "his sufferings are less than those of the free laborer at wages. As to actual freedom one has just about as much as the other. The laborer at wages has all

the disadvantages of freedom and none of its blessings, while the slave, if denied the blessings, is freed from the disadvantages." The wage-labor system was more oppressive—"and even more mischievous to morals"—than southern slavery, Brownson explained, because it imprisoned workers in abject poverty without offering them any hope of "becoming one whit better off than when they commenced labor."

Lashing out at the hypocrisy of many abolitionists, Brownson pointed to the bad faith of the capitalist master, a Christian and a republican, who shouts about liberty and equality but who smugly and serenely retains "all the advantages of the slave system, without the expense, trouble, and odium" of being a slaveholder. Turning the myth of southern leisure and indolence upside down, he contended that the northern capitalist, "revelling in luxury," was far more idle than the slaveowner.

These were radical arguments. But Brownson was surely right that neither northern capitalists nor abolitionists merited a pass. On the contrary, the hypocrisy on both sides was all too glaring. Alexander Hamilton, the president of the New York Manumission Society, believed that white women and children should toil in factories. And before him John Locke had proposed "working schools" where, from the age of three, the children of the poor would learn labor—and nothing but labor. The Virginia planters who opposed industrial development and the rise of an industrial working class were not merely indulging in spurious rationalizations of slavery; they were pointing to the miserable working and living conditions and the ruthless exploitation of a new class of industrial wage-workers.

The planters who defended slavery before the Civil War would have been saddened, but not surprised, to read, in the newspapers of 1892, that southern factory workers earned 36 cents a day for their labor. In the factory slums of the South one could see "rooms wherein eight and ten members of one family are stricken down, where pneumonia and fever and measles are attacking their emaciated bodies; where there is no sanitation, no help or protection from the city, no medicine, no food, no fire, no nurses—nothing but torturing hunger and death."

Is it true, then, that Virginia failed to industrialize? "Fail" would be the wrong verb. The men of the politically powerful planter class, who loved the land, cherished the uniqueness of their region, and viewed paper wealth, banking, and industrialization with suspicion, would not have agreed that they failed. They succeeded, at least for a while and at least partially, in *resisting* industrialization, in preventing the rise of a servile white working class, and in avoiding class conflict and labor unrest. They would have said that, more than Madison's far-sighted counsel to diversify their economic base, it was Jefferson's powerful agrarian vision and commitment to republican values that inspired them. Jefferson's unwavering belief that self-sufficient yeoman farmers made virtuous, civic-minded citizens encouraged them in their aversion to modernization, urbanization, and industrialization. Virginia had fortunately avoided most of the "evils" that stemmed from financial institutions, wrote one reader of the *Richmond Enquirer* in 1836. He credited the Old Dominion's "wisest and best men," who always sought the well-being of the cultivator of the soil. "Is there not already sufficient Banking capital in Virginia?" he asked. "We are now basking in the sunshine of prosperity."

And yet that "accomplishment" of halting the advance of industrialization also closed the doors of opportunity for all but the wealthiest Virginians and drained the state of energy, innovation, and hope. The myths of gracious plantation life and of the caring, paternal slaveowner ultimately provided no goals or purpose for society other than the consolidation of the planters' privileged status, the private, personal pursuit of leisure, and the illusory belief in slaveowners' "organic" relations with a servile black workforce. Virginia's ruling elite could offer no organizing principles, no positive agenda for improving the lives of ordinary white Virginians.

Virginia was "poor on principle," Philip Nicholas had declared in the state legislature in 1829. He was right; but a combination of a "principled" resistance to development and a sentimental fixation on arrested tradition guaranteed the continuance—and even the decline—of the status quo. Tomorrow would resemble yesterday.

6

The Case of
Virginia v. John Marshall

Though they were second cousins, Virginians Thomas Jefferson and John Marshall loathed each other. Marshall sneered at Jefferson, calling him "the most ambitious . . . and the most unforgiving of men," and Jefferson returned the compliment, lambasting Marshall's "twistifica- tions" of the Constitution and his "base prostitution of law to party pas- sions." The chief justice, Jefferson railed, was intent on deriving from the Constitution "any meaning which may subserve his personal malice."

Jefferson saw himself engaged in a struggle against judicial tyranny and a "despotic branch" of government, a battle for the future of the repub- lic—and for the soul of Virginia. Jefferson and Marshall indeed stood at different ends of the political spectrum, for Marshall, a moderate Federal- ist, held a broadly expansive view of national power. Marshall was hardly an imposing, charismatic presence; tall and thin, soberly dressed, he spoke with a hard, dry voice, and yet his logic as well as the skill and authority of his judicial opinions were commanding.

Infuriating to Jefferson were Marshall's nationalistic decisions overrul- ing state legislatures and state courts. In case after case, the chief justice asserted federal supremacy and dictated limits to the sovereign powers of the states. The federal judiciary, Jefferson fumed in 1820, "is the subtle corps of sappers and miners constantly working under ground to under- mine the foundations of our *confederated* fabric." The Constitution had become "a mere thing of wax" in the hands of the Supreme Court, he wrote to his friend Spencer Roane, the chief justice of the highest court in Virginia, the Supreme Court of Appeals. "They may twist and shape [it] into any form they please."

Jefferson would have agreed with the revolutionary statesman George Mason, who, as early as the Virginia Ratifying Convention in 1788, had warned that the effect of the federal judiciary "will be utterly to destroy the state governments." Would the states passively agree, Mason demanded, to be brought to the bar of the federal judiciary "like a delinquent individual? Is the sovereignty of the state to be arraigned like a culprit, or private offender? Will the states undergo this *mortification?*"

In the early decades of the nineteenth century, Chief Justice Marshall steadily expanded the authority of the Supreme Court: Not only would it overrule judicial decisions in the states, but it would even invalidate federal congressional legislation. The question was, How far were irate Virginians like Jefferson and Roane willing to go to assert the rights of the states and defend their understanding of the Constitution?

———

"This government is not a Virginian, but an American government," a distressed Patrick Henry had said in 1788 at the Virginia Ratifying Convention in Richmond, opposing the new Constitution and stricken by the possibility that Virginia might lose its autonomy. Only fourteen years earlier, glowing with revolutionary ardor, Henry had declared that he was "not a Virginian but an American." The Revolution might have made thirteen clocks strike together, as John Adams had memorably said, but that unity would not endure. At all the state ratifying conventions, antifederalists protested the idea of national consolidation at the expense of the independence of the states—and even delayed ratification in North Carolina and Rhode Island until after Washington's inauguration. But nowhere were the voices of antifederalists more passionate than in Virginia.

A fervent revolutionary, Patrick Henry had yearned for freedom and independence from Great Britain; but he was not willing to trade that hard-won freedom for the new shackles of a strong national union. So op-

posed was he to the idea of the consolidation of the states that he declined to participate in the Constitutional Convention in Philadelphia in
1787. But the following year, he did attend the Virginia Ratifying Convention, where he issued terrifying warnings about the "ropes and *chains
of consolidation.*" The new national government might impose a yoke as
unjust and arbitrary as Great Britain's had been, he railed. Henry feared
precisely what Jefferson would denounce thirty-two years later in his letter to Roane: a national takeover of the states and the constitutional and
judicial rape of Virginia.

Henry knew just how to strike emotional chords—he provoked people's fears, invigorated their Virginia patriotism, and turned them against
the unusual formula for sovereignty divided between the states and nation. Virginians would "sip sorrow," he predicted, if they placed their security in anything other than the laws of Virginia. He exhorted his
fellow Virginians not to give up their rights and sovereignty to men who
had "no fellow-feeling" for them and who shared no common interests
with them. Indeed, at the Philadelphia Convention, federalists like Gouverneur Morris had underscored their disdain for the states, asserting that
"state attachments and state importance have been the bane of this country." Disappointed that he could not simply "annihilate" the states, Morris hoped that his fellow federalists would at least "*take out the teeth* of
the serpents."

Henry was deeply concerned about the political rights and independence of the states, but he was equally sensitive to the rights of individuals to own private property—that is, human property. His great fear was
that such property might be heavily taxed or even taken away by the federal government. With northern states so hostile to slavery, Henry cried
out, might not the new Congress use its implied powers to liberate all
slaves? "Have they not power to provide for the general defence and welfare? . . . May they not think that these call for the abolition of slavery?"
Gouverneur Morris's comment in Philadelphia—that slavery defied "the
most sacred laws of humanity"—filled Henry with dread.

James Madison tried to reassure Henry and the other delegates in Richmond with conciliatory words. The new federal government, he said,
would not attempt a usurpation of power. On the contrary, it would show

such "an *irresistible bias*" toward the states that it would be impossible for it to subjugate them. There would be no change in Virginia's dominant, prestigious status, Madison promised; the Old Dominion would continue to be deferred to, as it always had been. As for the notion of the government emancipating slaves, that idea, Madison insisted, "never entered into any American breast."

Madison was not entirely candid. In reality, the prospect of state autonomy dismayed him. His original hope had been that the Constitution would give Congress, "*in all cases whatsoever*," the power to veto legislative acts of the states. The traditional "Kingly prerogative" of a negative on the states, he had written to George Washington before the Constitutional Convention, appeared to him absolutely necessary. Without it, he would argue in Philadelphia, there would be no way to prevent the states from going off, on their own, in different directions, no "check to the centrifugal Force which constantly operates in the several states to force them off from a common Centre."

George Washington, too, was already fed up in 1786 with "thirteen sovereignties pulling against each other, and all tugging at the foederal head." He did not doubt that they would "soon bring ruin on the whole." Washington represented the hopes of all federalists at the Constitutional Convention who believed that it was not only time to draft a national constitution with a strong central government but also time to return to the idealism and spirit of unity of the War of Independence, when American patriots believed, in the words of delegate James Wilson of Pennsylvania, that "Virginia is no more, Massachusetts is no more—we are one in name, let us be one in Truth & Fact."

Virginia is no more? No wonder frantic Virginians would balk at the prospect of a consolidated republic. The underlying question was whether the United States was a league—a kind of compact of convenience—of independent, sovereign states, or a unified, organic nation and a government, as Abraham Lincoln would later intone, "of the people, by the people, for the people." Like other federalists, George Washington viewed the people, not the states, as sovereign; the signers of the Constitution, after all, spoke in the name of "We the People," deriving their authority from them, not from their respective states.

Washington had no patience for Patrick Henry, the leading adversary in Virginia of his beloved national union. Though John Quincy Adams would later comment that Madison's "steady, unfaltering mind" had triumphed over the "dazzling but then beclouded genius of Patrick Henry," Madison himself was anything but sure that Virginians would ratify the Constitution. "The business is in the most ticklish state that can be imagined," he wrote nervously to Washington in the spring of 1788. "The majority will certainly be very small on whatever side it may finally lie; and I dare not encourage much expectation that it will be on the favorable side."

By the very close vote of 89 to 79, Virginia finally did ratify the Constitution. But Madison had not been deaf to the disquiet and mistrust expressed on the convention floor; he had grasped the delegates' panic and their sense of loss at joining the Union. The next year he would respond to some of their concerns about individual liberties and federal powers by steering a bill of rights through Congress that amended the Constitution. The Tenth Amendment addressed, though in the mildest of terms, the anxiety of Virginians and other Americans about federal encroachments on the sovereignty of states: "The powers not delegated to the United States by the Constitution, nor prohibited by it to the States, are reserved to the States respectively, or to the people."

But a few years later, Madison would make an about-face, distressed when he realized that Alexander Hamilton, spouting plans for a national bank and for vigorous industrial development, sought to turn the nation into precisely the kind of consolidated powerhouse that the antifederalists had feared. Madison even began to echo Patrick Henry as he wrote a series of articles in the *National Gazette* in 1792 warning against "a consolidation of the states into one government." And yet, Madison's retreat from his earlier nationalism was not entirely surprising. A decade earlier, there had already been signs of his identification with the interests of the South and mistrust of the northern states. In 1781, he had urged the creation of a national navy, not just to protect the Confederation against foreign aggression but also, as he wrote to Jefferson, "to protect the Southern States for many years to come against the *insults & aggressions of their Northern Brethren.*"

In early 1801, in the waning months of John Adams's presidency, the chief justice of the Supreme Court, Oliver Ellsworth, resigned. Many Virginians expected that incoming President Jefferson would appoint his successor and that his choice would be Jefferson's friend and fellow Virginian Spencer Roane. Who better than this son-in-law of antifederalist Patrick Henry to stand up to the Hamiltonian Federalists and their agenda of consolidation and expansion of federal power? But to their surprise and dismay, John Adams made a "midnight" appointment.

John Marshall, nationalist par excellence, became the new chief justice. Over the next thirty-five years, he would transform a weak institution—a branch of government that did not yet even have its own meeting place—into a powerhouse that would strike down federal and state legislation, overturn the decisions of state courts, and serve as the final arbiter of the meaning of the Constitution. Madison's idea of the "Kingly prerogative" of a peremptory veto had survived, as he had suspected it would, not in Congress but as a weapon of judicial power. And this weapon was shaped and wielded by the arch-nationalist and consolidationalist John Marshall.

A showdown between Marshall and the commonwealth of Virginia—a battle that Patrick Henry had dreaded and predicted—would indeed take place. It seemed highly likely that Jefferson would oppose Marshall to the end. But which way would Madison lean? Toward the authority of the Court and the national government, or toward the sovereignty of the states?

Jefferson would fume over his clash with Marshall in the 1803 case of *Marbury v. Madison* until the end of his life. Marshall's decision in that relatively insignificant case was a masterpiece of judicial strategy that established the principle of judicial review. The plaintiff in the case, William Marbury, a Federalist, had been appointed justice of the peace by President Adams in one of his last acts in office. But President Jefferson, loath to have more Federalist judges, withheld Marbury's commission from him. Marbury went to the high court to demand that James Madison, the secretary of state, deliver his commission to him.

Marshall believed that Marbury did have the right to the commission, and yet his tactic was not to rule for the plaintiff. If Marshall had demanded that Madison and Jefferson deliver the commission, they could simply have refused to do so. Instead, Marshall shrewdly declared that, de-spite an act of Congress that granted power to the high court in certain matters, the Court did not have jurisdiction in the Marbury case. Jeffer-son and his allies could hardly object to the Court's decision to *decline* to exercise power. But in his decision to invalidate a congressional act that granted power to the Court, Marshall was nevertheless establishing the Court's right to void an act of Congress. His shrewd move paid off: The Court had successfully asserted the power of judicial review, even though nothing in the Constitution had explicitly bestowed that power on it. The Marbury case may have been a weak precedent for judicial invalida-tion of congressional laws, but it was a precedent nonetheless—and one that left Jefferson baffled and frustrated.

Nowhere, Jefferson bristled, had the Constitution given the Court the power to "prescribe rules" for the other branches of government. Jefferson had long insisted that the three branches of the federal government were equal and independent; each branch had the right, he had written in 1801, to decide for itself "on the validity of an act according to its own judgment, and uncontrolled by the opinion of any other department." How such an arrangement could possibly work without some kind of um-pire Jefferson failed to explain. But Jefferson's idea was not any more il-logical than giving the unelected Supreme Court discretion to decide on the extent of its authority over the other elected branches of government; nor was it any less just than making the federal judiciary the umpire in disputes between the states and the federal government.

James Madison wholeheartedly agreed with Jefferson that the Supreme Court did not have the power to prescribe rules for the other branches of the federal government. Already in 1788, Madison insisted that judicial re-view of laws that were passed by democratically elected legislatures "was never intended and can never be proper." On this he never changed his mind. "In a Government whose vital principle is responsibility," Madison wrote to Jefferson in 1810, "it never will be allowed that the Legislative and Executive Departments should be compleatly subjected to the Judiciary."

But on the more crucial question—more crucial at least to Virginia—of the Supreme Court's role vis-à-vis the states, Madison and Jefferson dis-agreed. The authority of the Supreme Court to establish the dominance of the federal government over the states appeared to Madison entirely necessary. Indeed, after the delegates at the Constitutional Convention rejected his idea for a federal veto on the states, Madison had contented himself with the thought that the federal judiciary would supply that veto. The judiciary, he wrote to Jefferson, would "keep the states within their proper limits and supply the place of a negative on their laws."

But Virginians like Jefferson would be furious when they discovered that the states—and not just the legislative and executive branches of the federal government—would be subject to the authority of the federal judiciary. The case of *Fairfax's Devisee v. Hunter's Lessee*, in which the Supreme Court asserted its authority over state courts, drove that lesson home to them.

The *Fairfax* case involved conflicting claims to a small portion of the vast estate of the Loyalist Fairfax family. In that case, the Virginia high court in 1810 had upheld the state legislature's confiscation of the Fairfax land in 1782 as well as the state's sale of part of that land to a David Hunter. But in 1812, the Supreme Court overruled the state, giving the parcel in question, about 740 acres, back to the Fairfax heir, Denny Martin.

The Fairfax-Hunter scenario was George Mason's very own nightmare come true. At the Virginia Ratifying Convention, Mason had warned prophetically about federal intervention in land disputes, specifically pointing to the risk that the federal judiciary could overturn the General Assembly's 1782 confiscation of Lord Fairfax's 300,000 acres. Since it could be expected that the Supreme Court would give precedence to the 1783 peace treaty with Great Britain, which had prohibited the confiscation of Loyalists' property, the losses for landowners who had purchased the confiscated land could be catastrophic. "I dread the ruin that will be brought on thirty thousand of our people, with respect to disputed lands," Mason wrote.

Spencer Roane, the chief judge on the Virginia Supreme Court of Appeals, denied the Supreme Court's appellate jurisdiction in the Fairfax case, asserting that the Court did not have the authority to intervene in or overrule state court decisions. Although the Judiciary Act of 1789 had specifically permitted appeals from state court decisions to the Supreme Court, Roane and the Virginia court judged in 1815 that the Judiciary

Act was simply unconstitutional and held that both that act and the Supreme Court's ruling in the Fairfax case were void. The Union, Roane wrote, was but a confederacy of sovereign states whose governments would "remain in full force."

And so, with its authority challenged, the Supreme Court heard the case, now called *Martin v. Hunter's Lessee*, for the second time. Writing for the Court and representing Marshall's philosophy, Supreme Court Justice Joseph Story made the powerful argument that the people, not the states, were sovereign. In agreeing to the Constitution, the people had made clear that, in certain cases, sovereignty was to be vested in the national government and not in the states. For the second time, the Supreme Court reversed the opinion of the Virginia high court of appeals in the Fairfax case.

But even more outrageous than the *Fairfax* decision, for Jefferson and his friends, was the Supreme Court's ruling in the great bank case of *McCulloch v. Maryland* in 1819. The case pitted the Second Bank of the United States against the state of Maryland. Maryland had tried to curtail the bank as well as raise some revenue by requiring that federal banknotes circulated by the Baltimore branch of the bank be printed on heavily taxed paper issued by the state.

James McCulloch was the cashier at the national bank's Baltimore branch. When he circulated banknotes without Maryland's stamp, refusing to pay the state tax, the state successfully sued him in county court. After the Maryland Court of Appeals upheld the judgment against him, McCulloch brought his case to the Supreme Court. There the justices ruled unanimously for McCulloch, finding Maryland's tax on the bank unconstitutional.

Writing for the Court, Marshall crafted a sweeping, forceful decision that reached back to first principles. First of all, he dismissed the argument that the federal government derived its powers from the states. "The government of the Union," he wrote, "is, emphatically and truly, a government of the people. . . . Its powers are granted by them, and are to be exercised directly on them, and for their benefit."

But had Congress acted constitutionally in creating the bank in the first place? Marshall concluded that it had, grounding his opinion in a broad interpretation of the Constitution's "necessary and proper" clause, which, he contended, granted a variety of unspecified but implied powers to the federal government. That clause reads: "Congress shall have the power . . . to make all Laws which shall be necessary and proper for carrying into Execution" the powers invoked in the Constitution.

But how were these "implied powers" to be discerned? And, just as important, where were their limits to be found? "Let the end be legitimate," Marshall wrote in his *McCulloch* opinion, "let it be within the scope of the constitution, and *all means which are appropriate*, which are plainly adapted to that end, which are not prohibited, but which consist with the letter and spirit of the constitution, are constitutional." Marshall's assertive, far-reaching words seemed to invite the indefinite expansion of the powers of the federal government. Just what Jefferson—and Henry—had dreaded.

Reaction in the North to the Court's decision was favorable, but in the South and West it was decidedly hostile. The decision especially distressed many Virginians who were already deeply suspicious of the Bank of the United States, a symbol of the expansionist federal government. As early as 1790, when Hamilton had first proposed the bank, Madison and Jefferson had strenuously opposed it, fearful that it would introduce corruption into the government while chiefly benefiting northern merchants and speculators. The Panic of 1819 only intensified hostility to the bank; southerners blamed the economic downturn on the bank's inept management. The bank, they railed, had caused bankruptcies, a fall in land values, and a contraction of credit that strained the resources of state banks, causing many failures. The *McCulloch* decision, wrote Marshall to his young Massachusetts colleague, Justice Story, "has roused the sleeping spirit of Virginia—if indeed it ever sleeps."

Wide awake, Virginian Spencer Roane sprang into action, mobilizing opposition to the Supreme Court. Underneath his robes, the chief justice of the Virginia Supreme Court of Appeals was also a boss of bosses, running a political machine unrivaled in power and reach. The men he nominated to the state legislature were virtually certain of election, and the laws he favored almost always passed. At the end of the legislative sessions, assemblymen who were loyal to Roane received the kudos of the *Richmond Enquirer*, the newspaper he had founded in 1804. "Well Done, Good and Faithful Servants" was the typical headline approved by the editor, Thomas Ritchie, Roane's cousin. The fifty-seven-year old Roane was known as a sociable, good-tempered, even jocular man, but he was also fiercely partisan. He believed in states' rights and in limited federal power—and he was a declared enemy of John Marshall's brand of expansive nationalism.

In the spring of 1819, a few weeks after Marshall announced the *McCulloch* decision, Roane grabbed a pen and excitedly fired off two different series of letters to his newspaper, signing them "Hampden" and "Amphictyon." The fact that *McCulloch* did not involve Virginia was irrelevant. The Court's decision, Roane wrote, manifested a sinister design to overthrow the Constitution, prostrate the rights of the states and of the people, and establish a consolidated government of unlimited powers. It had been assumed, Roane wrote, that the Constitution could be changed by amendment. But the Supreme Court seemed to have appropriated for itself the authority to change the Constitution.

It was not the bank per se to which Roane objected; on the contrary, he admitted that a "great and general distress" would pervade all classes and interests if it were abolished. James Madison, moreover, had agreed with him. When President Madison had signed the bill creating the Second Bank of the United States in 1816, he had recognized that the force of precedent trumped his earlier doubts about the bank's constitutionality. After all, since the bank's founding, Congress as well as local authorities had always acquiesced in its operations.

What most troubled Roane was the Court's assertion of the primacy of the federal government over the states and its expansive formulation of "implied powers." Surely the word "necessary" (in the Constitution's "necessary and proper" clause) restricted the meaning of that phrase, Roane argued.

Jefferson was elated to read Roane's "Hampden" letters. Like Roane, he disputed the Supreme Court's claim to serve as the final arbiter of constitutional questions, either within the federal government or between the federal government and the states. He, too, lambasted Marshall for spearheading a movement designed to transform the American government into one "as venal and oppressive as the government from which we separated." Jefferson even took strong issue with Marshall's way of delivering court opinions as if they were unanimous, rarely recording minority opinions and thus virtually silencing any dissenting members of the Court. "An opinion is huddled up in conclave, perhaps by a majority of one," Jefferson wrote, "delivered as if unanimous, with the silent acquiescence of lazy or timid associates, by a crafty chief judge, who sophisticates the law to his mind, by the turn of his own reasoning."

The sweep of the *McCulloch* decision dismayed Madison, too. While the case had obviously called for a judicial decision, Madison wrote to Roane, it had not called for such a broad and expansive interpretation of the "necessary and proper" clause. Marshall's opinion in that case, Madison added, had the ominous effect of bestowing on Congress a discretion "to which no practical limit can be assigned." The Court's decision had simply empowered the "ingenuity" of the legislative branch to exercise any and all powers—including unconstitutional ones. The danger was that such judicial rulings might lead to a complete transformation of the federal system, converting "a limited into an unlimited Government."

Madison found himself even sympathizing with his old foes, the antifederalists. Many federalists, he ventured, would have joined forces with the antifederalists in rejecting the Constitution, had they suspected that the Court would impose such a "broad & pliant" construction of the Constitution.

While the imperious chief justice had no direct knowledge of Madison's or Jefferson's private wrath, he had carefully pored over Roane's published letters. They unleashed upon public opinion "a most serious hurricane," Marshall somberly wrote, the purpose of which was to impugn the judges and injure the Constitution. Though he found "Hampden's" principles "too palpably absurd for intelligent men," he understood that they could not simply be dismissed. More aroused than he had been by any other judicial controversy, Marshall dashed off nine lengthy letters of his own, signing them "A Friend to the Union" and publishing them in Philadelphia and Alexandria newspapers as well as in the *North American Review*. The Court's critics, he held, wanted to strip the government of its powers and "reinstate that miserable confederation."

Though Madison had been ambivalent about the Court's *McCulloch* decision, he supported the Court's opinion—and the Court's authority—in another case, *Cohens v. Virginia*. That support, however, would cause a breach between him and Jefferson.

In 1820, in the municipal court of Norfolk, a criminal indictment was brought against Philip and Mendes Cohen, brothers who managed the Norfolk branch of their family's Baltimore Lottery and Exchange Office. The two men were accused of selling National Lottery tickets in Virginia, which had prohibited the sale of unauthorized out-of-state lottery tickets. After their conviction and fine of $100, the Cohens decided to appeal the verdict. But since there was no appeal process in Virginia against municipal court rulings, the brothers took their case to the Supreme Court of the United States. Virginia, however, denied the Supreme Court's jurisdiction in a state criminal judgment. Not only did the Eleventh Amendment provide states with immunity from suits brought by citizens of other states, but, Virginia insisted, as a "sovereign and independent State," it could not be forced, without its consent, to appear as a defendant in federal court.

John Marshall himself, at the Virginia Ratifying Convention, had assured his fellow delegates that, under the new Constitution, a state would never be called to the bar of the federal court. "It is not rational to suppose that the sovereign power should be dragged before a court," Marshall had said at the convention. A state might be a plaintiff in a case, but never a defendant.

That was precisely the position that Virginia took in the *Cohens* case when it refused to appear as a defendant before the Supreme Court. But by then, Marshall had changed his mind on the issue. He had come to believe that there could be many instances that would compel states to surrender their sovereignty, especially when that surrender would benefit the people. Thus Marshall asked Boston lawyer Daniel Webster to defend the uncooperative state of Virginia; President Monroe's attorney general, William Wirt, would argue the case for the Cohen brothers.

Marshall's opinion in the *Cohens* case for a unanimous Supreme Court was another sweeping assertion of federal sovereignty and one more powerful blow to the doctrine of states' rights. First, Marshall established his Court's jurisdiction in the matter, arguing that since Congress had set up the National Lottery, the issue was a federal one. Second, he dismissed Virginia's "mischievous" claim that it need not submit to federal courts in such a matter. Such a claim, Marshall argued, would prostrate "the government and its laws at the feet of every State in the Union." If Virginia's claim went unchallenged, each state would possess a veto on the will of the federal Congress.

Surprisingly, the Court upheld the Cohens' conviction on the narrow grounds that Congress had not specifically authorized the sale of lottery tickets outside of the District of Columbia. But that favorable ruling hardly mollified embittered Virginians. The Court, they protested, had usurped even more power, reducing the states to nullities. But Marshall could scarcely have put it more bluntly: The laws of a state, he wrote, "so far as they are repugnant to the constitution and laws of the United States, are absolutely void." Because America had chosen to be a nation, he reasoned, the supreme power to make or to unmake a constitution resided only in the whole body of the people—and not in any or all of the states.

To Spencer Roane, Marshall's message was clear: The *Cohens* decision, Roane wrote, "negatives the idea that the states have a real existence." Standing at the "zenith of despotic power," the Court was operating on the principle that it could never be wrong. How could the federal system survive when one of the parties in the compact claimed the exclusive right to judge and decide upon the rights of the others?

So intense and unrelenting were the assaults on the authority of the Court that John Marshall suspected there might be a conspiratorial mastermind behind the scenes who was pulling the strings. The "whole attack," he wrote to Story, "if not originating with Mr. Jefferson, is obviously approved & guided by him." Mr. Jefferson's goal was clear, radical, and revolutionary: It was, Marshall wrote to Story, "the destruction of the government & the re-establishment of a league of sovereign states."

Marshall was wrong about Jefferson's role in orchestrating attacks on his Court, but he was right that Jefferson burned for something to be done. The former president was not only disgusted by the *Cohens* ruling—"ashamed that I was ever a lawyer"—but also frightened. While the Supreme Court noiselessly advanced like a thief, Jefferson wrote, the states had to rouse themselves from their apathy and meet the alarming judicial power grab head on.

The threat was so dire that every man, he wrote in a private letter to Thomas Ritchie, "should *uplift his arm*." Was the former president suggesting violent revolt? Another revolution—or disunion? If an indifferent Congress did nothing to shield the states from the judiciary, Jefferson wrote in early 1821, "the States must shield themselves, and meet the *invader* foot to foot." Not even Roane had been so rash.

But in the fall of 1821, a calmer, less impulsive, and less emotional Jefferson offered more cautious counsel. He advised Virginians to let northern states react first against overweening federal domination; then Virginia, in a supporting role, could helpfully follow their lead. Virginians would do best to lie low, he wrote to a friend, "until the shoe shall pinch an Eastern state. Let the cry be first raised from that quarter and we may fall into it with effect."

In the meantime, the only effective remedy for an overbearing, undemocratic Court—"unelected by, and independent of the nation"—was more democracy. "I know of no safe depository of the ultimate powers of the society but the people themselves," Jefferson wrote. When the elected members of the executive or legislative branches acted unconstitutionally, they were accountable to the voters; so should the judiciary be accountable to the people. The best solution that Jefferson could think of was to change the Constitution, eliminating lifetime Supreme Court appointments and instead limiting all judges to six-year terms, with the possibility of reappointment by the president with the approval of *both* houses of Congress. But Jefferson's bracing and refreshing position that democracy, majoritarian government, and accountability should apply to *all* branches of government was no match for a Constitution already venerated as if written in stone.

Though Jefferson and Madison had both objected to *McCulloch*, they parted ways with the *Cohens* decision. While Madison mildly regretted the Court's "propensity" for expanding the authority of the national government, he underscored that "the abuse of a trust does not disprove its existence." The Supreme Court, after all, was an essential component in the national structure that Madison had helped create and in which he still strongly believed. As president, he had even threatened to use force to uphold the Court's decisions. In 1809, the governor of Pennsylvania had called out the state militia to defy a Supreme Court order to collect funds that a state official had wrongly kept. Pennsylvania had maintained that it was acting to defend "State Rights," but after Madison issued a grave warning, the governor backed down. The president even had the militia officer who had carried out the governor's orders arrested; the man was tried and convicted—though, after having clearly established federal authority, Madison later pardoned him.

Following the *Cohens* decision, Madison again decided to stand firmly behind the federal system, expressing confidence that "sound arguments & conciliatory expostulations" would steer the government back on track. Though critical of the Supreme Court and occasionally venturing into Virginia localism, Madison remained a nationalist, actively resisting the trend toward state sovereignty, states' rights, sectionalism, and isolation.

But the fears of Virginians like Jefferson, Roane, and Ritchie—as well as Patrick Henry and George Mason before them—fears of consolidation and of a government of overbearing, if not unlimited, powers—were not imaginary. The powerful nationalist surge—the assertion of federal authority over the states—was unmistakable, and John Marshall's Supreme Court spearheaded it. To a fervent states' rights ideologue like Spencer Roane, who was hungry for some resolution to the problem, Madison's moderation, as well as Jefferson's recent, unexpected expression of caution, were unseasonable and cowardly. "Jefferson and Madison hang back too much in this great crisis," an agitated Roane objected at the end of 1821.

Martin, *McCulloch*, and *Cohens* were landmark Supreme Court cases. They signaled the beginning of a long, polarizing, and emotional struggle for states' rights that would preoccupy Virginians and other southerners for decades. When the increasingly embittered conflict finally exploded in violence, it sadly left Madison's moderation, Jefferson's caution, and even the excitable Roane's logical legal arguments far behind.

7

Another Constitutional Convention

"*The earth belongs to the living.*" While residing in his spacious townhouse on the Champs-Elysées in Paris during the revolutionary, explosive summer of 1789, Jefferson had the electrifying idea that each generation, not just his own, should possess the freedom and creative energy to renew society. "No society can make a perpetual constitution," he wrote to his faithful friend and correspondent James Madison, "or even a perpetual law. . . . Every constitution, then, and every law, naturally expires at the end of 19. years."

Madison was appalled. Though the federal Constitution he had recently helped draft did include a provision for future amendments, he saw in Jefferson's notion of continual change a dangerous formula for never-ending volatility. Attempting to temper his friend's exuberance, he suggested that a strong measure of continuity between generations contributed to the stability and well-being of a society. And the success of the American experiment notwithstanding, Madison cautioned that "experiments are of too ticklish a nature to be unnecessarily multiplied."

But the prospect of change—not stability or security—exhilarated Jefferson and ignited his imagination. Neither the cutting off of heads nor mobs roaming through the streets of Paris during the summer and fall of 1789 diminished his excitement about revolution. He only commented wryly to a friend that he was happy, upon awakening, to feel his head attached to his shoulders. Decades later, he still welcomed the idea of continuous renewal. Healthy societies as well as political institutions, he believed, could not survive without growth and revitalization. People should not be bound by the past, chained to obsolete governments and archaic ideas. Human beings, he was convinced, always strive for improvement.

In Jefferson's mind the American Revolution had not ended in 1783 when the peace treaty was signed with Great Britain; nor had it ended in 1789 with the ratification of the Constitution, or even in 1791 when the states approved the precious Bill of Rights. On the contrary, he conceived revolution as an ongoing process, an adventure that would never end. "I like a little rebellion now and then. It is like a storm in the Atmosphere," he had written to Abigail Adams in 1787, when enraged citizens in western Massachusetts took over the local courthouses to protest unfair taxation. And yet, he knew there were better ways to obtain truly significant reforms than armed takeovers and boisterous rallies. He believed in calm, reflective, and periodic constitutional change.

"Some men look at constitutions with sanctimonious reverence, and deem them like the ark of the covenant, too sacred to be touched," Jefferson wrote to his friend Samuel Kercheval in 1816. "They ascribe to the men of the preceding age a wisdom more than human." Conceding that frequent experimental changes in laws and constitutions might be harmful, he recommended instead that "moderate imperfections" be tolerated. But one of his core beliefs was that laws and institutions must change and evolve with the progress of the human mind. He thus suggested that regular opportunities for alteration be incorporated into the political calendar as well as into the constitution itself. Idealistically, he envisioned each generation, independent of all preceding generations, free and able to choose for itself the form of government it believed most conducive to its own happiness.

Jefferson knew by heart what those elements of political happiness were. He went on to outline a few essential ones for Kercheval: general suffrage; equal representation in the legislature; an executive chosen by the people; judges who were elected or removable from office; county officials who were elected; and periodic amendment of the constitution itself.

Alas, the constitution of his own state of Virginia allowed for *none* of those elements. As early as 1785, Jefferson had criticized the "capital defects" of the Virginia constitution. He recognized that it was written in 1776, not only under the stress of war but at a time when Virginians "were new and unexperienced in the science of government."

The flaws were legion. The right to vote was limited to a small class of white men. Every year, each county, regardless of population, elected two representatives to the House of Delegates, a system skewed toward the slaveholding counties. State senators were elected by senatorial districts, with a result that was no more proportional than in the House. The powerful House chose the governor as well as the members of the governor's council, who limited the governor's power and effectiveness. And it also appointed judges and local county officials.

Scarred by the colonial experience of arbitrary executive authority, Virginians had preferred in 1776 to concentrate power in the House of Delegates—even at the cost of eliminating checks and balances. Thus, in the executive branch, there was no strong, independent governor chosen by the people; in the judiciary, local justices of the peace, charged with administering county governments, were not chosen by or responsible to the people. Voters could not even cast secret ballots; instead they had to vote out loud. And the final blow: The constitution did not even include a provision for making amendments!

Virginia had rejected the kind of vital, democratic, self-governing townships that Jefferson admired in New England, where citizens took part in the administration of their public affairs and elected their own county judges and officers. Local government in the Old Dominion was imposed from above and remained unaccountable to the people. "An elective despotism," Jefferson complained, "was not the government we fought for."

James Madison agreed with Jefferson. He had long complained about Virginia's "bad" constitution, warning new states entering the Union not to copy it. As early as 1784, only eight years after Virginia's constitution was written, Madison had sponsored a bill in the House of Delegates for a new constitutional convention in Virginia—but his motion and others like it would lie dormant for decades. Virginia was suffering from a poverty of democratic institutions; two easy remedies that Madison suggested were the popular election of the governor and a judiciary independent of the legislature for everything but initial appointments. Madison would even come to believe in the Jeffersonian principle that men could not be bound by laws that they had no share in making.

State government in Virginia became even more unresponsive and archaic as the population shifted from the eastern to the western part of the state. The eastern Tidewater would have close to zero population growth in the early decades of the nineteenth century, while the population west of the Blue Ridge, from 1790 to 1830, increased by 500 percent. And yet citizens in the western part of the state went underrepresented in a legislature dominated by the Tidewater aristocracy. The east had twice as many representatives, in proportion to the number of qualified voters, as the west.

Indeed, bitter sectional rivalries divided Virginia. The Tidewater, the coastal plains that extended from the Chesapeake to the fall line of the eastern rivers, which was dominated by plantation owners and slaveholders, was the most conservative part of Virginia. The agriculturally diverse region of gentle hills and fertile soil from the Tidewater to the Blue Ridge Mountains was known as the Piedmont. The Valley, the region between the Blue Ridge on the east and the Allegheny Mountains on the west, was inhabited by small farmers who used mostly free labor. And to the far west was the Trans-Allegheny, a mineral-rich region of rugged hills and streams.

Suffrage in Virginia, like representation in both chambers of the General Assembly, favored the wealthier eastern part of the state, for it was limited to white men who owned either land or a house in a town, thereby excluding the majority of men from voting. Although Jefferson had always considered the independent, self-sufficient farmer and landowner the ideal citizen, he did not believe that citizenship should be defined by the ownership of land. It appeared that Virginia society was "instituted for the soil," he objected, "and not for the men inhabiting it." The state constitution had ensured "an usurpation of the minority over the majority," he said.

Far from being a living, inclusive document that enabled Virginians to govern themselves, the constitution of the Old Dominion was rigid, undemocratic, and archaic—deadening if not dead. And most of the men who had drafted it were dead. "The dead have no rights," Jefferson cried out in 1816. "They are nothing; and nothing cannot own something." Only the living, he wrote, "have a right to direct what is the concern of themselves alone." Only the living had the right "to make the constitution what they think will be the best for themselves."

In truth, Virginia had a stable if conservative government. The state had even managed to make a few important reforms over the years. Pressured by Jefferson, it abolished entail (which required that a family's property be left only to direct descendants) and primogeniture (which required that a family's property, in its entirety, be transferred to the oldest son), two laws that had made it possible for families to preserve their power and influence by passing undiluted economic power from one generation to the next. Virginia had also disestablished the Episcopal Church, permitting other competing religious denominations to flourish. In 1785 it reduced the property requirement for voting from 100 to 50 acres. And it could boast having two great documents: George Mason's declaration of rights of 1776, which became a model for bills of rights for all the other colonies, and Jefferson's revolutionary statute for religious freedom, written in 1779 and made law in 1786, which guaranteed the free exercise of religion according to the dictates of conscience.

Still, the state constitution paralyzed the state. With two-thirds of white males disenfranchised, and with voters prevented from electing their own local officials, Virginia did not have a body of citizens vitally engaged in self-government and in the politics and affairs of their state and communities. And by bestowing power on the state's backward-looking elite at the expense of average Virginians, the constitution ultimately inhibited the rise of an engaged, enterprising middle class and a new cadre of leaders—responsible, dynamic men interested in helping the state keep up with the changing times. In the inert political culture of the Old Dominion, there were few leaders excited by new ideas, energized by new challenges, and convinced that government should play an active, purposeful role in steering the state toward the future.

Virginia, the premier state, along with Massachusetts, in the 1770s, was no longer even in the mainstream by the 1820s. Not only did states like New York and Vermont have universal white male suffrage, but so did most of the other states in the South. Tennessee's first constitution of 1772 had provided for universal white male suffrage and even granted the vote to free blacks. Mississippi's 1817 constitution, as well as Alabama's 1819 constitution, provided for universal white male suffrage, legislatures based on the entire white population, and governors elected by the voters. By 1829, the restriction of voting rights to property holders survived in just two out of the twenty-four states in the Union, North Carolina and Virginia.

Some forward-looking Virginians, and especially many aggrieved westerners, urged constitutional change and a state government that would respond to their legitimate needs, whether for improved transportation, more banks, or better schools. They were interested in securing proportional representation in the legislature, extending political rights to all taxpayers, permitting the popular election of the governor, eliminating the governor's council, making officials of the county courts that administered local government accountable to the people, and, finally, providing for future changes and amendments. The goal was a democratic constitution and an active, receptive state government.

Almost a dozen times, between 1801 and 1813, progressive Virginians proposed holding another constitutional convention to revise the state's decades-old document. But each time, the General Assembly rejected their calls. The Old Dominion's wealthy and influential Tidewater planters had no incentive to transform an aristocratic, patriarchal government that served their interests into a democratic one. After all, the unproportional representation in the General Assembly favored them and shielded them from the taxation—especially taxation on their slave property—that they feared. Popular elections for governors, judges, and justices of the peace would only diminish their power, as would the extension of the franchise to men without land, breeding, and education. They would have disagreed with Jefferson that ordinary men "and not the rich, are our dependence for continued freedom." Those ordinary men would inevitably demand that the state play an active role in the life of society, and that kind of dynamic government represented the very antithesis of freedom as the planter elite understood it.

Still, pressure for constitutional reform continued to mount. Twice—in 1816 and 1825—unofficial reform conventions were held in Staunton, Virginia. Virginia's leading newspapers campaigned against "the rottenness of our state institutions," demanding that their gross problems and "defects" be repaired. At last, a statewide referendum put the issue to the people in 1828: A majority of voters agreed that the time had come to review the state's constitution.

Finally it would be possible to replace the privileged class that ruled Virginia with "responsible and accountable public servants," wrote "Videt" in a letter to the *Enquirer*. Virginia's rulers resembled the "old nobility of France, imbecile and incorrigible," wrote the editor of *Niles' Register*; and with their overthrow through expanded suffrage and fairer representation in the legislature, "a healthy and happy, bold and intelligent *middle class* will rise up to sweeten and invigorate society."

In the early fall of 1829, people began streaming into Richmond for the historic occasion, the first constitutional convention in the Old Dominion since 1776. Virginia's leaders would once again grapple with and debate fundamental questions of democracy and political equality.

The surviving greats of Virginia's illustrious revolutionary generation were all present: Madison, seventy-eight and weakened from a recent illness, had made the trip from Montpelier with Dolley; it was the first time in twelve years that they had left home. James Monroe, now seventy-one and showing signs of age, arrived from Oak Hill in Albemarle County dressed in the knee breeches that had been fashionable in the eighteenth century. The seventy-four-year-old Chief Justice John Marshall, who resided in an elegant Richmond home, made the short walk from 9th Street to the capitol. In the evenings there were dinners and receptions in the governor's mansion. James and Dolley Madison were delighted to attend the theatre. An observer admired Dolley's "countenance & manners"—"the finest I ever beheld," he remarked.

Also present were a host of eminent men representing the conservative eastern counties of Virginia: the ailing governor, William Branch Giles; the state's two United States senators, John Tyler and the ultra-conservative Littleton Waller Tazewell, as well as future senator Benjamin Watkins Leigh; the eccentric congressman John Randolph of Roanoke; former Speaker of the House Philip Barbour; Judge Abel Upshur, member of the House of Delegates and future secretary of state under Tyler; and the young Hugh Blair Grigsby, who would keep a diary of the proceedings and later write a history of the convention. Leading the western delegates were two soon-to-be members of the House of Representatives, Philip Doddridge and Bermuda-born John Cooke. Reformers from west of the Blue Ridge, counting for only thirty-six of the ninety-six delegates, knew that they would need support from moderates from northern Virginia and from counties close to the Blue Ridge.

On October 5, the men—eastern gentlemen in their dark, formal attire, westerners like Doddridge in their home-spun suits—all took their seats in the elegant delegates' chamber of the majestic capitol building, designed in 1786 by Jefferson. It was "a Glorious day—cool & pleasant—clear and bright," one of the many spectators recalled. From the visitors gallery, Vice President John Calhoun, from neighboring South Carolina, Secretary of State Martin Van Buren, Missouri Senator Thomas Hart Benton, and others keenly followed the debates, captivated by the prospect of hearing Virginians discuss equal rights and representation.

"The spectacle of so many distinguished men convened together for so solemn and important a purpose produced a sensation which baffles description," reported the *Enquirer*. When James Madison rose to call the assemblage to order and nominate James Monroe as president of the convention, "there were many a wet eye in the Hall," the *Enquirer* wrote. After Monroe's unanimous election, Madison, slightly unsteady on his feet, and John Marshall conducted the equally unsteady Monroe to the president's chair.

The initial work of the convention soon began, much of it performed in four committees concentrating on the executive, legislative, and judicial branches of state government as well as on the Virginia Declaration of Rights. Madison headed the committee charged with reviewing the state legislature. For the next three months, the men would gather in Jefferson's capitol building for five or six days a week.

The Sage of Monticello, Virginia's greatest advocate for constitutional reform, had died three years earlier. But his criticism of the Virginia constitution and his thirst for change had inspired the reformers and progressives at the convention. His spirit pervaded the chamber; delegates spoke of him as the "great Apostle of liberty" whose "spirit of reform has never slept." "Every principle for which we contend," said Philip Doddridge, "is supported by the deliberate opinions of Mr. Jefferson."

Democratic reformers like Doddridge quickly took the offensive, urging their fellow delegates to bring Virginia back into step with the times and reject the "idea of making Chinese shoes for American feet." It was no longer acceptable for a Tidewater county with only 620 free whites to have the same power as Shenandoah County with 17,000. The only path to meaningful change was to wrest political power from the Tidewater planters by remedying the defects in the constitution that Jefferson had outlined. Only by repealing property qualifications, granting universal white male suffrage, and reapportioning the legislature could new men play an active role in the affairs of the state; only then could a middle class emerge to diversify the economic arena and reinvigorate Virginia. In the Middle Ages, "for one noble Lord, there were ten thousand ignoble paupers," declared William Campbell. "I trust, Sir, we will rather strive to make *many middling men*, than a few great or noble men."

The true cost to the state of limiting suffrage to property holders, reformers argued, was in the exclusion from political participation of worthy citizens, men of talent and good character. William Campbell traced Virginia's backwardness in agriculture and industry to restraints on the right of suffrage. Also opposed to a property qualification was Thomas Bayly of Accomack County, on the eastern side of Chesapeake Bay, where many people earned their living, he remarked, by plowing the ocean, not the land. "I prefer residence and *a moral qualification* to a pecuniary or property qualification," Bayly declared. Eugenius Wilson of Monongalia pointed out that limitations on suffrage discouraged able, ambitious people from moving to Virginia while also driving "from the bosom of the Ancient Dominion, many of her most valuable sons."

The existing system of limiting suffrage to property owners and giving each county, regardless of population, the same number of representatives in the General Assembly had succeeded only in empowering an elite minority at the expense of the vast majority of Virginians. Lashing out at privilege, John Cooke demanded a government that derived its power "from the people and that was responsible to the people."

But the members of the old guard would not concede that they had created an aristocracy. "There exists not the slightest danger of a permanent concentration of wealth," contended Philip Barbour, for "the wheel of fortune never stands still, but is in a state of perpetual revolution." If property was taken into consideration, it was merely for the safety of society, Barbour said, and he asked the delegates to distinguish between civil liberty, which belonged to all citizens, and political liberty, which belonged to those best qualified to exercise it.

The paramount goal of the conservatives was to preserve tradition and bind society to the past. Dismissing Jefferson's famous enthusiasm for change and renewal and his insistence that "no society can make a perpetual constitution," they turned for political wisdom to the British statesman Edmund Burke, who had written the definitive primer for conservatives like themselves. His powerful book *Reflections on the Revolution in France*, published in 1790, described a society as a living, organic body whose strength and health lay in continuity, stability, and respect for its traditions and "prejudices."

Burke warned that heedless change driven by abstract theories of liberty, equality, and rights would bring chaos and bloodshed. Only with "infinite caution," he wrote, should men venture to alter a social edifice that has, "in any tolerable degree," served the purposes of society. Echoing Burke, Senator Tazewell lauded Virginia's traditional ways, admonishing Virginians against attempting thoughtless, rash innovations. Charging the verbs "change" and "reform" with ominous implications, he exclaimed that he would never consent "to pull down the whole venerated fabric to its foundation merely to build up another; to change everything, to reform everything, and to alter all."

Not surprisingly, the conservatives' most extravagant and provocative spokesman turned out to be none other than John Randolph of Roanoke, making one of his last public appearances. Announcing that he "never had any taste for Conventions or for new Constitutions" and that he had no confidence in Jefferson's theories, Randolph allowed that he was willing to aid in making some "*very small and moderate* reforms." And yet, he stressed that it was far safer that such changes *never* be made "and that our constitution remain *unchangeable* like that of Lycurgus." A Jefferson might thrive on the redesign of constitutions just as he had relished continuously redesigning Monticello, but for Randolph, the Jeffersonian "lust of innovation" was irrational, malignant, and damnable. "We are not struck down by the authority of Mr. Jefferson. Sir, if there be any point in which the authority of Mr. Jefferson might be considered valid, it is in the mechanism of a plough."

Addressing the most burning issue of the convention, universal white male suffrage, Randolph came out squarely for substantial property qualifications. Suffrage tied to the land, he declared, was the only safe foundation: "The moment you quit the land, (I mean no pun), that moment you will find yourselves at sea." After all, he quipped, Virginians were not drafting a constitution for Holland or Venice—or apparently for Accomack County. As for the county court system, which many people considered undemocratic and unaccountable, Randolph judged that it ensured a fair administration of public affairs and was mercifully free from the "instability of popular elections."

Randolph saved most of his contempt for the "monstrous tyranny" of what he called "King Numbers," that is, the principle of majority rule, the same principle that Jefferson had enshrined in his inaugural address. "The will of the majority is in all cases to prevail," Jefferson had declared in 1801. Jefferson, the idealistic democrat, trusted the people—educated, independent yeomen farmers—to govern themselves. There was no safer depository of the powers of society, he wrote, than the people themselves.

Ironically, the figure of the self-sufficient, self-governing, landowning yeoman farmer that Jefferson had held up as a model of virtue in a participatory democratic republic had been co-opted and distorted by the conservatives. In their hands, the yeoman became a lord, a vehicle for limiting participation in the political arena to a select few. *Actual* yeomen and other men who were "obliged to depend on their daily labor for daily subsistence" deserved no voice in political affairs, pronounced Benjamin Watkins Leigh. "Only *educated* people should vote," Tazewell explained to Hugh Grigsby, pointing out that "education can only be acquired by the fruits of property." Ergo, a hefty property qualification out of the reach of average Virginians. John Randolph despised Jefferson's egalitarian and democratic "ultra-Jacobinism." If he were still a young man, he proclaimed, he would flee the state: "I would not live under King Numbers. I would not be his steward, nor make him my taskmaster."

Conservatives like Randolph, Tazewell, and Leigh, closely following Burke, categorically rejected the principles of democracy, the sovereignty of the people, majority rule, and political equality. Burke, an unwavering believer in social hierarchy who branded equality a "monstrous fiction," had provided a solid ideological framework for Virginia conservatives.

And yet, constitutional revision was not only about ideology. On the contrary, it was also a familiar and mundane question of the planter class's abiding aversion to taxation. Under the existing constitution, the unproportional representation in the General Assembly, that was based on counties rather than population, was weighted heavily in favor of the wealthy Tidewater planters and slaveowners. But if suffrage were extended to all white males, and if representation were based solely on the white population, as the western reformers desired, then power would pass to the majority. Randolph feared that the majority would impose taxes—not just on land, horses, carriages, and some businesses, but also on slave property—in order to fund the schools, libraries, roads, canals, and railroads that western Virginians desperately needed.

Others at the convention, especially the conservative judge Abel Upshur, shared Randolph's dread of majority rule. Upshur, who had promised his constituents that he would block any alarming proposals to experiment with new reforms, declared that there was no "principle in the law of nature which gives to a majority a right to control a minority." Arguing that only landowners should be permitted to vote, and that wealth—in the form of slave property—should be recognized in calculating representation in the General Assembly, Upshur explained that there existed two different majorities: a majority of *interest* and a majority of *numbers*. Inasmuch as the very idea of society carried with it the idea of private property, the majority of interest, the guarantor of social order, should govern. "Take away all protection from property," he said, "and our next business is to cut each other's throats."

It stood to reason, Upshur said, that property owners had the greatest stake in the government and should therefore be entrusted with the greatest share of political power. And it was contrary to reason to permit those who possessed no property to dictate laws for regulating and taxing the property of others. So, he concluded, "Let us boldly take the bull by the horns . . . and incorporate this influence of property as a leading principle in our Constitution." A dozen years later, when Upshur served as John Tyler's secretary of the navy, he would continue to stress that the moment suffrage ceased to be tied to ownership of the soil, the "axe" would be laid to American institutions.

Others at the convention rushed to agree with Randolph and Upshur. The freehold, or property, requirement might not be a perfect rule, admitted Benjamin Watkins Leigh, for it excluded from political rights many women who were "fully equal to the most meritorious of the other sex, in intelligence, in public spirit and every other quality that constitutes a good citizen." And yet, Leigh could think of no better method than land ownership to identify those "whose own interests are the most completely identified with the interests of the Commonwealth." Any other system, such as Jefferson's dreamy, utopian ideas about universal suffrage, Leigh said, would merely lead to the "despotism" of "lazy and drunken men."

As the speeches continued, disgusted westerners saw through the charade. They grasped that they were being deprived of a meaningful political voice in the state because the planter class feared that new voters would impose taxes on their slave property. "Let it be once openly avowed," said one lucid delegate from western Virginia, "that the price which Western people must pay for the protection of your slaves, is the surrender of their power in the government, and you render that property hateful to them in the extreme."

After weeks of wrangling, the debate over suffrage and representation reached an impasse. Passions had been aroused, and "fraternal feelings

[were] exasperated into bitterness," remarked conservative Robert Sta-
nard. It seemed unlikely that grounds could be found for compromise.

The sole survivor of Virginia's constitutional convention of 1776—as well
as of the federal Constitutional Convention of 1787—sat quietly in the
chamber, taking notes, saying very little, especially during the convention's formal proceedings. But if anyone could bridge the gap between the
aristocrats and the democrats, perhaps it was the cool and dispassionate
Madison.

Still, it was not clear what position Madison would take on the most
crucial issue—majority rule in Virginia. Over the course of his political
life, he had stood on both sides of that issue. In his *Federalist* essays, he
had warned of oppressive majorities. He had even designed a system of
checks and balances—with its divided government, conflicting majorities, veto traps, and staggered elections—to counter them. Although
Madison would have said that he believed in majority rule, he had frag-
mented and undermined the potential force of the majority so as to render it largely ineffective. But in 1791 and 1792, in the series of articles he
wrote for the *National Gazette*, he had taken a very different stance, criti-
cizing President Washington's administration for representing the interests of a financial elite to the detriment of the majority of average citizens.

No one could predict what Madison would say in Richmond: In the
past he had feared unfettered democracy, calling it "despotism growing
out of anarchy." But he was equally apprehensive of "an oligarchy founded
on corruption."

On December 2, 1829, Madison rose from his seat to give his one and
only speech at the convention. It was an historic moment. Anxious to
hear his every word, many of the younger delegates rushed from their seats
and crowded around the mythic figure. His voice was "low and weak," reported the *Enquirer*, "but his sentences were rounding and complete; and
his enunciation, though tremulous and full of feeling, was distinct to
those who heard him."

Five weeks earlier, Madison had reported to the convention the con-
clusions of his committee, which had been charged with reviewing the
state legislature. He had announced that he and his colleagues favored

representation in the powerful House of Delegates based not on counties but exclusively on the white population. The human property of
slaveowners would go unrepresented, tilting the balance of power to the
western parts of the state. Had Madison joined a western cabal to destroy slavery? some conservatives frantically worried. Tazewell sneered
at the "fatuity" of Madison's proposal. Others ridiculed the idea of giving old men a role in public affairs.

But now, with hushed delegates hanging on his every word, Madison
made an unexpected about-face, abandoning the idea of a more democratic House of Delegates. In his weak voice and in a roundabout way, he
told the convention that the interests of slaveowners had to be recognized
in the state legislature by affording representation to three-fifths of the
slave population. If the legislature were "in the hands of a majority, who
have no interest in this species of property . . . injustice may be done to its
owners," he said softly. "It would seem, therefore, if we can incorporate
that interest into the basis of our system, it will be the most apposite and
effectual security that can be devised."

None of Randolph's hyperbole, none of his hysterical outbursts or
histrionic flourishes—and yet the message was virtually the same. Representation in the legislature should be based on three-fifths of the slave
population added to the white population, thereby incorporating the
recognition of property and wealth into political representation while
also slanting representation and power to the Tidewater planters and
slaveowners.

For Madison, the three-fifths basis for representation was both humane
and politic. Humane because slaves were human beings: Despite their
complexion, he argued, their humanity should be taken into account.
The use of a "white basis" for representation, as the westerners proposed,
Madison reasoned, would deny that black people existed in Virginia.
Politic because the weight of slave property would be incorporated into
the political power balance and would thus provide an effective safeguard
for the rights of the wealthy slaveowning minority. Politic, too, because
Virginia's use of the "three-fifths rule" would be consistent with the system of representation that the South had insisted upon in the federal government. In other words, the three-fifths rule would empower eastern

Virginia in the state government just as it empowered the South in the federal government.

Finally, in a "spirit of compromise," Madison added that perhaps representation in one of the two legislative chambers could be based on "federal numbers," while representation in the other chamber could be based solely on the white population, as westerners desired. This conclusion superficially seemed to align Madison with the men who represented the western part of the state. But eastern slaveowners felt that the victory would ultimately be theirs, for they realized that they could use Madison's argument in favor of the three-fifths rule in one house of the General Assembly to insist that those numbers be applied to both houses.

Surprisingly, Madison had come down on the conservative side of the most fundamental question at the convention. He had agreed that representation and political power should be weighted in favor of slaveowners. Citizens might be equal in their political rights, but the wealthy slaveholders in the eastern part of the state would continue to be more equal than others. Their ability to dominate the political life of the state would go unchallenged, perpetuating the status quo.

Madison had made an old and persuasive argument, but did it represent a shift in his political thinking, or a pragmatic attempt at compromise? In his *National Gazette* essays of 1791 and 1792, as well as in his notes for those essays, he had expressed radically different views from those he had voiced at the convention. A slaveholding society, he had written, was— and could only be—an aristocracy. "In proportion as slavery prevails in a State," he wrote, "the Government, however democratic in name, must be aristocratic in fact." In the southern states, the vast majority of inhabitants—slaves and propertyless white men (women went unmentioned), probably three-quarters of the population—could not vote; they had no political rights. Power resided in the minority, creating—by definition— an aristocracy. A combination of slavery and restricted suffrage, Madison wrote, "throws the power much more into the hands of property, than in the Northern states." This, he explained, was exactly the system that the entrenched ruling elite wanted.

Neither Madison nor Jefferson had ever been as preoccupied with the rights of property owners in America as the other wealthy men of their generation, who considered property a condition of political freedom. Men like Washington and John Adams had sought independence from Great Britain precisely because of the threats they perceived—in the form of taxation—to Americans' freedom to own and enjoy property. Anxious to safeguard both liberty and property, the wealthy, self-protective men who drafted many of the original state constitutions had insisted on property qualifications for voting as well as for holding office. Property owners, those who were presumed to have the most at stake in society, would govern. Men who were destitute of property, wrote John Adams, were "too little acquainted with public Affairs to form a Right Judgment."

But Madison and Jefferson had genuine and abiding democratic aims, realizing that political democracy required a measure of economic democracy. Hoping to establish a system that would allow all white men in Virginia to participate in public life, Jefferson had proposed in 1776 that all those without property be given 50 acres. Madison was also prepared to democratize the concept of property. In one of the most unusual of his *National Gazette* articles, he had sought to redefine the very concept of property—opening it up to the masses. Property, he wrote, had a "larger and juster meaning" than land or wealth—or slaves. A man's property included his labor, his opinions, his religious faith, his free use of his faculties, and "the most sacred of all property," his conscience.

Governments, Madison reminded his readers, were typically accorded high praise for protecting the property of the wealthy. But far more important to the health of a republic and to the vitality of an open political arena, he contended, was the government's protection of something that was both more democratic and more intangible: citizens' "free use of their faculties, and free choice of their occupations." Preserving and defending citizens' intangible property—that is, their rights and labor—was the primary role of government. Just as Jefferson had changed the classic Lockean formula from "life, liberty and estate" to "Life, Liberty, and the pursuit of Happiness," Madison was also drawing a distinction between a conservative government, which protects the material property of the wealthy few, and a truly "republican" government, which protects the interests and the freedom of expression of the many. Madison was awakening the class consciousness of average Americans, advising them that they, too, possessed "property" interests that were as worthy of their government's attention—and even intervention—as the economic interests of the moneyed elite.

Almost forty years after penning his *National Gazette* articles, at the Virginia convention of 1829, desperately searching for compromise and the middle ground, Madison backtracked on that expansive view of property. It would be "unsafe," he said in his low voice to his fellow delegates, to extend suffrage to all, including the "unfavored class" of white working men with no property other than their wages. He proposed instead a modest extension of the franchise to certain householders and leaseholders. The man who had lashed out at aristocracy in his 1792 essay on "Property" had reversed course, reverting to the antimajoritarian position of his *Federalist* essays of 1787 and 1788. At the 1829 convention he reminded delegates that the gravest danger in republics was "that the majority may not sufficiently respect the rights of the minority."

Ultimately Madison proved that over the years he had become, in the words of historian Drew McCoy, "ever more firmly bound to his native soil and its conventions." Fearful that the Virginia convention would result not only in "an abortion" but in the fatal division of Virginia into two separate states, he summoned his skill as a mediator to avoid that disaster. "The Convention is now arrived at a point where we must agree on some common ground," he told his listeners, casting himself as peacemaker. But although he claimed to want a compromise among the opposing parties, he admitted that it had been necessary to indulge the conservative faction, "whose defeat would have been most pregnant with danger." Unable to resist the hysteria of panic-stricken eastern Virginians who feared that the very foundation of their political influence and prestige might be toppled, Madison surrendered to them, sacrificing his political principles to the urgency of finding a pragmatic compromise.

Madison had always been a prudent, practical statesman who sought balance within an imperfect constitutional framework. In *Federalist* No. 37, he had noted that the Constitutional Convention of 1787 had "been compelled to sacrifice *theoretical propriety* to the force of extraneous considerations." Similarly, at the Virginia convention of 1829, he granted that it would be a "happy" situation if all citizens could have an equal voice in making laws. "But this is Theory, which like most theories, confessedly requires limitations and modifications," he said. And yet, the undemocratic configuration to which he consented would accomplish far more than the mere sacrifice of theoretical propriety. It empowered a slaveholding minority that, adamantly averse to taxation and to planning and funding improvements to the state, would systematically and consistently obstruct all efforts at modernization.

Ironically, Madison's shift to the right pleased virtually no one at the convention. "He voted with us and then against us, without explaining why or wherefore," wrote one perplexed reformer to Madison's friend Nicholas Trist. Eastern conservatives dismissed Madison's proposal. Indeed, immediately after Madison made his remarks, Abel Upshur took the floor, abruptly announcing that Madison had spoken in too low a voice to be heard and that he, Upshur, would therefore develop his own views "without regard to those remarks." It was as if the former president and coauthor of *The Federalist* had not even spoken.

In January 1830, after months of heated, acrimonious debate, weary delegates finally approved a new constitution. It was a triumph for the conservative majority; they considered it a victory over radicalism and a formula for maintaining their power. But for reformers, it was a fiasco: They viewed the new state constitution as an inherently undemocratic social contract that guaranteed the supremacy of the plantation-dominated Tidewater and Piedmont parts of the state.

Western Virginians saw almost all proposals for reform crushed. The Senate would continue to be malapportioned, while representation in the House of Delegates would be based on the three-fifths rule. In addition, it was decided that representation would be based on the already out-of-date 1820 census. This allowed for an increase in representation for western Virginia, but not as great an adjustment as its growing population warranted. The continued dominance of the old guard was guaranteed.

Suffrage was not accorded to all white males or even to all taxpayers. Instead, the right to vote was minimally expanded to include householders and certain kinds of leaseholders, a formula that still disenfranchised a third of the state's free white men. Virginia would continue to be one of only two states in which property determined the political rights of citizens. Voting aloud would continue. Also defeated was a proposal for the popular election of the governor, a move that would have stimulated grassroots participation in the political process and a more vibrant political culture. Instead, the House of Delegates hung on to the authority to choose the governor, and the power of that eminent personage would continue to be circumscribed by the legislature as well as by the governor's council, which, however, was reduced from eight men to three.

The local court system that administered counties went untouched; its officers would be appointed and thus unaccountable to voters. Also killed was the reform most ardently desired by Jefferson, a provision for allowing future amendments to the state constitution. John Randolph exulted that there would be no such invitation to constitutional tampering. "I should as soon think of introducing into a marriage contract a provision for divorce," he said. For some conservatives, even the minor changes agreed to by the convention went too far. "The extension of the Right of suffrage is perhaps too great," wrote Richmond lawyer Thomas Greene. But, he added, he had "no other objection to the new Constitution."

And no wonder. The eastern gentry had succeeded in blocking virtually all meaningful reform. They had held onto power. For them, after all, good government was simply government of, by, and for themselves and their interests. But for the great majority of the people of Virginia, this meant lifeless government, a government unresponsive to their needs and to a transforming world. Planters would continue to rule the state the way they had always ruled agrarian Tidewater, upholding "tradition" and the status quo. They would oppose taxation, public schools, banking, industry, and even improved roads. The new constitution represented a "static solution to a dynamic situation," commented historian Merrill Peterson.

Madison's voyage home to Montpelier from Richmond on Virginia's decomposing roads could have served as a warning of that grim future: "We reached home the fifth day after leaving Richmond," he wrote to James Monroe, "much fatigued, and with horses almost broken down by the almost impassable state of the roads."

Still, Madison tried to put a good face on the convention and claimed to be satisfied with the new constitution. Forwarding a copy of the constitution to a professor at the University of Virginia, Madison remarked that it was "very much a compound of compromising ingredients. It is pudding, with some good plums in it at least." A month after the convention ended, he informed Lafayette that Virginia's new constitution provided "evidence of the capacity of men for self-government." But in truth, by defining citizenship as well as representation in terms of property, and thereby limiting participation in the political process, the Virginia constitution of 1830, with Madison's unfortunate acquiescence, irremediably undermined self-government in the Old Dominion.

With its new constitution, the government of Virginia would look backward to the preindustrial past for guidance and inspiration for the next twenty years. The state's ruling elite would remain oblivious to the dynamic nineteenth century, preferring to believe that somehow everything would stay the same. As for western Virginians, they were left more than ever on their own, forced to forge economic ties with the Ohio Valley instead of with the Tidewater and the Piedmont.

Their hopes dashed, western reformers were distraught. Their defeat, said one of their leaders, Philip Doddridge, sealed the "political vassalage" of the Trans-Allegheny and struck a blow at democracy and republicanism. "No political body had ever done more to destroy the principles of free government than this convention," said another despondent reformer from the west, Mark Alexander. The reactionary, complacent Tidewater gentry, concerned only with their local and selfish interests, could not have been more different, Alexander continued, "from the virtuous, principled Southern gentlemen" who had created a nation in Philadelphia in 1787.

The acrimonious sectional conflict between the eastern and western parts of the state unsettled many Virginians, who foresaw the eventual splitting apart of their state. Governor Giles recognized the possibility of the "forcible separation of Virginia." And James Monroe, too, feared that the east-west clash might result in the "dismemberment" of Virginia. Might it also result in violence? "I tell you sir," westerner John Cooke had warned at the convention, "the separation of this Assembly, without redressing, in some measure at least, the grievances of the non-freeholders, will be the signal for resistance, passive at first, to the constituted authorities." Raising the specter of houses, villages, and towns reduced to ashes and fields strewn with mangled, bloodied corpses of Virginians, Cooke predicted that "Civil war will be the result."

Despite revisions finally made to the state constitution in 1851, western Virginia would indeed break away, at the outset of a different, wider civil war, when it refused to join the eastern part of the state in seceding from the Union. In 1861, western Virginians held a convention in Wheeling and elected their own governor. Two years later, with Richmond the capital of the Confederacy, the fifty western counties of Virginia won recognition as a new state in the Union. That breach within Virginia can be traced at least as far back as the convention of 1829, when Virginia conservatives crushed the hopes of reformers in the west, ensuring that Virginia would remain, for decades more, frozen in time.

8

Tariff Wars

Tariffs? What could be more tedious than these dull laws designed simply to produce revenue and encourage and protect domestic manufacturing? Yet they would provoke not only furious protests in Virginia but much more resentment, frustration, and defiance than either *McCulloch* or *Cohens*. And far more than those Court rulings, the outrage over tariffs would set Virginia and other southern states on a long and ultimately lethal collision course with the national government.

At the Constitutional Convention of 1787, few delegates had questioned the utility of giving Congress the power to regulate trade and impose tariffs. On the contrary, the convention had been called in part because, as George Washington remarked, the regulation of trade could not possibly be handled "by thirteen heads, differently constructed." Washington's fellow Virginian George Mason, however, took the opposite stance, leaving Philadelphia "in an exceeding ill humor," after declining to vote for the Constitution. Mason's principal objection, Madison reported to Jefferson, was none other than the federal government's power to regulate trade, an unacceptable restriction, in his opinion, on the autonomy of the states. But for Washington, there could have been no more convincing grounds for giving the federal government the power to regulate trade than the "extravagant and preposterous" prohibitory and retaliatory trade regulations that the Virginia legislature had almost passed; they were the most absurd statutes, Washington sneered, that he had ever read.

For his part, James Madison had no doubt that the new national government should be armed with the right to tax both exports and imports. He even proposed at the Constitutional Convention that the national government regulate not only interstate commerce but also trade *within* states, explaining that commerce was "indivisible" and should be "wholly under one authority." He disagreed strongly with George Mason's proposal that a two-thirds vote in each branch of the legislature be required to pass certain commerce and navigation acts. Only Maryland and Georgia had joined the Virginia delegation in supporting Mason's motion for a super-majority.

When Congress first convened in 1789, representatives quickly passed tariffs—15 percent on imports such as iron, nails, hemp, and glass, and 5 percent on all other imports—that President Washington signed into law. Their main purpose was to raise revenue for the new government. But Treasury Secretary Hamilton and others recognized that the levies on imports could also be used to protect and stimulate domestic industry and encourage diversification of the economy. Tariffs on imports, as Hamilton wrote in his "Report on Manufactures," would enable American manufacturers to undersell all their foreign competitors. Hamilton and Madison suspected that tariffs, which raised the cost of imported goods, might prove unpopular—that was even "to be expected," Madison wrote—but they never dreamt that tariffs might be considered unconstitutional.

And yet, only five years later, Madison would backtrack from his nationalist position on tariffs. In several articles that he wrote for the *National Gazette* in 1792, he launched an attack on Washington and Hamilton's economic and tariff policies. Tariffs on imported goods, he wrote, helped American manufacturers by raising the prices of competing European products, but they penalized farmers by forcing them to purchase more expensive American products. A good government, Madison wrote in the *Gazette*, should abstain "from measures which operate differently on different interests, and particularly such as favor one interest at the expence of another." Not only did tariffs favor manufacturing interests over agricultural interests, they also unfairly and arbitrarily favored certain manufacturing interests over others. In another article, he criticized the federal government for imposing tariffs on imported buttons, a tax that denied to both the manufacturer and the wearer of certain garments the "economical use of buttons," that is, the freedom of purchasing the cheapest buttons available.

But Madison would shift his opinion on tariffs again two dozen years later. Around the time of the War of 1812, from 1811 until 1815, there had been a temporary ban on imports from Europe. When the ban was finally lifted, the flood of foreign goods shipped to American ports threatened the survival of fledgling industries in cotton, woolens, iron, glass, and pottery. President Madison and his political allies realized that a protective tariff was urgently needed. In February 1816, for the first time, the federal government sought to impose tariffs designed primarily to protect domestic industries rather than simply to raise revenue.

Championed by Speaker of the House Henry Clay of Kentucky and Congressman John Calhoun of South Carolina, the tariff bill, imposing duties of about 20 percent on most imports, passed, despite the fierce opposition of southern agrarians like John Randolph of Roanoke. Tariffs may have been designed to protect domestic industry, but that industry was concentrated almost entirely in the North, while the South was almost entirely agricultural. As far as most southerners were concerned, tariffs were punitive legislation that raised their cost of living while forcing them to subsidize northern industry and prosperity. Randolph considered tariffs a direct attack on southern planters and farmers and their way of life. "No, I will buy where I can get manufactures cheapest," Randolph declared on the floor of Congress. "I will not agree to lay a duty on the cultivators of the soil to encourage exotic manufactures." With his usual extravagance, Randolph lashed out at industrialists and speculators, whom he fantasized living in "opulence, whirling in coaches, and indulging in palaces" and assembling every day on the Rialto to compare notes with Shylock.

John Tyler's complaint would be more succinct: "We sell cheap and are made to buy dear." And University of Virginia Professor George Tucker would teach in his course on political economy that "every citizen should have an unrestricted right to buy where he can obtain the cheapest and best articles."

Southerners objected to tariffs not only for economic reasons but also for ideological ones: Tariffs intruded on the autonomy and rights of the states as well as on the freedom of the individual. To force consumers to buy expensive American-made goods, wrote Professor Tucker, was "an act of tyranny and injustice." At least on economic grounds, Virginians and other southerners appeared to be justified in their protests. Tariffs on foreign products did increase the price of many of Virginians' imports—from textiles to farm machinery—and force them to buy higher-priced American goods, while offering no benefits to the southern economy.

But what about benefits to the northern economy? Can it at least be said that tariffs helped the economies of the Mid-Atlantic and northeastern states? Unfortunately, there is little evidence that they stimulated American industry or that they had more than negligible effects. More important to the rise of American industry, most economic historians conclude, were American inventiveness, the availability of capital, democratic political institutions, freedom of movement from place to place, and immigration, among many other factors. And so southerners—even eccentric conservatives like Randolph—could rightly protest the unjustifiable burden of tariffs on southern consumers.

Six years later, tariffs would climb even higher. Henry Clay's pro-growth "American System" of 1824 called for 30 percent duties on iron, lead, wool, hemp, and textile fabrics. Virginians cried that the higher prices on goods that resulted from tariffs were robbing them of their wealth, transferring it to manufacturers in the North. The tariff "takes property from one man and gives it to another without just compensation," declared politician William Branch Giles. He sardonically added that legislators justified this theft with the illusory idea that it was in the interest of southerners to finance manufacturing in the North; but for his part, Giles rejected this "enchanted notion of national unity." The Tariff Act of 1824 passed Congress with only one vote from the Virginia delegation in the House of Representatives and virtually no other support from the South.

Outraged Virginians decided to take matters into their own hands. In 1825, the General Assembly of the Old Dominion passed resolutions proposed by Giles that declared the tariff unconstitutional. And in 1827, when Congress considered increasing duties on woolen goods, Virginia again passed resolutions denying the constitutionality of tariffs. That attempt to raise the tariff was killed when Vice President John Calhoun cast a tie-breaking vote in the Senate.

But even worse was to come: In January 1828, Congress approved an even higher tariff, called the "tariff of abominations" by its many opponents, that hiked duties on cotton and woolen cloth up to 50 percent. That May, President John Quincy Adams signed it into law.

———

Could a minority rightly overrule the majority? Virginia had decided to assert the right of a state to declare federal legislation unconstitutional, transforming the simple subject of the fairness or unfairness of tariffs into an incendiary and divisive campaign for states' rights.

George Washington thought he had put the subject of minority resistance to rest once and for all in 1794 when his administration crushed the Whiskey Rebellion—the mob-violence provoked by farmers in Kentucky and western Pennsylvania who were irate at the federal excise tax on distilled spirits. In full military attire, the sixty-two-year-old president rode on horseback to western Pennsylvania at the head of more than 12,000 troops to crush the rebellion and uphold the principles of federal supremacy and majority rule. If a minority dictates to the majority, Washington wrote, "there is an end put, at one stroke, to republican government."

After the passage of the tariff of abominations, Madison decided to speak out on the side of the federal government and the congressional majority. Springing to action, he published letters and reports defending the constitutionality of protective tariffs and the authority of the federal government. In truth, Madison was no friend of that tariff, which he strongly opposed. But he did believe in the supremacy of the Constitution that he had helped draft.

The Constitution vested in Congress explicitly "the power to lay & collect taxes duties imposts & excises" along with the "power to regulate trade," Madison wrote in a 4,000-word public letter in the fall of 1828 to the *National Intelligencer* in Washington. One of the purposes of the regulation of trade, he explained, was to encourage domestic manufacturing, and among the government's tools for regulating trade was protective legislation. Indeed, it was absurd to think that the Congress's power to regulate trade did not "involve a power to tax it."

For many conservatives in the Old Dominion, Madison quickly became *persona non grata*. His defense of the constitutionality of tariffs was sufficient to discredit him in their eyes. They lumped him with activist nationalists like Henry Clay and attacked his position in the Virginia press. "Mr. Madison has chosen to throw the weight of his great name into the scale of unlimited power," editorialized the *Richmond Enquirer*.

But the *Enquirer* went further, embarking on a nasty campaign to denigrate Madison's knowledge and prestige. "The day of prophets and oracles has passed," wrote *Enquirer* editor Thomas Ritchie in early 1829, disparaging Madison's authority. Free citizens of a free country, Ritchie added, must think for themselves. Madison's arguments were "too farfetched, ambiguous, irrelevant, and unsatisfactory" to be useful in the debate, wrote one mocking writer to the *Enquirer*. The implication was that, while Madison could offer a font of insight into the original intentions of the founders, he was sadly out of step with the 1820s. Years earlier, in *Federalist* No. 14, Madison had praised Americans for *not* suffering "a blind veneration for antiquity, for custom, or for names." Happy to see them using their own rational faculties and imagination, he had encouraged them to embrace novelty and to dare to experiment. Now Virginians were taking him up on his advice.

The uproar over tariffs, especially over the tariff of abominations, proved to be far more than a banal dispute over expensive imports. On the contrary, it became a pivotal issue sparking a debate over the question of sovereignty. Did sovereignty lie in the national government or in the states—and what rights did the states have to assert a sovereignty of their own?

In the vanguard of the antitariff, states' rights movement was the vice president of the United States, John Calhoun of South Carolina. Calhoun had begun his political career as a fervent nationalist. He had been a chief backer of the 1816 tariff in the hope that it would eliminate the national debt, protect nascent industries in the North, and simultaneously secure strong northern markets for southern cotton and other crops. And that same year, he had also proposed the "Bonus Bill" to fund a national system of roads and canals. His goal had been to give the Union, through a transportation network, "strength and solidarity."

But over the course of the next decade, as cotton prices slumped and as the South declined economically, Calhoun inveighed against the tyranny of the majority. The manufacturing interests of the Northeast that demanded ever higher tariffs, Calhoun had come to believe, were assaulting the economic viability of the agricultural South as well as the slave-based social order that undergirded the southern economy. By the late 1820s, Calhoun had metamorphosed into an antitariff champion of small, limited government.

Calhoun decided to expand upon Virginia's decision to declare tariffs unconstitutional. Believing that mere protest was insufficient, he concluded that a program for active resistance was needed. He was convinced that Congress had no constitutional authority to promote certain sectors of the economy to the detriment of others. In late 1828, Vice President Calhoun carefully crafted an "Exposition and Protest," a fifty-page screed that he published anonymously, denouncing the tariff and postulating the right of any single state to nullify federal legislation.

In his "Exposition," Calhoun argued that, whereas the national government had the means to protect itself against the encroachments of the states, the states possessed no such means to defend themselves against the national government. Underscoring the crucial importance of minority rights, Calhoun wrote that the Constitution offered no real protection to states that believed themselves "injured" by legislation passed by Congress. They could count neither on the Supreme Court nor on a presidential veto, since both the judicial and executive branches were themselves part of the federal government. As for a constitutional amendment, that was possible only if three-quarters of the states agreed.

And yet, the final authority of constitutional review, Calhoun argued, should reside not in the government but in the governed, in the sovereign people. And those sovereign people, he reasoned, could be identified only through their states. "Not a particle of sovereignty," he wrote, resided in the fiction of a collective American people.

How then to protect the few against the many and return sovereignty to the people? Calhoun concluded that a state had not just the right but the "sacred duty" of "interposition"—that is, the right and obligation to assert its own authority against that of the Union, to overrule federal legislation, and to "arrest the progress of a usurpation" that would otherwise destroy the liberty of the country.

A few years later, after it became known that he was the author of the "Exposition," Calhoun elaborated on the high power of "interposition" that, he believed, states possessed. Without it, they would be forced to make "*an entire surrender of their sovereignty*" while the national government was left alone to determine the extent of its own powers. The right of states to declare a law unconstitutional, Calhoun summarily decided, "stands on clearer and stronger grounds than that of the Supreme Court."

How exactly would states exercise this power? Calhoun outlined certain procedures: He proposed that a state should be able to unilaterally nullify federal legislation and then call a convention of all the states; if three-quarters of them disagreed with the nullification, they could pass a constitutional amendment to render the disputed legislation constitutional. At that point, the nullifying states could either yield to the majority or secede from the compact of states. The nullifying power, Calhoun underscored, was to be reserved for cases of "dangerous infractions of the Constitution" when the alternative courses were either intolerable submission or violent resistance. For Calhoun, tariffs exemplified precisely such "dangerous infractions" and thus had brought Americans to a critical juncture in the life of the nation.

Calhoun had unknowingly set the stage for secession and civil war. And yet, in his mind, "interposition" was not a radical or even an inflammatory idea. It represented an "intermediate point . . . by which the Government may be brought to a pause," a basis for conciliation and compromise. He insisted that he was merely proposing a legal way to cancel an inadmissible law while also saving the Union. He emphasized that he was speaking out of "strong attachment" to the Constitution and that he was proud to have spent half of his life in the service of the Union. But union, he wrote, meant "not a nation, but . . . a confederacy of equal and sovereign states." And the crucial principle of this union was minority power. No government based on the will of the majority could "preserve its liberty even for a single generation," Calhoun wrote, turning Washington's dictum about majority rule upside-down. Calhoun was pleased that his ideas had been accepted in Virginia and Georgia, and especially in his own state of South Carolina, the trailblazer in the nullification movement.

Another politician had preceded Calhoun by three decades in articulating the theory of state interposition. Ironically, this man was none other than James Madison, the defender of tariffs and of the authority of the national government. In 1798 he and Jefferson, working in tandem, had made similar arguments in their Kentucky and Virginia Resolutions, written in protest of the Sedition Act.

Congress had passed the Sedition Act against the background of the war fever that was gripping the nation in the late 1790s. Angered by a trade treaty that the United States had negotiated with Great Britain, France was permitting private, armed French vessels to raid or capture American ships. Fearing an imminent conflict, Congress called up a provisional army of 12,000 men. Even President Washington was willing to come out of retirement and serve as commander.

In that heated crisis atmosphere, amid calls for national unity, Congress decided to make it a criminal offense to criticize the government's policies or malign its elected officials. Only seven years after the Bill of Rights was ratified, the people's elected representatives overruled the First Amendment—"Congress shall make no law . . . abridging the freedom of speech, or of the press." Journalists, newspaper editors, and a few ordinary citizens who had dared to criticize President John Adams or other officers of the national government were fined and thrown into jail.

Searching for a remedy against such overweening and clearly unconstitutional federal power, Jefferson and Madison drafted the Virginia and Kentucky Resolutions. The two friends, along with their political allies, hoped that those two states would adopt the resolutions and that other states would follow suit.

In his Kentucky Resolutions, drafted in secret, Jefferson, then the vice president, explained that the federal union was a compact among states which had delegated only "certain definite powers" to the national government, reserving all other powers to themselves. Thus, Jefferson argued that if any acts of the federal government went beyond the powers that had been delegated to it, every state had the right "to *nullify* of their own authority all assumptions of power." Since Congress had trampled upon the Constitution, Jefferson considered it crucial to reestablish a "rampart" to protect the minority "against the passions and the powers of a majority."

Madison's Virginia Resolutions were slightly more moderate in tone than Jefferson's. Like Jefferson, Madison portrayed the union as a "compact to which the states are parties" and issued an impassioned warning against federal legislation that represented a deliberate and dangerous exercise of power not granted to the national government by the Constitution. But, instead of using Jefferson's belligerent scare word "nullification," Madison used the blander verb "interpose," asserting that states were "in duty bound to *interpose* for arresting the progress" of unconstitutional legislation.

In truth, Jefferson and Madison were less interested in offering a new theory of nullification or in asserting state sovereignty than in protecting the integrity of the First Amendment. Madison excoriated the Sedition Act's violation of First Amendment rights of conscience and freedom of the press as well as the "right of freely examining public characters and measures." The results of the intimidating Sedition Act, he had warned, would be citizens' withdrawal from public life and the ensuing "deadly lethargy" that always characterizes despotic regimes. But Jefferson had ventured farther into dangerous territory, arguing that any additional unconstitutional assumptions of power and violations of rights would "necessarily drive these States into revolution and blood." Freedom of the mind, he believed, mattered even more than constitutional government and union. If called to defend that freedom, Jefferson wrote to a friend in 1799, "every spirit should be ready to devote itself to *martyrdom*."

In the end, how critical a role did the resolutions play? Not only had the Kentucky legislature deleted Jefferson's references to nullification in the final version of the resolutions that they approved, no other states joined Virginia and Kentucky in their protest. On the contrary, ten state legislatures censured Kentucky and Virginia. And even the then-governor of Virginia, James Monroe, never sought to prevent the enforcement of the Sedition Act.

And yet, some southerners would never forget the principles embedded in those resolutions. Far from disappearing, they became the impassioned rallying cry of the states' rights movement, reawakened and mobilized by John Calhoun. Terms like "nullification," "interposition," and "state sovereignty" would become the mantra of states' rights proponents.

Guilt-stricken that he had provided the foundational arguments for Calhoun's states' rights doctrine—a theory that threatened the very survival of the Constitution and the nation—Madison, during the last years of his life, would painstakingly strive to argue the resolutions away and to underscore their benign intentions.

Anxious to exculpate himself of the taint of the states' rights ideology, Madison presented his own explication of the Virginia Resolutions, presenting a panoply of sensible thoughts. He pointed out that the utterly banal—and constitutional—matter of a protective tariff on imported woolen goods paled in importance next to the government's unconstitutional violation of the Bill of Rights. He insisted that he believed fervently in a perpetual union and had never intended to suggest that the minority could overrule the majority or that states could withdraw from the union. The Virginia Resolutions had referred only to the rights of the states *in the plural* to nullify federal laws and not, as Calhoun contended, to the right of a single state to nullify a law; and the verb "interpose" was meant only to suggest an appeal to public opinion, not resistance. It could even be argued that the immediate goal of the resolutions was to empower the majority of Americans in the next election by inspiring them to overthrow the Federalists in 1800. In that electoral campaign, the resolutions indeed proved supremely effective, for they played a vital role in galvanizing public opinion on behalf of Thomas Jefferson, who defeated Federalist John Adams.

Still, Madison's efforts in the early 1830s to deny that the resolutions had made the case for states' rights came too late. By then, the Virginia and Kentucky Resolutions already symbolized a potent strain of southern thought that would be used to buttress Calhoun's doctrine of nullification—and more. The ideas that Madison and Jefferson had expressed in 1798, intentionally or not, had ignited a fire that would be impossible to quench.

Despite Madison's attempt to dilute the import and the repercussions of his resolutions, Senator Robert Hayne of South Carolina would thank him in early 1830 for the contribution that his Virginia Resolutions had made to the nullification cause. It was unfortunate that the resolutions of 1798 had been forgotten by so many citizens, Hayne told Madison, for the result of that forgetfulness was "the alarming assumptions of power on the part of the federal government." Now, nothing could save southerners, the South Carolinian wrote, "from consolidation and its inevitable consequences, the separation of the States, but the restoration of the principles of '98."

But Madison longed only to affirm his nationalist credentials. Though his defense of tariffs had already provoked opposition, at the risk of inciting still more attacks on himself, he responded to Hayne's letter of praise with a long and scholarly denunciation of nullification, published in 1830 for all to read in the *North American Review*.

The Constitution, Madison argued in his essay, could not be "altered or annulled at the will of the individual states." With twenty-four states already in the Union, a multiplicity of independent decisions was untenable; indeed, the vital principle could only be uniform laws for all. Nullification would simply overturn the fundamental principle of free government—majority rule—with the ultimate effect of overturning the government itself.

Madison did not deny that egregious legislation—like the Alien and Sedition Acts—might be passed. But the most effective means for opposing such intolerable legislation, he now argued, was not nullification, but rather a variety of constitutional remedies: the influence of senators and representatives in Congress; the power of the Supreme Court to determine the parameters of state and national authority; the responsibility of the president to the people; the liability of the executive and the judiciary to impeachment; and, finally, the ballot box. Indeed, he reminded his readers that, in the first presidential election following the Alien and Sedition Acts, Jefferson had triumphed, and that the new president, a champion of freedom of speech and the press, had let the Sedition Act expire. Failing the ballot box, there was still another option available to the states: a constitutional amendment. Only if every constitutional resort collapsed, then and only then, he allowed, could states assert "their original rights and the law of self-preservation."

Chief Justice John Marshall hailed Madison's letter. "Mr. Madison is himself again," he crowed, elated that Madison had distanced himself from the Virginia Resolutions and taken a firm, clear stand in favor of the federal government and majority rule. But the nullifiers simply turned from Madison to Jefferson, celebrating the Sage of Monticello for having warned against consolidation, despotism, and unlimited government. "They have rallied only with the more zeal under the authority of Mr. Jefferson," a friend in Charleston informed Madison, "and endeavor to array his authority against . . . your own."

The nullifiers of 1830 showered Jefferson with praise and admiration for having explicitly used the word "nullification" in the Kentucky Resolutions, lauding him for making the radical claim that nullification was a "rightful remedy" and for asserting the rights of the minority against the majority. In Jefferson, the nullifiers had found a guardian and a shield; he would legitimize their movement, protecting them with the prestige of his name, absolving them of any accusation of extremism. Calhoun himself had quoted from Jefferson's Kentucky Resolutions in his "Exposition." At a dinner in 1830 in honor of Jefferson's birthday at Brown's Indian Queen Hotel in Washington, southern politicians toasted their political father. It mattered not a whit to them that Jefferson had proclaimed in his first inaugural address in 1801 that the "vital principle" of republics was "absolute acquiescence in the decision of the majority."

It was a posthumous return to grace for Jefferson. During his presidency, Virginia's conservative political elite had considered him harebrained and reckless on issues like equality, suffrage, democracy, slavery, and the expansion of the national government. They had harshly maligned his "fatal legacies." But now, three decades later, they succeeded in the improbable feat of simultaneously repudiating his democratic vision and extolling his authority on nullification. They explicated and quoted from his writings on states' rights as if they were holy texts.

"Take care of me when dead," Jefferson had implored Madison in 1826, five months before he died. Now Madison had his work cut out for him. He had to defend not only his own reputation and nationalist credentials but Jefferson's too. In an attempt to varnish over Jefferson's impulsive words in the Kentucky Resolutions, he explained to his friend Nicholas Trist that allowances ought to be made for the habit of men of "great genius" like Jefferson "of expressing in strong and round terms, impressions of the moment." But nothing that Madison could say or write was enough to cement the reputation of his friend as a nationalist, committed to the Union and to the principle of majority rule.

But even more depressing to Madison were the continuing misrepresentations of his own positions that were used by the states' rights advocates to buttress their attacks on the Constitution and on the Union itself. Those poisonous attacks, moreover, were hitting their target, dangerously undermining the constitutional foundation of the nation. "Take the linch-pins from a carriage," Madison darkly wrote, "and how soon would a wheel be off its axle." The "anarchical" doctrine of nullification could very well bring the whole federal system down; it was impossible not to envision the "disastrous consequences of disunion."

Infinitely saddened by the thought that the constitutional republic, the masterpiece that he had helped create, might be "broken up and scattered to the winds," Madison branded the states' rights agenda "monstrous." The idea of breaking up the Union, he confessed to Trist in the spring of 1832, "is more painful than words can express." Closing his letter, he wrote, "I am much exhausted and can only add an affectionate adieu."

Representatives in Washington decided that it was time to defuse the crisis over nullification by lowering tariffs. In July 1832, Congress did just that, reducing them to their 1824 level, about 33 percent. But that wasn't good enough for Calhoun's state of South Carolina. In November 1832, South Carolina belligerently passed its Ordinance of Nullification, basing its claim to the constitutional right of nullification on Madison's Virginia Resolutions. The state prohibited federal officers from collecting duties in the state. If any forcible attempt were made to collect the duties, the ordinance warned, South Carolina would secede from the Union.

Now the president of the United States had to take a stand. The following month, on December 10, 1832, five days after winning overwhelming reelection to the presidency in the Electoral College, President Andrew Jackson issued his own proclamation. Sharp and succinct, he dismissed South Carolina's claims and asserted that the Constitution was a binding contract that had created "*one* people." No state could secede from the Union "because each secession destroys the unity of a nation." While Jackson believed that his proclamation did not clash "in the slightest" with the principles of Jefferson and Madison, many South Carolinians and other southerners greeted it with derisive laughter. Vice President Martin Van Buren of New York had predicted such a negative reaction, advising Jackson against making a proclamation that would bring him onto a "collision" course with his southern supporters, especially in Virginia.

Following Jackson's proclamation, the Virginia legislature also took up the question of nullification. Recognizing that the debate in Virginia could be a pivotal turning point in the nation's history, citizens throughout the country intensely followed the Virginia debate in their newspapers. "All eyes are at this moment turned to the Old Dominion," editorialized a newspaper in Maine. "Should she adopt South Carolina principles in practice, disunion would seem inevitable."

At first, Virginia was in a secessionist mood. Its governor, John Floyd, supported Calhoun's theory of nullification. "Constitutions are intended to protect the rights of the minority," Floyd declared in a speech to the General Assembly in December 1832. "If the majority be permitted to become the interpreters of their own powers, there ceases to be any limit to the Government." Some advocates of nullification reprinted 500 copies of the report that Madison had written in 1800 elaborating on his Virginia Resolutions, but, when asked, they refused to reprint and circulate his more recent letter in the *North American Review*. Nor would the state legislature agree to print a letter that Madison had written in 1821 to Judge Spencer Roane upholding the authority of the Supreme Court. "We do not believe that the fabric raised by a youthful Hercules," said one representative from Prince William County, "can be thrown down by him in the weakness and decrepitude of old age." "Was the legislature to be dictated to by the mere *name* of Madison?" asked a representative from Mecklenburg County.

And yet, the efforts of Madison and his friends and defenders to publicize his opposition to nullification began to bear fruit. The *Enquirer* and other newspapers, though they had previously opposed tariffs, realized that the fate of the nation was at stake. Now they came to the defense of the Union and condemned the movement toward separation. "Are these men mad—or are they worse?" the *Enquirer* editorialized in 1832. "Instead of striving to do all in their power to save the Union from convulsion and war, [they] are plunging us at once . . . into all the horrors of intestine commotion." As people became more informed about the issues and their potential consequences, they wrote letters to the editor and published articles and pamphlets. Public opinion shifted away from secession.

Virginia had approached the brink—and stepped back. After much intense debate, the General Assembly passed resolutions similar to the ones of 1798. The new resolutions, however, omitted any mention of secession and implored South Carolina to withdraw its Ordinance of Nullification. And, as a way of defusing the situation, it asked Congress to lower the tariff. Given the passions that had been unleashed, Virginia's resolutions were, finally, moderate and prudent. And the state's reasoned and cogent appeal to South Carolina to abandon any thoughts of disunion, wrote Madison's biographer Irving Brant, "could as well have been written by Madison himself."

In Washington, too, the crisis seemed to dissipate when Congress passed Henry Clay's Compromise Tariff Bill in February 1833. The bill lowered some duties and eliminated them on goods that did not compete with American products. The nullifiers could congratulate themselves on having won a victory—but their celebration was short-lived. That same month, Congress passed the "Force Bill," giving Jackson's administration new powers to enforce tariff acts. When the Force Bill came up for a vote in the Senate, its bitter opponents walked out of the chamber, leaving only one senator, John Tyler of Virginia, to vote nay, exciting wild praise at home. The Force Bill, the *Enquirer* declared, was "unnecessary and unseasonable."

Still, Madison was relieved. The "feverish excitement" of the past few years, he wrote to Clay, was almost instantly soothed by the compromise on tariffs. The principle of majority government had survived. And yet, Madison was still mulling over his ideas for the most effective way to deal with unpopular or unconstitutional legislation. In truth, he was concerned not just with the current issues of tariffs and nullification but also with preserving his own legacy and his reputation as a nationalist. Thus, in 1833, he drafted still another position paper in which he tried to reconcile the problems of unpopular legislation and majority rule.

A government representing a majority of citizens could indeed pass obnoxious legislation, Madison recognized. Unfortunately, there did not exist an antidote. "No government of human device and human administration can be perfect," he wrote, underlining that the least imperfect system was to obey the will of the majority.

But it was also possible that obnoxious legislation could be passed by an administration that represented a "constitutional" majority but not a "numerical" majority. Indeed, the Constitution designed by Madison and his colleagues had created an Electoral College in which the candidate who wins the greatest number of popular votes might not receive a majority of electoral votes; in the Senate, in which every state, regardless of population, had equal representation, a majority of senators would not necessarily represent a majority of voters in the nation. Hence a "constitutional majority"—though not a "numerical majority"—might very well pass legislation. In such cases, did a majority of citizens have any recourse?

Citizens might find relief by attempting to pass a constitutional amendment or, failing that, by mobilizing public opinion. But, other than that, Madison maintained, their obligation was to acquiesce to constitutional government, however flawed. Three decades after penning the Virginia Resolutions, Madison asserted unequivocally that there was no place in constitutional government for "nullification" or even "interposition."

Other Virginians, too, celebrated the compromise tariff and the end of the nullification crisis. They would not become "parricides" of their nation, proclaimed the *Enquirer*. "We will cherish the patriotic sentiment which makes the North and the South feel that they are portions of the same people and bound to each other by the ties of a common interest, a common honor, and a common liberty."

The storm subsided, the skies cleared—temporarily. When the commotion seemed over, Madison wondered what it had all been about. How

could something as banal as tariffs have been at the root of so much turmoil in Virginia?

The whole tariff uproar and the subsequent nullification movement,
Madison would contend in 1833, had all been a grand ruse, a camouflage,
that enabled Virginians to shift the blame for their economic decline to
the North and to the federal government instead of courageously placing
it at home. At bottom, the tariff question masked the anguish of Virginians—which was about Virginia.

The "finest talents" of the Old Dominion were exerting themselves,
Madison wrote in a lengthy letter addressed to a Professor Davis, to promote the false belief that the tariff was "the cause, the sole cause" of all
the private and public suffering in the state. They blindly insisted that the
tariff itself "had occasioned the distressing fall in the value of land and in
the price of its staple productions; that it had converted the splendid
mansions of the rich into decaying abodes of embarrassment and degradation; that it ground to dust the faces of the poor and drove them from
their ancient homes to look for better in the wilderness of the West; that
it threw the whole burden of taxes on the southern planters."

Even if tariffs were abolished altogether, Madison suspected, "the relief
would be but little felt." Only when the "paroxysm of fever" was over
would the public realize that it had been "misled from the *real causes* of
the suffering." Virginia's economic decline could be reversed only by enlightened policies in land management, industrial development, and
eventual emancipation. "Our country must be a manufacturing as well as
an agricultural one," he judged.

As for the canker of slavery, in a letter to the pro-slavery polemicist
Thomas Roderick Dew, he noted that the process of withdrawing slaves
from the Virginia labor force and diversifying the economic base by attracting free and skilled labor from outside the state would be slow. But,
he asked Dew, "is it not preferable to a torpid acquiescence in a perpetuation of slavery?" Unconvinced, Dew continued to insist that it was the
tariff, and the tariff alone, that discouraged southern industry and caused
the economic deterioration of the South. "It is not slave labour which has
produced our depression," he wrote, deaf to Madison's arguments, "but it
is the action of the federal government which is ruining slave labour."

As Madison suspected, tariffs had bestowed on conservative Virginians like Dew an invaluable gift. They provided an all-purpose scapegoat onto which Virginians could project all their pent-up frustrations and anxieties. Instead of addressing the problems of exhausted soil, the decline of property values, economic stagnation, and the blight of slavery, they could sputter on endlessly about tariffs, states' rights, and nullification. At bottom, their opposition to the tariff was fueled by their determination to defend their agrarian civilization, by their defensiveness about their increasingly marginal role in the nation, and, perhaps most of all, by their fear of the power of the national government. Indeed, there was little that frightened southerners more than the idea that, one day, the Supreme Court or Congress, having already intruded on the sovereignty of the states, might redefine property rights—and then move to abolish slavery.

Even if the antipathy of Virginians to tariffs was genuine and justified, the nullification crisis provided a tantalizing excuse to do nothing about Virginia's decline. Once again, Virginia's leaders faced a choice: They could reform and modernize the state and improve the lives of ordinary Virginians, or they could defend their agrarian vision of the state and focus all their energy and attention on their grievances. They made a conscious choice—and chose the latter. It was back to square one. As so often in the past, they would let themselves be seduced by the myth of an idyllic, agrarian state, free from the constraints and intrusions of the federal government.

And yet, the decision of mediocre, short-sighted leaders to do nothing to improve their state should not have come as a surprise or a shock to Madison, for it was he who had collaborated in empowering those very men, to the detriment of the reformers of western Virginia, during the state constitutional convention of 1829.

If states are unable to check federal usurpation of their rights, declared the fiery Virginia governor, John Floyd, in late 1833, "secession becomes the rightful remedy." Even with the immediate crisis passed, it was clear to Madison that the nullification disease had not disappeared but, on the contrary, was continuing to spread its venom. "What more dangerous than nullification," he wrote in 1834 to his friend and former secretary Edward Coles, "or more evident than the progress it continues to make, either in its original shape or in the disguises it assumes?" Madison recognized that the explosive potential of the doctrine of nullification had not been extinguished: It still had the effect, he wrote, "of putting powder under the Constitution and Union, and a match in the hand of every party to blow them up at pleasure." "The first and most obvious step is nullification," he wrote to Coles. "The next, secession; and the last, a farewell separation."

And yet how ironic that the persuasive notion of states' resistance to the national government had first been expressed by Jefferson and Madison in their resolutions of 1798. That perilous idea, Madison wrote in 1834, seemed destined to break "a more beautiful China vase than the British Empire ever was, into parts which a miracle only could reunite."

9

Abolitionists and Other Enemies

"The unexpected evil is now upon us; it has invaded our firesides, and under our own roofs is sharpening the dagger for midnight assassination!" proclaimed Senator John Tyler of Virginia in the late summer of 1835. What was this sudden atrocity? The post office department, explained an agitated Tyler, had been "converted into a vehicle for distributing incendiary pamphlets, with which our land is at this moment deluged."

The crisis had begun in South Carolina when thousands of antislavery tracts overwhelmed the postmaster of Charleston. Three hundred enraged citizens, led by the ex-governor, Robert Hayne, took matters into their own hands, breaking into the post office in the middle of the night and confiscating and destroying the bags of mail. The following day, crowds burned effigies of abolitionists. But frenzied rage quickly yielded to organization: Some people formed an ad hoc committee to search boats carrying mail, while others closed schools for free blacks and suspended religion classes for slaves; still others formed vigilance committees.

Throughout the South, postmasters protested the invasion of antislavery propaganda. In October, the *Richmond Enquirer* reported on a meeting in Prince Edward County at which citizens resolved to "*prepare their own ample means of defence.*" At an anti-abolition meeting in Fredericksburg, citizens agreed that only their own "watchfulness" could protect them against "incendiary proceedings and inflammatory publications."

Much of the turmoil was the work of two wealthy New York brothers, Arthur and Lewis Tappan, crusaders who had launched the American Anti-Slavery Society with William Lloyd Garrison in late 1833. Their fiery pamphlets and articles called for immediate emancipation. It was a wild demand, for slavery was in fact tolerated by the vast majority of Americans. Presidents deferred to it; northern politicians accepted it. Slavery was embedded in American society and in the political life of the nation.

Most northerners were uninterested in—or hostile to—the antislavery campaign. What they *were* interested in was the need to arrest the expansion of slavery and ban it from new territories. But as for the abolitionists, many in the North viewed them as a subversive element. The editor of the *Philadelphia National Gazette* criticized the abolitionists for sending their publications to the southern states and advised the postmaster general to exclude such publications from the mails.

People in the North flocked to rallies and demonstrations—not to demand emancipation, but to protest the radical abolitionists. A mob tied a rope around William Lloyd Garrison and dragged him through the streets of Boston. Even Unitarian minister William Ellery Channing and former president John Quincy Adams, both sympathetic to abolition, criticized the crusaders' hyperbolic attacks on slaveholders. For his part, Adams feared that the "great excitement and fermentation in all parts of the Union" caused by the abolitionists' fiery pamphlets would ultimately be counterproductive.

Indeed, many of Virginia's politicians and newspaper editors stoked citizens' anger and feelings of persecution, encouraging them to cling ever more tightly to slavery and to the principle of states' rights. The editor of the *Richmond Whig,* enraged by the antislavery tracts, accused the editor of the *Richmond Enquirer* of "keeping the peddle soft" when writing about the northern "fanatics." Governor Littleton Waller Tazewell, in December 1835, pointed to the "undisguised purpose" of the abolition societies—"the immediate emancipation of our slaves"—and called for urgent talks among the slaveholding states to deal, in a united manner, with the threatening abolitionist propaganda.

For Tazewell and other conservative Virginians, the real cause for concern was the same one that had preoccupied them at many times in the past: when they opposed federal planning for roads and canals; when they bridled at the authority of the Supreme Court; when they resisted changes to the state's constitution in 1829; when they opposed a system of public schools; when they debated slavery in 1831; and when they decried tariffs in 1828 and 1832. Little had changed: They were still fearful of the federal government, fearful of taxation, and, above all, fearful for the security of their property—their human property, the principal source of their wealth. That was always the bottom line. "A society has sprung up," Senator Tyler had cried out, referring to the abolitionists, "whose avowed object it is to despoil us of our *property*."

Their fears were understandable, for the property of slaveowners was unique: It possessed reason and a will of its own. No other form of property could contest its status as property or revolt against its owner. This "property" had ideas and emotions that could boil to the surface. Could Virginians rely on the federal government to use all of its authority—and even its might—to protect and guarantee slaveholders' property? It was a question that had troubled them since 1787.

Even George Mason, who hated slavery and frowned on the slave trade, had worried about the security of the South's human property. "There is no clause in the Constitution," he objected at the Virginia Ratifying Convention, "that will prevent the Northern and Eastern states from meddling with our whole *property of that kind*. There is a clause to prohibit the importation of slaves after twenty years but there is *no provision* made for securing to the Southern States those they now possess."

Although in 1787 James Madison had said that it would be "wrong to admit in the Constitution that there could be property in men," at the Virginia Ratifying Convention he tried to allay the qualms of slaveowners. He pointed out, for example, that South Carolina and Georgia had insisted upon writing into the Constitution explicit protection for fugitive slave property. That clause, in Article IV on Interstate Relations, Madison said, had been purposefully inserted in order to enable owners of fugitive slaves to reclaim them. The Framers had also deferred to the South by permitting three-fifths of the slave population to be included in the census, thereby boosting the number of southern representatives in Congress. And southerners believed that they could head off any change to the Constitution that might be proposed, since three-quarters of the states had to approve any amendment. Still, when Virginia finally agreed to ratify the Constitution, many in the Old Dominion remained dubious about the new national government.

The events of that tumultuous summer of 1835 revived those doubts. Union might be important, but not as important as half of the state's wealth.

The flood of abolitionist literature would put the national government to the southern test. Southerners anxiously waited to see if Washington would stop the postal service from acting as the agent of abolitionists and halt the circulation of antislavery literature in the South.

The president of the United States would pass their test, for Andrew Jackson sympathized completely with the southerners' concerns. While he officially informed his postmaster general, Amos Kendall, that "the inflammatory papers" had to be delivered, he also suggested that the names of subscribers to abolitionist literature be recorded so that "every moral and good citizen" could avoid their company. For his part, Kendall unofficially encouraged individual postmasters to exclude abolitionist literature from the southern mails. Although people owed an obligation to the law, he wrote to one postmaster, they owed "a higher one to the communities in which we live."

But Jackson wanted more than mere suggestions and unofficial ploys: He demanded that Congress take action and pass a federal censorship law. The antislavery tracts were "unconstitutional and wicked," he told Congress in December 1835, and the conduct of abolitionists was "destructive of the harmony and peace of the country and so repugnant to the principles of our national compact." He proposed that Congress prohibit the circulation of incendiary abolitionist publications through the mail in the southern states. Whereas the national postal system had been created to promote harmony among the states, the antislavery tracts, Jackson argued, aimed at instigating slaves to insurrection.

The head of the select committee in the Senate charged with drafting the legislation was none other than John Calhoun. For Calhoun, the opportunity was an unexpected boon. He was happy to ratchet up the level of anxiety of southerners, thinking that their alarm would help to unite the South. Though he knew that most people in the North did not approve of the antislavery agitation, he nevertheless issued dire warnings that the abolitionists were "numerous, zealous, and active."

On the question of federal censorship of the mails, however, Calhoun disagreed with Jackson. If the federal government could censor antislavery mail, Calhoun reasoned, it could also censor pro-slavery mail. If there was to be censorship, he advised, it should be done by the states. The bill that Calhoun proposed modified the bill suggested by Jackson by calling for postmasters to recognize the authority of the states in determining what was incendiary material.

Senators were divided on the proposed legislation, many agreeing with Massachusetts senators Daniel Webster and John Davis that any censorship was a blatant violation of the First Amendment. When the censorship bill came up for a vote, it was defeated by 25 to 19. Censorship would be left to local officials. That year, the Virginia legislature passed a law requiring postmasters to notify the county justice of the peace when they received publications that denied a slaveowner's right to his property. Then the justice of the peace was authorized to do as he wished with the mail. Virginia Senator Benjamin Watkins Leigh proposed a statewide boycott of newspapers that favored emancipation. Virginians, Leigh wrote, had the right "to suppress to the utmost of our power what we deem inflammatory, dangerous, mischievous."

What would Thomas Jefferson have thought of these efforts to boycott newspapers and ban free speech? No one believed more strongly than he in giving "a full scope to reason." "Were it left to me to decide whether we should have a government without newspapers or newspapers without a government," Jefferson had written in 1787, "I should not hesitate a moment to prefer the latter." But whereas Jefferson believed that the free flow of information was essential to a democracy (he had even proposed that newspapers be sent free through the mails), the new generation of Virginians insisted that order and security had to precede liberty.

Without order in society, they reasoned, liberty was irrelevant. Distressed by the northern zealots, they were therefore willing to relinquish the free circulation of ideas and information and close the state's borders to critical voices. In truth, they only bought time—not security. Perhaps if southerners had permitted the free flow of information and opened their minds to criticism of slavery, they might have recognized the urgency of finding real solutions to the problem of slavery. And perhaps if that criticism of slavery had been less violent and abusive, it might have opened channels of communication and inspired a rational quest to find ways of both emancipating the slaves and avoiding civil war. Instead, moderation and tolerance were abjured by both sides, and both sides would lose.

The excitement over the abolitionist tracts and the subject of censorship subsided. But the abolitionists did not give up—on the contrary, they discovered a more effective strategy: a campaign focused on the House of Representatives in Washington. The American Anti-Slavery Society submitted thousands of antislavery petitions to Congress. These petitions demanded the immediate abolition of slavery in the District of Columbia, over which Congress had authority. It was an ominous proposal, one that future United States Senator William Grayson had feared and predicted as early as the 1788 Virginia Ratifying Convention. Since the 10 square miles that would form the new capital were subject to the exclusive legislation of Congress, Grayson had worried that both slaves and fugitive slaves might receive the protection of Congress and be set free.

The antislavery petitions in Washington unnerved the members of the House of Delegates in Richmond, some of whom demanded that the state prepare for war. "Ought not our constituents to be *placed on their guard to prepare for the worst?*" asked Peter Daniel. Virginians must be ready to protect their soil from invasion, said another delegate. There was no point in disguising or hiding from the imminent danger. "I exhort every Virginian to be ready now for action," he cried.

And those who counseled restraint did so in equally apocalyptic terms. Delegate George Hopkins hoped that feelings of hostility between North and South would not be excited; he feared "a dreadful conflict between the two sections of the country will ensue—civil war with all its horrors will pervade this now happy land." "Has it come to this?" James Garland wondered aloud. "Are gentlemen prepared for this rupture? . . . Shall we embroil ourselves with citizens of a common country—imbrue our hands in a brother's blood?"

But the militants in Richmond prevailed, threatening to dissolve the union of states. Late in January 1836, before any petitions were even accepted in Washington, the House of Delegates passed a resolution stating that any action by Congress to regulate slavery in the District of Columbia would "afford just cause of alarm . . . and bring the Union into imminent peril."

What would the House of Representatives do with the thousands of antislavery petitions that continued to pour in? Some of them were provocatively introduced by Representative John Quincy Adams of Massachusetts. "Why bring this subject here every day, every hour?" asked a pro-slavery representative, desperate to put the subject to rest. In the past, abolitionist petitions had been sent to a Committee on the District of Columbia where they had been filed and forgotten. Another possible way to defuse the tension was for the House to simply refuse to accept the petitions.

And yet, Congress was constitutionally bound to consider them. The First Amendment guaranteed citizens' right to "petition the government for a redress of grievances." The denial of that right could be expected to fuel and even radicalize the abolitionist movement, handing abolitionists the powerful argument that the masters of slaves sought to deny white people, too, their civil liberties.

Though battle lines between the pro- and antislavery forces hardened in Congress, the majority in the House of Representatives was clearly on the pro-slavery side. It was imperative, the majority believed, to quickly arrest the agitation and, in the words of the House Select Committee, "restore tranquility to the public mind." The key, the majority believed, was to establish the federal government's neutrality in the matter of slavery.

The solution was a "gag" resolution, which passed in the spring of 1836 by a wide margin. Petitions involving slavery would be accepted but then immediately "laid on the table," where they could gather appropriate dust. A few hot-headed Virginians, like the young representative Henry Wise, objected, contending that the mere act of accepting petitions amounted to "treason to the South." Though Wise lost that round in the House, a few years later, as governor of Virginia, he would push through the Virginia legislature a rule stating that no antislavery petitions "shall be received by this House or entertained in any way whatever." Still, the gag rule passed by the House of Representatives was hardly ineffectual; it not only required tabling the petitions but also prohibited the House from printing, debating, or even mentioning the contents of petitions related to slavery. Case closed.

A few men, like John Quincy Adams, were preoccupied with the morality of slavery. But for the majority of representatives, more important than burning questions of morality was the preservation of the Union. Thus they decided that the federal government would not intervene in the regulation of slavery or in the affairs of the South. Predictably, the gag rule resulted in a new flood of petitions, which in turn was matched by an even stricter gag rule that would be renewed every year until 1844.

The Senate, too, would take a harsh stand against petitions. Months earlier, John Tyler, disgusted that Washington had been turned into "a slave mart," had proposed that the slave trade be prohibited in the District of Columbia. But now, responding to the furor back home, Tyler demanded a resolution stating that the Senate "was not competent to interfere with the question of slavery, either in the States or in the District of Columbia." The Senate passed, again by a wide margin, its own gag bill, proposed by Senator James Buchanan of Pennsylvania. According to this legislation, the Senate would receive, but then instantly reject, antislavery petitions.

James Madison, in his eighty-fifth year, was unpersuaded that the fiery pamphlets from the North ever posed any threat to slavery. On the contrary, he predicted that abolitionist propaganda, like the slavery debate of 1831, would have the reverse effect and incite southerners to speak out ever more passionately in favor of slavery. To "modern abolition, to it alone," Madison said in 1836, "we owe not only the lamentable *arrest* of onward emancipation, but till it intruded no Governor in Carolina extolled slavery as a happy balance of her Government, no Virginia professor vindicated its moral advantages." In reaction to the vituperative denunciations of northern abolitionists, most southerners, Madison predicted, would embrace slavery ever more ardently, convincing themselves of its beneficence. "The worst effect of the abolition excitement," he told a friend in 1836, "would be to lead the minds of southern men from looking upon slavery as a necessary evil, to looking upon it as one of the *greatest blessings* they could enjoy."

If the abolitionist movement was so small, unpopular, and ineffectual, why then were so many southern politicians sounding the alarm? Madison suggested that they were exploiting abolitionism for their own ends: first, to foment panic about a supposed northern scheme to abolish slavery, and then to use that panic to fuel a movement for southern secession. "It is painful to observe the unceasing efforts to alarm the South by imputations against the North of unconstitutional designs on the subject of the slaves," a disgusted Madison wrote to Henry Clay in 1833. He saw no evidence of an "intermeddling disposition" among the majority of northerners. On the contrary, the self-interest of northern textile manufacturers, ship-owners, merchants, bankers, and insurance companies assured their desire to preserve a union with the slaveholding states, a union in which northern and southern economies were entwined and mutually sustaining.

The problem lay not in the North but in the overreaction in the South. "What madness in the south," Madison wrote to Clay, "to look for greater safety in disunion. It would be worse than jumping out of the Frying-pan into the fire: it would be jumping into the fire for fear of the Frying-pan." The pride and resentment that southerners were whipping up would overwhelm, he warned, prudence and restraint. Their panic would "insidiously revive" the project of a southern confederacy.

Other Virginians also sought to uncover the real agenda of their most fiery politicians. It appeared to James Garland that Governor Tazewell deliberately wanted "to excite a panic, to agitate, agitate, agitate—to throw the country into confusion and ride into power on the terrors of the people." Indeed, Tazewell was a "fanatic," a writer to the *Enquirer* remarked in 1835. "We had hoped that our governor would have . . . calmed the raging storm . . . but instead he has thrown himself into the exciting elements to lash up the tempest. . . . Let us not be driven into war, or revolution, either to please Southern or Northern Fanatics." The only enemies the South had in the North were a handful of wild religious fanatics who were crazy on the subject of slavery, the *Enquirer* editorialized that fall, retreating from its initial aggressive stance. The abolitionists, the *Enquirer* assured its readers, represented absolutely no threat either in the North or in the South. "Their leaders are hunted from town to town like wild beasts—their meetings are broken up and their amalgamation schools destroyed."

A reader calling himself "Anti-Tappan" complained that the *Enquirer* paid too much attention to the "agitation" of abolitionists and attached too much importance to their "false philanthropic ebullitions." "I would lay them aside," he wrote, "as spurious coin." Still other readers issued perspicacious warnings that any laws censoring the mail and restricting the freedom and civil liberties of abolitionists would backfire, making the abolitionists "more potent than all their philanthropy. . . . They will make more converts in one day by preaching up the right of discussion, the freedom of speech and freedom of the press than they could make in a century by talking about the hardships of our slaves."

One man, writing to the *Enquirer* under the name "Cassandra," appeared to agree with Madison that if there was any conspiracy, it emanated not from the North but from the South. The impudent northern fanatics would have sunk into merited oblivion, had radical southern demagogues not rushed to exploit the situation and enshrine the abolitionists' "diabolical purpose." What exactly was that diabolical purpose? "To introduce misery into their country and *themselves into office*. . . . The Union dissolved—the South disturbed and devastated, they vainly imagine they will be called to office and then be able to claim the character of peace-makers and restorers. Before them, convulsions, and convulsions of their own creation will cease."

If northern abolitionists posed no real danger to slavery, neither did the federal government. Slaveholders and pro-slavery interests would continue to have their way in every branch of American government. For fifty of the first seventy-two years of the republic, the president's office was occupied by slaveholders. Of the six presidents elected from northern states before the Civil War, only two were hostile to slavery, John Adams and his son John Quincy, neither of whom was elected to a second term. Martin Van Buren of New York promised voters that Congress had no power to interfere with the "domestic institutions" of the states. His fellow New Yorker Millard Fillmore deemed it "an especial duty to guard against any infringement on the just rights of the States." Franklin Pierce of New Hampshire would select Mississippian Jefferson Davis, the future president of the Confederacy, as his secretary of war. And with the nation on the verge of Civil War, lame-duck Pennsylvanian James Buchanan would propose in early 1861 a constitutional amendment expressly recognizing slavery.

Congress, too, with its powerful and energetic southern bloc, was deferential to the interests of slaveowners through the mid–nineteenth century. In 1790, after Quakers petitioned the House of Representatives to abolish slavery, the House debated the issue and then resolved that Congress had "no authority to interfere in the emancipation of slaves," leaving the regulation of slavery to the states. The "very mal-apropos" Quaker petition had been "put to sleep," wrote a relieved President Washington. In 1804, southerners quickly quashed the attempt of Massachusetts senators to abolish the three-fifths rule, successfully defending southern clout in the House of Representatives. Indeed, until the 1850s, the South had a virtual veto over any policy affecting slavery. Though some antislavery measures passed the House between 1800 and 1860, all were killed in the Senate. And during most of the years between 1789 and 1850, southerners—including Virginians Philip Barbour and his brother James—controlled the speakership of the House and the chairmanship of the House Ways and Means Committee.

On the Supreme Court, a majority of the justices were slaveowners. In 1857, in the *Dred Scott* decision, the Court ruled against Scott, a slave from Missouri who, because he had lived with his owner in the free state of Illinois for four years, sued for his liberty. Chief Justice Roger Taney's majority decision held that not even free blacks could be citizens and thus could have no access to the courts. But, going even further, Taney ruled that the Missouri Compromise of 1820, which had barred slavery from the northern part of the Louisiana territories, was unconstitutional. Though the Compromise had worked reasonably well for almost four decades, the Court judged that Congress had no constitutional power to exclude slavery from any parts of the nation and its territories. Not only would slavery be permitted everywhere, but blacks, Taney reasoned, "had no rights which the white man was bound to respect." "The negro might justly and lawfully be reduced to slavery for his benefit," he concluded.

Before the Civil War, American abolitionists failed to achieve any reforms or to realize any of their goals. Presidents, senators, representatives, and justices together all made sure that slaveowners could not be deprived of their human property. No wonder that some northerners lent credence to the idea of a Great Slavepower Conspiracy. They were convinced that aggressive southern slaveowners had seized control of the federal government.

And yet, although in the 1830s there were no effective challenges or threats to the institution of slavery, and no peril whatsoever to the property of slaveholders, southern politicians wildly overreacted to the abolitionists.

It was a response that would ultimately have terrible consequences. By inflating the influence and impact of the antislavery movement, these leaders and many of their followers diminished their confidence in their own political clout. And the more insecure they felt, the more defensive and belligerent they became. Though most Virginians were moderate on the subject of slavery, the furor over the abolitionist threat only intensified their commitment to slavery, dampening any interest they might have had in reform or compromise. Just as the Virginia debate on slavery in 1831 had led to the defiant expression of pro-slavery positions, overreaction to the abolitionist propaganda and petitions deepened southerners' intransigence, encouraging them to identify slavery as the key feature of their society. Their tenacious resistance blinded many Virginians to the need to modernize their state as well as to temper and renovate their ideas.

Thomas Ritchie, the editor of the *Richmond Enquirer*, would express regret in 1840 that "the fanatics of the North have taken the most effective means not to leave a single friend of emancipation in the Southern states." The "efforts of abolitionists," Virginia professor George Tucker would write in 1843, "have hitherto made the people in the slaveholding States cling to [slavery] more tenaciously." All the habits and prejudices of southerners, he concluded, "have struck their roots the deeper for the rudeness with which they have been assailed." A former governor of Virginia, James McDowell, bitterly blamed northern abolitionists for having made slavery "a forbidden topic with us."

The cultural chasm between North and South would widen even more as southern censorship and intransigence invigorated the antislavery movement. Indeed, the southern overreaction to the small abolitionist movement would backfire by creating precisely the situation the South most feared. It empowered the unpopular abolitionists, and by fueling moral outrage in the North, it propelled slavery to center stage of the nation's collective conscience. Newspapers, presses, and religious organizations began churning out enormous amounts of abolitionist publications. Membership in the American Anti-Slavery Society mushroomed in just a few short years: Whereas in 1835 it had 400 chapters, by 1838 it had 1,350 chapters and more than 250,000 members. Other antislavery societies sprang up, too: Philadelphia alone was home to three different antislavery organizations. Apprehensive, insecure, and simultaneously self-protective and aggressive, southern leaders accomplished the impossible: They turned their own potent political bloc into a beleaguered, rigid, and vulnerable one.

And yet, perhaps Virginians were not totally wrongheaded to doubt their political strength. The number of representatives from Virginia in Congress shrank from twenty-three in 1810 to a mere ten in 1860. Nor were they irrational to feel insecure about their wealth and property— that "special" form of property that had reason as well as will and locomotion. On the contrary, they realistically and correctly intuited that slavery could not survive indefinitely in an accelerating, industrializing, and urbanizing nation and in a democracy that was slowly becoming more inclusive.

In 1860, Abraham Lincoln could assure his listeners in Cooper Union that northerners had left southerners alone and "never disturbed them." He explained that "after all, it is what we *say* which dissatisfies them. They will continue to accuse us of *doing*, until we cease *saying*." But

words—about equality, justice, and emancipation as well as about nullification and separation—have consequences; indeed, words and ideas are
the motor of history. And people in the South could reasonably expect
that words would eventually be followed by deeds. Perhaps it was emi-
nently rational of them to anticipate and psychologically prepare themselves for an inevitable showdown.

In 1835, a year before James Madison's death, Nathaniel Beverley Tucker,
a lawyer and professor at the College of William and Mary, asked his
friend John Calhoun to help him publish his novel, *The Partisan Leader*,
privately and "secretly." Appearing in 1836, it was an "historical novel"
set in the future. Tucker told the dramatic story of a war that takes place
in 1848, a struggle between North and South, in which courageous Virginians lead the southern effort to throw off the federal government,
controlled by the North. Politically, the Virginians in the novel feel
themselves the victims of a Constitution that, though designed to secure
freedom for Americans, has been "perverted" to destroy liberty in the
South. Economically, they feel they are the victims of predatory northerners determined "to plunder and desolate the South." Rebelling against
"northern cupidity and northern fanaticism," Tucker's Virginians seek
release from a government "the benefits of which have all been theirs, the
burdens ours."

Oddly, the book ends inconclusively, the outcome of the struggle un-
certain. Tucker had envisioned publishing further installments of the
tale until, as a later editor of the volume wrote, "the whole South should
have become impregnated with disunion." But he abandoned the project, and no other installments ever appeared. Still, we know Tucker's
vision: an independent, agrarian, slaveholding southern confederacy,
free from punitive tariffs, able to trade freely with all nations. His wish
was to be remembered as the founder of a "glorious Southern Confederacy." Although *The Partisan Leader* was not a best-seller, it nevertheless
helped spread and popularize the idea of a violent resolution to the differences between North and South. The resentment and frustration felt

by Tucker and other Virginians about northern hegemony and the declining importance of Virginia found a release in the contemplation of war and disunion.

As the decades passed, and as the modernizing northern states, not the agrarian, slaveholding, southern ones, shaped the American republic and gave definition to mainstream American values, northern and southern mentalities grew ever more distinct and alien to each other. Indeed, Virginians and other southerners became both more aware of their marginalization and more assertive of their difference from the rest of the nation.

And why *wouldn't* Virginia wish to remain distinct from the rest of the nation? As materialistic, predatory northerners worked obsessively for more wealth and power, trampling anyone in their path, the inhabitants of the Old Dominion believed that they had already glimpsed—if not momentarily captured—the essence of the good life. Surely it was not surprising that wealthy and politically powerful Virginians, unmoved by the suffering of blacks and the indigence of most whites, preferred the plantation idyll of gracious living, elegant manners, and warm hospitality to the dull depersonalization and cacophonous din of industrialized society. While much of the rest of the nation charged ahead, nostalgic Virginians longed for stasis or even retrogression—a secure, serene haven from the dislocations of a threatening and dehumanized future.

While the nation, as defined by the North, was becoming a more democratic, open, and nationalistic society, welcoming more voters, accepting wave upon wave of foreign immigrants speaking strange tongues, Virginia continued to uphold its traditional ways and principles: government by the elite and states' rights. While the northern "nation" was embracing industrial capitalism, Virginia clung to its agrarian traditions. While, in the North, armies of boys and girls, men and women, were abandoning the countryside to become anonymous wage-workers in regimented factory towns, Virginians clung to the Jeffersonian ideal of the independent, self-sufficient yeoman, deeply believing in the importance of their civilization's rootedness in the soil. And while northerners could conceive of no place whatsoever in a modern, free, democratic state for the institution of chattel slavery, Virginians congratulated themselves on their moral beneficence in caring for an inferior, illiterate caste of slaves, taking

pride in the social stability and absence of labor unrest in the Old Dominion. With both sections of the country asserting their differences in
increasingly emotional terms, the widening gulf between them—deepened by ineffectual national and party leaders and a southern ruling class
that was economically, emotionally, and intellectually invested in slavery—left little or no opportunity for a collective search for solutions,
whether incremental or definitive, to the wrenching problem of slavery.
At least Beverley Tucker's *Partisan Leader* offered a solution—albeit a
lethal one.

Should North and South have taken amicable leave of each other far earlier? At the Constitutional Convention of 1787, even the nationalist
James Madison recognized that the greatest danger to the new national
government came from "the great southern and northern interests of the
continent, being opposed to each other." But Gouverneur Morris of Pennsylvania airily dismissed geographical distinctions as "groundless." And
yet, if delegates truly believed them to be real, he added, "instead of attempting to blend incompatible things, let us at once take a friendly leave
of each other." For his part, President Washington wondered what Virginia and the other states that were "inclined to join her" would gain by
separation. "Would they not, most unquestionably," he perspicaciously
asked, "be the weaker party?"

Over the next decades, the distinctions between North and South did
not appear groundless to many northerners, who themselves occasionally
toyed with secession, or to some Virginians. Disunion might indeed be
preferable, Henry Lee had written to Madison in 1790, to living with "an
insolent northern majority." In 1795, the future senator and president
John Tyler expressed regret that temperaments, customs, manners, and "a
thousand things more" had not been well weighed before union took
place. Virtually every feature of American life proved to him how unfit
the states were to form one nation.

And Jefferson himself, while frowning at the idea of separation, had
nevertheless found it possible to imagine that the South might have no

choice but to separate from the Union. Rather than forfeit the rights of self-government, he wrote to Madison in 1799, Virginians would "sever ourselves from that union we so much value." Two decades later, he again considered the possibility of disunion, though he noted that separation could be considered only "when the sole alternatives left, are the dissolution of our union with them or submission to a government without limitation of powers." George Washington would have shuddered—or wept.

But those intemperate and rash pronouncements were relatively rare and never persuaded most Virginians that it was in their interest to sever themselves from the Union. Unlike South Carolinians, who believed that slavery should exist in perpetuity in their midst, most Virginians were ambivalent enough about slavery to vaguely hope for its eventual termination. And even if they were convinced that the federal government and the Supreme Court possessed too much power and that the states should be the locus of sovereignty, few Virginians were prepared to seriously contemplate disunion.

During the tumultuous decades that led up to the Civil War, as political tensions mounted, and as some hotheads—especially in South Carolina—screamed for separation, most Virginians would remain attached to the nation and the Constitution, the political masterpiece of their Virginia forebears. They remained largely restrained and calm as the nation grappled with the question of slavery in Texas, California, Kansas, and Nebraska; as a southern convention on the deteriorating relations between North and South was held in Jackson, Mississippi, in the summer of 1849; as states like Vermont and Wisconsin refused to obey the Fugitive Slave Act; and as Congress responded with an even stricter version of that act.

Through all the commotion, Virginians would prove to be among the most temperate and unionist of southerners. Even Hugh Blair Grigsby, the unhappy Yale student who had become a historian of Virginia politics and who had once written that Madison's Constitution had "the hand of bastardy on its face," became a unionist. He warned in 1855 that disunion and civil war, far from bestowing on the South the blessings that some people anticipated, "would open a hundred new questions of peace and war more perplexing and more difficult of solution" than the annoying and paltry ones of tariffs and states' rights. After all, the Union had always protected slavery, but who could predict the policies of a new, untested southern confederacy—or the reaction of the North to secession?

After decades of inconclusive sectional and ideological conflict in which the fundamental issue was always slavery, the crisis finally arrived: In December 1860, southern states began to secede from the Union. Virginians, however, hesitated to follow them into the unknown. The governor, John Letcher, searched for the middle ground, sending a commission to other southern states to discover if conditions could be found for their return to the Union.

Virginia's General Assembly, in which secessionists held only 30 percent of the seats, proposed a national peace conference in Washington in early February 1861, inviting all the states to attend. The conference had the support of William Henry Seward, soon to be named Lincoln's secretary of state, and was presided over by former president Tyler. Although neither the seven states of the lower South nor the state of Arkansas sent delegates, representatives from the other slave states were present. But many of the northern states that did attend instructed their delegates to resist making concessions to the South—and so the conference utterly failed. In Virginia's conservative southern and eastern regions, secession fever seemed to be spreading, perhaps becoming, some people felt, irresistible. "Virginia will not act hastily," Hugh Blair Grigsby insisted in March, "but as yet we cannot say what that action will be."

The secessionist southern states awaited Virginia's decision. A legitimate and full-blooded southern nation surely required the participation of the Old Dominion—the Revolution's premier state, the home of four of the first five presidents, the protector of southern agrarian traditions.

What advice might James Madison have given his fellow Virginians on the eve of their fateful decision? Would he have been able to convince them not to abandon a national Constitution that, as he wrote, had "brought such a happy order out of so gloomy a chaos"?

"The essential difference between a free government and governments not free," he wrote in his typical careful, constitutionalist prose in 1833, "is that the former is founded in compact, the parties of which are mutually and equally bound by it." Saddened by intemperate politicians in Virginia who rashly called for their state to separate from the Union, Madison defended constitutional government. In the 1820s he had defended the authority of the Supreme Court, and in the 1830s, that of Congress to authorize tariffs. It was high time, he wrote, that "the claim to secede at will should be put down by the public opinion." In 1833, public opinion in the Old Dominion favored union, but, as Madison surely knew, the majority did not make decisions in elitist Virginia. The state's antidemocratic constitution, which he had played a role in shaping in 1829, had deprived western reformers and antislavery advocates of an effective voice in Virginia politics.

In 1834, two years before he died, Madison penned a short public letter, a message he called "Advice to My Country." In this 200-word farewell to his fellow Americans, he reminded them that he had served his country in various ways over a period of forty years and had always espoused the cause of its liberty. Then, turning to "the advice nearest to my heart and deepest in my conviction," he implored Americans to "cherish" and "perpetuate" the union of the states. He urged them to beware of the Union's enemies—declared enemies as well as clandestine ones. The "open enemy [should] be regarded as a Pandora with her box opened; and the disguised one, as the Serpent creeping with his deadly wiles into Paradise." It is unclear exactly who Madison believed those "enemies" were. Perhaps by "open enemy," he had in mind those who embraced the new doctrine of nullification with its far-reaching, fatal consequences; and by "disguised enemy," he may have meant those who made the false, insidious claim that nullification did not constitute a betrayal of the core principles of the Constitution.

Still, Madison's final advice to his nation was understated and not explicit. Had he been less of an Orange County gentleman, he might have gone further, offering more pointed advice not just to the nation but especially to the South and to his own beleaguered state.

For the Old Dominion was surely in dire need of inspiration and counsel. It, too, had "open enemies"—judges and politicians like Roane, Giles, Floyd, and Tazewell who played light and easy with disunion and separation, opening a Pandora's box of alluring promises of sovereignty, free trade, and prosperity. In fact, the category of open enemies might have encompassed the whole leadership caste of the Old Dominion—the elitist Tidewater politicians who trumpeted the rights of the aristocratic minority and ignored the cries pouring out of the western part of the state for more democracy.

Unlike the men of the founding generation of Virginians whose reputations would ever be secure, Virginia's leaders in the second generation of constitutional government were indeed a dismal failure. Their failure was one of will, insight, vision, and moral conscience—all of the elements that constitute genuine leadership. Again and again, confronted with a variety of options and choices, Virginia's politicians exercised power not to improve their state but rather to arrest change and progress and keep most Virginians walled within an economic prison. They made conscious, elaborately justified decisions *not* to improve agriculture in the state, or to tax property to fund public education, or to open the polls to more voters. Nor did they make state government more open and accountable, seek a solution to the affliction of slavery, diversify the economy, or encourage the rise of an educated, upwardly mobile, white working class. Under their passive watch, Virginia's government did not construct a coherent network of roads, canals, and railroads, encourage industry and banking, support civic and cultural institutions, or attempt to stem the stream of Virginia families moving west.

Ironically, their antipathy for the kind of energetic planning and active government that could transform Virginia into a modern, prosperous, and developed state was not the result of their shallowness or their intellectual paralysis. On the contrary, they were loyally following Jefferson and Madison's lead, inspired by the principled, if mistaken, stands the great founders had taken, again and again, against the broadening of federal power, against federal intrusion in the regulation of slavery, against federal planning of internal improvements, and against the authority of the Supreme Court. Virginia's new cohort of leaders could trumpet their fidelity to Madison and Jefferson's belief in the power of the states to resist federal legislation they considered unconstitutional. Indeed, the seeds of Virginia's decline had been adroitly planted in fertile soil by the great patriarchs themselves.

In addition to everything that Virginia's new cohort of leaders did *not* want to do, did they have any positive agenda? In truth, they sought only to perpetuate the status quo with passive government, nurture a spirit of assertive provincialism averse to outside interference, and defend their own self-interest. Ironically, they did not even succeed well in that self-serving cause, for they failed to grasp that energy, ideas, and reform are necessary merely to maintain the status quo.

A more forthright and less gentlemanly Madison might have aggressively condemned these men as Virginia's "open enemies." He might also have unmasked Virginia's "disguised enemies"—all those nostalgic, pining dreamers so tied to agrarianism and slavery, so apprehensive of the changing, modernizing world. Serpent-like, spinning their languid tales of gentle, aristocratic plantations, these men sought to seduce Virginians from the "paradise" of union with charming memories of dominion.

And a more probing and self-critical Madison might have assumed some responsibility himself for the looming crisis—by expressing regret for his impulsive authorship of the Virginia Resolutions of 1798, which set the stage for nullification and disunion. And he might have found other grounds for regret: the cramped "limited government" platform of his and Jefferson's Republican Party in the 1790s, which had the effect of undergirding Virginia's economic decline; his vacillating and compromising role in drafting the antimajoritarian state constitution of 1829, which empowered the do-nothing Virginia elite at the expense of average Virginians and the people of western Virginia; and his short-sighted veto in 1817 of the Bonus Bill, legislation that deprived Virginia of internal improvements while assuaging the fears of slaveholders nervous about federal power. For a modern transportation system and a more democratic and dynamic state government would together have spurred a vital economy, spread prosperity, and alleviated the cultural and political isolation of Virginia and the South, helping to counter an insular mentality and pernicious tendencies toward disunion.

Still, Madison's final message to the nation and to Virginia was a supremely rational one—union and vigilance—though he offered it in vain. But what advice could have reached his fellow Virginians, whose prescription for the future lay in an imaginary past?

At a rally in Richmond in March 1861, Madison's protégé and biographer William Cabell Rives, a former minister to France and United States senator, was still valiantly trying to negotiate a compromise, imploring Virginians not to "wander and lose ourselves hopelessly in the dreary and perplexed wilderness of secession." How could Virginia exit willingly from a republic "of which she may be considered, emphatically, the founder?" Rives asked, resurrecting the spirit of Madison.

But in April 1861—five days after the fall of Fort Sumter and more than five months after Lincoln's election—delegates to the Virginia Secession Convention voted 90 to 45 to secede and join the Confederacy. This time there would be no turning back, as Virginia plunged into the abyss.

Epilogue:
Jefferson and Virginia, A Hundred Years Later

"I am seventy-six years old in *genuine Jefferson Democracy*," declared Virginia Senator Carter Glass in 1934, "and I do not care to mar the record before I die by embracing brutal and despicable bureaucracy."

The atrocious bureaucracy to which Glass objected was Franklin D. Roosevelt's New Deal, the proliferation of government programs and agencies designed to alleviate the widespread suffering caused by the Depression. Glass was not opposed to reform, but his idea of reform resembled that of nineteenth-century leaders in Virginia like Spencer Roane and John Randolph, who believed in good, clean, paternalistic government by the elite. Like those backward-looking men captivated by tradition, Glass frowned at the prospect of making any deep changes to his state or nation. Ironically, Glass had been an early supporter of Roosevelt. "Holding fast to sound Jeffersonian principles," he said in a 1932 radio endorsement of FDR, "we shall hope to rescue the government and the country from the unendurable confusion and distress into which the Republican maladministration has thrust us." A delighted FDR sent a telegram to Glass: "Wonderful speech last night . . . sincere appreciation." Roosevelt even offered Glass, who had been Woodrow Wilson's secretary of the treasury, that same post in his own administration.

At first, Glass welcomed FDR's emergency legislation of early 1933, but he soon balked when he realized that Roosevelt sought not just economic recovery but real, enduring reform. Glass loathed—and tried to derail—bills like the National Labor Relations Act, which protected the rights of working people to organize; the Fair Labor Standards Act, which sought to raise wages and limit working hours; and the Social Security Act, which guaranteed economic security to the elderly. In his mind, Social Security was a "Frankenstein." The premise of New Deal programs like Social Security was that people not only had the right to be free *from* government, but also had certain rights to freedom *through* government—rights to decent jobs, medical care, education, and security in old age. But the newspaper Glass owned, the *Lynchburg News*, editorialized in 1935 that government had no obligation to provide security to the nation's citizens. "Is there no responsibility resting upon the individual to secure himself against the 'major hazards' and vicissitudes of life?" the editor asked. Americans should "work out their own problems," Glass advised. "There is entirely too much running to Washington by business, by agriculture and by labor. That way lies paternalism, with socialism just beyond."

Glass's protégé, Virginia's junior senator Harry Byrd, had been a moderately progressive governor in the 1920s, overseeing the construction of highways and working to expand business and manufacturing in the Old Dominion. But, like Glass, as well as like the generation of Randolph and Roane, Byrd held that the first purpose of government was to produce a balanced budget on an annual basis at the lowest level of taxation. "I do not believe a government can borrow and spend its way to prosperity," he declared in 1935.

Byrd's own program for recovery was "wait and see": "Great public works and social service," he improbably advised, "should await recovery." He opposed farm bills, labor bills, unemployment bills, public works programs, housing—virtually all the legislation that comprised the New Deal. He and Carter Glass were among only six senators who voted against the Social Security Act. "Children are supposed to look after their parents," Byrd sermonized, remarking that old-age pensions had the unhappy effect of "relieving . . . children of this responsibility." Byrd gave the impression, the *Richmond Times-Dispatch* wrote, that he lived in the nineteenth century, "when anybody who advanced the idea that governments were socially responsible for their citizens was regarded as a radical or a crank."

For inspiration, Glass and Byrd turned to Thomas Jefferson: He was the pillar of their conservatism, the defender of small government, states' rights, and a rural, agrarian nation of independent landowners. Like the Sage of Monticello, they believed in maximizing individual freedom and limiting government involvement in citizens' lives. Glass even railed against some southern Democrats who claimed to be Jeffersonians while supporting certain federal programs. They "betrayed the Jeffersonian doctrine every time," Glass cried, scoffing that "Jefferson would not speak to one of them."

Had Jefferson lived in the twentieth century, would he have agreed with Glass and Byrd, or would he have been a partisan of the New Deal? Jefferson would have been "unequivocally on the side of a New Deal that assumes the priority of the welfare of all the people over the privilege of the few," wrote University of Virginia professor Robert Gooch in 1935. "It is inconceivable that he should stand on any other side."

President Roosevelt, the father of the New Deal, was also convinced that Jefferson stood with him. Indeed, Jefferson was his hero. FDR admired the Virginian for championing ordinary citizens, for declaring war on the privileged few, and for forming an opposition party to wrest power from the aristocratic Federalists and the nation's financial elite. That agenda seemed to mirror FDR's own.

Roosevelt broke ground for the Jefferson Memorial in Washington, placed the Virginian's face on the first-class three-cent postage stamp as well as on the popular nickel, and hailed him as "the savior of the deeper ideals of the Revolution" as well as "the consummate politician." And yet, it is not at all inconceivable that Jefferson might have opposed Roosevelt's New Deal.

Jefferson's legacy was a complex one. He believed in continual change and progress, jubilantly writing to James Madison that the "earth belongs to the living" and asserting that laws, constitutions, and institutions must evolve "with the progress of the human mind." He advocated democracy in economics as well as in politics, proposing that every white male in Virginia receive 50 acres in order to be able to vote and participate in self-government. But Jefferson had also warned against an expansive federal government: He opposed federal planning of internal improvements; feared industrialization, factories, cities, wage-workers, and immigrants; and, above all, stressed the importance of individual self-sufficiency. In the tug of war over the right to own Jefferson, conservatives as well as progressives could reasonably claim victory.

Glass and Byrd passionately believed that Jefferson would have opposed any federal legislation that impinged on the sovereignty of the Old Dominion—whether to establish a minimum wage or regulate crop production. Though the South was the only region in the country without a minimum wage, southern conservatives had no interest in raising the low living standards of working southerners, especially African American ones, or in empowering the working class. Glass loathed FDR's National Recovery Act, the heart of the early New Deal. This act, which established a variety of codes—for fair competition, wages, and hours—was designed to stimulate the economy while improving conditions for both business and labor. To Glass, the Blue Eagle—the omnipresent symbol of the NRA, displayed on store fronts and on flags—was a "blue buzzard," a "bird of prey." He even objected to the Agricultural Adjustment Act for its regulation of crop production. "Were we to depend on Washington to tell us when to sow and when to reap," he wrote, "we should soon want for bread."

Ironically, Roosevelt's administration had designed much of its New Deal legislation with an eye to improving the dismal conditions of the South. "It is my conviction," Roosevelt told the American people in 1938, "that the South presents right now the Nation's No. 1 economic problem—the Nation's problem, not merely the South's." A month after he created a blue ribbon panel of experts to report on conditions in the South, the panel returned with a diagnosis and a host of remedies. "The paradox of the South," their report read, "is that while it is blessed by Nature with immense wealth, its people as a whole are the poorest in the country." The report pounded on the region's low wages, ramshackle

housing, inadequate schooling, and scarcity of industry. It even agreed
with southerners—starting with John Calhoun—that high tariffs and
"outside financiers" were partly to blame for the economic backwardness of the South.

Even so, Roosevelt's vast array of New Deal government programs and
entitlements came as a shock—and a threat—to Virginia's politicians. It
triggered, first of all, their instinctual aversion to public debt and high
taxes and their loathing for the intrusion of the federal government in the
affairs of their state. But they seemed also to fear that New Deal programs,
designed to help the poor and secure for workers, farmers, miners, women,
and children a host of improvements and rights, would overturn Virginia's
traditional hierarchical social structure. Their own political power and
prestige might be jeopardized if average Virginians could turn to the federal government and not to them for help—and if a more prosperous and
politically active electorate could challenge their leadership.

And so leaders like Glass and Byrd waged war against the New Deal, re-
peating ad infinitum that it was not by government handouts, programs,
and regulations that Virginians would recover from the economic collapse,
but rather by a reliance on their own resourcefulness and on the paternalism of the state's political elite. Thus they could make the accusation that
New Dealers not only spent excessively and vastly expanded federal control but also weakened the moral character of Americans.

Admirers of Byrd and Glass hailed them for resurrecting what was best
in their state's past. One contemporary Virginia writer and historian,
Agnes Rothery, called the two senators the "worthy successors" of Jefferson, John Randolph, John Marshall, and James Monroe. Ultimately, Virginia owed its success, she explained, to "the fact that its leaders have
come and are still coming not from the lower but from the upper stratum."
It was a source of pride, at least to some people, that a white male elite
continued to govern the state from the top down.

Fortunately, the Depression was relatively mild in Virginia. Having diversified its agriculture as well as its economy, the Old Dominion was able
to emerge more swiftly from the economic crisis than many other states,
making it less politically risky for its senators and congressmen to oppose
the New Deal. Not that they had much to worry about.

Virginia, like the rest of the South, was a one-party land, run by the Democratic Party. With uncontested elections controlled by an iron-fisted statewide Democratic machine, it was hardly surprising that there was monumental voter apathy. Even more, poll taxes, and registration quizzes (Which counties constitute the 27th Judicial District of Virginia? How many men signed the Declaration of Independence?) ensured that the principal victims of the Depression—poor whites and blacks—had no political voice. Virginia's "oligarchs," as the great historian of southern politics, V. O. Key, called them, could count on their minute electoral bases to win primaries that were tantamount to reelection. So tiny a fraction—less than 10 percent—of Virginia's potential electorate voted, Key wrote, that compared to the Old Dominion, Mississippi was a "hotbed of democracy." Throughout the New Deal period, wrote another political scientist, Larry Sabato, "politics in the Old Dominion seemed so predictable that one wonders how the voters managed to stay awake."

But did they really need to stay awake? Virginia politics had scarcely changed from the early decades of the nineteenth century and had retained many of the same features: one ruling party, uncontested elections, and the sense that the ballot was a privilege, not a right. Already in 1921, the popular Virginia novelist Ellen Glasgow described the "lifeless atmosphere" of the political culture of Virginia. "The political soil has become so impoverished and the political air so stagnant that names have passed for ideas and personalities have been mistaken for principles," she wrote. Twenty years later, in his book *Southern Politics*, V. O. Key entitled a chapter "Virginia: Political Museum Piece." Just as Spencer Roane's political machine had dominated Virginia politics in the early nineteenth century, the "Byrd Organization" in the 1930s and 1940s had political power in the Old Dominion all sewn up.

In the statehouse in Richmond, most politicians were determined to maintain the status quo, hoping to block or at least delay all efforts to bring the New Deal to Virginia. The General Assembly refused to raise the age at which children could work from fourteen to sixteen and declined to set a minimum wage or reduce the workday of women. It rejected legislation for mine safety, workman's compensation, unemployment insurance, old-age pensions, and elimination of the poll tax. The Assembly was "remarkable for its negativism," wrote the *Richmond Times Dispatch*, and would "go down in history as one of the most reactionary legislatures." When Virginia finally agreed to appropriate money for old-age assistance in 1938, in order to qualify for federal matching funds, it was the very last state to do so.

Despite the negativity of Virginia's politicians, average Virginians—working people, farmers, miners, teachers, and blacks—all cheered for FDR. Yearning for meaningful reform and economic growth, most citizens of this largely rural state welcomed agricultural reform, rural electrification, and old-age security. And they cheered, too, for a bill providing low-interest, long-term loans to sharecroppers and tenant farmers that enabled them to own their own land. That bill, sponsored by Alabama Senator John Bankhead, indeed responded to Jefferson's belief in the importance of independent farmers and small landowners.

"VIRGINIA PROSPERS; ROOSEVELT STRONG" read the headline in the *New York Times* on December 4, 1935. Farm income in the Old Dominion had tripled since 1933. Sixty Civilian Conservation Corps camps had been established in the state; and more people were at work in the industrialized northern section of Virginia than at any time in its previous history. "Roosevelt couldn't possibly lose Virginia," said one citizen to the *Times* reporter. "Every section of the state has been so well watered with Federal benefits and Federal money that potential votes lie out there in bunches." That sentiment was corroborated by a poll conducted by the *Richmond Times-Dispatch* that found overwhelming popular sentiment throughout the state for the president.

As the 1936 election approached, Byrd, who was up for reelection, and Glass had no choice but to recognize Roosevelt's popularity and tone down their attacks. They even sought a rapprochement, however halfhearted, with the president. Expediency trumped principle. Whereas Republican Herbert Hoover had won all but one congressional district in Virginia in 1928, eight years later FDR captured 70.2 percent of the popular vote—despite the tepid support of Virginia's powerbrokers. In Virginia's rural communities, his vote was even higher: 90 percent. The people of Virginia did not share the politicians' fears of expansive government.

"I often think of those great Virginians," said Senator Byrd in 1961, "who established our form of government—Jefferson, Washington, Madison, and Mason—on the basis that the states were sovereign. . . . I wonder what those great men would think of a Federal bureau established to go into Southern States originating suits against their citizens." Senator Byrd was again summoning the ghosts of Jefferson and the other revolutionary Virginians—this time to encourage defiance of the 1954 Supreme Court ruling in *Brown v. Board of Education*.

Thomas Jefferson, the inspiration for segregation, inequality, and the status quo? Jefferson, the polestar of reactionary politicians? The great leaders of Virginia's revolutionary past followed "not a dead star, but a living one," novelist Ellen Glasgow had remarked in the 1920s, desperately trying to rouse her fellow Virginians from their lethargy. "Washington, Marshall, Jefferson, Henry—these were dynamic spirits, not static," she wrote. Still, even in the second half of the twentieth century, Harry Byrd would continue to invoke Thomas Jefferson to keep integration and civil rights, as well as the federal government, at bay.

On May 17, 1954, in its unanimous *Brown* decision, the Supreme Court ruled that racially segregated public schools were in violation of the Fourteenth Amendment's clause that no state could "deny to any person within its jurisdiction the equal protection of the laws." The decision was breathtaking: It hit the front pages of newspapers throughout the country like a cyclone. Hundreds of thousands of African American children were legally entitled to take their places alongside white children in the nation's public schools.

On the day the Supreme Court announced its *Brown* decision, Senator Byrd released a terse statement: The Court's judgment, he declared, "will be deplored by millions of Americans, and, instead of promoting the education of our children, it is my belief that it will have the opposite effect in many areas of the country. In Virginia we are facing now a crisis of the first magnitude." The Court had inflicted upon the Old Dominion, Byrd bristled, "the most serious blow that has yet been struck against the rights of the states."

In the past, Byrd had rarely played the race card or enthused about the old nineteenth-century credo of states' rights and Virginia localism. But now, facing the prospect of radical change, he was determined to defend what he could of the southern traditions of state sovereignty and white supremacy.

The immediate reaction of other Virginia politicians to *Brown* was restrained. Governor Tom Stanley said he found the decision "unwelcome and distasteful," but he rejected the idea of defying the high court. Virginia's state superintendent of public education was willing to consider how to resolve the question of desegregation "gradually, calmly, and with an open mind." In 1955, a commission reported to the governor, recommending that localities decide for themselves whether or not to integrate.

But that restraint and moderation were short-lived. In 1956, Governor Stanley would propose that Virginia adopt a "total resistance line," and Senator Byrd would place himself at the head of a reactionary movement calling for "massive resistance" to school desegregation.

The resistance movement had been sparked by a suggestion from James Kilpatrick, the editor of the *Richmond News Leader*, that Virginia revive John Calhoun's old theory of nullification. Reprinting Jefferson's Kentucky Resolutions, Madison's "Report on the Alien and Sedition Acts," and Calhoun's "Exposition," Kilpatrick proposed that Virginia revert to the antebellum principles of southern ideology, assert Jefferson and Calhoun's doctrine, and simply declare the *Brown* ruling null and void. The state General Assembly did just that, passing a nullification resolution. "If Virginia surrenders, the rest of the South will go down too," Byrd warned.

On one level, Byrd's support for resistance represented sheer opportunism: He was exploiting the race issue to reanimate the fortunes of his sagging political machine. "This will keep us in the saddle for 25 years," one Byrd aide was quoted as saying in the *Washington Post*. But fueling the resistance movement more than cynical opportunism were deeply held convictions—about white superiority, black inferiority, and state sovereignty. Byrd and other Virginians denounced the *Brown* decision and assailed the Supreme Court, as had Jefferson and Roane more than a century earlier, as a "despotic branch" of government. "I am convinced," Byrd declared, echoing Jefferson, "that the decision of the Supreme Court was illegal and a usurpation of power."

With Strom Thurmond of South Carolina, Byrd rounded up seventeen other United States senators and eighty-two congressmen, including the entire Virginia delegation, to join them in issuing a Southern Manifesto in the spring of 1956. Read out loud on the Senate floor by Walter George of Georgia, and presented by Virginian Howard Smith in the House, the Manifesto declared that the Supreme Court was "destroying the amicable relations between the white and Negro races" and was "encroach[ing] on the rights reserved to the States and to the people." It was back in time 130 years to nullification, interposition, and resistance. Among southern senators, only Albert Gore, Sr. and Estes Kefauver of Tennessee and Lyndon Johnson of Texas demurred.

In the statehouse in Richmond, politicians decided that public schools in the Old Dominion would remain segregated and that no state funds would be allocated to integrated schools. The governor could close integrated schools and then attempt to reopen them as voluntarily segregated schools. Tuition grants would be given to white pupils "forced" to attend private schools. That November, campaigning for governor, Attorney General Lindsay Almond vowed that he would cut off his right arm before allowing a black child to enter a white school.

But within two years, influential business leaders and editors began complaining that the economy in Virginia was suffering. Whereas North Carolina, a state that did not resist *Brown,* had seen an inflow of a billion dollars from outside the state, no outside money had recently been invested in industry in Virginia. Finally, after both the Virginia Supreme Court of Appeals and a federal court ruled in early 1959 that Virginia's laws closing integrated schools were unconstitutional, Governor Almond, in an about-face—and with both arms still attached—admitted that Virginia could no longer afford to defy the courts. The General Assembly passed his proposals to permit some degree of school integration. It would be a snail-like pace, but at least the process of integration had begun.

One man, however, remained steadfast. "I stand now as I stood when I first urged massive resistance," pronounced Senator Byrd. He applauded enthusiastically when Prince Edward County decided to close its public schools in 1959 rather than comply with the new state law and admit black pupils. For five years, that county would provide vouchers to white parents to operate segregated private schools for their children, while leaving almost 2,000 black children out in the cold to fend for themselves. Hailing the "gallant little county," Byrd announced that he took "pride in the fortitude demonstrated by the citizens of Prince Edward in defense of principles which they believe and rights they hold dear." If black children had nowhere to go for an education, people could blame the NAACP, he said. Instead of organizing black-only schools, the NAACP, he charged, stubbornly chose to pursue the matter in the courts.

A few years later, in 1964, Byrd would resurrect the spirit of Jefferson one final time. On the Senate floor, he rose to filibuster the Civil Rights Act, the landmark bill that prohibited discrimination in public accommodations and public schools as well as employment. Joining other southern senators in their three-month filibuster of that bill—the longest filibuster in Senate history—Byrd reminded his fellow senators (or at least the few present to hear the Dixiecrats drone on) that "it was in Virginia that we learned from Thomas Jefferson that the safeguard against despotic Central Government lies in decentralization of power through the exercise of States rights." Byrd's conclusion came as no surprise: The government in Washington stood "in violation of the principles of Jefferson."

Would a twentieth-century Jefferson, with all that he would have learned in two centuries, have defended states' rights instead of civil rights? Would he have closed his mind and his heart to the vestiges of slavery and injustice? Would Jefferson, the champion of universal education, have blasted the Supreme Court's decision to reopen public schools in Prince Edward County, calling it, as Byrd did, "tyrannical"? It was one thing to summon Jefferson to defend the honored conservative vision of small, frugal, limited federal government, but it was surely another to use the name of the man who wrote "all men are created equal" to promote the continuation of injustice and inequality. Byrd was indeed engaged in a doomed struggle; it was the last gasp of old men determined to hold back time and shut out a changing world.

Half a century after Prince Edward County closed the doors of its public schools to avoid desegregation, the General Assembly, in 2004, announced the creation of the "Brown v. Board of Education Scholarship Program and Fund."

In an act of contrition and redemption, the state promised financial assistance for up to five years of study to students who had been deprived of a public school education between 1959 and 1964. State legislators, supported by Governor Mark Warner and some newspaper editors, acknowledged and apologized for the racist past and offered reparations. Dozens of African American Virginians, now in their fifties, made plans to go back to school or college. Still, they had not forgotten the scars of the past. "I lived behind one of those schools," said a fifty-eight-year-old woman. "I looked at it every day of my life. If I close my eyes, I can still see those doors chained up."

Carter Glass, born in 1858, died in office in 1946; Harry Byrd, who lived from 1887 to 1966, resigned from the Senate in 1965, after condemning the Voting Rights Act as "grossly offensive to Virginia."

"The torch has been passed to a new generation," said John F. Kennedy, a bit prematurely, in his inaugural address in 1961. But almost half a century later, the fate of our democracy indeed lies in the hands of new generations.

To what use will Virginians and other Americans put the rich but ambiguous legacies of Thomas Jefferson and James Madison? Will the memories of Jefferson and Madison buttress a cramped and provincial idea of government and an elitist attitude toward political leadership? Or will the brilliance and idealism of those two founders and friends inspire us to seek grander, more expansive and creative ways to revitalize our democracy, to extend freedom, security, and prosperity to all, to enhance equality, and to walk, as they as young men did, not only in step with the times, but boldly ahead of them?

NOTES

Prologue

1   *"Let me once more have the happiness"*: Jefferson to Lafayette, 3 September 1824, in *The Writings of Thomas Jefferson*, ed. Paul Leicester Ford, 10 vols. (New York: G. P. Putnam's Sons, 1892–1899), 10:319.

1   *Embraced and wept*: Dumas Malone, *Jefferson and His Time*, vol. 6, *The Sage of Monticello* (Boston: Little, Brown, 1981), 404.

1   *"In full possession"*: Lafayette, "Memoirs," 8 November 1824, in Gilbert Chinard, ed., *Letters of Lafayette and Jefferson* (Baltimore: Johns Hopkins Press, 1929), 358–359. See also Malone, *The Sage of Monticello*, 405.

1   *Increased in bulk*: James Morton Smith, ed., *The Republic of Letters: The Correspondence Between Thomas Jefferson and James Madison, 1776–1826*, 3 vols. (New York: W. W. Norton, 1995), 3:1889.

1   *Banquet and toast*: A. Levasseur, *Lafayette in America in 1824 and 1825: Journal of a Voyage to the United States*, translated by John D. Godman, 2 vols. (Philadelphia: Carey and Lea, 1829), 1:220.

2   *They revived memories*: Lafayette to Jefferson, 26 January 1825, in Chinard, ed., *Letters of Lafayette and Jefferson*, 430.

2   *Declined to express his feelings*: Madison to Cox, 1 March 1823, in Madison, *Letters and Other Writings of James Madison*, eds. William C. Rives and Philip R. Fendall, 4 vols. (Philadelphia: J. B. Lippincott, 1865), 3:304–305.

2   *"Delightfully situated"; "beautiful village"*: Levasseur, *Lafayette in America*, 1:30 and 40.

2   *Six hours to travel 25 miles*: Ibid., 1:211–212.

2   *"Her true interests better"*: Ibid., 1:203.

2   *Israel Jefferson*: "Reminiscences of Israel Jefferson," in Fawn Brodie, *Thomas Jefferson: An Intimate History* (New York: W. W. Norton, 1974), 481.

2 *"Inflict on his fellow men"*: Jefferson to Jean Nicholas Demeunier, 26 June 1786, in *Papers of Thomas Jefferson*, ed. Julian P. Boyd et al., 32 vols. (Princeton, N.J.: Princeton University Press, 1950–2005), 10:63.

3 *He was more concerned with rescuing white people*: Ari Helo and Peter Onuf, "Jefferson, Morality, and the Problem of Slavery," *William and Mary Quarterly*, July 2003, http://www.historycooperative.org/journals/wm/60.3/helo.html.

3 *While politely praising Jefferson's plan*: Lafayette to Jefferson, 9 December 1824, in Chinard, ed., *Letters of Lafayette and Jefferson*, 426 and 359.

3 *"Importance and urgency"*: Lafayette to Jefferson, 25 February 1826, in ibid., 362.

3 *"I would like, before I die"*: Lafayette to Jefferson, 1 June 1822, in ibid., 409.

3 *"These partings and many others"*: Lafayette, "Memoirs," 28 August 1825, in ibid., 361.

4 *"The most spirited"*: John Adams, "Diary," 2 September 1774, in Charles Francis Adams, ed., *The Works of John Adams*, 10 vols. (Boston: Charles C. Little and James Brown, 1850), 2:362.

4 *"We all look up"*: Adams to Patrick Henry, 3 June 1776, in ibid., 9:387.

4 *"Bostonians are mere Milksops"*: Jack N. Rakove, *The Beginnings of National Politics: An Interpretive History of the Continental Congress* (New York: Alfred A. Knopf, 1979), 45.

4 *"I look back with rapture"*: Adams to Jefferson, 25 February 1825, in *The Adams-Jefferson Letters*, ed. Lester J. Cappon, 2 vols. (Chapel Hill: University of North Carolina Press, for the Institute of Early American History and Culture, 1959), 2:610.

4 *"Equal to any standard"*: James MacGregor Burns, *The Vineyard of Liberty* (New York: Vintage, 1982), 257.

5 *"A systematic design"*: "Exposition of Motives for Opposing the Nomination of Mr. Monroe for the Office of President of the United States" (City of Washington: Jonathan Elliot, 1816), 10–11.

5 *Block the political rise of any potential rival*: Jabez Hammond, *The History of Political Parties in the State of New-York* (Syracuse, N.Y.: Hall, Mills, 1852), 405–406.

5 *John Quincy Adams*: "Exposition of Motives," 1–12.

5 *Lord Liverpool*: *The Diary of John Quincy Adams, 1794–1845*, ed. Allan Nevins (New York: Frederick Ungar, 1969), 25 August 1816, 175.

5 *"Wrest the sovereignty"*: William G. Morgan, "The Congressional Nominating Caucus of 1816: The Struggle Against the Virginia Dynasty," *Virginia Magazine of History and Biography*, 1972, 461–475. See also Charles Francis Adams, ed., *Memoirs of John Quincy Adams*, 10 vols. (Philadelphia: J. B. Lippincott, 1874–1877), 5:475.

6   *But neither caucuses, nor political maneuvers:* Hammond, *History of Political Parties in the State of New-York*, 412.

6   *"That nothing less than a Virginian":* Adams, ed., *Memoirs of John Quincy Adams*, 4:120.

6   *"As a republican & a lover of the Union":* Story to Marshall, 27 June 1821, in Charles Warren, "The Story-Marshall Correspondence (1819–1831)," *William and Mary Quarterly Historical Magazine*, 2nd ser., vol. 21, no. 1, January 1941, 6.

6   *"Our Views [are] too confined":* Washington to Thomas Johnson, 20 July 1770, in Washington, *Writings*, ed. John Rhodehamel (New York: Library of America, 1997), 139.

6   *"Our interest, however diversified":* Washington to Madison, 20 May 1792, in ibid., 805.

6   *"The most malignant":* Washington to David Stuart, 2 December 1788, in *The Writings of George Washington*, ed. John C. Fitzpatrick, 39 vols. (Washington, D.C.: U.S. Government Printing Office, 1931–1944), 30:146.

7   *"Tory":* Jefferson to Madison, 15 October 1810, in Smith, ed., *Republic of Letters*, 3:1647.

7   *"The times are hard":* Madison to Corbin, 26 November 1820, in Madison, *Letters and Other Writings*, ed. Rives and Fendall, 3:193.

7   *"During the voyage":* Irving Brant, *James Madison*, vol. 6, *Commander in Chief, 1812–1836* (Indianapolis: Bobbs-Merrill, 1961), 420.

7   *Books and farm:* Jefferson to Madison, 15 April 1817, in Smith, ed., *Republic of Letters*, 3:1785.

7   *A turnpike company:* Brant, *James Madison: Commander in Chief*, 6:446.

8   *"As if he had never been young":* Ibid., 6:421.

8   *"Virginia—poor Virginia":* James Mercer Garnett to John Randolph, 16 October 1827, in Robert P. Sutton, "Nostalgia, Pessimism, and Malaise: The Doomed Aristocrat in Late Jeffersonian Virginia," *Virginia Magazine of History and Biography* 76, 1968, 42.

8   *"Dilapidation and ruin"; "an aspect of forlorn neediness"; "how the spot would be treasured":* William Rasmussen and Robert Tilton, *Old Virginia: The Pursuit of a Pastoral Ideal* (Charlottesville: Howell Press, 2003), 70.

8   *"Tied together, two and two":* Doris Kearns Goodwin, *Team of Rivals: The Political Genius of Abraham Lincoln* (New York: Simon and Schuster, 2005), 78.

8   *"Mass of the citizen class"; "slovenly"; statistics about life in the North and South:* Frederick Law Olmsted, *The Cotton Kingdom: A Traveller's Observations on Cotton and Slavery in the American Slave States*, ed. Arthur M. Schlesinger (New York: Modern Library, 1969), 11, 31, 33, 89, 520, 559, 589.

9   *Less than one-eighth as much per acre:* Olmsted, quoted in Eugene Geno-
     vese, *The Political Economy of Slavery: Studies in the Economy and Society of
     the Slave South* (New York: Vintage Books, 1967), 135.

9   *1800 and 1820 elections:* Richard R. Beeman, *The Old Dominion and the
     New Nation, 1788–1801* (Lexington: University Press of Kentucky,
     1972), 239.

9   *Illiteracy among whites:* "Ratio of Pupils and Illiterate in the Great Sec-
     tions, 1840–1850," in U.S. Census Bureau, *Compendium of the Seventh
     Census,* ed. J. D. B. De Bow, Superintendent of U.S. Census (New York:
     Norman Ross, 1990), Table, clvi, 152.

10   *Exports:* U.S. Census Bureau, *Compendium of the 7th Census,* 186. See
     also David Hackett Fischer and James C. Kelly, *Bound Away: Virginia and
     the Westward Movement* (Charlottesville: University of Virginia Press,
     2000), 284.

10   *"Flush times":* Joseph Baldwin, *The Flush Times of Alabama and Mississippi*
     (Americus, Ga.: Americus Book Company, 1853).

10   *"We slight the warnings":* Address to the Virginia Agricultural Society,
     1852, in Clement Eaton, *Freedom of Thought in the Old South* (Durham,
     N.C.: Duke University Press, 1940), 47.

10   *"Nothing can be more melancholy":* John Randolph to Josiah Quincy, 1814,
     in Edmund Quincy, *Life of Josiah Quincy of Massachusetts* (Boston: Tick-
     nor and Fields, 1867), 351. See also Phillip Hamilton, *The Making and
     Unmaking of a Revolutionary Family: The Tuckers of Virginia, 1752–1830*
     (Charlottesville: University of Virginia Press, 2003), 1–2.

10   *Richard Randolph died prematurely:* Hamilton, *The Making and Unmaking of
     a Revolutionary Family,* 102–105.

10   *Dejected novelists:* George Tucker, *Valley of Shenandoah: Or Memoirs of the
     Graysons* (New York, 1824); Nathaniel Beverley Tucker, *George Balcombe*
     (New York, 1836).

10   *"Whither has the Genius":* Robert P. Sutton, "Nostalgia, Pessimism, and
     Malaise: The Doomed Aristocrat in Late-Jeffersonian Virginia," *Virginia
     Magazine of History and Biography* 76, 1968, 47.

11   *"I am a disappointed man":* Ibid., 43–45.

11   *"Where are our men of abilities?":* Washington to George Mason, 27 March
     1779, in Washington, *Writings,* ed. Rhodehamel, 340–341.

11   *"Aversion to change":* Henry St. George Tucker to St. George Tucker, 1
     March 1810, in Hamilton, *The Making and Unmaking of a Revolutionary
     Family,* 147.

11   *"Earth belongs to the living":* Jefferson to Madison, 6 September 1789, in
     Jefferson, *Writings,* ed. Merrill D. Peterson (New York: Library of Amer-
     ica, 1984), 959.

11   *"No parallel"*: Madison, *Federalist* No. 14.

12   *"My dearest grandfather"*: Ellen Coolidge to Thomas Jefferson, 1 August
      1825, in *Family Letters of Thomas Jefferson*, ed. Edwin Betts and James
      Bear (Charlottesville: University of Virginia Press, 1995), 454–457. See
      also Ellen Coolidge to Thomas Jefferson, 8 March 1826, in ibid.,
      473–474.

13   *"One fatal stain"*: Jefferson to Ellen Coolidge, 27 August 1825, in ibid.,
      457–458. Italics added.

14   *A way of life—and a civilization*: Herman Clarence Nixon, "Whither
      Southern Economy," in *I'll Take My Stand: The South and the Agrarian
      Tradition*, by Twelve Southerners (New York: Harper's, 1930), 199. See
      also Rasmussen and Tilton, *Old Virginia*, 14–15; and Francis W. Coker,
      "Are There Distinctive Political Traditions for the South?" *Journal of Pol-
      itics* 2, no. 1, February 1940, 3–22.

14   *"It all comes down to the most practical"*: Stark Young, "Not in Memoriam
      But In Defense," in *I'll Take My Stand*, 358.

14   *"I linger still"*: John Esten Cooke, *Henry St. John, Gentleman, A Tale of
      1774–'75* (New York: Harper and Brothers, 1859), 488–489.

Chapter 1

15   *"Let me then describe"*; *"No object"*: Chastellux, 13 April 1782, 14–16
      April 1782, in *Visitors to Monticello*, ed. Merrill D. Peterson (Char-
      lottesville: University of Virginia Press, 1989), 12–13.

16   *"No quarter of the globe"*: Jefferson to Alexander Donald, 30 May 1795, in
      Papers of Thomas Jefferson, ed. Julian P. Boyd et al., 32 vols. (Princeton,
      N.J.: Princeton University Press, 1950–2005), 28:368.

16   *"Where all is love and peace"*: Jefferson to Maria Eppes, 15 February 1801,
      in *The Republic of Letters: The Correspondence Between Thomas Jefferson
      and James Madison, 1776–1826*, ed. James Morton Smith, 3 vols. (New
      York: W. W. Norton, 1995), 2:1143.

16   *"Preservatives of our peace"*: Jefferson to Thomas Jefferson Randolph, 24
      November 1808, in *Writings of Thomas Jefferson*, ed. Paul Leicester Ford,
      10 vols. (New York: G. P. Putnam's Sons, 1892–1899), 9:231.

16   *"Giving a pleasing"*: Ibid., 9:232.

16   *"Smooth handle"*: Jefferson to Paul Clay, in ibid., 10:93n.

16   *"Never enter into dispute"*: Jefferson to Thomas Jefferson Randolph, 24
      November 1808, in ibid., 9:231–232.

16   *"Severest of . . . intellectual labors"*: Madison to Nicholas Biddle, 17 May
      1827, in *The Writings of James Madison*, ed. Gaillard Hunt, 9 vols. (New
      York: G. P. Putnam's Sons, 1900–1910), 9:288.

16 *Pursue and practice his personal happiness:* Arthur M. Schlesinger, Sr., "The Lost Meaning of the Pursuit of Happiness," *William and Mary Quarterly,* 3rd ser., vol. 21, no. 3, July 1964, 325–327.

16 *"The art of avoiding pain":* Jefferson to Maria Cosway, 12 October 1786, in Jefferson, *Writings,* ed. Merrill Peterson (New York: Library of America, 1984), 872.

17 *Symbolized the social domination:* Eugene D. Genovese, *The Political Economy of Slavery: Studies in the Economy and Society of the Slave South* (New York: Vintage Books, 1967), 18.

17 *Equal because they were free and not slaves:* Edmund Morgan, *American Slavery, American Freedom: The Ordeal of Colonial Virginia* (New York: W. W. Norton, 1975), 381.

17 *Self-reliant whites:* See William W. Freehling, *The Road to Disunion: Secessionists at Bay, 1776–1854* (New York: Oxford University Press, 1990), 167.

17 *"My first wish":* Jefferson to John Randolph, 25 August 1775, in Ford, ed., *Writings of Thomas Jefferson,* 1:482.

17 *"I have taken my final leave":* Jefferson to Edmund Randolph, 16 September 1781, in Boyd, ed., *Papers of Thomas Jefferson,* 6: 118.

18 *"My only object now":* Jefferson to Chastellux, 26 November 1782, in ibid., 6:203–204.

18 *"The ravages of overseers":* Jefferson to Washington, 14 May 1794, in Ford, ed., *Writings of Thomas Jefferson,* 6:509.

18 *"Unfit for society"; "Happiness . . . requires":* Jefferson to Maria Jefferson Eppes, 3 March 1802, in *The Family Letters of Thomas Jefferson,* eds. Edwin Betts and James Bear (Charlottesville: University of Virginia Press, 1995), 219.

18 *"I do expect that your farm":* Jefferson to Monroe, 8 February 1798, in Ford, ed., *Writings of Thomas Jefferson,* 7:198.

19 *"Circumstances of our country":* Margaret Bayard Smith, *The First Forty Years of Washington Society,* ed. Gaillard Hunt (New York: Scribner, 1906), 80–81.

19 *"A return of those halcyon Days":* George Mason to Washington, 2 April 1776, in *The Papers of George Mason, 1725–1792,* Robert A. Rutland, ed., 3 vols. (Chapel Hill: University of North Carolina Press, 1970), 1:267.

19 *"I am become a private citizen":* Washington to Lafayette, 1 February 1784, in Washington, *Writings,* ed. John Rhodehamel (New York: Library of America, 1997), 553–554.

19 *"When I dream":* Jan Lewis, "The Blessings of Domestic Society," in *Jeffersonian Legacies,* ed. Peter S. Onuf (Charlottesville: University of Virginia Press, 1993), 109.

20   No "corruption of morals": Jefferson, Notes on the State of Virginia, ed. William Peden (Chapel Hill: University of North Carolina Press, 1995), Query 19, "Manufactures," 165.

20   Proportion of its "healthy parts": Ibid., 164–165.

20   50 acres: Drew McCoy, The Elusive Republic: Political Economy in Jeffersonian America (Chapel Hill: Published for the Institute of Early American History and Culture, Williamsburg, Va., by the University of North Carolina Press, 1980), 67. See also Dumas Malone, Jefferson and His Time, vol. 1, Jefferson the Virginian (Boston: Little, Brown, 1948), 252, 217, 235–240.

20   Entails, primogeniture: Malone, Jefferson the Virginian, 252–253.

20   "Half dozen aristocratical gentlemen": Jefferson to Benjamin Franklin, 13 August 1777, in Boyd, ed., Papers of Thomas Jefferson, 2:26.

20   Top 10 percent: John Majewski, A House Dividing: Economic Development in Pennsylvania and Virginia Before the Civil War (Cambridge: Cambridge University Press, 2000), 15.

20   More property owners: Malone, Jefferson the Virginian, 259.

20   Louisiana Purchase: Jefferson, 28 December 1805, speech on the territory of Indians, in McCoy, The Elusive Republic, 203.

21   "I cherish a narrow attachment": Proceedings and Debates of the Virginia State Convention of 1829–30 (Richmond: Samuel Shepherd, for Ritchie and Cook, 1830), 401.

21   "Never part with your land": Henry Adams, John Randolph (Boston: Houghton Mifflin, 1899), 8.

21   "Will melt like Snow": Washington to John Parke Custis, 26 May 1778, in The Writings of George Washington, ed. John C. Fitzpatrick, 39 vols. (Washington, D.C.: U.S. Government Printing Office, 1931–1944), 11:457.

21   "We are now taught to believe": Jefferson to Yancey, 6 January 1816, in Ford, ed., Writings of Thomas Jefferson, 10:2. On the cult of the soil, see also Susan Dunn, "French Anti-Semitism and the Cult of the Soil," Partisan Review 61, no. 4, Fall 1994, 592–599.

21   Great Seal: Richard Beeman, The Varieties of Political Experience in Eighteenth-Century America (Philadelphia: University of Pennsylvania Press, 2004), 31.

22   Washington was willing to probe: Washington to John Sinclair, 11 December 1796, in Fitzpatrick, ed., Writings of Washington, 35:327ff.

22   "No resource but in the sale"; "paper property": Madison to F. Corbin, 26 November 1820, in Madison, Letters and Other Writings of James Madison, eds. William C. Rives and Philip R. Fendall, 4 vols. (Philadelphia: J. B. Lippincott, 1865), 3:193. See also Madison to Nicholas Trist, 26 January 1828, in Hunt, ed., Writings of James Madison, 9:302–303.

22   *Federal bankruptcy laws:* Charles Warren, *Bankruptcy in United States History* (Cambridge: Harvard University Press, 1935), 12–17. See also McCoy, *The Elusive Republic*, 179–180.

22   *"Render almost all the landholders":* Jefferson to Thomas Mann Randolph, 21 December 1792, in Ford, ed., *Writings of Thomas Jefferson*, 6:149.

22   *"Should not all laws be made":* "Thoughts and Doubts over the Bankrupt Bill," December 1792, in Ford, ed., *Writings of Thomas Jefferson*, 6:145.

22   *Jefferson himself feared:* Jefferson to Archibald Stuart, 20 July 1795, in Boyd, ed., *Papers of Thomas Jefferson*, 28:410.

22   *"Many planters had been swindled":* Warren, *Bankruptcy in United States History*, 21.

23   *Bankruptcy act at bay:* Ibid., 79.

23   *La Rochefoucauld–Liancourt:* Avery Craven, *Soil Exhaustion as a Factor in the Agricultural History of Virginia and Maryland, 1606–1860* (Urbana: University of Illinois Press, 1926), 83.

23   *"A scene of desolation":* Farmer's Register, in Craven, *Soil Exhaustion*, 83.

23   *Unsightly woods:* Jane Louise Mesick, *The English Traveller in America, 1785–1835* (New York: Columbia University Press, 1922), 157.

23   *No real system of agriculture:* Washington to Arthur Young and Sir John Sinclair, 6 August 1789, quoted in Craven, *Soil Exhaustion*, 82.

23   *"Scarcely any part of America":* Washington to Arthur Young, 1 November 1787, in Fitzpatrick, ed., *Writings of George Washington*, 29:298.

23   *Cultivation of tobacco:* See Ford, ed., *Writings of Thomas Jefferson*, 7:309.

24   *"Nothing is more wanting":* Washington to Jefferson, 6 July 1796, in Washington, *Writings*, ed. Rhodehamel, 954.

24   *He experimented:* Craven, *Soil Exhaustion*, 88–89.

24   *900 volumes:* Richard Beale Davis, *Intellectual Life in Jefferson's Virginia, 1790–1830* (Chapel Hill: University of North Carolina Press, 1964), 89.

24   *Experimental seed:* Davis, *Intellectual Life in Jefferson's Virginia*, 149, 168.

24   *"Essence of dung":* Jefferson to George Washington, 14 May 1794, in Ford, ed., *Writings of Thomas Jefferson*, 6:509.

24   *He hoped that different grasses:* Craven, *Soil Exhaustion*, 97.

24   *John Alexander Binns:* Ibid., 94–95.

24   *Addressing the Agricultural Society:* 12 May 1818, in Madison, *Letters and Other Writings*, ed. Rives and Fendall, 3:63–95.

24   *An agricultural college in Virginia:* Charles W. Turner, "Virginia Agricultural Reform," *Agricultural History* 26, July 1952, 85.

24   *"Details, unentertaining":* John Taylor, *Arator* [1810], ed. M. E. Bradford (Indianapolis: Liberty Classics, 1977), 146.

24   *By constantly replenishing his land:* See John Grammer, *Pastoral and Politics in the Old South* (Baton Rouge: Louisiana State University Press, 1996), 30.

25   *"Best architect of a complete man":* Taylor, *Arator,* ed. Bradford, 316.

25   *Hazelwood:* Grammer, *Pastoral and Politics in the Old South,* 42.

25   *Ruffin's study of chemistry:* Craven, *Soil Exhaustion,* 137–140, 143.

25   *Farmers' and planters' associations:* Turner, "Virginia Agricultural Reform," 85. See also Davis, *Intellectual Life in Jefferson's Virginia,* 170; Charles Turner, "Virginia State Agricultural Societies, 1811–1860," *Agricultural History* 38, July 1964, 164–177.

25   *Farmers were left completely ignorant:* Turner, "Virginia Agricultural Reform," 85.

25   *New plows sent:* Address to Frederick Agricultural Society, 14 November 1822, *American Farmer,* in Craven, *Soil Exhaustion,* 109.

25   *Overworking the soil:* Craven, *Soil Exhaustion,* 84, 118.

26   *"Incompatible":* Madison to F. Corbin, 26 November 1820, in Madison, *Letters and Other Writings,* ed. Rives and Fendall, 3:193.

26   *Too numerous . . . impoverishing him:* Irving Brant, *James Madison,* vol. 6, *Commander in Chief, 1812–1836* (Indianapolis: Bobbs-Merrill, 1961), 510, 517. See also Genovese, *Political Economy of Slavery,* 138.

26   *Expressed admiration:* Brant, *James Madison: Commander in Chief,* 6:510, 517. See also Genovese, *Political Economy of Slavery,* 138.

26   *"In spite of all I can say":* Washington to Jefferson, 4 October 1795, in Ford, ed., *Writings of George Washington,* 13:112.

26   *Exhausted state of his fields:* Washington to James Anderson, 10 December 1799, in Fitzpatrick, ed., *Writings of George Washington,* 37:460.

26   *"Save us and our children":* Jefferson to Mary Jefferson Eppes, 7 January 1798, in Betts and Bear, eds., *Family Letters of Thomas Jefferson,* 152.

26   *"All Virginia would soon be a perfect garden":* Farmer's *Register,* in Craven, *Soil Exhaustion,* 111.

26   *Gypsum seemed only to impoverish:* Ibid., 111–112.

27   *"The great evils":* Drew Faust Gilpin, *A Sacred Circle: The Dilemma of the Intellectual in the Old South, 1840–1860* (Baltimore: Johns Hopkins University Press, 1977), 12.

27   *"All wished to sell":* Avery Odelle Craven, *Edmund Ruffin, Southerner: A Study of Secession* (Baton Rouge: Louisiana State University Press, 1966), 52–53.

27   *Grandiose plans:* Ruffin, in Genovese, *The Political Economy of Slavery,* 127.

27   *Survey of South Carolina:* Faust, *A Sacred Circle,* 1. See also K. R. Constantine Gutzman, "Old Dominion, New Republic: Making Virginia

Republican, 1776–1840," Ph.D. dissertation (University of Virginia, 1999), 361.

27 *"What inducement"*: Francis Eppes to Nicholas Trist, 2 March 1828, in Drew McCoy, *The Last of the Fathers: James Madison and the Republican Legacy* (Cambridge: Cambridge University Press, 1989), 220.

27 *"No smiling pastures"*: *Farmer's Register,* in Craven, *Soil Exhaustion,* 113.

28 *"Abject depression"*: Jefferson to Madison, 17 February 1826, in Smith, ed., *Republic of Letters,* 3:1966.

28 *"No resources but in the earth"*: Madison to Jefferson, 24 February 1826, in ibid., 3:1967.

28 *Virtually penniless:* Harry Ammon, *James Monroe: The Quest for National Identity* (New York: McGraw-Hill, 1971), 571.

28 *"Southern interest"*: Jefferson to Madison, 27 April 1795, in *Papers of James Madison,* ed. William T. Hutchinson et al., 17 vols. (Charlottesville: University of Virginia Press, 1962–1991), 16:2 and note 2. See also James R. Sharp, *American Politics in the Early Republic: The New Nation in Crisis* (New Haven, Conn.: Yale University Press, 1993), 158–159.

28 *"Last asylum and bulwark"*: Jefferson to Henry Middleton, 8 January 1813, in *The Writings of Thomas Jefferson,* eds. Andrew Lipscomb and Albert Bergh, 20 vols. (Washington, D.C.: Thomas Jefferson Memorial Association, 1904), 13:203. Italics added.

29 *"Mimicry of an Amsterdam"*; *"'let us separate'"*: Jefferson to William Crawford, 20 June 1816, in Ford, ed., *Writings of Thomas Jefferson,* 10:34–35. Italics added.

29 *"Pseudo-citizens"*; *"afford themselves bread"*: Ibid., 10:34–35.

Chapter 2

31 *"Enemy within our bowels"*: Thomas Jefferson, *Notes on the State of Virginia,* ed. William Peden (Chapel Hill: University of North Carolina Press, 1995), Query 13, "Constitution," 125.

31 *"Insoluble fifty years hence"*: Jefferson to John Page, 30 July 1776, in *Papers of Thomas Jefferson,* ed. Julian P. Boyd et al. (Princeton, N.J.: Princeton University Press, 1950–2005), 1:482.

31 *"Enterprising temper"*: Jefferson, *Notes on the State of Virginia,* ed. Peden, "Observations of Charles Thompson," 197.

31 *"Indolent"*: Jefferson, *Notes on the State of Virginia,* ed. Peden, Query 13, "Constitution," 125.

31 *In the North, people were sober:* Jefferson to Chastellux, 2 September 1785, in Jefferson, *Writings,* ed. Merrill Peterson (New York: Library of America, 1984), 827.

31   *"Vanity and sloth"*: James C. Cobb, *Away Down South: A History of Southern Identity* (New York: Oxford University Press, 2005), 11.

32   *Dominating every important room was a chiming clock*: Robert A. Ferguson, *Reading the Early Republic* (Cambridge: Harvard University Press, 2004), 224. See also Mark M. Smith, *Mastered by the Clock: Time, Slavery and Freedom in the American South* (Chapel Hill: University of North Carolina Press, 1997).

32   *"Wretched" of the earth*: Jefferson to Martha Jefferson, 21 May 1787, in Jefferson, *Writings*, ed. Peterson, 896.

32   *"A suspension of healthy exercise"*: Jefferson to William Short, 31 October 1819, in *The Writings of Thomas Jefferson*, ed. Paul Leicester Ford, 10 vols. (New York: G. P. Putnam's Sons, 1892–1899), 10:145.

32   *"Habituate yourself to walk"*: Jefferson to Peter Carr, 19 August 1785, in Jefferson, *Writings*, ed. Peterson, 816–817.

32   *6 or 8 miles*: Jefferson to Dr. Vine Utley, 21 March 1819, in ibid., 1417.

32   *"Of all the cankers"*: Jefferson to Martha Jefferson, 28 March 1787, in *Family Letters of Thomas Jefferson*, eds. Edwin Betts and James Bear (Charlottesville: University of Virginia Press, 1995), 34.

32   *Never to be idle*: Jefferson to Martha Jefferson, 5 May 1787, in Boyd, ed., *Papers of Thomas Jefferson*, 11:349.

32   *"Business becomes a mere chaos"*: Washington to James Anderson, 10 December 1799, in *Writings of George Washington*, ed. John C. Fitzpatrick, 39 vols. (Washington, D.C.: U.S. Government Printing Office, 1931–1944), 37:460.

32   *"Waste of time or idleness"*: Washington to unknown recipient, 10 December 1799, in ibid., 37:472. Italics added.

32   *Modern clock consciousness*: Mark Smith, "An Old South by the Clock," in *The Old South*, ed. Mark Smith (Malden, Mass.: Blackwell, 2001), 43ff.

32   *Tocqueville and Adams*: G. W. Pierson, *Tocqueville and Beaumont in America* (New York: Oxford University Press, 1938), 418–419.

33   *Tocqueville and Alabama lawyer*: Ibid., 640–641.

34   *"Strong, regular"*: Ibid., 509.

34   *Lackadaisical workers*: Frederick Law Olmsted, *The Cotton Kingdom: A Traveller's Observations on Cotton and Slavery in the American Slave States*, ed. Arthur M. Schlesinger (New York: Modern Library, 1969), 9.

34   *"Unambitious, indolent"*: Lewis Perry, *Boats Against the Current: American Culture Between Revolution and Modernity, 1820–1860* (New York: Oxford University Press, 1993), 39.

34   *"He called to a young ploughman"*: Andrew Nelson Lytle, "The Hind Tit," in *I'll Take My Stand: The South and the Agrarian Tradition*, by Twelve Southerners (New York: Harper's, 1930), 211–212.

35 *Pursued with intelligence and leisure:* John Crowe Ransom, "Reconstructed but Unregenerate," in ibid., 12.

35 *"Respectable, and kind-hearted"; "give a hearty welcome":* William Robert Taylor, *Cavalier and Yankee* (New York: George Braziller, 1961), 157.

35 *"I only want a thousand acres":* John Pendleton Kennedy, *Swallow Barn, or A Sojourn in the Old Dominion,* ed. William Osborne (New York: Hafner, 1962), 27, 451–453.

35 *More sensitive to questions of time and efficiency:* Smith, *Mastered by the Clock,* 100–107.

36 *"A class of masters":* Henry Wise, "The Wealth, Resources, and Hopes of Virginia," *De Bow's Review* 23, 1857, 60–61.

36 *The taste for the unhurried life:* David Bertelson, *The Lazy South* (New York: Oxford University Press, 1967).

36 *"The category of consequences":* C. Vann Woodward, "The Southern Ethic in a Puritan World," in *Myth and Southern History: The Old South,* ed. Patrick Gerster and Nicholas Cords (Chicago: Rand McNally College, 1974), 46.

36 *"Almost all the differences":* Alexis de Tocqueville, *De la Démocratie en Amérique,* ed. François Furet (Paris: Garnier Flammarion, 1981), 1:463.

36 *Robert Beverley; William Byrd:* Bertelson, *The Lazy South,* 67–68, 81, 83. See also A. Cash Koeniger, "Climate and Southern Distinctiveness," *Journal of Southern History* 54, no. 1, February 1988, 21–44.

37 *Virginians were "cavaliers":* Joseph C. Robert, *The Road from Monticello: A Study of the Virginia Slavery Debate of 1832* (Durham, N.C.: Duke University Press, 1941), 81–82.

37 *"No man will labour for himself":* Jefferson, *Notes on the State of Virginia,* ed. Peden, Query 18, "Manners," 163.

37 *"Incentive to enterprise":* Robert, *The Road from Monticello,* 22, 77.

37 *"Slavery . . . retards improvements":* John McCardell, *The Idea of a Southern Nation: Southern Nationalists and Southern Nationalism, 1830–1860* (New York: W. W. Norton, 1979), 52.

37 *Samuel Moore:* Robert, *The Road from Monticello,* 63.

38 *"Where there is Negro slavery":* Francis Corbin to Madison, 24 September 1818 and 10 October 1819, in Drew McCoy, *The Last of the Fathers: James Madison and the Republican Legacy* (Cambridge: Cambridge University Press, 1989), 222.

38 *"Stately name of planter":* Cobb, *Away Down South,* 27.

38 *Surrounded from infancy:* Michel Chevalier, *Society, Manners and Politics in the United States* [1837], ed. John William Ward (Garden City, N.Y.: Doubleday, 1961), 103–104.

38 *"Every kind of labour"*: Charles Ball, quoted in Joyce Appleby, *Inheriting the Revolution: The First Generation of Americans* (Cambridge: Belknap Press of Harvard University Press, 2000), 156.

38 *Habits of labor*: Hamilton to Robert Morris, 30 April 1781, in *The American Enlightenment*, ed. Adrienne Koch (New York: G. Braziller, 1965), 575.

38 *Mistress of a plantation*: Edmund Morgan, *Virginians at Home: Family Life in the Eighteenth Century* (Williamsburg, Va.: Colonial Williamsburg, 1952), 43. See also Richard Brown, *Modernization: The Transformation of American Life, 1600–1865* (New York: Hill and Wang, 1976), 147.

38 *Dissipated gamesters*: William Rasmussen and Robert Tilton, *Old Virginia: The Pursuit of a Pastoral Ideal* (Charlottesville: Howell Press, 2003), 100.

38 *"My life has been one uninterrupted series"*: Phillip Hamilton, *The Making and Unmaking of a Revolutionary Family: The Tuckers of Virginia* (Charlottesville: University of Virginia Press, 2003), 171–172.

39 *"Get a few slaves"*: Bertelson, *The Lazy South*, 109.

39 *"One portion of mankind"*: Abel Upshur, "Domestic Slavery," *Southern Literary Messenger*, 1839, quoted in Laurence Shore, *Southern Capitalists: The Ideological Leadership of an Elite, 1832–1885* (Chapel Hill: University of North Carolina Press, 1986), 29.

39 *Menial work*: George Fitzhugh, *Sociology for the South*, in *Ante Bellum: Writings of George Fitzhugh and Hinton Rowan Helper on Slavery*, ed. Harvey Wish (New York: Capricorn Books, 1960), 94.

39 *"Bound to labour"*: Morgan, *Virginians at Home*, 13.

39 *"Slavery makes all work"*: Bertelson, *The Lazy South*, 199.

39 *"Natural and habitual repugnance"*: Madison to Fanny Wright, 1 September 1825, in *The Mind of the Founder: Sources of the Political Thought of James Madison*, ed Marvin Meyers (Hanover, N.H.: University Press of New England, 1981), 330.

39 *No moral necessity*: Jefferson to William Short, 8 September 1823, in *The Writings of Thomas Jefferson*, eds. Andrew Lipscomb and Albert Bergh, 20 vols. (Washington, D.C.: Thomas Jefferson Memorial Association, 1904), 15:469.

39 *George Summers*: Robert, *The Road from Monticello*, 85.

40 *"To be idle, to bribe them"*: Washington to Anthony Whiting, 30 December 1792, in Fitzpatrick, ed., *Writings of George Washington*, 32:281.

40 *"Our bodies, as well as our minds"*: McCardell, *The Idea of a Southern Nation*, 25.

40 *"An evil uppermost"*: Appleby, *Inheriting the Revolution*, 225.

40 *"Egyptian darkness"*: David Hackett Fischer and James C. Kelly, *Bound Away: Virginia and the Westward Movement* (Charlottesville: University of Virginia Press, 2000), 290.

40 *Leaving behind . . . the abject culture*: See Philip J. Schwarz, *Migrants Against Slavery: Virginians and the Nation* (Charlottesville: University of Virginia Press, 2001).

40 *Henry St. George Tucker left the Tidewater*: Hamilton, *The Making and Unmaking of a Revolutionary Family: The Tuckers of Virginia*, 109.

41 *Slavery devalued free labor*: Schwarz, *Migrants Against Slavery*, 10.

41 *"How poor a thing a poor white man"*: Allan Nevins, *Ordeal of the Union* (New York: Charles Scribner's Sons, 1947), 1:492.

41 *"Depend as little as possible"*: Madison to Edmund Randolph, 26 July 1785, in Irving Brant, *James Madison*, vol. 2, *Madison the Nationalist, 1780–1787* (Indianapolis: Bobbs-Merrill, 1948), 337.

41 *"No local partialities"*: Madison to Caleb Wallace, 23 August 1785, in *The Writings of James Madison*, ed. Gaillard Hunt, 9 vols. (New York: G. P. Putnam's Sons, 1900–1910), 2:166. Italics added.

41 *"125 Cents per acre"*: Madison to Thomas Dew, 23 February 1833, in ibid., 9:501.

41 *160 acres*: Richard Beale Davis, *Intellectual Life in Jefferson's Virginia, 1790–1830* (Chapel Hill: University of North Carolina Press, 1964), 417. See also Dumas Malone, *Jefferson and His Time*, vol. 6, *The Sage of Monticello* (Boston: Little, Brown, 1981), 326.

41 *Coles and his slaves*: Nevins, *Ordeal of the Union*, 1:502. See also D. B. Davis, *Was Thomas Jefferson an Authentic Enemy of Slavery?* (Oxford: Clarendon Press, 1970), 18.

42 *Henry Clay*: Fischer and Kelly, *Bound Away*, 287.

42 *230 men; "surplus talent"*: Ibid., 276. See also Richard Beale Davis, "The Jeffersonian Expatriate in the Building of the Nation," *Virginia Magazine of History and Biography* 70, January 1962, 49–61.

42 *"Emigration to the West"*: Jefferson to Albert Gallatin, 24 November 1818, in *Writings of Thomas Jefferson*, ed. Ford, 10:115.

42 *"To submit to any personal inconveniences"*: Mary Jefferson Randolph to Ellen Coolidge, 25 January 1827, in Ellen Wayles Coolidge Letters, Albert and Shirley Small Special Collections Library, University of Virginia.

42 *"How much trouble and distress"*: Martha Jefferson Randolph to Ellen Wayles Coolidge, 2 August 1825, in Ellen Wayles Coolidge Letters, UVA.

42 *Vetoing legislation*: "A Summary View of the Rights of British America," in Jefferson, *Writings*, ed. Peterson, 115–116.

42 *Northwest Ordinance*: Dumas Malone, *Jefferson and His Time*, vol. 1, *Jefferson the Virginian* (Boston: Little, Brown, 1948), 413–414.

42 *"Whole commerce between master and slave"*: Jefferson, *Notes on the State of Virginia*, ed. Peden, Query 18, "Manners," 162–163.

43   *"Habits of the governed"*: Jefferson to Dupont de Nemours, 18 January 1802, in Jefferson, *Writings*, ed. Peterson, 1101.

43   *"Uncontrouled dispersion"*: Madison to Monroe, 23 February 1820, in Hunt, ed., *Writings of James Madison*, 9:25. Italics added.

44   *"Declare that the condition"*: Jefferson to Albert Gallatin, 26 December 1820, in Jefferson, *Writings*, ed. Peterson, 1449–1450.

44   *"Absolutely void"*: Robert Ernst, *Rufus King: American Federalist* (Chapel Hill: University of North Carolina Press, 1968), 372.

44   *"Third persons"*: Jefferson to Edward Everett, 8 April 1826, in Lipscomb and Bergh, eds., *Writings of Thomas Jefferson*, 16:163.

44   *Went on to propose in 1824*: Jefferson to Jared Sparks, 4 February 1824, in Jefferson, *Writings*, ed. Peterson, 1484–1487.

44   *"Justice is in one scale"*: Jefferson to John Holmes, 22 April 1820, in Jefferson, *Writings*, ed. Peterson, 1434.

44   *Evacuate their states*: Jefferson to Albert Gallatin, 26 December 1820, in Ford, ed., *Writings of Thomas Jefferson*, 10:177.

44   *Preserving the leverage*: William W. Freehling, *The Road to Disunion: Secessionists at Bay, 1776–1854* (New York: Oxford University Press, 1990), 146.

45   *"Interest is really going over to the side of morality"*: Jefferson to William Burwell, 28 January 1805, in Ford, ed., *Writings of Thomas Jefferson*, 8:30. See also D. B. Davis, *Was Thomas Jefferson an Authentic Enemy of Slavery?* 1.

45   *Some planters considered slavery repugnant*: Davis, *Intellectual Life in Jefferson's Virginia*, 414.

45   *Closed its ports to the foreign slave trade*: Garry Wills, *"Negro President": Jefferson and the Slave Power* (Boston: Houghton Mifflin, 2003), 131.

45   *Chief entrepreneurial activity*: Appleby, *Inheriting the Revolution*, 70.

45   *Worth $300*: Clement Eaton, *The Civilization of the Old South*, ed. Albert D. Kirwan (Lexington: University of Kentucky Press, 1968), 107.

45   *"Almost boundless reservoir"*: Dice Robins Anderson, *William Branch Giles: A Study in the Politics of Virginia and the Nation from 1790 to 1830* (Menasha, Wis.: George Banta, 1914), 227.

45   *"The loss of 5 little ones"*; *"Providence . . . has made"*: *Thomas Jefferson's Farm Book*, ed. Edwin Morris Betts (Charlottesville: University of Virginia Press, 1976), 42–43. See also Eaton, *The Civilization of the Old South*, 123.

46   *"No lover of his country"*: Jefferson to Edward Coles, 25 August 1814, in Jefferson, *Writings*, ed. Peterson, 1345.

46   *"Recoiled more from the children"*: Peter S. Onuf, "Every Generation Is an 'Independent Nation': Colonization, Miscegenation, and the Fate of

Jefferson's Children," *William and Mary Quarterly*, 3rd ser., vol. 57, no. 1, January 2000, 160.

46   *"My proposition would be"*: Jefferson to Albert Gallatin, 26 December 1820, in Jefferson, *Writings*, ed. Peterson, 1450.

47   *"It is impossible to look at the question"*: Jefferson to Jared Sparks, 4 February 1824, in Jefferson, *Writings*, ed. Peterson, 1485.

47   *Ceded its immense western territory*: Ibid., 1485–1486.

47   *"Some scruples of humanity"*: Ibid., 1487.

47   *Calculations quickly overcame*: Onuf, "Every Generation Is an 'Independent Nation,'" 166–168.

48   *In 1820, east of the Blue Ridge*: McCoy, *Last of the Fathers*, 272.

48   *"Dammed up in a land of slaves"*: James Simon, *What Kind of Nation: Thomas Jefferson, John Marshall, and the Epic Struggle to Create a United States* (New York: Simon and Schuster, 2002), 279.

49   *American Colonization Society*: Robert, *The Road from Monticello*, 13.

49   *"A spark to a mass"*: Madison to Lafayette, 1 February 1830, in Madison, *Letters and Other Writings of James Madison*, eds. William C. Rives and Philip R. Fendall, 4 vols. (Philadelphia: J. B. Lippincott, 1865), 4:60.

49   *"Our wisest men"*: *Richmond Enquirer*, 7 January 1832.

49   *"I wish from my soul"*: Washington to Lawrence Lewis, 4 August 1797, in Washington, *Writings*, ed. Rhodehamel, 1002.

50   *"This is the act"*: Robert, *The Road from Monticello*, 20.

50   *"Better fed, better clad"*: Madison to Robert Walsh, 2 March 1819, in Madison, *Letters and Other Writings*, eds. Rives and Fendall, 3:121–122.

50   *"Dreadful calamity"*: Madison to R. R. Gurley, 28 December 1831, in Hunt, ed., *Writings of James Madison*, 9:469.

50   *"That liberty for which we have paid the price"*: Madison to James Madison, Sr., 8 September 1783, in ibid., 2:15.

50   *"Universally obnoxious"*: Madison to Lafayette, 20 February 1828, in ibid., 9:311.

50   *"Unalterable"*: Madison to Robert Evans, 15 June 1819, in Madison, *Writings*, ed. Jack N. Rakove (New York: Library of America, 1999), 728–729.

50   *Dearth of acceptable places*: Madison to R. R. Gurley, 28 December 1831, in Hunt, ed., *Writings of James Madison*, 9:469.

50   *"Vacant"*: Madison to Robert Evans, 15 June 1819, in Meyers, ed., *Mind of the Founder*, 316.

50   *"Emancipating disposition"*: Madison to Lafayette, November 1826, in Madison, *Letters and Other Writings*, eds. Rives and Fendall, 3:539.

50   *"Horror of going to Liberia"*: Madison to Harriet Martineau, in Irving Brant, *James Madison*, vol. 6, *Commander in Chief, 1812–1836* (Indianapolis: Bobbs-Merrill, 1961), 511. See also David Brion Davis, *Challenging the Boundaries of Slavery* (Cambridge: Harvard University Press, 2003), 63.

50   *"I will not rest"*: "The Diary of Governor John Floyd," in *The Southampton Slave Revolt of 1831: A Compilation of Source Material*, ed. Henry Irving Tragle (New York: Vintage Books, 1973), 262. See also Robert, *The Road from Monticello*, 13–14.

51   *Deportation Debate*: Freehling, *The Road to Disunion*, 195.

51   *Samuel McDowell Moore; George Williams; James McDowell*: Robert, *The Road from Monticello*, 21, 101, 27.

52   *Madison's reaction to McDowell's speech*: Robert Winthrop to William Rives, 24 June 1856, Rives Papers, in Nevins, *Ordeal of the Union*, 1:499.

52   *Thomas Jefferson Randolph; Henry Berry*: Robert, *The Road from Monticello*, 97, 99. Italics added.

52   *George Summers*: Ibid., 22.

52   *Charles Faulkner; Samuel Garland*: Ibid., 23, 77, 92.

52   *John Thompson Brown*: Ibid., 90.

53   *"Bands which bind society"*: Dickson Bruce, *The Rhetoric of Conservatism: The Virginia Convention of 1829–30 and the Conservative Tradition in the South* (San Marino, Calif.: Huntington Library, 1982), 178–179.

53   *Militant pro-slavery ideology*: Larry Tise, *Proslavery: A History of the Defense of Slavery in America* (Athens: University of Georgia Press, 1987), 308.

53   *Principle of states' rights*: Louis P. Masur, *1831: Year of Eclipse* (New York: Hill and Wang, 2001), 56.

53   *William Goode*: Robert, *The Road from Monticello*, 107.

53   *John Shell*: Ibid., 24.

53   *Gholson*: Ibid., 67. See also *Proceedings and Debates of the Virginia State Convention of 1829–1830* (Richmond: Samuel Shepherd, for Ritchie and Cook, 1830), 324.

54   *"Give up slavery and tobacco"*: Alexis de Tocqueville, *De la Démocratie en Amérique* (Paris: Garnier-Flammarion, 1981), Bk. 1, pt. 2, ch. 10, 463–464. See also Pierson, *Tocqueville and Beaumont in America*, 652.

54   *Preamble*: Alison Goodyear Freehling, *Drift Toward Dissolution: The Virginia Slavery Debate of 1831–1832* (Baton Rouge: Louisiana State University Press, 1982), 148.

54   *"Entering wedge"*: *Richmond Enquirer*, 17 January 1832, in Freehling, *Drift Toward Dissolution*, 148.

54   *$50,000*: Robert, *The Road from Monticello*, 40. See also A. Upshur, "Northampton County Petition to Virginia Legislature," 1831, in *The*

Southern Debate over Slavery, ed. Loren Schweninger (Urbana: University of Illinois Press, 2001), 128–131.

54   *Illegal to teach slaves:* Edgar Knight, ed., *A Documentary History of Education in the South Before 1860*, 5 vols. (Chapel Hill: University of North Carolina Press, 1949–1953), 5:475.

55   *"This lamentable evil":* William Wirt Henry, *Patrick Henry: Life, Correspondence and Speeches*, 3 vols. (New York: Charles Scribner's Sons, 1891), 1:152–153.

55   *"To whine over it":* John Taylor, *Arator* [1810], ed. M. E. Bradford (Indianapolis: Liberty Classics, 1977), 180.

55   *"We must submit to our destiny":* Griggs, in Debate in the House of Delegates, quoted in *Richmond Enquirer*, 27 February 1836.

55   *"Be that property an evil":* Robert, *The Road from Monticello*, 43.

56   *"Unto death"; "wheedled":* Ibid.

56   *"Quit at once":* Jane Randolph to Sarah Nichols, undated, in Freehling, *The Road to Disunion*, 182.

56   *"Our political power is fast passing away":* *Richmond Enquirer*, 18 May 1832.

56   *"Arguments in favor of negro emancipation"; another half century:* George Tucker, *Progress of the United States in Population and Wealth in Fifty Years* (New York: Press of Hunt's Merchants' Magazine, 1843), 108–109.

56   *"Inflammatory and mischievous":* Wiley Hodges, "Pro-Governmentalism in Virginia, 1789–1836: A Pragmatic Liberal Pattern in the Political Heritage," *Journal of Politics* 25, no. 2, May 1963, 341.

56   *"We will never witness":* Melvin Urofsky, "The Virginia Historical Society: The First 175 Years," *Virginia Magazine of History and Biography* 114, 2006, 19.

56   *"Virginia is no longer a home":* Martha Randolph to Ellen Coolidge, 15 September 1833, in Ellen Wayles Coolidge Letters, Albert and Shirley Small Special Collections Library, University of Virginia.

56   *"An alien":* Merrill Peterson, *The Jefferson Image in the American Mind* (New York: Oxford University Press, 1960), 39.

57   *Dew's "Review of the Debate":* Robert, *The Road from Monticello*, 46; Dickson Bruce, *The Rhetoric of Conservatism*, 180.

57   *"Misguided philanthropy"; "stupendous piece of folly":* Thomas Roderick Dew, "Review of the Debate in the Virginia Legislature," reprinted as "Abolition of Negro Slavery," in *The Ideology of Slavery: Proslavery Thought in the Antebellum South, 1830–1860*, ed. Drew Gilpin Faust (Baton Rouge: Louisiana State University Press, 1981), 27–28, 44.

57   *Protection of private property:* Ibid., 40–41.

57   *Biblical and ancient history:* Ibid., 58, 61–62, 66.

58   *Consolidating and codifying:* Ibid., 64–67.

58   *State of war:* Peter Onuf and Ari Helo, "Jefferson, Morality, and the Problem of Slavery," *William and Mary Quarterly*, July 2003, http://www.historycooperative.org/journals/wm/60.3/helo.html.

58   *"In 1929 . . . our police":* Dew, "Abolition of Negro Slavery," in Faust, ed., *The Ideology of Slavery,* 70.

58   *"Nursed, educated":* Jefferson, *Notes on the State of Virginia,* ed. Peden, Query 18, "Manners," 162.

58   *Dew on Jefferson:* Dew, "Abolition of Negro Slavery," in Faust, ed., *The Ideology of Slavery,* 63–65.

59   *"I am obliged to say":* Madison to Thomas Dew, 23 February 1833, in Meyers, ed., *Mind of the Founder,* 333–336.

59   *Accepting the presidency:* Madison to R. R. Gurley, 19 February 1833, in McCoy, *Last of the Fathers,* 301.

59   *"As one of the greatest blessings":* Charles Ingersoll's account of conversation with Madison, May 1836, in Brant, *James Madison: Commander in Chief,* 6:517. Italics added.

Chapter 3

61   *"Permit me to say"; "Your children . . . would regard":* Dwight-Taylor Correspondence, in *Tyler's Quarterly Historical and Genealogical Magazine* 32, October 1950, 82–86.

61   *"The faculty do not treat the Southerners":* Hugh Blair Grigsby to Dr. Nathan Colgate Whitehead, 25 December 1825, in Grigsby Family Papers, Virginia Historical Society (VHS), Richmond. See also Alden Griswold Bigelow, "Hugh Blair Grigsby: Historian and Antiquarian," Ph.D. dissertation (University of Virginia, 1957).

62   *"So many Southerners have been rather wild":* Hugh Blair Grigsby to Dr. Nathan Colgate Whitehead, 16 February 1825, in Grigsby Family Papers, VHS.

62   *"A diminutive and low-minded set":* Hugh Blair Grigsby, 17 February 1825, Grigsby Family Papers, VHS. See also Fitzgerald Flourney, "Hugh Blair Grigsby at Yale," *Virginia Magazine of History and Biography* 22, April 1954, 166–190.

62   *"Can't be a gentleman":* Dr. Nathan Colgate Whitehead to Hugh Blair Grigsby, 3 April 1825, Grigsby Family Papers, VHS.

62   *"We always call each other 'Virginian'":* Hugh Blair Grigsby to Dr. Nathan Colgate Whitehead, 12 December 1824, Grigsby Family Papers, VHS.

62   *"Dirty tea"; the sheets:* Hugh Blair Grigsby to Dr. Nathan Colgate Whitehead, 1 May 1825, Grigbsy Family Papers, VHS.

62   *"Young Judases":* H゙ugh Blair Grigsby to Dr. Nathan Colgate Whitehead, 25 January 1825, Grigsby Family Papers, VHS. See also Flourney, "Hugh Blair Grigsby at Yale," 174.

62   *Yankee beau:* Lelia Grigsby to Hugh Blair Grigsby, 1 March 1825, Grigsby Family Papers, VHS.

62   *"Well recognized"; gentleman's library:* Dr. Nathan Colgate Whitehead to Hugh Blair Grigsby, 25 September 1825, Grigsby Family Papers, VHS. See also Flourney, "Hugh Blair Grigsby at Yale," 177.

63   *"Sustain and advance":* Littleton Waller Tazewell to John Tazewell, 17 November 1825, in Tazewell Family Papers, State Library of Virginia, Richmond.

63   *Louis Agassiz:* John Hope Franklin, *A Southern Odyssey: Travelers in the Antebellum North* (Baton Rouge: Louisiana State University Press, 1976), 77.

63   *"Bladders of conceit":* William Robert Taylor, *Cavalier and Yankee* (New York: George Braziller, 1961), 238.

63   *"The young Southerner comes here"; "The Southerner asks":* The Journals of *Ralph Waldo Emerson,* eds. E. W. Emerson and W. E. Forbes, 10 vols. (Boston: Houghton Mifflin, 1910), 4:312, 275.

63   *"Roony" Lee:* Henry Adams, *The Education of Henry Adams,* ed. Ira B. Nadel (Oxford: Oxford University Press, 1999), 52–54.

64   *"In one sentiment we agree"; "Consider, sir, the consequences":* John Taylor to Timothy Dwight, September 1805, in *Tyler's Quarterly Historical and Genealogical Magazine* 32, October 1950, 82–86.

64   *"A century in the ordinary intercourse"; "Young men from different parts":* Washington to Hamilton, 1 September 1796, in *The Writings of George Washington,* ed. John C. Fitzpatrick, 39 vols. (Washington, D.C.: U.S. Government Printing Office, 1931–1944), 35:199–200.

64   *"Do away with local attachments":* Washington, "Testament," 14 December 1799, in Fitzpatrick, ed., *Writings of George Washington,* 37:60.

64   *"Where too often principles":* Washington to Jefferson, 15 March 1795, in ibid., 34:149.

65   *"But why send an American youth to Europe":* Jefferson to John Banister, Jr., 5 October 1785, in Jefferson, *Writings,* ed. Merrill Peterson (New York: Library of America, 1984), 837–839.

65   *Half the students at Princeton:* Jefferson to Cabell, 31 January 1821, in *The Writings of Thomas Jefferson,* eds. Andrew Lipscomb and Albert Bergh, 20 vols. (Washington, D.C.: Thomas Jefferson Memorial Association, 1904), 15:311.

65   *"Imbibed opinions"*: Jefferson to John Taylor, 14 February 1821, in Jefferson Papers, *Collections of the Massachusetts Historical Society*, 7th ser. (Boston: Massachusetts Historical Society, 1900), 1:305–306.

65   *"Fanatics & tories"*: Jefferson, 22 January 1820, quoted in Cameron Addis, *Jefferson's Vision for Education, 1760–1845* (New York: Peter Lang, 2003), 93.

65   *"The signs of the times"*: Jefferson to John Taylor, 14 February 1821, in Jefferson Papers, *Collections of the Massachusetts Historical Society*, 7th ser., 1:305–306.

65   *"Every attempt to alienate"*: Washington, Farewell Address, 19 September 1796, in Washington, *Writings*, ed. John Rhodehamel (New York: Library of America, 1997), 964–965.

65   *George Washington Lafayette*: Washington to Henry Knox, 20 September 1795, in ibid., 917.

66   *"Inert"*: James Thomas Flexner, *George Washington: Anguish and Farewell, 1793–1799* (Boston: Little, Brown, 1965–1972), 4:347.

66   *"Less prone to dissipation"*: Washington to David Stuart, 22 January 1798, in Fitzpatrick, ed., *Writings of George Washington*, 36:136.

66   *"Generally spent much money"*: Thomas Jefferson Coolidge, *T. Jefferson Coolidge, 1831–1920: An Autobiography* (Boston: Houghton Mifflin, 1923), 7.

66   *"Rather than anywhere northwardly"*: Jefferson to Dr. Thomas Cooper, 14 August 1820, in Lipscomb and Bergh, eds., *Writings of Thomas Jefferson*, 15:264.

66   *"The discipline is more lax"*: Coolidge Collection of Thomas Jefferson Manuscripts, Massachusetts Historical Society, Accession 36713, Misc. reel, 2045.

66   *"Minds and affections"*: Jefferson to James Breckinridge, 15 February 1821, in Lipscomb and Bergh, eds., *Writings of Thomas Jefferson*, 15:315. Italics added.

67   *"Sacred principles"*: Jefferson to Cabell, 31 January 1821, in ibid., 15:311.

67   *"Canker"*; *"be beyond remedy"*: Jefferson to James Breckenridge, 15 February 1821, in ibid., 15:315.

67   *"So miserable are the means"*: Jefferson to Francis Eppes, 17 November 1821, in *Family Letters of Thomas Jefferson*, eds. Edwin Betts and James Bear (Charlottesville: University of Virginia Press, 1995), 441.

67   *"Bestow on us"*: Jefferson to Cabell, 28 November 1820, in *Early History of the University of Virginia as Contained in the Letters of Thomas Jefferson and Joseph C. Cabell* (Richmond: J. W. Randolph, 1856), 185.

67   *"If knowledge is power"*: Jefferson to John Taylor, 14 February 1821, *Collections of the Massachusetts Historical Society*, 7th ser. (Boston: Massachusetts Historical Society, 1900), 1:305–306.

67   *Best school in the nation*: Jefferson to Francis Eppes, 28 July 1787, in *Papers of Thomas Jefferson*, ed. Julian P. Boyd et al. (Princeton, N.J.: Princeton University Press: 1950–2005), 11:635.

67   *"I know of no place in the world"*: Jefferson to Ralph Izard, 17 July 1788, in ibid., 13:372.

67   *The removal of the state capital*: Rosemarie Zagarri, "Representation and the Removal of State Capitals, 1776–1812," *Journal of American History* 74, 1988, 1240–1241.

67   *"It is over with the college"*: Jefferson to Thomas Cooper, 16 January 1814, in Lipscomb and Bergh, eds., *Writings of Thomas Jefferson*, 14:60.

67   *"Decaying institution"*: Isaac Coles, quoted in Susan H. Godson et al., *The College of William and Mary: A History*, 2 vols. (Williamsburg: King and Queen Press, 1993), 1:177.

67   *Dilapidated buildings*: Godson et al., *The College of William and Mary*, 1:218.

68   *"Den of noise, of filth"*: Jefferson to Trustees of East Tennessee College, 6 May 1810, in Lipscomb and Bergh, eds., *Writings of Thomas Jefferson*, 12:387.

68   *"What service can we ever render"*: Jefferson to Cabell, 31 January 1821, in *Early History of the University of Virginia*, 202.

68   *Regenerate Virginia*: "Thoughts on Lotteries," February 1826, in *The Writings of Thomas Jefferson*, ed. Paul Leicester Ford, 10 vols. (New York: G. P. Putnam's Sons, 1892–1899), 10:371.

68   *"More beautiful than anything architectural"*: Addis, *Jefferson's Vision for Education*, 118. See also Philip Bruce, *History of the University of Virginia, 1819–1919*, 4 vols. (New York: Macmillan, 1920).

68   *Nor did Jefferson want hierarchy*: Addis, *Jefferson's Vision for Education*, 117.

68   *Mission . . . to train priests*: Godson et al., *The College of William and Mary*, 1:212.

68   *Not hire a professor of divinity*: Jefferson to Thomas Cooper, 2 November 1822, in Ford, ed., *Writings of Thomas Jefferson*, 10:243.

68   *"By avoiding too much government"*: Jefferson to George Ticknor, 16 July 1823, in Lipscomb and Bergh, eds., *Writings of Thomas Jefferson*, 15:455.

69   *"We shall be reduced to six professors"*: Jefferson to Cabell, 31 January 1821, in *Early History of the University of Virginia*, 201.

69   *Enough qualified scholars in America*: Adams to Jefferson, 22 January 1825, in *The Adams-Jefferson Letters*, ed. Lester J. Cappon, 2 vols. (Chapel Hill: Published for the Institute of Early American History and Culture at

Williamsburg, Va., by the University of North Carolina Press, 1959),
2:607.

69   *"Lay down the principles"*: Jefferson to Madison, 1 February 1825, in *The Republic of Letters: The Correspondence Between Thomas Jefferson and James Madison, 1776–1826*, ed. James Morton Smith (New York: W. W. Norton, 1995), 3:1923.

69   *No professors would be hired*: Madison to Jefferson, 17 February 1825, in ibid., 3:1927.

69   *"Amiableness of temper"*: Madison to Jefferson, 17 February 1825, in ibid., 3:1928.

69   *"Nursery of republican patriots"*: Madison to Samuel Smith, 4 November 1826, in *The Writings of James Madison*, ed. Gaillard Hunt, 9 vols. (New York: G. P. Putnam's Sons, 1900–1910), 9:257. See also Madison to Jefferson, 24 February 1826, in Smith, ed., *Republic of Letters*, 3:1967.

69   *Hamiltonian vision*: Jefferson to unknown recipient, 3 February 1825, in Lipscomb and Bergh, eds., *Writings of Thomas Jefferson*, 16:104.

70   *"Correct principles"*: Jefferson to William Giles, 26 December 1825, in Jefferson, *Writings*, ed. Peterson, 1512.

70   *"If we are true and vigilant"*: Jefferson to Madison, 17 February 1826, in ibid., 1514.

70   *Lomax*: Addis, *Jefferson's Vision for Education*, 124.

70   *"Hamiltonian in Disguise"*: Merrill Peterson, *The Jefferson Image in the American Mind* (New York: Oxford University Press, 1960), 123. See also Tipton Snavely, *The Department of Economics at the University of Virginia, 1825–1956* (Charlottesville: University of Virginia Press, 1967).

70   *Colleagues who used their talents*: George Tucker, *Progress of the United States in Population and Wealth in Fifty Years* (New York: Press of Hunt's Merchants' Magazine, 1843), 108.

70   *"Freer intellectual air"*: Peterson, *The Jefferson Image*, 123.

70   *"I am never afraid of the issue"*: Jefferson to Diodati, 3 August 1789, in Jefferson, *Writings*, ed. Peterson, 958.

70   *"A full scope to reason"*: Jefferson to David Humphreys, 18 March 1789, in Boyd, ed., *Papers of Thomas Jefferson*, 14:677.

70   *"Academical village"*: Jefferson to Hugh White, 6 May 1810, in Jefferson, *Writings*, ed. Peterson, 1222–1223.

70   *"Bulwark of the human mind"*: Jefferson to Thomas Cooper, 14 August 1820, in Lipscomb and Bergh, eds., *Writings of Thomas Jefferson*, 15:269.

70   *"Illimitable freedom"*: Jefferson to William Roscoe, 27 December 1820, in ibid., 15:303.

70   *"Centre of ralliance"*: "Thoughts on Lotteries," February 1826, in Ford, ed., *Writings of Thomas Jefferson*, 10:371.

70   *"Vestal flame"*: Jefferson to Madison, 17 February 1826, in Smith, ed., *Republic of Letters*, 3:1965.

71   *Cooler subjects; "We are forbidden to speak"*: Philip Alexander Bruce, *History of the University of Virginia, 1819–1919* (New York: Macmillan, 1921), 3:176–177.

71   *"Has a State the right . . . ?"; "In case of the election"*: Ibid., 262.

71   *"It is safer"*: Jefferson to Cabell, 13 January 1823, in *Early History of the University of Virginia*, 267–268.

71   *Academic pyramid*: Addis, *Jefferson's Vision for Education*, 12.

71   *Elementary schools at the base*: Jefferson, Autobiography, in Ford, ed., *Writings of Thomas Jefferson*, 1:66.

72   *"Mass of talents"*: Jefferson to Jose Correa de Serra, 25 November 1817, in Lipscomb and Bergh, eds., *Writings of Thomas Jefferson*, 15:156.

72   *Blow against aristocracy*: Merle Curti, *Social Ideas of American Educators* (Totowa, N.J.: Littlefield, Adams, 1974), 44.

72   *"A popular government without popular information"*: Madison to W. T. Barry, 4 August 1822, in Hunt, ed., *Writings of James Madison*, 9:103.

72   *"Must arm themselves"*: Ibid., 9:105–108.

72   *Literary Fund*: J. L. Blair Buck, *The Development of Public Schools in Virginia, 1607–1952* (Richmond: State Board of Education, 1952), 28.

72   *"While you get millions"*: Jefferson to De Witt Clinton, 19 March 1822, in Andrew Burstein, *Jefferson's Secrets: Death and Desire at Monticello* (New York: Basic Books, 2005), 82.

72   *"Pigmy"*: Jefferson to Cabell, 28 November 1820, in Lipscomb and Bergh, eds., *Writings of Thomas Jefferson*, 15:292.

72   *"Fall into the ranks"*: Jefferson to Cabell, 28 November 1820, in *Early History of the University of Virginia*, 185.

73   *"The fact is"*: Mark Hopkins to his parents, 16 June 1821, in *Early Letters of Mark Hopkins* (New York: John Day, 1929), 86; see also 6 October 1820, 64; and 4 July 1820, 52.

73   *Bronson Alcott*: Joyce Appleby, *Inheriting the Revolution: The First Generation of Americans* (Cambridge: Belknap Press of Harvard University Press, 2000), 105, 108.

73   *"Education can only be acquired"*: Hugh Blair Grigsby, Diary, 4 January 1828, Grigsby Family Papers, VHS. See also Alden G. Bigelow, "Hugh Blair Grigsby," 23.

73   *"That all things must be done for them"*: John Randolph, Speech at Virginia Convention, 1829, "King Numbers," in Russell Kirk, *John Randolph of Roanoke* (Indianapolis: Liberty Press, 1978), 563–564.

73   *"Throw on wealth"*: Jefferson, Autobiography, in Ford, ed., *Writings of Thomas Jefferson*, 1:67.

73   *Violation of their property rights*: Robert Woodburn, "An Historical Investigation of the Opposition to Jefferson's Educational Proposal in the Commonwealth of Virginia," Ph. D. dissertation (American University, 1974), 117–119.

73   *"I will put it in the power of no man"*: Randolph, "King Numbers," 558.

74   *"Let any plan be proposed"*: William M. Rives, 21 January 1832, quoted in Joseph C. Robert, *The Road from Monticello: A Study of the Virginia Slavery Debate of 1832* (Durham, N.C.: Duke University Press, 1941), 69.

74   *"Indisposition to labor"*: "A Constituent," *Richmond Enquirer*, 8 January 1818, 3 January 1818.

74   *"Have no leisure for mental culture"*: Matthew Estes, "Defence of Negro Slavery" [1846], in Rush Welter, *Popular Education and Democratic Thought in America* (New York: Columbia University Press, 1962), 133.

74   *"Educate the wealthy"*: De Bow's Review, 1856, quoted in Carl Kaestle, *Pillars of the Republic: Common Schools* (New York: Hill and Wang, 1983), 207.

75   *"Ought to reflect that"*: Madison to W. T. Barry, 4 August 1822, in Hunt, ed., *Writings of James Madison*, 9:105–108.

75   *"Perform the part expected"*: Charles Lowery, *James Barbour: A Jeffersonian Republican* (University: University of Alabama Press, 1984), 215.

75   *"Objects of deeper interest"*: Marshall to Charles Fenton Mercer, 7 April 1827, in Curti, *Social Ideas of American Educators*, 46.

75   *"Let your common school system"*: Abbott Lawrence to William Rives in Curti, *Social Ideas of American Educators*, 76.

75   *E. W. Newton*: Charles Ambler, "The Cleavage Between Eastern and Western Virginia," *American Historical Review* 15, no. 4, July 1910, 768.

75   *Many counties did not even bother*: Addis, *Jefferson's Vision for Education*, 47, 51.

75   *Ignored the directive*: Buck, *The Development of Public Schools in Virginia*, 39, 41.

76   *"Banner state of ignorance"*: Carl Kaestle et al., eds., *Literacy in the United States: Readers and Reading Since 1880* (New Haven, Conn.: Yale University Press, 1991), 200.

76   *"A plan of female education"; "solid education"*: Jefferson to Nathaniel Burwell, 14 March 1818, in Ford, ed., *Writings of Thomas Jefferson*, 10:104.

76   *"A due reference"; "would require more consideration"*: Madison to Albert Picket, September 1821, in Madison, *Letters and Other Writings of James Madison*, eds. William C. Rives and Philip R. Fendall, 4 vols. (Philadelphia: J. B. Lippincott, 1865), 3:232.

76   *"The only chance a man has"*: Una Pope-Hennessy, *The Aristocratic Journey: Being the Outspoken Letters of Mrs. Basil Hall Written During a Four-*

teen Months' Sojourn in America, 1827–1828 (New York: G. P. Putnam's Sons, 1931), 232–233.

76   "The time has arrived"; "Boarding School Miss": Edgar Knight, ed., A Documentary History of Education in the South Before 1860, 5 vols. (Chapel Hill: University of North Carolina Press, 1949–1953), 5:403.

76   Education for slaves: "It is most particularly to be remembered that all the information necessary for (the slaves) must be communicated orally. ... We do not believe in imparting knowledge in any other way to a laboring class." ("Religious Instruction of Slaves," Southern Quarterly Review 12, 1848, 179–180.) They also felt that white laborers should not be educated; a South Carolina man wrote: "The privileged few must govern." (James Simmons, "Instruction in Schools and Colleges," Southern Quarterly Review 22, 1852.)

76   Fines and prison sentences: Knight, ed., Documentary History of Education in the South, 5:491–493.

76   A special state law: Ibid., 5:485–486.

77   Illiteracy among whites: Robert L. Church and Michael W. Sedlak, Education in the United States (New York: The Free Press, 1976), 121. See also Drew Gilpin Faust, A Sacred Circle: The Dilemma of the Intellectual in the Old South, 1840–1860 (Baltimore: Johns Hopkins University Press, 1977), 8.

77   "I should blush": Robert, The Road from Monticello, 22.

77   Would not begin to establish: Buck, The Development of Public Schools in Virginia, 46.

77   No statewide public school system: Addis, Jefferson's Vision for Education, 32.

77   "Scarcely begun": Warren, "The Briar Patch," in I'll Take My Stand: The South and the Agrarian Tradition, by Twelve Southerners (New York: Harper's, 1930), 249.

77   "That peculiar system"; "destroy that peculiar character": Carl Kaestle et al., eds., Literacy in the United States: Readers and Reading Since 1880 (New Haven, Conn.: Yale University Press, 1991), 212.

77   "Capital races": Jane Louise Mesick, The English Traveller in America, 1785–1835 (New York: Columbia University Press, 1922), 206–207.

77   "I could not help regretting": Cornelius Felton to Hugh Blair Grigsby, 17 April 1861, in Grigsby Family Papers, VHS.

78   "I wish we had energy": James Heath to CC, 27 August 1839, in Michael O'Brien, Conjectures of Order: Intellectual Life and the American South, 1810–1860 (Chapel Hill: University of North Carolina Press, 2004), 1:47.

78   "Why should not we profit": James Mercer Garnett, "An Address on the Subject of Literary Associations to Promote Education," 25 September

1834, in *Six Addresses on the State of Letters and Science in Virginia*, ed. Alfred Morrison (Roanoke, Va.: Stone Print and Manufacturing, 1917), 35.

78 *"Honor to the literature of the South"*: 16 January 1824, John Rice, James Marsh, Jonathan Cushing, in Morrison, ed., *Six Addresses*, 4–5.

79 *Defending . . . and explaining southern values*: Faust, *A Sacred Circle*, 131.

79 *"First great object"*: Ibid., 93.

79 *"Speculative doubts"; "genuine southern literature"*: Robert E. Morrow, "The Proslavery Argument Revisited," *Mississippi Valley Historical Review* 48, no. 1, June 1961, 87.

79 *"Great imaginative moment"*: Louis Hartz, *The Liberal Tradition in America* (New York: Harcourt, Brace, 1955), 147, 149, 176.

80 *Wild and chaotic clash; slavery . . . created order*: Faust, *A Sacred Circle*, 53, 121.

80 *Bound to God*: Ibid., 122.

80 *"Affair of the heart"; "It protects"*: Ibid., 53, 121.

80 *Marching toward slavery*: George Fitzhugh, "Southern Thought," in *The Ideology of Slavery*, ed. Drew Gilpin Faust (Baton Rouge: Louisiana State University Press, 1981), 275.

80 *"Safe, efficient"; "all is peace, quiet"*: George Fitzhugh, *Sociology for the South*, quoted in John Grammer, *Pastoral and Politics in the Old South* (Baton Rouge: Louisiana State University Press, 1996), 112–113.

81 *"Moral stewards"*: Faust, *A Sacred Circle*, 53, 122, 115–116.

81 *Emphatic assertions*: Grammer, *Pastoral and Politics in the Old South*, 14.

81 *"Consistent with the purest justice"*: Robert E. Morrow, "The Proslavery Argument Revisited," *Mississippi Valley Historical Review* 48, no. 1, June 1961, 89.

81 *"Who is forced into a position"; "upon the degree of obedience"*: Faust, *A Sacred Circle*, 120. Italics added.

81 *"To protect the weak"; "Is necessary as an educational institution"*: George Fitzhugh, *Southern Thought* [1857], in Faust, ed., *The Ideology of Slavery*, 292–293.

81 *"Why the devil"*: *Daily Palladium* (New Haven), 22 March 1855, in Harvey Wish, *George Fitzhugh, Propagandist of the Old South* (Baton Rouge: Louisiana State University Press, 1943), 133.

82 *"Trumpeting their own praise"*: "Educational Reform at the South," *De Bow's Review* 20, no. 1, January 1856, 68, 76.

82 *"Who of the North"*: 1851, in O'Brien, *Conjectures of Order*, 1:46.

82 *Virginia Society for the Promotion of Useful Knowledge; Virginia Historical Society*: Melvin I. Urofsky, "The Virginia Historical Society: The First 175 Years," *Virginia Magazine of History and Biography* 114, no. 1, 2006, 12.

82   *"So difficult is a diffusion"*: Madison to G. W. Featherstonhaugh, 5 April 1821, in Madison, *Letters and Other Writings*, eds. Rives and Fendall, 3:207–208.

82   *Circulation of Harper's*: Allan Nevins, *Ordeal of the Union* (New York: Charles Scribner's Sons, 1947), 1:93.

83   *"Odd, eccentric"*: Harvey Wish, *George Fitzhugh, Propagandist of the Old South* (Baton Rouge: Louisiana State University Press, 1943), 126–127. See also George Fitzhugh, *Cannibals All!*, ed. C. Vann Woodward (Cambridge: Belknap Press of Harvard University Press, 1960), x.

83   *"Is the Nineteenth Century"*: Adams to Jefferson, 1815, in Cappon, ed., *Adams-Jefferson Letters*, 2:456.

83   *"I never conversed with a cultivated Southerner"*: Frederick Law Olmsted, *The Cotton Kingdom: A Traveller's Observations on Cotton and Slavery in the American Slave States*, ed. Arthur M. Schlesinger (New York: Alfred A. Knopf, 1953), 475.

83   *Fear of miscegenation*: John Hope Franklin, *A Southern Odyssey: Travelers in the Antebellum North* (Baton Rouge: Louisiana State University Press, 1976), 73.

83   *"Under slavery we live surrounded by prostitutes"*: Charles Grier Sellers, "The Travail of Slavery," in *The Southerner as American*, ed. Charles Grier Sellers (Chapel Hill: University of North Carolina Press, 1960), 49.

83   *"Perpetual suspicion"*: Madison's remarks to Harriet Martineau in Irving Brant, *James Madison*, vol. 6, *Commander in Chief, 1812–1836* (Indianapolis: Bobbs-Merrill, 1961), 504. See also "Reminiscences of Madison Hemmings," in Fawn M. Brodie, *Thomas Jefferson: An Intimate History* (New York: W. W. Norton, 1974), 473.

83   *"Political prostitution of their sons"*: John McCardell, *The Idea of a Southern Nation: Southern Nationalists and Southern Nationalism, 1830–1860* (New York: W. W. Norton, 1979), 204.

83   *"Just self-respect"*: "Resolve of Citizens of Richmond," 1854, in Knight, ed., *Documentary History of Education in the South*, 5:292–293.

83   *"Southern heads and hearts"*: "Report of the Committee on Education, Louisiana," 1844, in Knight, ed., *Documentary History of Education in the South*, 5:285.

84   *Medical students arrive home; "Let us have our own schools"*: *Richmond Daily Dispatch*, 23 December 1859, in Knight, ed., *Documentary History of Education in the South*, 5:308–314.

84   *Southern students left Princeton*: Edward Mark Norris, *The Story of Princeton* (Boston: Little, Brown, 1917), 186.

84   *Thomas Jefferson Coolidge*: Coolidge, *T. Jefferson Coolidge*, 7.

Chapter 4

85 *"P.S. Have you considered"; "bridging of rivers":* Jefferson to Madison, 6 March 1796, in Smith, ed., *Republic of Letters,* 2:923.

85 *"Extensive work": The Republic of Letters: The Correspondence Between Thomas Jefferson and James Madison, 1776–1826,* ed. James Morton Smith (New York: W. W. Norton, 1995), 2:923n.

85 *"Our country is too large":* Jefferson to Gideon Granger, 13 August 1800, in *The Writings of Thomas Jefferson,* ed. Paul Leicester Ford, 10 vols. (New York: G. P. Putnam's Sons, 1892–1899), 7:451.

86 *"I tried the road by Ravensworth":* Jefferson to Madison, 30 April 1801, in Smith, ed., *Republic of Letters,* 2:1176.

86 *Conceding that there was indeed doubt:* "Report on Manufactures," in *The Papers of Alexander Hamilton,* ed. Harold C. Syrett, 26 vols. (New York: Columbia University Press, 1961–1987), 10:310. See also Madison to Reynolds Chapman, 6 January 1831, in *The Writings of James Madison,* ed. Gaillard Hunt, 9 vols. (New York: G. P. Putnam's Sons, 1900–1910), 9:435.

86 *"To the great purposes"; "New channels of communication":* Jefferson, Sixth Annual Message, 2 December 1806, in Jefferson, *Writings,* ed. Merrill Peterson (New York: Library of America, 1984), 529.

86 *Gallatin's report:* Dumas Malone, *Jefferson and His Time,* vol. 4, *Jefferson the President: First Term, 1801–1805* (Boston: Little, Brown, 1970), 558.

87 *Pennsylvania localists:* John Lauritz Larson, "Bind the Republic Together: The National Union and the Struggle for a System of Internal Improvements," *Journal of American History* 74, no. 2, September 1987, 371.

87 *"I am held by the cords of love":* Jefferson to Baron Alexander von Humboldt, 6 March 1809, in Dumas Malone, *Jefferson and His Time,* vol. 6, *The Sage of Monticello* (Boston: Little, Brown, 1981), 12.

87 *"Companions in sentiments":* Jefferson to Edward Livingston, 4 April 1824, in Ford, ed., *Writings of Thomas Jefferson,* 10:300.

87 *"The best that is published":* Jefferson to William Short, 8 September 1823, in *The Writings of Thomas Jefferson,* ed. Andrew Lipscomb and Albert Bergh, 20 vols. (Washington, D.C.: Thomas Jefferson Memorial Association, 1904), 15:468–469.

88 *"Very active, lively":* James MacGregor Burns, *The Vineyard of Liberty* (New York: Vintage, 1982), 255.

88 *"Under the authority to establish post roads":* Jefferson to William Giles, 26 December 1825, in Ford, ed., *Writings of Thomas Jefferson,* 10:355.

88 *Jurisdictions . . . belonged "exclusively" to the states:* Jefferson, "Declaration and Protest of the Commonwealth of Virginia, on the Principles of the

Constitution of the United States of America, and on the Violations of Them" [December 1825], in Jefferson, *Writings*, ed. Peterson, 483.

88   *"Solemn Declaration and Protest"*: Jefferson to Madison, 24 December 1825, in Smith, ed., *Republic of Letters*, 3:1943–1946.

88   *"Internal weakness"*: Madison to Jefferson, 28 December 1825, in ibid., 3:1948.

88   *"Often knee-deep in mud"*: Thomas Jefferson Coolidge, *T. Jefferson Coolidge, 1831–1920, An Autobiography* (Boston: Houghton Mifflin, 1923), 2.

88   *Covered with saplings*: Matthew Page Andrews, *Virginia, The Old Dominion* (Garden City, N.Y.: Doubleday, 1937), 411.

88   *"Rainy spells"*: Hugh Blair Grigsby, *The History of the Virginia Federal Convention of 1788* (Richmond: Virginia Historical Society, 1890), 25.

89   *"Mud pikes"*: Samuel Mordecai, *Richmond in By-Gone Days* [1856] (New York: Arno Press, 1975), 239–240.

89   *"Embryo metropolis"*: Morris Birkbeck, *Notes on a Journey in America from the Coast of Virginia to the Territory of Illinois* [1818] (New York: Augustus M. Kelley, 1971), 29.

89   *"If you would see the last resting-place"*: "An Hour at Mount Vernon," *New England Magazine* 7, 1934.

89   *"Such is the state of the roads"*: Madison to Nicholas Trist, 23 December 1832, in Madison, *Letters and Other Writings of James Madison*, eds. William C. Rives and Philip R. Fendall, 4 vols. (Philadelphia: J. B. Lippincott, 1865), 4:229.

89   *Observed Frederick Law Olmsted*: Lewis Perry, *Boats Against the Current: American Culture Between Revolution and Modernity, 1820–1860* (New York: Oxford University Press, 1993), 135.

89   *"Bad roads meant bad morals"*: Henry Adams, *The Education of Henry Adams*, ed. Ira B. Nadel (Oxford: Oxford University Press, 1999), 44–45.

90   *"Hundreds of large ships"*: Gouverneur Morris to James Parish, January 1801, in William Howard Adams, *Gouverneur Morris: An Independent Life* (New Haven, Conn.: Yale University Press, 2003), 289.

90   *"We rely on your patriotism"*: Richard Brookhiser, *Gentleman Revolutionary: Gouverneur Morris, The Rake Who Wrote the Constitution* (New York: Free Press, 2003), 190.

90   *"In the strongest lights"*: Madison, "Special Message to Congress," 23 December 1811, in Hunt, ed., *Writings of James Madison*, 8:172–173.

90   *Land grant in northern Indiana*: Brookhiser, *Gentleman Revolutionary*, 190.

90   *"Microcosmic minds"*: Ibid., 191.

91   *Growth of upstate towns*: Sean Patrick Adams, *Old Dominion, Industrial Commonwealth: Coal, Politics, and Economy in Antebellum America* (Baltimore: Johns Hopkins University Press, 2004), 85.

91   *Explosion of prosperity: Commercial Advertiser* (New York), 11 October
      1822, in Allan Nevins, *American Press Opinion* (New York: D. C. Heath,
      1928), 63–64. See also Carter Goodrich et al., *Canals and American Eco-
      nomic Development* (New York: Columbia University Press, 1961), 228,
      229, 235, 241.

91   *"Sounder calculating mind"*: Jefferson to De Witt Clinton, 12 December
      1822, in David Hosack, *Memoir of De Witt Clinton* (J. Seymour, 1829),
      347. Also see Burns, *Vineyard of Liberty*, 306.

91   *"Little short of madness"*: Hosack, *Memoir of De Witt Clinton*, 347.

91   *Reapportionment bill:* Irving Brant, *James Madison*, vol. 5, *The President,
      1809–1812* (Indianapolis: Bobbs-Merrill, 1956), 382–383. See also
      Adams, *Gouverneur Morris*, 290ff.

91   *"What a monument to your retirement"*: Jefferson to Washington, 15
      March 1784, in Jefferson, *Writings*, ed. Peterson, 787–789. See also Madi-
      son to Jefferson, 16 March 1784, in Smith, ed., *Republic of Letters*, 1:299ff.

92   *Rivanna River:* "Services of Jefferson," 1800, in Ford, ed., *Writings of Thomas
      Jefferson*, 7:475–476. See also Jefferson, *Notes on the State of Virginia*, ed.
      William Peden (Chapel Hill: University of North Carolina Press, 1995), 6.

92   *Magnitude of the project:* Madison to Jefferson, 9 January 1785, in Smith,
      ed., *Republic of Letters*, 1:357.

92   *"For the trade of a rising empire"*: Washington to Thomas Johnson, 20 July
      1770, in Washington, *Writings*, ed. John Rhodehamel (New York: Library
      of America, 1997), 137–140.

92   *"To the poor, the needy"*: Washington to Lafayette, 25 July 1785, in *The
      Writings of George Washington*, ed. John C. Fitzpatrick, 39 vols. (Wash-
      ington, D.C.: U.S. Government Printing Office, 1931–1944), 28:206.

92   *"Quite a distinct People"*: Washington to James Warren, 7 October 1785,
      in Washington, *Writings*, ed. Rhodehamel, 592.

92   *The plan was to broaden the Potomac:* James Thomas Flexner, *Washington,
      The Indispensable Man* (Boston: Little, Brown, 1974), 196.

93   *"The earnestness"*: Madison to Jefferson, 9 January 1783, in Smith, ed.,
      Republic of Letters, 1:359.

93   *Create greater economic opportunity:* Madison to Jefferson, 9 January 1783,
      in ibid., 1:359.

93   *Wealthy elite:* Washington to Thomas Johnson, 20 July 1770, in Fitz-
      patrick, ed., *Writings of George Washington*, 2:19.

93   *Sail upstream:* Washington to Benjamin Harrison, 10 October 1784, in
      Washington, *Writings*, ed. Rhodehamel, 566.

93   *Mount Vernon Conference:* Madison to Washington, 9 December 1785, in
      Madison, *Writings*, ed. Jack N. Rakove (New York: Library of America,
      1999), 48.

93   *"A power to provide for cutting canals"*: The Records of the Federal Convention of 1787, ed. Max Farrand (New Haven, Conn.: Yale University Press, 1986), 2:615–616, 620. See also John Lauritz Larson, *Internal Improvement: National Public Works and the Promise of Popular Government in the Early United States* (Chapel Hill: University of North Carolina Press, 2001), 18.

93   *"Not even an earthquake"*: Norman K. Risjord, *The Old Republicans: Southern Conservatism in the Age of Jefferson* (New York: Columbia University Press, 1965), 173.

94   *"A comprehensive system"*: "Eighth Annual Message," 3 December 1816, in Hunt, ed., *Writings of James Madison*, 8:379–380.

94   *"National jurisdiction"*: "Seventh Annual Message," 5 December 1815, in ibid., 8:342. See also Drew R. McCoy, *The Last of the Fathers: James Madison and the Republican Legacy* (Cambridge: Cambridge University Press, 1989), 93.

94   *Bonus Bill passed*: Larson, "Bind the Republic Together," 384.

94   *"I am constrained"; "I have no option"*: "Veto Message to Congress," 3 March 1817, in Madison, *Writings*, ed. Rakove, 718–720. See also Madison to Monroe, 29 November 1817, in Madison, *Letters and Other Writings*, eds. Rives and Fendall, 3:50.

95   *"Defect" of constitutional authority*: "Message to Congress," 5 December 1815, in Hunt, ed., *Writings of James Madison*, 8:342.

95   *"I had not supposed that my view"*: Madison to Monroe, 29 November 1817, in ibid., 8:397.

95   *"I am not unaware that my belief"*: Madison to Henry St. George Tucker, 23 December 1817, in McCoy, *Last of the Fathers*, 97.

96   *"Recount every minutiae"*: "Debate in the House," 18 August 1789, *Annals of Congress*, 1st Cong., 1st sess., 761. See also Jesse Carpenter, *The South as a Conscious Minority, 1789–1861: A Study in Political Thought* (New York: New York University Press, 1930), 41.

96   *Proposed a clause*: Farrand, ed., *Records of the Federal Convention*, 2:611, 615–616. See also Larson, *Internal Improvement*, 18.

96   *Survey Bill; "the great temptation"*: Madison to Jefferson, 17 February 1825, in Smith, ed., *Republic of Letters*, 3:1927.

97   *Madison's search for political stability*: McCoy, *Last of the Fathers*, 80–83.

97   *Fears of unlimited government*: Madison to Thomas Ritchie, 18 December 1825, in Hunt, ed., *Writings of James Madison*, 9:235.

97   *Fourteen of Virginia's eighteen representatives*: Charles D. Lowery, *James Barbour: A Jeffersonian Republican* (University: University of Alabama Press, 1984), 97.

97   *"Gulph of consolidation"*: Ibid., 99.

97 *"Grammatical quibble"*: Jefferson to Albert Gallatin, 16 June 1817, in Ford, ed., *Writings of Thomas Jefferson*, 10:91.

98 *Access to markets*: Raymond Dingledine, "The Political Career of William Cabell Rives," Ph.D. dissertation (University of Virginia, 1947), 95.

98 *Had deserted the agricultural states*: Jefferson to Richard Rush, 13 October 1824, in Ford, ed., *Writings of Thomas Jefferson*, 10:322.

98 *"Injudicious"*: Harry Ammon, *James Monroe: The Quest for National Identity* (New York: McGraw-Hill, 1971), 931.

98 *"So ineffably stupid"*: Larson, *Internal Improvement*, 159.

98 *"I ask gentlemen"*: Russell Kirk, *John Randolph of Roanoke* (Indianapolis: Liberty Press, 1978), 434.

99 *Pennsylvania congressman . . . proposed Survey Bill*: Larson, *Internal Improvement*, 147.

99 *Randolph cut a strange, outlandish figure*: Burns, *Vineyard of Liberty*, 258. See also Benjamin Perley Poore, *Perley's Reminiscences of Sixty Years in the National Metropolis*, 2 vols. (Philadelphia: Hubbard Brothers, 1886), 1:68–69.

99 *"His speech, as usual, had neither beginning"*; *"rabid foam"*: *Memoirs of John Quincy Adams*, ed. Charles Francis Adams, 10 vols. (Philadelphia: J. B. Lippincott, 1875), 4:532, 7:366.

99 *Union and sense of connectedness*: Washington to Lafayette, 27 July 1785, in Washington, *Writings*, ed. Rhodehamel, 583.

99 *Randolph . . . cared not a whit*: Daniel P. Jordan, *Political Leadership in Jefferson's Virginia* (Charlottesville: University of Virginia Press, 1983), 168.

99 *"No Government can be safe for Virginia"*: Larson, *Internal Improvement*, 169.

100 *"Under this power to make war"*: Kirk, *John Randolph of Roanoke*, 434ff.

100 *"They may emancipate"*: Ibid. Italics added.

100 *"Like Aaron's serpent"*: Lowery, *James Barbour*, 138.

100 *"When they cease to be united"*: Ibid., 138–139.

100 *Tyler warned in 1826*: 4 December 1826, in Kevin R. Gutzman, "Preserving the Patrimony: William Branch Giles and Virginia Versus the Federal Tariff," *Virginia Magazine of History and Biography* 104, no. 2, Summer 1996, 355.

101 *The effort drowned*: Larson, *Internal Improvement*, 172–173.

101 *"Arresting the rage of encroachment"*: *Richmond Enquirer*, 1 June 1830, in Nevins, *American Press Opinion*, 80.

101 *Swallow Barn*: John Pendleton Kennedy, *Swallow Barn; or a Sojourn in the Old Dominion* [1832], ed. Jay Hubell (New York: Harcourt, Brace, 1929), 131–136.

102 *Board of Public Works*; *"stationary"*: Larson, *Internal Improvement*, 94.

102   *"Without calling upon Hercules?"*: Richmond Enquirer, 28 August 1829.

102   *Tobacco prices; wheat and corn prices*: John McCardell, *The Idea of a Southern Nation: Southern Nationalists and Southern Nationalism, 1830–1860* (New York: W. W. Norton, 1979), 21–22.

102   *Entrepreneurs furnished three-fifths of the capital*: Wiley Hodges, "Pro-Governmentalism in Virginia, 1789–1836: A Pragmatic Liberal Pattern in the Political Heritage," *Journal of Politics* 25, no. 2, May 1963, 346.

102   *"Capitalists like no interregnum"*: Richmond Whig, 10 April 1838, in Robert Hunter, "The Turnpike Movement in Virginia, 1816–1860," *Virginia Magazine of History and Biography* 69, July 1961, 287–288.

102   *"What the Old Dominion required"*: Larson, *Internal Improvement*, 96.

103   *Zero-sum game*: John D. Majewski, *A House Dividing: Economic Development in Pennsylvania and Virginia Before the Civil War* (Cambridge: Cambridge University Press, 2000), 25.

103   *Buffalo–New Orleans turnpike*: Charles Henry Ambler, *Sectionalism in Virginia from 1776–1861* (Chicago: University of Chicago Press, 1910), 175–177.

103   *Projects were unprofitable*: Robert Hunter, "The Turnpike Movement in Virginia, 1816–1860," *Virginia Magazine of History and Biography* 69, July 1961, 285–286.

103   *Competition among the different companies*: Philip Morrison Rice, "Internal Improvements in Virginia, 1775–1860," Ph.D. dissertation (University of North Carolina, 1948), 275.

103   *Board found itself reduced*: Ibid., 457.

103   *"Cannot be delayed much longer"*: Richmond Enquirer, 3 March 1829.

103   *"Cannot Virginia do what New York has done . . . ?"*: Richmond Enquirer, 28 August 1829.

103   *"Government, rightly understood"*: 21 February 1827, in Gutzman, "Preserving the Patrimony," 357.

103   *"The lowlands and the plains"*: Jean François Chastellux, *Travels in North America, in the Years 1780, 1781, and 1782*, ed. Howard C. Rice, Jr. (Chapel Hill: Published for the Institute of Early American History and Culture at Williamsburg, Va., by the University of North Carolina Press, 1963), 451, 461, 463.

104   *Improving water transportation*: Carter Goodrich et al., *Canals and American Economic Development* (New York: Columbia University Press, 1961), 221.

104   *Connecting the James with the Kanawha River*: Blair Niles, *The James: From Iron Gate to the Sea* (New York: Farrar and Rinehart, 1945), 208.

104   *Monopolized the resources*: K. R. Constantine Gutzman, "Old Dominion, New Republic: Making Virginia Republican, 1776–1840," Ph.D. dissertation (University of Virginia, 1999), 377–378.

105 *"We too of the Ancient Dominion"*: Majewski, A House Dividing, 32–35.

105 *"The dream of the great canals"*: George Bagby, Canal Reminiscences: Recollections of Travel in the Old Days on the James River and Kanawha Canal (Richmond: West, Johnston, 1879), 33–34.

105 *"The canal, after a fair and costly trial"*: Ibid., 33.

106 *Steam engines and locomotives*: Burns, Vineyard of Liberty, 430–433.

106 *"All local attachments"*: Madeline Sadler Waggoner, The Long Haul West: The Great Canal Era, 1817–1850 (New York: Putnam, 1958), 275–276.

106 *Canal interests ultimately hampered*: Rice, Internal Improvements in Virginia, 465.

106 *Westerners found themselves obliged*: Ibid., 466–468, 209, 302.

106 *No effort to assert state power*: Angus J. Johnston, "Virginia Railroads in April 1861," Journal of Southern History 23, no. 3, August 1957, 315.

107 *Rival towns*: Majewski, A House Dividing, 62.

107 *Claudius Crozet*: Rice, Internal Improvements in Virginia, 317–319.

107 *Not begin work . . . until the 1850s*: Ibid., 319.

107 *"A reproach to our republican system"*: Madison to Reynolds Chapman, 6 January 1831, in Hunt, ed., Writings of James Madison, 9:432.

107 *Convention on internal improvements*: Adams, Old Dominion, Industrial Commonwealth, 84–85.

107 *"Want of facilities for developing"*: "Agricola," Richmond Enquirer, 2 October 1835.

107 *"Or shall we quietly rest . . . ?"*: Richmond Enquirer, 16 October 1835.

108 *"The immense interests"*: Richmond Enquirer, 15 December 1835.

108 *"The gigantic system of roads and canals"*: House of Delegates, quoted in Richmond Enquirer, 17 March 1836.

108 *"Every day increases the distance"*: David Bertelson, The Lazy South (New York: Oxford University Press, 1967), 196.

108 *Bridge near Farmville; "My native state"*: Peter S. Carmichael, The Last Generation: Young Virginians in Peace, War, and Reunion (Chapel Hill: University of North Carolina Press, 2005), 40, 37.

109 *Returned to the idea of a federal program*: Address to Memphis Convention, fall 1845, in Allan Nevins, Ordeal of the Union (New York: Charles Scribner's Sons, 1947), 155. See also Drew Gilpin Faust, A Sacred Circle: The Dilemma of the Intellectual in the Old South, 1840–1860 (Baltimore: Johns Hopkins University Press, 1977), 102.

109 *"In wealth and numbers"*: Thomas Roderick Dew, "Abolition of Negro Slavery," in Ideology of Slavery, ed. Drew Gilpin Faust (Baton Rouge: Louisiana State University Press, 1981), 72–73.

109 *"Connect in pleasant communion"*: Hugh Blair Grigsby, The Convention of 1776, in Michael O'Brien, Conjectures of Order: Intellectual Life and the

American South, 1810–1860 (Chapel Hill: University of North Carolina Press, 2004), 2:653.

109   *"Never to eat brown bread"*: McCardell, *The Idea of a Southern Nation*, 104.

109   *"To resolve and resolve"*: Ibid., 106.

109   *Charlottesville and Scottsville*: Majewski, *A House Dividing*, 66–68.

109   *Lynchburg Daily Virginian*: Ibid., 132–133. See also Charles H. Ambler, "Cleavage Between Eastern and Western Virginia," *American Historical Review* 15, no. 4, July 1920, 773.

109   *Southern Planter*: Majewski, *A House Dividing*, 133.

110   *No central depot*: Ibid., 134.

110   *Half of the 12,000 troops*: George Edgar Turner, *Victory Rides the Rails: The Strategic Place of Railroads in the Civil War* (Indianapolis: Bobbs-Merrill, 1953), 282–286.

110   *Few rail lines connected; Baltimore and Ohio*: Johnston, "Virginia Railroads," 330.

110   *One of the causes of the Confederacy's defeat*: McCardell, *The Idea of a Southern Nation*, 127.

110   *The point of constructing*: Ulrich Bonnell Phillips, *The Slave Economy of the Old South*, ed. Eugene Genovese (Baton Rouge: Louisiana State University Press, 1968), 167.

110   *Populations in 1840*: George Tucker, *Progress of the United States in Population and Wealth in Fifty Years* (New York: Press of Hunt's Merchants' Magazine, 1843), 128.

110   *William Barton Rogers*: Clement Eaton, *The Mind of the Old South* (Baton Rouge: Louisiana State University Press, 1964), 141–142.

111   *Salt- and coal-producing state*: See Adams, *Old Dominion, Industrial Commonwealth*, 92–100.

111   *Tredegar Iron Works*: Charles Dew, *Ironmaker to the Confederacy: Joseph R. Anderson and the Tredegar Iron Works* (New Haven, Conn.: Yale University Press, 1966), 22, 2–3. See also "The Baltimore and Ohio Railroad," *Baltimore Gazette*, 30 April 1828, in Nevins, *American Press Opinion*, 76.

111   *"Emporium"*: Duc de la Rochefoucauld-Liancourt, *Travels in North America*, 2:21–22, in Avery Craven, *Soil Exhaustion as a Factor in the Agricultural History of Virginia and Maryland, 1606–1860* (Urbana: University of Illinois Press, 1926), 77.

111   *"Grass grown streets"*: Craven, *Soil Exhaustion*, 81.

111   *Demanded that the sleepy port secede*: Majewski, *A House Dividing*, 131–132.

112   *"The blessing of being located"*: Eudora Welty, quoted in C. Vann Woodward, "The Search for Southern Identity," in *The South and the Sectional*

Image, ed. Dewey W. Grantham, Jr. (New York: Harper and Row, 1967), 185.

112	*"I don't deny that the steamboat is destined"*: John Pendleton Kennedy, *Swallow Barn*, 59. Italics added.

Chapter 5

113	*"The soil is a gift"*: Jefferson to John Eppes, 24 June 1813, in Jefferson, *Writings*, ed. Merrill Peterson (New York: Library of America, 1984), 1282.

113	*Hume*: Drew McCoy, *The Elusive Republic: Political Economy in Jeffersonian America* (Chapel Hill: Published for the Institute of Early American History and Culture, Williamsburg, Va., by the University of North Carolina Press, 1980), 81.

113	*"Amass wealth"*: Benjamin Rush, "Thoughts upon the Mode of Education Proper in a Republic" [1786], in *Colonies to Nation, 1763–1789*, ed. Jack P. Greene (New York: McGraw Hill, 1967), 401.

113	*"The art of acquisition"*: John Danford, "Riches Valuable at All Times and to All Men": Hume and the 18th Century Debate on Commerce and Liberty," in *Liberty and American Experience in the Eighteenth Century*, ed. David Womersley (Indianapolis: Liberty Fund, 2006), 552–590.

114	*"Our citizens have had too full a taste"*: Jefferson to Washington, 15 March 1784, in Jefferson, *Writings*, ed. Peterson, 787ff.

114	*"While we have land to labour"*: Jefferson, *Notes on the State of Virginia*, ed. William Peden (Chapel Hill: University of North Carolina Press, 1995), Query 19, "Manufactures," 165. Italics added.

114	*"Manufactures of all sorts"*: David Bertelson, *The Lazy South* (New York: Oxford University Press, 1967), 135.

114	*"Most favourable to the freedom"*; *"contrariety of interests"*; *"the common error"*: "Report on Manufactures," in *The Papers of Alexander Hamilton*, ed. Harold C. Syrett, 26 vols. (New York: Columbia University Press, 1961–1987), 10:236, 258–293.

115	*"Having no manufactories of their own"*: Bertelson, *The Lazy South*, 86.

116	*"Not a sprig"*: Jefferson to his daughter, in James MacGregor Burns, *The Deadlock of Democracy* (Englewood Cliffs, N.J.: Prentice-Hall, 1963), 25.

116	*"Unable to afford themselves bread"*: Jefferson to William Crawford, 20 June 1816, in *The Writings of Thomas Jefferson*, ed. Paul Leicester Ford, 10 vols. (New York: G. P. Putnam's Sons, 1892–1899), 10:33–35.

116	*Enterprise, opportunity, creativity*: Richard Brown, *Modernization: The Transformation of American Life, 1600–1865* (New York: Hill and Wang, 1976), 170, 146.

116   *"I found my farms so much deranged"*: Jefferson to Jean Démeunier, 29
       April 1795, in Ford, ed., *Writings of Thomas Jefferson*, 7:14.

117   *"A dozen little boys"*: Jefferson to Jean Démeunier, 29 April 1795, in ibid.,
       7:14.

117   *"Of literally domesticating"*: McCoy, *The Elusive Republic*, 230.

117   *"We must now place"*; *"To be independent for the comforts"*: Jefferson to
       Benjamin Austin, 9 January 1816, in Ford, ed., *Writings of Thomas Jeffer-
       son*, 10:10.

117   *"Satanic"*; *"peaceable and agricultural nation"*; *"our first parents"*: Jefferson
       to William Short, 28 November 1814, in Jefferson, *Writings*, ed. Peterson,
       1357.

118   *New York a sewer; Virginia rational, moral, and "affectionate"*: Jefferson to
       William Short, 8 September 1823, in *The Writings of Thomas Jefferson*,
       eds. Andrew Lipscomb and Albert Bergh, 20 vols. (Washington, D.C.:
       Thomas Jefferson Memorial Association, 1904), 15:469.

118   *Two-thirds of his own slaves; "spoke often and anxiously"*: Irving Brant,
       James Madison, vol. 6, *Commander in Chief, 1812–1836* (Indianapolis:
       Bobbs-Merrill, 1961), 517.

118   *""No problem in political OEconomy"*: Madison to Jefferson, 19 June 1786,
       in *The Republic of Letters: The Correspondence Between Thomas Jefferson
       and James Madison, 1776–1826*, ed. James Morton Smith (New York: W.
       W. Norton, 1995), 1:424.

118   *Economic diversification; "have sunk most in their value"*: Madison to Pro-
       fessor Davis, 1832 [1833], in Madison, *Letters and Other Writings of James
       Madison*, eds. William C. Rives and Philip R. Fendall, 4 vols. (Philadel-
       phia: J. B. Lippincott, 1865), 4:262–263.

119   *"A manufacturing as well as an agricultural"*: Madison to Professor Davis, in
       ibid., 4:263–264.

119   *"Sagacity of individuals"*; *"certain limits"*: Madison to D. Lynch, 27 June
       1817, in ibid., 3:43.

119   *"Without public patronage"*: Madison to Clarkson Crolius, December
       1819, in ibid., 3:160.

119   *"Virginia has every element and every advantage"*: William Shade, *Democra-
       tizing the Old Dominion: Virginia and the Second Party System* (Char-
       lottesville: University of Virginia Press, 1996), 37.

120   *"It appears incumbent on Virginia"*: Richmond Enquirer, 27 November 1835.
       Italics added.

120   *"Soon lift up her head high"*: Richmond Enquirer, 22 December 1836.

120   *"We want more Banking Capital"*: Richmond Enquirer, 16 March 1837.

120   *"Suicidal neglect"*: Richmond Enquirer, 4 December 1835.

120   *"We must keep pace"*: "A Consumer," *Richmond Enquirer*, 10 December 1836.

120   *House of Delegates defeated a proposal*: Shade, *Democratizing the Old Dominion*, 41.

121   *Capital and credit in Virginia banks in 1840*: Howard Bodenhorn, *A History of Banking in Antebellum America* (Cambridge: Cambridge University Press, 2000), Table 2.2, 63–64.

121   *Decimal currency system*: "Notes on the Establishment of a Money Unit," April 1784, in Ford, ed., *Writings of Thomas Jefferson*, 3:446–447.

121   *Looked "forward to the abolition of all credit"*: Jefferson to A. Donald, 25 July 1787, in ibid., 4:414.

121   *Happy to reduce the national debt*: Jefferson to Thaddeus Kosciusko, 2 April 1802, in Peterson, ed., *Writings*, 1103.

121   *"Not only unconstitutional"; Giles and Brent: The Letters and Times of the Tylers*, ed. Lyon Tyler, 3 vols. (Richmond: Whittet and Shepperson, 1884), 1:274.

122   *"Our wise men flattered us"*: John Tyler to Dr. Curtis, 18 December 1818, in ibid., 1:303.

122   *"I believe the Bank"*: John Tyler to Littleton Waller Tazewell, 23 June 1834, in ibid., 1:499.

122   *"Money is the great corrupter"*: John Tyler to Dr. Curtis, 13 April 1832, in ibid., 1:439.

122   *"Let us expel the money-changers"*: 1816, in ibid., 1:412.

122   *"Represented a people"*: House of Delegates, quoted in *Richmond Enquirer*, 28 January 1836.

122   *"It would be better if we had no banks"*: Mr. Watkins, House of Delegates, quoted in *Richmond Enquirer*, 28 January 1836.

122   *"Just to be in fashion"*: Letter, "To the Farmers of Virginia," *Richmond Enquirer*, 27 February 1836.

122   *"It is always better to do too little"*: Letter from "A.B." in *Richmond Enquirer*, 6 February 1836.

123   *Every earthly blessing*: *Richmond Enquirer*, 3 April 1829.

123   *Before Virginia had banks*: *Richmond Enquirer*, 26 February 1829. See also *Richmond Enquirer*, 3 March 1829.

123   *"Land, slaves, and live stock"*: *Richmond Enquirer*, 26 June 1829.

123   *Entrepreneurs and speculators should be given no help*: *Richmond Enquirer*, 3 April 1829, 26 February 1829. See also *Richmond Enquirer*, 3 March 1829.

123   *"Fangs"*: "Against Banking," by "George Clinton," *Richmond Enquirer*, 21 February 1829.

123   *"An explosion must take place"*: *Richmond Enquirer*, 19 June 1829.

123   *"Offered a single syllable of argument"*: Richmond Enquirer, 26 June 1829.

123   *Mobilization of capital*: Lance Davis, "Capital Immobilities and Finance Capitalism," in *Purdue Faculty Papers in Economic History* (Homewood, Ill.: Richard D. Irwin, 1967), 593.

123   *Southern banks were not sources of industrial capital*: Eugene Genovese, *The Political Economy of Slavery: Studies in the Economy and Society of the Slave South* (New York: Vintage Books, 1967), 21–22.

123   *Putting their profits and capital*: Fred Bateman and Thomas Weiss, "Manufacturing in the Antebellum South," in *Research in Economic History*, ed. Paul Uselding (Greenwich, Conn.: JAI Press, 1976), 1:14, 39, 21.

123   *An excellent speculative risk*: Stanley Engerman, "The Effects of Slavery upon the Southern Economy: A Review of the Recent Debate," in *Explorations in Entrepreneurial History* 4, no. 2, Winter 1967, 92.

123   *Hardly economic masochists*: Fred Bateman and Thomas Weiss, *A Deplorable Scarcity: The Failure of Industrialization in the Slave Economy* (Chapel Hill: University of North Carolina Press, 1981), 163.

123   *The worth of the slaves; the value of the planters' land*: James L. Huston, *Calculating the Value of the Union: Slavery, Property Rights, and the Economic Origins of the Civil War* (Chapel Hill: University of North Carolina Press, 2003), 27–29.

123   *Far from being irrational precapitalists; fared well in their capitalist investments*: Anna J. Schwartz, 2006, correspondence with the author.

124   *"Rear of our neighbors"*: Henry Clay, 17 December 1829, in *Papers of Henry Clay*, ed. James F. Hopkins et al., 11 vols. (Lexington: University of Kentucky Press, 1959–1972), 8:142.

124   *"Clog . . . weighed down her enterprise"*: Allan Nevins, *Ordeal of the Union*, 2 vols. (New York: Charles Scribner's Sons, 1947), 1:462.

124   *Textile manufacturing*: Bateman and Weiss, *A Deplorable Scarcity*, 58–59.

124   *Neither Virginia nor Virginia slaveowners*: Bateman and Weiss, *A Deplorable Scarcity*, 163. See also Stanley Engerman, "A Reconsideration of Southern Economic Growth, 1770–1860," *Agricultural History* 49, 1975, 346.

124   *Not a cause of stagnation or retardation*: Bodenhorn, *A History of Banking in Antebellum America*, 110n.

124   *"Where enterprise leads"*: Joan Robinson, quoted in Bodenhorn, *A History of Banking in Antebellum America*, 86.

124   *Not as many entrepreneurs*: Ibid., 110n.

125   *Not necessarily an inefficient or unproductive system*: David Brion Davis, *Challenging the Boundaries of Slavery* (Cambridge: Harvard University Press, 2003), 77.

125   *Tredegar Iron Works*: Charles Dew, *Ironmaker to the Confederacy: Joseph R. Anderson and the Tredegar Iron Works* (New Haven, Conn.: Yale Univer-

sity Press, 1966), 22–28. See also Charles Dew, "Disciplining Slave Iron-workers in the Antebellum South," *American Historical Review* 79, no. 2, 1974; Kathleen Bruce, *Virginia Iron Manufacture in the Slave Era* (New York: Century, 1931).

125 *Slaves were more efficient than whites:* Batemen and Weiss, *A Deplorable Scarcity*, 32.

125 *Irish laborers:* Clement Eaton, *The Civilization of the Old South: Writings of Clement Eaton*, ed. Albert D. Kirwan (Lexington: University of Kentucky Press, 1968), 125.

125 *Hesitant entrepreneurs:* Bateman and Weiss, *A Deplorable Scarcity*, 37.

126 *White equality in a slave society:* Edmund Morgan, *American Slavery, American Freedom: The Ordeal of Colonial Virginia* (New York: W. W. Norton, 1975), 380–381.

126 *"Constant whirl and deafening roar":* Ellen Randolph Coolidge to Thomas Jefferson, 1 August 1825, in *The Family Letters of Thomas Jefferson*, eds. Edwin Betts and James Bear (Charlottesville: University of Virginia Press, 1995), 456.

126 *"Trooping to their prisons"; "degraded population":* "A Virginian," "One Day of a Foot Tour in Connecticut," *Southern Literary Messenger*, 14 June 1858, quoted in John Hope Franklin, *A Southern Odyssey: Travelers in the Antebellum North* (Baton Rouge: Louisiana State University Press, 1976), 48.

127 *To greet President Andrew Jackson:* Laurence Gross, *The Course of Industrial Decline: The Boott Cotton Mills of Lowell, Massachusetts, 1835–1955* (Baltimore: Johns Hopkins University Press, 1993), 19.

127 *Dickens visit to Lowell in 1842:* Charles Dickens, *American Notes and Pictures from Italy* [1842] (Oxford: Oxford University Press, 1997), 66–70.

127 *Maximum efficiency:* Richard Brown, *Modernization: The Transformation of American Life* (New York: Hill and Wang, 1976), 128.

127 *Supervisors who received bonuses:* Joseph W. Lipchitz, "The Golden Age," in *When Cotton was King*, ed. Arthur Eno (Lowell: Lowell Historical Society, 1976), 94.

128 *Sarah Bagley:* Gross, *The Course of Industrial Decline*, 21.

128 *Schools . . . established by the citizens:* Lipchitz, "The Golden Age," 95.

128 *"An industrious, sober":* Gross, *The Course of Industrial Decline*, 10–11. Italics added.

128 *Crushed workers' sense of importance:* Ibid., 12. See also Charles Sellers, *The Market Revolution: Jacksonian America, 1815–1846* (New York: Oxford University Press, 1991), 289.

128 *"UNION IS POWER"; Massachusetts legislature:* James MacGregor Burns, *The Vineyard of Liberty* (New York: Vintage, 1982), 399.

128   *White female slaves:* The Journals and Miscellaneous Notebooks of Ralph
       Waldo Emerson, ed. Merton M. Sealts (Cambridge: Harvard University
       Press, 1973), 102–103.

128   *"In a state little better":* Avery Craven, *Civil War in the Making, 1815–1860*
       (Baton Rouge: Louisiana State University Press, 1959), 15.

128   *Moral stewardship:* Ibid., 12.

129   *Fear of want:* Ibid., 15.

129   *"Brute force"; "as from bees":* Jefferson to William Johnson, 12 June 1823,
       in Ford, ed., *Writings of Thomas Jefferson,* 10:226.

129   *Lived as well as many free workers:* Jefferson to William Short, 8 Septem-
       ber 1823, in Lipscomb and Bergh, eds., *Writings of Thomas Jefferson,*
       15:469.

129   *"Moral features of Virginia"; "in every respect":* Madison to Robert Walsh,
       2 March 1819, in Madison, *Letters and Other Writings,* eds. Rives and
       Fendall, 3:122.

129   *"Cunning device":* Robert E. Shalhope, *John Taylor of Caroline: Pastoral
       Republican* (Columbia: University of South Carolina Press, 1980), 192,
       203, 171.

129   *Abel Upshur:* Claude Hampton Hall, *Abel Parker Upshur, Conservative
       Virginian, 1790–1844* (Madison: State Historical Society of Wisconsin,
       1963), 76–77.

129   *"Much more cruel and exacting":* George Fitzhugh, "Southern Thought,"
       in *De Bow's Review,* 1857, 339.

129   *"Vampire capitalist class"; "sooner subject his child":* George Fitzhugh, *Can-
       nibals All!* [1859], ed. C. Vann Woodward (Cambridge: Harvard Univer-
       sity Press, 1960), xxv, 109.

130   *"To die in the highway":* George Fitzhugh, *Sociology for the South, or the
       Failure of Free Society* (Richmond: A. Morris, 1854), 233.

130   *"It has been confidently alleged":* Morris Birkbeck, *Notes on a Journey in
       America from the Coast of Virginia to the Territory of Illinois* [1818] (New
       York: Augustus M. Kelley, 1971), 21–23.

130   *"Starved & rickety":* Jefferson to Pierre Samuel Du Pont de Nemours, 31
       December 1815, in *Correspondence Between Thomas Jefferson and Pierre
       Samuel Du Pont de Nemours, 1798–1817* (Boston: Houghton Mifflin,
       1930), 73.

130   *"Most distinguishing characteristic":* James Kirke Paulding, *Slavery in the
       United States* (New York: Harper and Brothers, 1836), 88.

130   *"His sufferings are less than those of the free laborer"; "and even more mis-
       chievous"; "all the advantages of the slave system":* Orestes Brownson, "The
       Laboring Classes," *Boston Quarterly Review* 3 (Boston: Benjamin H.
       Greene, 1840), 368–370.

131   *John Locke:* Morgan, *American Slavery, American Freedom,* 381.

131   *"Rooms wherein eight and ten members":* C. Vann Woodward, *Tom Watson: Agrarian Rebel* (New York: Macmillan, 1938), 225.

132   *"Evils"; "We are now basking":* Letter from "Gloucester," *Richmond Enquirer,* 7 January 1836. See also letter from "A Voice in the Country," *Richmond Enquirer,* 21 January 1836.

132   *Private, personal pursuit of leisure:* See Bertelson, *The Lazy South,* 242.

132   *"Poor on principle":* Proceedings and Debates of the Virginia State Convention of 1829–1830 (Richmond: Samuel Shepherd, 1830), 324.

Chapter 6

133   *"The most ambitious":* Marshall to Joseph Story, 13 July 1821, in "Story-Marshall Correspondence," ed. Charles Warren, *William and Mary Quarterly,* 2nd ser., vol. 21, January 1941, 13–14.

133   *"Twistifications":* Jefferson to Madison, 25 May 1810, in *The Republic of Letters: The Correspondence Between Thomas Jefferson and James Madison, 1776–1826,* ed. James Morton Smith (New York: W. W. Norton, 1995), 3:1632.

133   *"Base prostitution"; "personal malice":* Jefferson to John Tyler, 26 May 1810, in *The Writings of Thomas Jefferson,* ed. Paul Leicester Ford, 10 vols. (New York: G. P. Putnam's Sons, 1892–1899), 9:276.

133   *"Despotic branch":* Jefferson to Abigail Adams, 11 September 1804, in ibid., 8:311n.

133   *"Subtle corps of sappers":* Jefferson to Thomas Ritchie, 25 December 1820, in Jefferson, *Writings,* ed. Merrill Peterson (New York: Library of America, 1984), 1446. Italics added.

134   *"A mere thing of wax"; "They may twist":* Jefferson to Judge Spencer Roane, 6 September 1819, in ibid., 1426.

134   *"Will be utterly to destroy"; "like a delinquent individual":* Jonathan Elliot, ed., *The Debates in the Several State Conventions on the Adoption of the Federal Constitution* (Philadelphia: J. B. Lippincott, 1937), 3:524, 521, 527.

134   *"This government is not a Virginian":* Ibid., 3:55.

134   *"Not a Virginian but an American":* William Wirt Henry, *Patrick Henry: Life, Correspondence and Speeches* (New York: 1891), 1:222.

135   *"Ropes and chains of consolidation":* Elliot, ed., *Debates,* 3:54. Italics added.

135   *"Sip sorrow":* Ibid., 3:156.

135   *"No fellow-feeling":* Ibid., 3:29–34, 3:589–590.

135   *"State attachments and state importance":* Irving Brant, *James Madison,* vol. 3, *Father of the Constitution, 1787–1800* (Indianapolis: Bobbs-Merrill, 1950), 93. Italics added.

135   *"Have they not power to provide . . . ?"*: Elliot, ed., *Debates*, 3:590.

135   *"The most sacred laws"*: *The Records of the Federal Convention of 1787*, ed. Max Farrand (New Haven, Conn.: Yale University Press, 1986), 2:221–223.

136   *"An irresistible bias"*: Elliot, ed., *Debates*, 3:258–259, 617. Italics added.

136   *"Never entered into any American breast"*: Ibid., 3:621–622.

136   *"In all cases whatsoever"*; *"Kingly prerogative"*: Madison to Washington, 16 April 1787, in Madison, *Writings*, ed. Jack N. Rakove (New York: Library of America, 1999), 81. Italics added.

136   *"Check to the centrifugal Force"*: 8 June 1787, in Farrand, ed., *Records of the Federal Convention*, 1:171–172.

136   *"Thirteen sovereignties"*: Washington to Madison, 5 November 1786, in Washington, *Writings*, ed. John Rhodehamel (New York: Library of America, 1997), 622.

137   *"Steady, unfaltering mind"*: John Quincy Adams, *The Lives of James Madison and James Monroe* (Buffalo, N.Y.: George Derby, 1850), 48.

137   *"The business is in the most ticklish state"*: Madison to Washington, 13 June 1788, in *The Writings of James Madison*, ed. Gaillard Hunt, 9 vols. (New York: G. P. Putnam's Sons, 1900–1910), 5:179.

137   *"A consolidation of the states"*: "Consolidation," *National Gazette*, 5 December 1791, in Madison, *Writings*, ed. Rakove, 499.

137   *"To protect the Southern States"*: Madison to Jefferson, 16 April 1781, in ibid., 14. Italics added.

138   *Veto had survived*: See Madison to Jefferson, 24 October 1787, in ibid., 148.

138   *Marbury v. Madison*: James MacGregor Burns, *The Vineyard of Liberty* (New York: Vintage, 1982), 187–189.

139   *"On the validity of an act"*: Richard Ellis, "The Path Not Taken: Virginia and the Supreme Court," in *Virginia and the Constitution*, eds. A. E. Dick Howard and Melvin Urofsky (Charlottesville: Virginia Commission on the Bicentennial of the United States Constitution: Center for Public Service, University of Virginia, 1992), 33.

139   *Discretion to decide*: "Draft of the Kentucky Resolutions," October 1798, in Jefferson, *Writings*, ed. Peterson, 449.

139   *"Was never intended"*: Madison, "Observations on Jefferson's Draft," 1788, in *Papers of James Madison*, eds. Robert Allen Rutland and Charles F. Hobson (Charlottesville: University of Virginia Press, 1977), 11:293.

139   *"In a Government whose vital principle"*: Madison to Jefferson, 4 June 1810, in Smith, ed., *Republic of Letters*, 3:1734.

140   *"Keep the states within their proper limits"*: Madison to Jefferson, 24 October 1787, in ibid., 1:500.

140   *"I dread the ruin"*: Elliot, ed., *Debates*, 3:528–529.

141   *"Remain in full force"*: Jean Edward Smith, *John Marshall: Definer of a Nation* (New York: Henry Holt, 1996), 428.

142   *Reaction in the North*: Anonymous, "Judge Spencer Roane of Virginia: Champion of States' Rights, Foe of John Marshall," *Harvard Law Review* 66, no. 7, May 1953, 1252.

142   *"Has roused the sleeping spirit"*: Marshall to Joseph Story, 24 March 1819, in *Papers of John Marshall*, ed. Herbert Johnson (Chapel Hill: University of North Carolina Press for the Omohundro Institute of Early American History and Culture, 1947–2006), 8:280.

143   *Running a political machine*: William E. Dodd, "Chief Justice Marshall and Virginia, 1813–1821," *American Historical Review* 12, no. 4, July 1907, 777.

143   *Sociable, good-tempered, even jocular*: *Richmond Enquirer*, 17 September 1822.

143   *Overthrow the Constitution*: Johnson, ed., *Papers of John Marshall*, 8:285, editor's note.

143   *Supreme Court seemed to have appropriated*: Judge Spencer Roane, "Hampden" letters, no. 1, 11 June 1819, in *Richmond Enquirer*.

143   *"Great and general distress"*: Judge Spencer Roane to James Barbour, 16 February 1819, in "Letters of Spencer Roane, 1788–1822," *Bulletin of the New York Public Library* 10, no. 3, March 1906, 172.

143   *Acquiesced in its operations*: Madison to Charles Ingersoll, 25 June 1831, in Madison, *Letters and Other Writings of James Madison*, eds. William C. Rives and Philip R. Fendall, 4 vols. (Philadelphia: J. B. Lippincott, 1865), 4:183–187. See also Drew McCoy, *Last of the Fathers: James Madison and the Republican Legacy* (Cambridge: Cambridge University Press, 1989), 81–82.

143   *Roane on "necessary and proper"*: Jesse Carpenter, *The South as a Conscious Minority, 1789–1861* (New York: New York University Press, 1930), 53.

144   *"As venal and oppressive"*: Jefferson to Charles Hammond, 18 August 1821, in *The Writings of Thomas Jefferson*, eds. Andrew Lipscomb and Albert Bergh, 20 vols. (Washington, D.C.: Thomas Jefferson Memorial Association, 1904), 15:332.

144   *"An opinion is huddled up"*: Jefferson to Thomas Ritchie, 25 December 1820, in Ford, ed., *Writings of Thomas Jefferson*, 10:171.

144   *"Ingenuity"; "a limited into an unlimited"*: Madison to Judge Spencer Roane, 2 September 1819, in Hunt, ed., *Writings of James Madison*, 8:447–452.

144   *"Broad & pliant"*: Madison to Judge Spencer Roane, 2 September 1819, in ibid., 8:450.

144   *"A most serious hurricane"*: Marshall to Bushrod Washington, 17 June 1819, in Johnson, ed., *Papers of John Marshall*, 8:316–317.

144   *"Too palpably absurd"*: Marshall to Joseph Story, 27 May 1819, in ibid., 8:314.

144   *More aroused*: Marshall to Bushrod Washington, 17 June 1819, in ibid., 8:316–317.

144   *"Reinstate that miserable confederation"*: "A Friend of the Constitution," No. 1, 30 June 1819, in ibid., 8:318.

145   *"It is not rational to suppose"*: Marshall, 20 June 1788, in Elliot, ed., *Debates*, 3:555–556.

146   *Cohens v. Virginia decision*: Johnson, ed., *Papers of John Marshall*, 9:113–146.

146   *The exclusive right to judge*: K. R. Constantine Gutzman, "Old Dominion, New Republic: Making Virginia Republican, 1776–1840," Ph.D. dissertation (University of Virginia, 1999), 402.

146   *"Whole attack"; "re-establishment of a league"*: Marshall to Joseph Story, 13 July 1821, in Johnson, ed., *Papers of John Marshall*, 9:179.

146   *"Ashamed"*: Jefferson to John Taylor, 14 February 1821, quoted in Warren, ed., "Story-Marshall Correspondence," 6.

146   *Noiselessly advanced; rouse themselves from their apathy*: Jefferson to Charles Hammond, 18 August 1821, in Lipscomb and Bergh, eds., *Writings of Thomas Jefferson*, 15:331–332.

147   *"Should uplift his arm"*: Jefferson to Thomas Ritchie, 25 December 1820, in Jefferson, *Writings*, ed. Peterson, 1446.

147   *"The states must shield themselves"*: Jefferson to Archibald Thweat, 19 January 1821, in Ford, ed., *Writings of Thomas Jefferson*, 10:184. Italics added.

147   *"Until the shoe shall pinch"*: Jefferson to Nathaniel Macon, 20 October 1821, in ibid., 10:193–194n.

147   *"Unelected by, and independent of"*: Jefferson to Judge Spencer Roane, 6 September 1819, in Jefferson, *Writings*, ed. Peterson, 1426.

147   *"I know of no safe depository"*: Jefferson to William Jarvis, 28 September 1820, in Ford, ed., *Writings of Thomas Jefferson*, 10:161.

147   *Limiting all judges*: Jefferson to James Pleasants, 26 December 1821, in ibid., 10:198.

147   *"The abuse of a trust"*: Madison to Jefferson, 27 June 1823, in Smith, ed., *Republic of Letters*, 3:1869–1870.

148   *Madison later pardoned him*: *United States v. Peters*, in Ellis, "The Path Not Taken," 34.

148   *"Sound arguments"*: Madison to Judge Spencer Roane, 6 May 1821, in Smith, ed., *Republic of Letters*, 3:1870–1873, enclosure in letter to Jefferson.

148   *"Jefferson and Madison hang back too much"*: Judge Spencer Roane to
        Archibald Thweat, 24 December 1821, in Anonymous, "Judge Spencer
        Roane of Virginia: Champion of States' Rights, Foe of John Marshall," 1257.

Chapter 7

149   *"The earth belongs to the living"*; *"No society can make a perpetual constitution"*:
        Jefferson to Madison, 6 September 1789, in *The Republic of Letters: The Cor-*
        respondence Between Thomas Jefferson and James Madison, 1776–1826, ed.
        James Morton Smith (New York: W. W. Norton, 1995), 1:635.

149   *Continuity between generations*: Madison to Jefferson, 4 February 1790, in
        ibid., 1:651.

149   *"Experiments are of too ticklish a nature"*: Madison, *Federalist* No. 49.

149   *Cutting off of heads*: Jefferson to Diodati, 3 August 1789, in *Papers of*
        Thomas Jefferson, ed. Julian P. Boyd et al. (Princeton, N.J.: Princeton
        University Press: 1950–2005), 15:325.

150   *"I like a little rebellion"*: Jefferson to Abigail Adams, 22 February 1787, in
        Jefferson, *Writings*, ed. Merrill Peterson (New York: Library of America,
        1984), 890.

150   *"Some men look at constitutions"*: Jefferson to Samuel Kercheval, 12 July
        1816, in ibid., 1401–1402.

151   *"Capital defects"*; *"new and unexperienced"*: Jefferson, *Notes on the State of*
        Virginia, ed. William Peden (Chapel Hill: University of North Carolina
        Press, 1995), Query 13, "Constitution," 118.

151   *Self-governing townships*: Jefferson to Kercheval, 12 July 1816, in Jefferson,
        Writings, ed. Peterson, 1399.

151   *"An elective despotism"*: Jefferson, *Notes on the State of Virginia*, ed. Peden,
        Query 13, "Constitution," 120.

151   *"Bad" constitution*: Madison to Caleb Wallace, 23 August 1785, in *The*
        Mind of the Founder: Sources of the Political Thought of James Madison, ed.
        Marvin Meyers (Hanover, N.H.: University Press of New England for
        Brandeis University Press, 1981), 28.

152   *Two easy remedies*: Meyers, ed., *Mind of the Founder*, 30ff.

152   *Men could not be bound by laws*: Irving Brant, *James Madison*, vol. 6, *Com-*
        mander in Chief, 1812–1836 (Indianapolis: Bobbs-Merrill, 1961), 462.

152   *Population west of the Blue Ridge*: William W. Freehling, *The Road to Dis-*
        union: Secessionists at Bay, 1776–1854 (New York: Oxford University
        Press, 1990), 170.

152   *Twice as many representatives*: Brant, *James Madison: Commander in Chief*,
        6:462.

152   *"Instituted for the soil"*: Jefferson to John Taylor, 28 May 1816, in *The Writings of Thomas Jefferson*, ed. Paul Leicester Ford, 10 vols. (New York: G. P. Putnam's Sons, 1892–1899), 10:30.

152   *"Usurpation of the minority"*: Jefferson to James Pleasants, 19 April 1824, printed in the *Richmond Enquirer*, 27 April 1824, in William G. Shade, *Democratizing the Old Dominion: Virginia and the Second Party System, 1824–1861* (Charlottesville: University of Virginia Press, 1996), 60.

153   *"The dead have no rights"*: Jefferson to Samuel Kercheval, 12 July 1816, in Jefferson, *Writings*, ed. Peterson, 1402.

154   *Assembly rejected their calls*: Shade, *Democratizing the Old Dominion*, 57.

154   *"And not the rich"*: Jefferson to Samuel Kercheval, 12 July 1816, in Jefferson, *Writings*, ed. Peterson, 1400.

155   *"The rottenness of our state institutions"*: Shade, *Democratizing the Old Dominion*, 61.

155   *"Defects" be repaired*: Richmond Enquirer, 2 October 1816.

155   *"Responsible and accountable public servants"*: Letter to the editor from "Videt," *Richmond Enquirer*, 3 March 1829.

155   *"Old nobility of France"*; *"healthy and happy"*: Niles' Register, 31 October 1829. Italics added.

155   *James and Dolley Madison*: Joanne Gatewood, "Richmond During the Virginia Constitutional Convention," *Virginia Magazine of History and Biography* 84, 1976, 304n.

155   *"Countenance & manners"*: Thomas Greene (Richmond attorney), in ibid., 296.

156   *Reformers from west of the Blue Ridge*: Merrill Peterson, ed., *Democracy, Liberty, and Property: The State Constitutional Conventions of the 1820s* (Indianapolis: Bobbs-Merrill, 1966), 274.

156   *"The spectacle of so many"*: Richmond Enquirer, 6 October 1829.

156   *Virginia constitutional convention*: See Peterson, ed., *Democracy, Liberty, and Property*; Shade, *Democratizing the Old Dominion*; Dickson Bruce, *The Rhetoric of Conservatism: The Virginia Convention of 1829–30 and the Conservative Tradition in the South* (San Marino, Calif.: Huntington Library, 1982); Robert P. Sutton, *Revolution to Secession: Constitution Making in the Old Dominion* (Charlottesville: University of Virginia Press, 1989); David L. Pulliam, *The Constitutional Conventions of Virginia from the Foundation of the Commonwealth to the Present Time* (Richmond, 1901).

157   *"Great Apostle"*; *"spirit of reform"*: Proceedings and Debates of the Virginia State Convention of 1829–30 (Richmond: Samuel Shepherd, for Ritchie and Cook, 1830), 57.

157   *"Every principle for which we contend"*: Peterson, ed., *Democracy, Liberty, and Property*, 273.

157   *"Idea of making Chinese shoes"*: Proceedings and Debates of the Virginia State Convention, 389.

157   *A Tidewater county*: Peterson, ed., *Democracy, Liberty, and Property*, 273–274.

157   *"For one noble Lord"*: Proceedings and Debates of the Virginia State Convention, 390. Italics added.

157   *Virginia's backwardness*: Ibid., 651.

157   *Plowing the ocean*: Ibid., 372.

157   *"I prefer residence"*: Ibid., 386. Italics added.

157   *"The bosom of the Ancient Dominion"*: Ibid., 352–353.

158   *Power "from the people"*: Sutton, Revolution to Secession, 83.

158   *"There exists not the slightest danger"; distinguish between civil liberty*: Proceedings and Debates of the Virginia State Convention, 96–97.

158   *"Perpetual constitution"*: Jefferson to Madison, 6 September 1789, in Smith, ed., *Republic of Letters*, 1:635.

158   *"Infinite caution"*: Edmund Burke, *Reflections on the Revolution in France* [1790], ed. Conor Cruise O'Brien (New York: Penguin, 1984), 152.

158   *"To pull down the whole venerated fabric"*: Proceedings and Debates of the Virginia State Convention, 335.

159   *"Never had any taste"; "very small"*: Ibid., 532. Italics added.

159   *"And that our constitution remain unchangeable"*: Ibid., 320. Italics added.

159   *"Lust of innovation"*: Ibid., 492.

159   *"We are not struck down"*: Ibid., 533.

159   *"The moment you quit the land"*: Ibid., 430.

159   *"Instability of popular elections"*: Ibid., 532.

159   *"Monstrous tyranny"*: Ibid., 313.

159   *The yeoman became a lord*: See Philip Nicholas, in ibid., 366.

159   *"Obliged to depend"*: Proceedings and Debates of the Virginia State Convention, 158.

160   *"Only educated people should vote"*: Hugh Blair Grigsby, Diary, 4 January 1828, Grigsby Family Papers, Virginia Historical Society. Italics added.

160   *"I would not live under King Numbers"*: Proceedings and Debates of the Virginia State Convention, 321.

160   *Believer in social hierarchy*: Edmund Burke, "Thoughts on French Affairs" [1791], in *Further Reflections on the Revolution in France*, ed. Daniel Ritchie (Indianapolis: Liberty Fund, 1992), 211–212.

160   *"Monstrous fiction"*: Burke, *Reflections on the Revolution in France*, ed. O'Brien, 124, 191.

160   *Any alarming proposals*: Claude Hall, *Abel Parker Upshur* (Madison: University of Wisconsin Press, 1964), 44.

160 *"Principle in the law of nature"*: Proceedings and Debates of the Virginia State Convention, 66.

161 *The very idea of society;* *"Take away all protection"*: Ibid., 71.

161 *Greatest stake:* Ibid., 66.

161 *"Let us boldly take the bull by the horns"*: Ibid., 73.

161 *Suffrage ceased to be tied; "axe":* Abel Upshur to Beverley Tucker, 13 March 1843, in William W. Freehling, *The Reintegration of American History: Slavery and the Civil War* (New York: Oxford University Press, 1994), 126.

161 *"Fully equal to the most meritorious of the other sex":* Proceedings and Debates of the Virginia State Convention, 400.

161 *"Despotism":* Shade, *Democratizing the Old Dominion,* 67.

161 *"Let it be once openly avowed":* Avery Craven, *The Growth of Southern Nationalism, 1848–1861* (Baton Rouge: Louisiana State University Press, 1953), 17.

161 *"Fraternal feelings":* Proceedings and Debates of the Virginia State Convention, 312.

162 *"Despotism growing out of anarchy":* Madison to John Brown, 15 October 1788, "Remarks on Mr. Jefferson's Draught of a Constitution," in Meyers, ed., *Mind of the Founder,* 37.

162 *Delegates rushed from their seats:* The Writings of James Madison, ed. Gaillard Hunt, 9 vols. (New York: G. P. Putnam's Sons, 1900–1910), 9:358n.

162 *"Low and weak":* Ralph Ketchum, *James Madison, A Biography* (Charlottesville: University of Virginia Press, 1991), 639.

163 *Based exclusively on the white population:* Madison, 24 October 1829, in *Proceedings and Debates of the Virginia State Convention,* 39.

163 *"Fatuity":* Brant, *James Madison: Commander in Chief,* 6:463.

163 *Others ridiculed the idea:* Hugh Blair Grigsby, Diary at Virginia Convention, October 1829, Grigsby Family Papers, Virginia Historical Society.

163 *Deny that black people existed:* Madison, Speech in the Virginia Constitutional Convention, 2 December 1829, in Hunt, ed., *Writings of James Madison,* 9:362.

163 *Provide an effective safeguard:* Ibid., 9:361.

164 *"Spirit of compromise":* Ibid., 9:364. See also Brant, *James Madison: Commander in Chief,* 6:466; Robin L. Einhorn, *American Taxation, American Slavery* (Chicago: University of Chicago Press, 2006), 251–255.

164 *"In proportion as slavery prevails":* Notes for *National Gazette* essays, in *Papers of James Madison,* eds. Robert Rutland and Thomas Mason (Charlottesville: University of Virginia Press, 1983), 14:160.

164 *"Throws the power much more":* Ibid., 14:160 and 163–164.

165   *Property qualifications for voting*: Willi Paul Adams, *The First American Constitutions: Republican Ideology and the Making of the State Constitutions in the Revolutionary Era*, Rita and Robert Kimber, trans. (Chapel Hill: University of North Carolina Press for the Institute of Early American History and Culture, 1980), ch. 9, "Property."

165   *"Too little acquainted"*: John Adams to James Sullivan, 26 May 1776, in *Papers of John Adams*, ed. Robert Taylor et al. (Cambridge: Belknap Press of Harvard University Press, 1977–), 4:208–212.

165   *Madison's essay on "Property"*: "Property," 29 March 1792, *National Gazette*, in Madison, *Writings*, ed. Jack N. Rakove (New York: Library of America, 1999), 515–517. On other aspects of Madison's political and economic agenda in the *National Gazette*, see Paul Rahe, *Republics Ancient and Modern*, vol. 2, *Inventions of Prudence* (Chapel Hill: University of North Carolina Press, 1994), 61–62. See also Susan Dunn, *Jefferson's Second Revolution: The Election Crisis of 1800 and the Triumph of Republicanism* (Boston: Houghton Mifflin, 2004).

166   *"That the majority may not sufficiently respect"*: Madison, Speech in the Virginia Constitutional Convention, 2 December 1829, in Hunt, ed., *Writings of James Madison*, 9:361.

166   *"Ever more firmly bound"*: Drew McCoy, *Last of the Fathers: James Madison and the Republican Legacy* (New York: Cambridge University Press, 1989), 236.

166   *"An abortion"*: Madison to C. J. Ingersoll, 8 January 1830, in Madison, *Letters and Other Writings of James Madison*, eds. William C. Rives and Philip R. Fendall, 4 vols. (Philadelphia: J. B. Lippincott, 1865), 4:57.

166   *"The Convention is now arrived"*: Madison, Speech in the Virginia State Convention, 2 December 1829, in Madison, *Letters and Other Writings*, eds. Rives and Fendall, 4:54.

166   *"Whose defeat"*: Douglass Adair, ed., "James Madison's Autobiography," *William and Mary Quarterly*, 3rd ser., vol. 2, 1945, 208.

166   *Madison surrendered to them*: Brant, *James Madison: Commander in Chief*, 6:467.

167   *"But this is Theory"*: Madison, Speech in the Virginia Constitutional Convention, 2 December 1829, in Hunt, ed., *Writings of James Madison*, 9:359.

167   *"He voted with us and then against us"*: Brant, *James Madison: Commander in Chief*, 6:466.

167   *"Without regard"*: *Proceedings and Debates of the Virginia State Convention*, 539.

168   *"Introducing into a marriage contract"*: Ibid., 789.

168   *"The extension of the Right of suffrage"*: Gatewood, "Richmond During the Virginia Constitutional Convention," 328.

168   *Oppose taxation*: A county tax could be rescinded by the petition of twenty-four citizens. See Einhorn, *American Taxation, American Slavery*, 230.

168   *"Static solution"*: Peterson, ed., *Democracy, Liberty, and Property*, 278–279.

168   *"We reached home"*: Madison to Monroe, 21 January 1830, in Brant, *James Madison: Commander in Chief*, 6:466.

169   *"Very much a compound of compromising ingredients"*: Madison to Professor Long, 30 March 1830, in McCoy, *Last of the Fathers*, 249.

169   *"Evidence of the capacity of men"*: Madison to Lafayette, 1 February 1830, in Madison, *Letters and Other Writings*, eds. Rives and Fendall, 4:59.

169   *"No political body"*: *Proceedings and Debates of the Virginia State Convention*, 715.

169   *"Forcible separation"*: Ibid., 253.

169   *"Dismemberment"*: Ibid., 148.

169   *"I tell you sir"*; *"Civil war will be the result"*: Ibid., 692.

Chapter 8

171   *Few delegates had questioned*: *The Records of the Federal Convention of 1787*, ed. Max Farrand (New Haven, Conn.: Yale University Press, 1986), 2:625.

171   *"By thirteen heads"*: Washington to James Warren, 7 October 1785, in Washington, *Writings*, ed. John Rhodehamel (New York: Library of America, 1997), 592.

171   *"In an exceeding ill humor"*; *Mason's principal objection*: Madison to Jefferson, 24 October 1787, in Madison, *Writings*, ed. Jack N. Rakove (New York: Library of America, 1999), 153.

171   *"Extravagant and preposterous"*: Washington to Lafayette, 28 April 1788, in Washington, *Writings*, ed. Rhodehamel, 677.

172   *Right to tax both exports and imports*: Madison to Washington, 16 April 1787, in Madison, *Writings*, ed. Rakove, 81.

172   *"Indivisible"*: Madison, 15 September 1787, in Farrand, ed., *Records of the Federal Convention*, 2:625.

172   *Two-thirds vote*; *Maryland and Georgia*: Farrand, ed., *Records of the Federal Convention*, 2:631.

172   *Undersell all their foreign competitors*: "Report on Manufactures" [1791], in Alexander Hamilton, *Writings*, ed. Joanne B. Freeman (New York: Library of America, 2001), 697.

172 *"To be expected"*: Madison to Richard Rush, 17 January 1829, in Madison, *Letters and Other Writings of James Madison*, eds. William C. Rives and Philip R. Fendall, 4 vols. (Philadelphia: J. B. Lippincott, 1865), 4:6.

172 *Tariffs might be considered unconstitutional*: See Madison to Richard Rush, 4 December 1820, in Madison, *Letters and Other Writings*, eds. Rives and Fendall, 3:195.

172 *"From measures which operate differently"*: Madison, "Parties," *National Gazette*, 23 January 1787, in Madison, *Writings*, ed. Rakove, 504.

173 *"Economical use of buttons"*: Madison, "Property," *National Gazette*, 29 March 1792, in ibid., 516.

173 *Ban on imports*: Donald R. Hickey, "American Trade Restrictions During the War of 1812," *Journal of American History* 68, no. 3, December 1981, 517–538.

173 *"No, I will buy where I can get"*; *"Opulence, whirling in coaches"*; Shylock: John Randolph, 16 January 1816, *Annals of Congress*, 14th Congress, vol. 29, 687–688.

173 *"We sell cheap"*: John Tyler, 1832, in *Letters and Times of the Tylers*, ed. Lyon G. Tyler, 3 vols. (Richmond: Whittet and Shepperson, 1884–1896), 1:435.

173 *"Every citizen should have an unrestricted right"*: George Tucker, *Political Economy for the People* (Philadelphia: C. Sherman and Son, 1859), 118. Italics added.

174 *"Act of tyranny and injustice"*: Ibid., 118.

174 *Unfortunately, there is little evidence*: Sidney Ratner, *The Tariff in American History* (New York: D. Van Nostrand, 1972), 82. See also F. W. Taussig, *The Tariff History of the United States* (New York: G. P. Putnam's Sons, 1931), 60–61.

174 *"Takes property from one man"*; *"enchanted notion"*: William Branch Giles, "Political Disquisitions on Raymond's *Elements of Political Economy*" [1825] in Giles, *Political Miscellanies* (Richmond, 1830), 39.

174 *One vote from the Virginia delegation*: Joseph Johnson from northwestern Virginia: See Raymond Dingledine, "The Political Career of William Cabell Rives," Ph.D. dissertation (University of Virginia, 1947), 72. See also *Annals of Congress*, 18th Cong., 1st sess., 1467–1468.

174 *General Assembly . . . passed resolutions*: Irving Brant, *James Madison*, vol. 6, *Commander in Chief, 1812–1836* (Indianapolis: Bobbs-Merrill, 1961), 469.

175 *"There is an end put, at one stroke"*: Washington to Charles Mynn Thruston, 10 August 1794, in Washington, *Writings*, ed. Rhodehamel, 874.

176   *"Involve a power to tax it"*: Madison to Cabell, 18 September 1828, in *The Writings of James Madison*, ed. Gaillard Hunt, 9 vols. (New York: G. P. Putnam's Sons, 1900–1910), 9:316–340.

176   *"Mr. Madison has chosen"*: *Richmond Enquirer*, 13 March 1829.

176   *"The day of prophets"*: *Richmond Enquirer*, 3 January 1829, 16 February 1828.

176   *"Too far-fetched"*: *Richmond Enquirer*, 13 March 1829.

177   *"Strength and solidarity"*: John C. Calhoun, "Speech on the Bonus Bill," 4 February 1819, in *The Papers of John C. Calhoun*, ed. Robert Meriwether, 28 vols. (Columbia: University of South Carolina Press, 1959), 1:401.

177   *Were assaulting the economic viability*: Lacy K. Ford, Jr., "Inventing the Concurrent Majority: Madison, Calhoun, and the Problem of Majoritarianism in American Political Thought," *Journal of Southern History* 60, no. 1, February 1994, 43.

177   *"Not a particle"*: John C. Calhoun, "Speech Introducing Resolutions Declaratory of the Nature and Power of the Federal Government," 22 January 1833, in Ford, "Inventing the Concurrent Majority," 49.

178   *"Sacred duty"*; *"arrest the progress"*: John C. Calhoun, "Exposition and Protest" [19 December 1828], in *Union and Liberty: The Political Philosophy of John C. Calhoun*, ed. Ross M. Lence (Indianapolis: Liberty Fund, 1992), 361. See also Theodore R. Marmor, "Anti-Industrialism and the Old South: The Agrarian Perspective of John C. Calhoun," *Comparative Studies in Society and History* 9, no. 4, July 1967, 377–406.

178   *"Stands on clearer and stronger grounds"*: Calhoun, "Exposition and Protest," 352.

178   *"Intermediate point"*: John C. Calhoun, "Fort Hill Address," in Calhoun, *Union and Liberty*, ed. Lence, 371, 384.

178   *"Not a nation"*: John C. Calhoun, in Joyce Appleby, *Inheriting the Revolution: The First Generation of Americans* (Cambridge: Belknap Press of Harvard University Press, 2000), 242.

178   *"Preserve its liberty"*: Calhoun, "Exposition and Protest," 341.

179   *Virginia and Georgia*: Drew McCoy, *Last of the Fathers: James Madison and the Republican Legacy* (New York: Cambridge University Press, 1989), 120.

179   *"Certain definite powers"*; *"nullify of their own authority"*: Jefferson, "Draft of the Kentucky Resolutions," in Jefferson, *Writings*, ed. Merrill Peterson (New York: Library of America, 1984), 449, 453. Italics added. See also Adrienne Koch and Harry Ammon, "The Virginia and Kentucky Resolutions: An Episode in Jefferson's and Madison's Defense of Civil

Liberties," *William and Mary Quarterly*, 3rd ser., vol. 5, no. 2, April 1948, 157.

180   *"Rampart"*: Jefferson, "Draft of the Kentucky Resolutions," 453–454.

180   *"Compact to which the states"*; *"in duty bound to interpose"*: "Virginia Resolutions Against the Alien and Sedition Acts," 21 December 1798, in Madison, *Writings*, ed. Rakove, 589–591. Italics added.

180   *"Right of freely examining"*: Ibid., 590.

180   *"Deadly lethargy"*: Madison, "The Alien and Sedition Acts: Address of the General Assembly," 23 January 1799, in Adrienne Koch, *The American Enlightenment* (New York: G. Braziller, 1965), 515.

180   *"Necessarily drive these States"*: "Draft of the Kentucky Resolutions," October 1798, in Jefferson, *Writings*, ed. Peterson, 454.

180   *"Every spirit should be ready"*: Jefferson to William Munford, 18 June 1799, in Koch and Ammon, "The Virginia and Kentucky Resolutions," 152. Italics added.

180   *Ten state legislatures*: Sean Wilentz, *The Rise of American Democracy: Jefferson to Lincoln* (New York: W. W. Norton, 2005), 80.

181   *States in the plural*: See Madison to Nicholas Trist, 23 December 1832, in Madison, *Writings*, ed. Rakove, 862; see also Madison, "Notes on Nullification," 1835–1836, in *The Mind of the Founder: Sources of the Political Thought of James Madison*, ed. Marvin Meyers (Hanover, N.H.: University Press of New England for Brandeis University Press, 1981), 419ff.

181   *Election of 1800*: Richard E. Ellis, *The Union at Risk: Jacksonian Democracy, States' Rights, and the Nullification Crisis* (New York: Oxford University Press, 1987), 4.

182   *"The alarming assumptions of power"*: Robert Hayne to Madison, 5 March 1830, in McCoy, *Last of the Fathers*, 140.

182   *He responded to Hayne's letter*: See McCoy, *Last of the Fathers*, 141.

183   *"Their original rights"*: Madison to Edward Everett, 28 August 1830, in Madison, *Writings*, ed. Rakove, 843–851.

183   *"Mr. Madison is himself again"*: Marshall to Joseph Story, 15 October 1830, in Brant, *James Madison: Commander in Chief*, 6:484.

183   *"They have rallied only with the more zeal"*: John Townsend to Madison, October 1831, in ibid., 6:487–488.

183   *"Fatal legacies"*: *Richmond Whig*, in Merrill Peterson, *The Jefferson Image in the American Mind* (New York: Oxford University Press, 1960), 51.

183   *"Take care of me"*: Jefferson to Madison, 17 February 1826, in *The Republic of Letters: The Correspondence Between Thomas Jefferson and James Madison, 1776–1826*, ed. James Morton Smith (New York: W. W. Norton, 1995), 3:1967.

184   *"Great genius"*: Madison to Nicholas Trist, May 1832, in Madison, *Writings*, ed. Rakove, 860.

184   *"Take the linch-pins"*: Madison to Cabell, 16 September 1831, in Madison, *Letters and Other Writings*, eds. Rives and Fendall, 4:196.

184   *"Anarchical"*: Madison to Nicholas Trist, December 1831, in ibid., 4:206.

184   *"Disastrous consequences"*: Madison to Henry Clay, 22 March 1832, in ibid., 4:217.

184   *"Is more painful"*: Madison to Nicholas Trist, May 1832, in Madison, *Writings*, ed. Rakove, 860.

184   *Ordinance of Nullification*: Brant, *James Madison: Commander in Chief*, 6:493.

185   *"One people"*; *"because each secession"*; *"in the slightest"*: Proclamation quoted in Andrew Jackson to Thomas Ritchie, 1837, in Peterson, *The Jefferson Image in the American Mind*, 61n. *Italics added.*

185   *Jackson's proclamation*: Merrill Peterson, *Olive Branch and Sword: The Compromise of 1833* (Baton Rouge: Louisiana State University Press, 1982), 47.

185   *"Collision" course*: Martin Van Buren to Andrew Jackson, 27 December 1832 and 10 February 1833, in William W. Freehling, *The Road to Disunion, Secessionists at Bay, 1776–1854* (New York: Oxford University Press, 1990), 281.

185   *"If the majority be permitted"*: Ellis, *Union at Risk*, 128.

185   *Letter . . . to Judge Spencer Roane*: Brant, *James Madison: Commander in Chief*, 6:496.

185   *"Fabric raised by a youthful Hercules"*; *"mere name of Madison"*: Ibid., 6:495–496.

186   *"Are these men mad . . . ?"*: Richmond Enquirer, 8 May 1832.

186   *"Could as well have been written by Madison"*: Brant, *James Madison: Commander in Chief*, 6:496.

186   *Only one senator*: Tyler, ed., *Letters and Times of the Tylers*, 1:461.

186   *"Unnecessary and unseasonable"*: Ibid., 1:462.

186   *"Feverish excitement"*: Madison to Henry Clay, 2 April 1833, in Madison, *Letters and Other Writings*, eds. Rives and Fendall, 4:567.

187   *"No government of human device"*: Madison, "Majority Governments," 1833, in Meyers, ed., *Mind of the Founder*, 416.

187   *"Constitutional" majority but not a "numerical" majority*: Ibid.

187   *"Parricides"*; *"We will cherish"*: Richmond Enquirer, 2 October 1835.

188   *"Finest talents"*; *"the relief would be but little felt"*; *"misled"*: Madison to Davis, 1832 [1833], in Madison, *Letters and Other Writings*, ed. Rives and Fendall, 4:259–261. *Italics added.*

188   *"Our country must be"*: Madison to Davis, 1832 [1833], in ibid., 4:261–264.

188   *"Is it not preferable . . . ?"*: Madison to Thomas Dew, 23 February 1833, in Hunt, ed., *Writings of James Madison*, 9:500.

188   *"It is not slave labour"*: Thomas Dew, "Abolition of Negro Slavery" [1832], in Drew Gilpin Faust, ed., *The Ideology of Slavery: Proslavery Thought in the Antebellum South, 1830–1860* (Baton Rouge: Louisiana State University Press, 1981), 76.

189   *"Secession becomes the rightful remedy"*: Brant, *James Madison: Commander in Chief*, 6:509.

189   *"What more dangerous"*; *"putting powder under the Constitution"*; *"The first and most obvious step"*: Madison to Edward Coles, 29 August 1834, in Madison, *Letters and Other Writings*, eds. Rives and Fendall, 4:357.

190   *"A more beautiful China vase"*: Madison to Edward Coles, 29 August 1834, in ibid., 4:357.

Chapter 9

191   *"The unexpected evil"*: 22 August 1835, in *Letters and Times of the Tylers*, ed. Lyon G. Tyler, 3 vols. (Richmond: Whittet and Shepperson, 1884–1896), 1:574. See also Clement Eaton, "Censorship of the Southern Mails," *American Historical Review* 48, no. 2, January 1943, 266–280.

191   *The crisis had begun*: William W. Freehling, *Prelude to Civil War: The Nullification Controversy in South Carolina, 1816–1836* (New York: Harper and Row, 1965), 340ff.

191   *"Prepare their own ample means"*: *Richmond Enquirer*, 6 October 1835. Italics added.

192   *Editor of the Philadelphia National Gazette*: *National Gazette*, 8 August, 22 August 1836, in Eaton, "Censorship of the Southern Mails," 274.

192   *"Great excitement and fermentation"*: John Quincy Adams, *Memoirs*, ed. Charles Francis Adams (Philadelphia: J. B. Lippincott, 1874–1877), 9:257.

192   *Would ultimately be counterproductive*: See William W. Freehling, *The Road to Disunion: Secessionists at Bay, 1776–1854* (New York: Oxford University Press, 1990), 343.

192   *"Keeping the peddle soft"*: *Richmond Whig*, 24 July 1835, in Eaton, "Censorship of the Southern Mails," 273.

192   *"Undisguised purpose"*: "Governor's Message," *Richmond Enquirer*, 8 December 1835.

193   *"A society has sprung up"*: David Brion Davis, ed., *The Fear of Conspiracy: Images of Un-American Subversion from the Revolution to the Present* (Ithaca, N.Y.: Cornell University Press, 1971), 414–442. Italics added.

193   *It possessed reason*: See James L. Huston, *Calculating the Value of the Union: Slavery, Property Rights, and the Economic Origins of the Civil War* (Chapel Hill: University of North Carolina Press, 2003), 44.

193   *"There is no clause"*: *The Debates in the Several State Conventions on the Adoption of the Federal Constitution*, ed. Jonathan Elliot, 5 vols. (Philadelphia: J. B. Lippincott, 1937), 3:269–270. Italics added.

193   *South Carolina and Georgia*: Madison to Robert Walsh, 27 November 1819, in Gaillard Hunt, ed., *The Writings of James Madison*, 9 vols. (New York: G. P. Putnam's Sons, 1900–1910), 9:2.

194   *"Inflammatory papers"*: Freehling, *Prelude to Civil War*, 342; Eaton, "Censorship of the Southern Mails," 269–270.

194   *"A higher one"*: Freehling, *Prelude to Civil War*, 342.

195   *"Numerous, zealous"*: John Calhoun to Armistead Burt, 28 June 1836, in Eaton, "Censorship of the Southern Mails," 272.

195   *Calhoun's bill*: Freehling, *The Road to Disunion*, 310. See also Kevin R. Kemper, "'We Shall Not Submit': How the Twenty-Fourth Congress and the Jackson Administration Attempted and Failed to Stop the Circulation of Abolitionist Publications Through the United States Post Office During the Late 1830s," unpublished paper, University of Missouri, Columbia, 2004; "Bill from the Select Committee on the Circulation of Incendiary Publications, in the Senate, February 4, 1836," in *The Papers of John C. Calhoun, 1835–1837*, ed. Clyde N. Wilson (Columbia: University of South Carolina Press, 1959), 13:67–69.

195   *Requiring postmasters to notify*: Eaton, "Censorship of the Southern Mails," 269.

195   *"To suppress to the utmost"*: William Shade, *Democratizing the Old Dominion: Virginia and the Second Party System, 1824–1861* (Charlottesville: University of Virginia Press, 1996), 212.

195   *"A full scope to reason"*: Jefferson to David Humphreys, 18 March 1789, in *Papers of Thomas Jefferson*, ed. Julian P. Boyd et al. (Princeton, N.J.: Princeton University Press: 1950–2005), 14:677.

195   *"Were it left to me"*: Jefferson to Edward Carrington, 16 January 1787, in Jefferson, *Writings*, ed. Merrill Peterson (New York: Library of America, 1984), 880.

196   *William Grayson*: Elliot, ed., *Debates*, 3:435.

196   *"Ought not our constituents"*: "Report on House of Delegates," *Richmond Enquirer*, 23 January 1836. Italics added.

196   *"I exhort every Virginian"*: *Richmond Enquirer*, 7 January 1836.

196   *"A dreadful conflict"*: "Report on House of Delegates," *Richmond Enquirer*, 14 January 1836.

196   *"Has it come to this?"*: *Richmond Enquirer*, 7 January 1836.

197   *"Why bring this subject here"*: John McFaul, "Expediency vs. Morality: Jacksonian Politics and Slavery," *Journal of American History* 62, no. 1, June 1975, 37.

197   *Wide margin*: The vote in favor of the gag rule was 117 to 68. In the Senate the vote was 34 to 6.

197   *"Treason to the South"*: Freehling, *The Road to Disunion*, 332.

198   *"Shall be received by this House"*: Shade, *Democratizing the Old Dominion*, 217.

198   *"A slave mart"*: John Tyler, 10 February 1835, in Tyler, ed., *Letters and Times of the Tylers*, 1:571.

198   *"Was not competent to interfere"*: John Tyler, 7 January 1836, reported in *Richmond Enquirer*, 21 January 1836.

198   *Its own gag bill*: Freehling, *The Road to Disunion*, 325.

198   *"Modern abolition"*: Ingersoll's account of conversation with Madison, May 1836, in Irving Brant, *James Madison*, vol. 6, *Commander in Chief, 1812–1836* (Indianapolis: Bobbs-Merrill, 1961), 517. Italics added.

199   *"The worst effect of the abolition excitement"*: Madison's conversation with Ingersoll, May 1836, in ibid., 517. Italics added.

199   *"It is painful to observe"; "what madness"; "insidiously revive"*: Madison to Henry Clay, June 1833, in Madison, *Letters and Other Writings of James Madison*, eds. William C. Rives and Philip R. Fendall, 4 vols. (Philadelphia: J. B. Lippincott, 1865), 4:301.

199   *"To excite a panic"*: *Richmond Enquirer*, 7 January 1836.

199   *"We had hoped that our governor"*: *Richmond Enquirer*, 19 December 1835.

200   *The only enemies; "Their leaders are hunted"*: *Richmond Enquirer*, 6 October 1835.

200   *"Anti-Tappan"*: Ibid.

200   *"More potent than all their philanthropy"*: *Richmond Enquirer*, 2 January 1836.

200   *"Cassandra"*: *Richmond Enquirer*, 17 November 1835.

201   *"Domestic institutions"*: Shade, *Democratizing the Old Dominion*, 217.

201   *"An especial duty"*: Millard Fillmore, "First Annual Message," 1851.

201   *"Very mal-apropos"*: Washington to David Stuart, 28 March 1790, in Washington, *Writings*, ed. John Rhodehamel (New York: Library of America, 1997), 758.

201   *South had a virtual veto*: Barry R. Weingast, "Political Stability and Civil War: Institutions, Commitment, and American Democracy," in *Analytic Narratives*, ed. Robert H. Bates et al. (Princeton, N.J.: Princeton University Press, 1988), 148–193, 166, and Table 4.3, 168.

202   *"Had no rights"*: *Dred Scott v. Sanford*, 60 U.S. 393 (1857).

202   *Abolitionists failed to achieve any reforms*: David Brion Davis, *Challenging the Boundaries of Slavery* (Cambridge: Harvard University Press, 2003), 75. See also Huston, *Calculating the Value of the Union*, 27, 29.

202   *"The fanatics of the North"*: *Richmond Enquirer*, 18 February 1840, in Eaton, "Censorship of the Southern Mails," 279.

202   *"Efforts of abolitionists"*: George Tucker, *Progress of the United States in Population and Wealth in Fifty Years* (New York: Press of Hunt's Merchants' Magazine, 1843), 108–109.

203   *"A forbidden topic with us"*: Allan Nevins, *Ordeal of the Union*, 8 vols. (New York: Scribner, 1947–1971), 1:500.

203   *"Never disturbed them"*; *"after all, it is what we say"*: Lincoln, "Cooper Union Speech," 27 February 1860, in *The Life and Writings of Abraham Lincoln*, ed. Philip van Doren Stern (New York: Modern Library, 1940), 590. Italics added.

204   *"Secretly"*: Beverley Tucker of Virginia, *The Partisan Leader* [1836] (New York: Rudd and Carleton, 1861), vi.

204   *"Perverted" to destroy liberty*: Ibid., 323.

204   *"To plunder and desolate"*; *"northern cupidity"*: Ibid., 40.

204   *"The benefits . . . the burdens"*: Ibid., 206.

204   *"The whole South should have become impregnated"*: Ibid., vii.

204   *"Glorious Southern Confederacy"*: Beverley Tucker, quoted in Susan H. Godson et al., *The College of William and Mary: A History*, 2 vols. (Williamsburg, Va.: King and Queen Press, 1993), 255.

206   *"The great southern and northern"*: *The Records of the Federal Convention of 1787*, ed. Max Farrand (New Haven, Conn.: Yale University Press, 1986), 14 July 1787, 2:10.

206   *"Instead of attempting to blend"*: Ibid., 13 July 1787, 1:604.

206   *"Would they not, most unquestionably"*: Washington to David Stuart, 28 March 1790, in Washington, *Writings*, ed. Rhodehamel, 757.

206   *Toyed with secession*: See Peter Onuf, "The Origins of American Sectionalism," in *All Over the Map: Rethinking American Regions*, by Edward Ayers et al. (Baltimore: Johns Hopkins University Press, 1996), 25.

206   *"An insolent northern majority"*: Madison to Henry Lee, 2 April 1790, in Richard Beeman, *The Old Dominion and the New Nation* (Lexington: University Press of Kentucky, 1972), 77.

206   *John Tyler expressed regret*: John Tyler to St. George Tucker, 10 July 1795, in ibid., 142.

207   *"Sever ourselves"*: Jefferson to Madison, 23 August 1799, in *The Republic of Letters: The Correspondence Between Thomas Jefferson and James Madi-*

son, 1776–1826, ed. James Morton Smith (New York: W. W. Norton, 1995), 2:1119.

207   *"When the sole alternatives":* Jefferson to William Branch Giles, 26 December 1825, in Jefferson, *Writings,* ed. Peterson, 1510.

207   *"The hand of bastardy":* Hugh Blair Grigsby, *The History of the Virginia Federal Convention of 1788* [1855] (Richmond: Virginia Historical Society, 1890), 1:18, 42n, 31.

207   *"Would open a hundred new questions":* Ibid., 1:23.

208   *Irresistible:* Avery Craven, *The Growth of Southern Nationalism, 1848–1861* (Baton Rouge: Louisiana State University Press, 1953), 385.

208   *"Virginia will not act hastily":* Hugh Blair Grigsby to Henry S. Randall, 18 March 1861, in *The Correspondence Between Henry Stephens Randall and Hugh Blair Grigsby, 1856–1861* (Berkeley: University of California Press, 1952), 181.

208   *"Brought such a happy order":* Madison to Edward Everett, 14 November 1831, Everett Papers, quoted in Drew McCoy, *Last of the Fathers: James Madison and the Republican Legacy* (New York: Cambridge University Press, 1989), 133.

208   *"The essential difference"; "the claim to secede":* Madison to Nicholas Trist, 23 December 1833, in Madison, *Writings,* ed. Jack N. Rakove (New York: Library of America, 1999), 862–863.

209   *"Advice to My Country":* 1834, in ibid., 866.

209   *Those who made the false, insidious claim:* Professor Ralph Lerner, 23 April 2006, correspondence with the author.

212   *Protégé and biographer:* William C. Rives, *History of the Life and Times of James Madison,* 3 vols. (Boston: Little, Brown, 1859).

212   *"Turn back to wander":* Robert Gunderson, "William C. Rives and the 'Old Gentlemen's Convention,'" *Journal of Southern History* 22, November 1956, 475.

212   *"Of which she may be considered":* Raymond Dingledine, "The Political Career of William Cabell Rives," Ph.D. dissertation (University of Virginia, 1947), 109.

212   *Voted 90 to 45: Proceedings of the Virginia State Convention of 1861,* ed. George H. Reese, 4 vols. (Richmond: Virginia State Library, Historical Publications Division, 1965), 4:144.

Epilogue

213   *"I am seventy-six years old in genuine Jefferson Democracy":* Ronald Heinemann, *Depression and New Deal in Virginia* (Charlottesville: University of Virginia Press, 1983), 138.

213   *"Holding fast to sound Jeffersonian principles"*: Carter Glass, 1 November 1932, in Rixey Smith and Norman Beasley, *Carter Glass* (New York: Longmans, Green, 1939), 319.

214   *"Frankenstein"*: Robert F. Hunter, "Virginia and the New Deal," in *The New Deal: The State and Local Levels*, ed. John Braeman (Columbus: University of Ohio Press, 1975), 124.

214   *"Is there no responsibility"*: *Lynchburg News*, 1935, in Heinemann, *Depression and New Deal in Virginia*, 140.

214   *"Work out their own problems"*: Smith and Beasley, *Carter Glass*, 410. See also A. Cash Koeniger, "Carter Glass and the National Recovery Administration," *South Atlantic Quarterly* 74, no. 3 (Summer 1975), 349–364.

214   *A moderately progressive governor*: See Raymond Pulley, *Old Virginia Restored: An Interpretation of the Progressive Impulse, 1870–1930* (Charlottesville: University of Virginia Press, 1968), 180ff.

214   *"I do not believe a government can borrow"*: Harry Byrd, quoted in George Brown Tindall, *The Emergence of the New South, 1913–1945* (Baton Rouge: Louisiana State University Press, 1967), 612.

214   *"Great public works and social service"*: Hunter, "Virginia and the New Deal," 113.

214   *He opposed . . . virtually all the legislation*: Ibid., 109.

214   *"Children are supposed to look after"*: Ronald Heinemann, *Harry Byrd of Virginia* (Charlottesville: University of Virginia Press, 1996), 155.

215   *"Betrayed the Jeffersonian doctrine"*: "Address of Senator Carter Glass," in *University of Virginia Institute of Public Affairs Proceedings*, 1929, quoted in Tindall, *Emergence of the New South*, 358.

215   *"Unequivocally on the side"*: Robert Gooch, "Reconciling Jeffersonian Principles with the New Deal," *Southwestern Social Science Quarterly* 16, June 1935, 1.

215   *"The savior of the deeper ideals"*: Franklin D. Roosevelt, "Is There a Jefferson on the Horizon?" *New York Evening World*, 3 December 1925, in *The Roosevelt Reader*, ed. Basil Rauch (New York: Rinehart, 1957), 44–47.

215   *Earth belongs to the living"; "with the progress of the human mind"*: Jefferson to James Madison, 6 September 1789; and Jefferson to Samuel Kercheval, 12 July 1816, in Jefferson, *Writings*, ed. Merrill Peterson (New York: Library of America, 1984), 959, 1401.

216   *"Blue buzzard"*: in Smith and Beasley, *Carter Glass*, 361.

216   *"Bird of prey"*: Carter Glass to Walter Lippmann, 1933, in Koeniger, "Carter Glass and the National Recovery Administration," 358.

216   *"Were we to depend on Washington"*: Smith and Beasley, *Carter Glass*, 392.

216   *Report on Economic Conditions in the South*: See brandywinesources.com.

217   *Glass and Byrd waged war against the New Deal:* Heinemann, *Depression and New Deal in Virginia,* 187–188.

217   *"Worthy successors":* Agnes Rothery, *Virginia: The New Dominion* (New York: D. Appleton-Century, 1940), 31–32.

218   *Registration quizzes:* Andrew Buni, *The Negro in Virginia Politics, 1902–1965* (Charlottesville: University of Virginia Press, 1967), 124–125.

218   *No political voice:* Bruce J. Dierenfield, *Keeper of the Rules: Congressman Howard W. Smith of Virginia* (Charlottesville: University of Virginia Press, 1987), 54.

218   *"Hotbed of democracy":* V. O. Key, *Southern Politics in State and Nation* (New York: Alfred A. Knopf, 1949), 20.

218   *"Politics in the Old Dominion seemed so predictable":* Larry Sabato, *The Democratic Party Primary in Virginia Tantamount to Election No Longer* (Charlottesville: University of Virginia Press, 1977), 54.

218   *"The political soil":* Ellen Glasgow, "My Fellow Virginians," 1921, in *Ellen Glasgow's Reasonable Doubts: A Collection of Her Writings,* ed. Julius Rowan Raper (Baton Rouge: Louisiana State University Press, 1988), 57.

218   *"Remarkable for its negativism":* Heinemann, *Depression and New Deal in Virginia,* 159.

219   *Virginia finally agreed to appropriate money:* Hunter, "Virginia and the New Deal," 123–124.

219   *"VIRGINIA PROSPERS"; "Roosevelt couldn't possibly lose":* Turner Catledge, "Virginia Prospers; Roosevelt Strong," *New York Times,* 4 December 1935, 6.

219   *Hoover in 1928:* Heinemann, *Harry Byrd of Virginia,* 94.

220   *"I often think of those great Virginians":* *Lynchburg News,* 31 May 1961.

220   *"Not a dead star":* Glasgow, "My Fellow Virginians," 65.

220   *"Will be deplored by millions":* Heinemann, *Harry Byrd of Virginia,* 325.

221   *"Unwelcome and distasteful"; "gradually, calmly":* Ibid., 325–326.

221   *"Total resistance line":* Ibid., 337.

221   *"Massive resistance":* See James Ely, *The Crisis of Conservative Virginia: The Byrd Organization and the Politics of Massive Resistance* (Knoxville: University of Tennessee Press, 1976); Benjamin Muse, *Virginia's Massive Resistance* (Bloomington: Indiana University Press, 1961); J. Harvie Wilkinson, *Harry Byrd and the Changing Face of Virginia Politics, 1945–1966* (Charlottesville: University of Virginia Press, 1968).

221   *Kilpatrick:* Joseph J. Thorndike, "'The Sometimes Sordid Level of Race and Segregation': James J. Kilpatrick and the Virginia Campaign Against Brown," in *The Moderates' Dilemma: Massive Resistance to School Desegregation in Virginia,* ed. Matthew D. Lassiter and Andrew B. Lewis

(Charlottesville: University of Virginia Press, 1998). See also Heine-mann, *Harry Byrd of Virginia*, 332.

221 *"If Virginia surrenders"*: Heinemann, *Harry Byrd of Virginia*, 335.

221 *"This will keep us in the saddle"*: *Washington Post*, 19 June 1957, in Ely, *The Crisis of Conservative Virginia*, 90.

221 *"Despotic branch"*: Jefferson to Abigail Adams, 11 September 1804, in *The Writings of Thomas Jefferson*, ed. Paul Leicester Ford, 10 vols. (New York: G. P. Putnam's Sons, 1892–1899), 8:311n.

221 *"I am convinced . . . that the decision"*: Harry Byrd to Samuel M. Bemiss, 24 September 1956, in Ely, *The Crisis of Conservative Virginia*, 91.

222 *Manifesto presented by Smith*: Dierenfield, *Keeper of the Rules*, 148.

222 *"Destroying the amicable relations"*: *Congressional Record*, 84th Cong., 2nd sess., vol. 102, part 4, March 12, 1956 (Washington, D.C.: U.S. Govern-ment Printing Office, 1956), 4459–4460.

222 *Lindsay Almond*: Heinemann, *Harry Byrd of Virginia*, 342.

222 *Business leaders . . . began complaining*: Ibid., 346.

222 *Snail-like pace*: Ibid., 351.

222 *"I stand now"*: Ibid.

223 *"Gallant little county"*: Ibid., 390.

223 *"Pride in the fortitude"*: http://www.vcdh.virginia.edu/reHIST604/images/1961speecha.jpg.

223 *Longest filibuster in Senate history*: Heinemann, *Harry Byrd of Virginia*, 403.

223 *"It was in Virginia that we learned"*: *Congressional Record*, 20 May 1964, 11520–11522.

223 *Supreme Court's decision to reopen public schools*: See Griffin v. Board of Ed-ucation of Prince Edward County, 377 U.S. 218 (1964).

223 *"Tyrannical"*: Byrd joined other southerners to filibuster the bill, arguing that the bill represented "a monstrous grab for federal power . . . the worst legislation ever introduced." Heinemann, *Harry Byrd of Virginia*, 403.

224 *"I lived behind one of those schools"*: *New York Times*, 31 July 2005.

ACKNOWLEDGMENTS

I am deeply indebted to many generous colleagues and friends for their contributions to this project. Joyce Appleby inspired me with her pioneering work on the American Revolution and rescued me more than once from making errors about Virginia and Jefferson. Joseph J. Ellis made invaluable suggestions for my manuscript, encouraging me with his exhilarating enthusiasm. Peter Onuf offered excellent advice about Thomas Jefferson and slavery. Drew McCoy and Ralph Lerner shared with me their subtle understanding of James Madison. Anna J. Schwartz helpfully answered my economic questions. John Danford introduced me to the economic ideas of David Hume; and David Carrithers made many useful suggestions on Madison.

I owe special thanks to generous colleagues at Williams College: Robert Dalzell offered many perspicacious suggestions. Charles Dew was a penetrating reader of portions of the manuscript. Gary Jacobsohn once again advised me on constitutional questions; and Frederick Rudolph was a fount of knowledge on the subject of education.

Deep gratitude goes to Milton Djuric who tirelessly helped me research questions pertaining to Virginia during the New Deal and offered innumerable substantive and stylistic suggestions for the manuscript. My editor, Lara Heimert, cemented her reputation as a talented editor. And my agent, Ike Williams, contributed his insights and knowledge and energetically cheered me on.

I am also very grateful to the professional staffs at the State Library of Virginia, the Virginia Historical Society, and the Manuscripts Department of the University of Virginia Library who, time and again, helped me navigate the waters of their astounding collections.

Alison O'Grady, Walter Komorowski, Jo-Ann Irace, and Sandy Brooke at the Williams College Library, and Robin Keller, Donna Chenail, and my other friends in the Faculty Secretarial Office at Williams College all assisted me in this project. My student Matthew Ressiger aided me in compiling useful statistics on Virginia. And I am grateful to Thomas Kohut and William Wagner, Deans of Faculty at Williams College, for their collegial support for my research and my teaching.

My deepest appreciation goes to James MacGregor Burns, my infinite source of wisdom, patience, and love, who eagerly read and reread my manuscript, contributing his vast knowledge, always encouraging, energizing, and inspiring me with his Jeffersonian optimism and profound generosity of spirit.

Williamstown, Massachusetts, February 2007

INDEX

abolitionism, abolition of slavery:
abolition societies and, 203;
antislavery petitions and, 196–198;
antislavery propaganda and,
191–192, 194–196, 198–199, 203;
censorship and, 194–196; cost of,
47–48, 53; deportation and, 50;
"gag" resolution and, 197–198;
Jefferson, Thomas and, 42–43, 51;
Lincoln, Abraham and, 203–204;
Madison, James and, 59, 193;
secession and, 206–207; societies
for, 192; Union, preservation of and,
198; Virginia slavery debate of
1831–1832 and, 49–60;
Washington, George and, 49
Adams, Abigail, 150
Adams, Henry, 4, 63, 89
Adams, John, 5, 134, 179; education
and, 63, 69, 83; Election of 1800
and, 9, 181; First Continental
Congress (1774) and, 4; internal
improvements and, 87; Marshall,
John appointment and, 138; slavery
and, 201; Virginia, University of
and, 69
Adams, John Quincy, 11; abolitionism
and, 192, 197; internal

improvements and, 87, 98, 99; as
minister to Russia, 5; pro-slavery
arguments and, 59–60; slavery and,
33, 198, 201; Virginia presidential
monopoly and, 6; Virginia Ratifying
Convention (1788) and, 137
"Advice to My Country" (Madison),
209
Africa, 50, 57, 59
Agassiz, Louis, 63
"Agricola," 107
Agricultural Adjustment Act (1933),
216
Agricultural Society of Albemarle
County, 24, 25
agriculture: economic diversification
and, 114; industrialization and,
113–121, 123–124; knowledge of,
14; manufacturing and, 114–115;
rational farming and, 25; republican
virtue and, 24–25, 28; single-crop
farming and, 23–24; slavery and, 26;
time, meaning of and, 34–35;
Virginia, decline of and, 8, 12;
Virginia reliance of, 118; wealth
and, 26. *See also* soil exhaustion
Alabama, 10, 154
Alcott, Bronson, 73

Alexander, Mark, 169
Alien and Sedition Acts of 1798, 180,
    182, 221
Almond, Lindsay, 222
American Anti-Slavery Society, 192,
    203
American Colonization Society, 49, 59
The American Farmer, 25
American Philosophical Society, 82
American Revolution, 65, 134, 136;
    as ongoing process, 150; Virginia
    and, 4
"Amphictyon." *See* Roane, Spencer
Annapolis Convention (1785), 93
Anti-Federalists, Constitution, U. S.,
    ratification of and, 134–137, 148.
    See also Henry, Patrick; Mason,
    George
Arator (John Taylor of Caroline), 24
aristocracy, Virginia: economic decline
    of, 10; land, accessibility of and, 20;
    moral decline of, 10; public
    education and, 72; resistance to
    democratization, 158–161, 168;
    resistance to industrialization and,
    97, 99, 100, 119, 125–126, 131–132,
    205; slavery, defense of and, 14,
    80–81
Aristotle, 113
Articles of Confederation, 7, 96

Bagby, George, 105
Bagley, Sarah, 128
Baldwin, Joseph Glover, 42
Ball, Charles, 38
Baltimore and Ohio Railroad, 106,
    110
Bankhead, John, 219
banking: antibanking movement and,
    122–123; Bank of the United

States, 28, 96, 119, 121, 122;
    capital, mobilization of and,
    120–123; capital, scarcity of and,
    120–121; Constitution, U. S. and,
    122, 141–142; First Bank of the
    United States, rechartering and,
    122–123; Hamilton, Alexander and,
    121; Jefferson, Thomas and, 121; in
    Massachusetts, 121; Second Bank of
    the United States, 94, 96, 121–122;
    Second Bank of the United States,
    creation of and, 143; Second Bank
    of the United States, rechartering
    and, 56; Second Bank of the United
    States and, 141–142; states' rights
    and, 121; Supreme Court, U. S.
    and, 141–142; Virginia House of
    Delegates and, 121–122
Bank of the United States, 28, 96, 119,
    122
bankruptcy, land value and, 22–23
Barbour, James, 11, 75, 94, 201
Barbour, Philip, 11, 95, 100, 156, 158,
    201
Barry, William, 8
Bayly, Thomas, 157
Beauregard, Pierre, 84
Benton, Thomas Hart, 156
Berry, Henry, 52
Bertelson, David, 36
Beverley, Robert, 36
Biddle, Nicholas, 28
"Bill for the More General Diffusion of
    Knowledge" (Jefferson), 71–72
Bill of Rights, 137, 150, 179, 181
Binns, John Alexander, 24
Birkbeck, Morris, 40, 89, 129
blacks. *See* slavery; slaves
Blue Ridge Railroad tunnel, 125
Board of Public Works, 102–103

Bonus Bill of 1816, 94–97, 107, 176–178. *See also* internal improvements

Brent, Richard, 121–122

British Board of Trade, 115

Brown, John, 83–84

Brown, John Thompson, 52–53

Brown v. Board of Education, 220–221

Brown v. Board of Education Scholarship Program and Fund, 224

Brownson, Orestes, 130–131

Buchanan, James, 198, 201

Burke, Edmund, 158, 160

Byrd, Harry: *Brown v. Board of Education* and, 220–221; New Deal and, 214–217, 219; segregation and, 220–223

Byrd, William, 36

Cabell, Joseph, 57

Calhoun, John, 94, 173; antislavery propaganda and, 194–195; Bonus Bill of 1816 and, 177–178; internal improvements and, 100–101; nationalism of, 176; nullification and, 179, 183, 185, 221; secession and, 178; states' rights and, 108–109, 181; tariff wars and, 175, 176, 177–178; Virginia Constitutional Convention of 1829–1830 and, 156

California, 207

Cambridge, Mass., 2, 63

Campbell, William, 157

canals, 90–101, 104–107; Bonus Bill of 1816 and, 94–98; Erie Canal, 90–91, 98, 105, 107; Illinois and Michigan Canal, 105; James Canal, 104, 105, 106; Miami Canal, 105;

national building of, 104–105; Potomac Canal, 91–93, 104, 105, 106; railroads and, 106; Survey Bill (1824) and, 98–101; trade and, 91. *See also* internal improvements

Cannibals All! (Fitzhugh), 130

capitalism, 117; laissez-faire, 14; slavery and, 124. *See also* banking

censorship, 194–196, 203

Channing, William Ellery, 192

Chastellux, François Jean, Marquis de, 15, 31, 103–104

children: education and, 71, 73, 76; labor and, 131, 218; race-mixing and, 46; slavery and, 8, 45–47

Christianity, 68, 80

Civilian Conservation Corps (1933), 219

Civil Rights Act of 1964, 223

Civil War, U. S., 35, 55, 57, 84, 178; beginning of, 84, 212; *Dred Scott v. Sandford* and, 3

Clay, Henry, 42, 93; slavery and, 124, 199; tariff wars and, 173, 174, 176, 186

Clinton, De Witt, 72, 90, 91, 105

Clinton, George, 5

Clinton, George (pseudonym), 122–123

Cocke, John, 105

Cohen, Philip and Mendes, 145

Cohens v. Virginia, 145–146, 171

Coles, Edward, 26, 41–42, 189–190

Coles, Isaac, 66

College of South Carolina, 66

College of William and Mary, 57, 67–68, 78

colonization, 3, 43, 47, 57. *See also* deportation; slavery

Compromise Tariff Bill (1833), 186

Confederacy. *See* Confederate States of America

Confederate Provisional Congress, 3

Confederate States of America, 3; Virginia and, 55, 212

Connecticut, 61, 77

conscience, freedom of, 16

Constitution, U. S.: amendment of, 182–183, 194; banking and, 122, 141–142; Bill of Rights, 137, 150, 179, 181; Bonus Bill of 1816 and, 94, 95–96; censorship and, 195; education and, 69; Eleventh Amendment, 145; federal government vs. states and, 134–136; Federalist Party, Federalists and, 136; First Amendment, 179, 180, 195, 197; Fourteenth Amendment, 220; "general welfare" clause of, 88, 95, 97, 100; judicial review and, 139; Marshall, John and, 11, 133, 138; Missouri Compromise of 1820 and, 201–202; "necessary and proper" clause of, 142, 143, 144; nullification and, 190; ratification of, 134; state sovereignty and, 137, 141; states' rights and, 181; Supreme Court, U. S. interpretation of, 133–134, 143–144; tariff wars and, 172, 173–174, 175–176, 177; Tenth Amendment, 95–96, 137; veto power and, 136; Virginia Ratifying Convention (1788) and, 134–137

Constitutional Convention (1787): Henry, Patrick and, 135; internal improvements and, 96; slavery and Southern work ethic and, 37; Virginia and, 4

Constitutional Whig, 54, 55

Cooke, John Esten, 14, 156, 158, 170

Coolidge, Ellen Randolph, 12–14, 19, 42, 126

Coolidge, Joseph, 12–13

Coolidge, Thomas Jefferson, 66, 84, 88

Corbin, Francis, 38

Covington and Ohio Railroad, 109

Crawford, William, 5

Crozet, Claudius, 107

Cumberland Road, 98

Cumberland Road Act (1806), 87

Curtis, Josiah, 128

Custis, George Washington, 66

Daniel, Peter, 3, 196

Davis, Jefferson, 201

Davis, John, 195

De Bow, J. D. B., 108

De Bow's Review, 74, 78, 81, 82

debt, bankruptcy, and land value and, 27–28

Declaration of Independence, 4, 51

Declaration of Rights of 1776, 153

democracy: equality and, 17; Jefferson, Thomas and, 11, 151–152, 159; speech, freedom of and, 195. *See also* aristocracy

Democracy in America (Tocqueville), 33

Democratic Party, Democrats, 215, 218

deportation, 3, 43, 46–47, 50, 51; *See* colonization; slavery

Depression: *See* Great Depression

Dew, Charles B., 125

Dew, Thomas Roderick, 78; internal improvements and, 109; slavery, defense of by, 57–60; tariff wars and, 188–189

Dickens, Charles, 127

District of Columbia, 146; slavery in, 196–197; slave trade in, 198

Doddridge, Philip, 156, 157, 169

Dred Scott v. Sandford, 3, 201–202
Dwight, Timothy, 61, 64

economic diversification: agriculture
  and, 114; Hamilton, Alexander and,
  114, 137; Jefferson, Thomas and,
  113–114, 116–117; Madison, James
  and, 132; manufacturing and, 114,
  114–115; Virginia, decline of and,
  118–119; Washington, George and,
  114–115
education: *Brown v. Board of Education*
  and, 220–221; Constitution, U. S.
  and, 69; funding for, 9, 14, 71–77;
  government and, 72; importance of,
  65; Jefferson, Thomas and, 65,
  66–68, 71–72, 76; Madison, James
  and, 76; Missouri Compromise of
  1820 and, 66–67; national
  university and, 64–66; in North,
  61–63, 65, 77; primary, 71–77;
  property and, 160; public, 71–77;
  religion and, 68–69; segregation in,
  220–224; of slaves, 54–55, 76; social
  distinctions and, 74–75; state
  responsibility for, 75–76; suffrage
  and, 160; taxation and, 9, 14, 72,
  73–74, 128; universal, 72, 74;
  Virginia, decline of and, 9; Virginia,
  University of and, 1–2, 56, 62,
  68–71; of women, 76
Election of 1796, 5
Election of 1800, 9, 181
Election of 1816, 5–6
Election of 1820, 9
Election of 1824, 2
Eleventh Amendment, 145
Ellsworth, Oliver, 138
emancipation: compensated, 47–48,
  53; cost of, 45, 47–48; gradual, 54;

importance of, 3; Jefferson, Thomas
  and, 46–48; Virginia slavery debate
  of 1831–1832 and, 51–52
Emerson, Ralph Waldo, 63, 78, 81,
  128
emigration, 40–42, 91, 110
Enlightenment, 60, 68, 70;
  "reactionary," 78; Scottish, 66
entail, abolition of, 20, 153
Episcopal Church, 153
Eppes, Francis, 27, 56, 66, 67
Eppes, John, 113
equality, 126; democracy and, 17;
  Jefferson, Thomas and, 11, 17, 46;
  pro-slavery arguments and, 58;
  slaves and, 46–47
Erie Canal, 90, 98, 105, 107
Europe, cities in, 114; slavery in, 57
expatriation, 47, 50
"Exposition and Protest" (Calhoun),
  177, 183, 221

Fairfax's Devisee v. Hunter's Lessee,
  140–141
Farmer's Register, 25
farming. *See* agriculture; land; soil
  exhaustion
Faulkner, Charles J., 37, 52
Federal Aid Road Act (1916), 111
federal government: education and,
  72; Federalist Party, Federalists and,
  69, 116; internal improvements
  and, 85–88, 91, 94–98, 98–101,
  107; Jefferson, Thomas philosophy
  of, 5; Missouri Compromise of 1820
  and, 44; object of, 57; Republican
  Party, Republicans and, 116; slavery
  and, 200–202; Southern view of,
  44–45; states vs., 134–136; tariffs
  and, 171–172; taxation and, 97;

federal government (*continued*)
    trade, regulation of and, 171–172;
    Virginia's doubts about, 6
The Federalist, 95, 96, 162, 166, 167,
    176
Federalist Party, Federalists, 133, 181,
    215; Constitution, U. S. and, 136;
    federal government and, 69, 116;
    Virginia presidential monopoly and,
    5
federal judiciary. *See* Supreme Court,
    U. S.
Felton, Cornelius, 77
Fillmore, Millard, 201
First Amendment, 179, 180, 195, 197
First Continental Congress (1774), 4, 5
Fitzhugh, George: internal
    improvements and, 109; pro-slavery
    literature and, 78, 80, 81, 83;
    slavery, defense of by, 39; slavery
    and class conflict and, 129–130
Floyd, John, 11, 48, 49, 185; secession
    and, 189; Virginia slavery debate of
    1831–1832 and, 50–51
Force Bill (1833), 186
Fourteenth Amendment, 220
Franklin, Benjamin, 82, 93
freedom: of conscience, 16; Jefferson,
    Thomas and, 16; land and, 27; of
    press, 180; pro-slavery arguments
    and, 58, 81; of religion, 16, 153;
    right to, 3, 51–52; slavery and, 2; of
    speech, 180, 195–196; Virginia
    slavery debate of 1831–1832 and,
    51–52
Free Soil Party, 42
French Revolution, 2, 149
"A Friend to the Union," 144. *See also*
    Marshall, John
Fugitive Slave Act (1850), 207

Gallatin, Albert, 5, 97; internal
    improvements and, 86–87, 90,
    101
Garland, James, 196–197, 199–200
Garland, Samuel, 52
Garnett, James Mercer, 8, 78
Garrison, William Lloyd, 192
Genovese, Eugene D., 123
George, Walter, 222
George III, King, 42
Georgia, 48–49, 85, 172
Gholson, James, 52–54
Giles, William Branch, 11, 169;
    banking and, 121–122; limited
    government and, 103; slavery and,
    45; tariffs and, 174; Virginia
    Constitutional Convention of
    1829–1830 and, 156
Gilmer, Francis Walker, 69, 70
Glasgow, Ellen, 218
Glass, Carter, 213–215, 216, 217, 219,
    224
Gooch, Robert, 215
Goode, William, 53
Gore, Albert, Sr., 222
government. *See* federal government
Grayson, William, 39, 196
Great Britain, 28; Reform Act of 1832
    of, 56; slavery in, 57
Great Depression, 213, 216, 218. *See
    also* New Deal
Great Slavepower Conspiracy,
    202
Greeley, Horace, 8
Greene, Thomas, 168
Grigsby, Hugh Blair, 77, 109, 160;
    education and, 62, 73; secession
    and, 207, 208; Virginia
    Constitutional Convention of
    1829–1830 and, 156

Hamilton, Alexander, 69, 70; agriculture, importance of and, 114; banking and, 96, 121; consolidation and, 137; economic diversification and, 114; immigration policies of, 116; industrialization and, 115, 116, 117; internal improvements and, 86; modernization and, 115; tariff wars and, 172; wage-labor system and, 131; work ethic of, 38

Hammond, James Henry, 78

"Hampden," 143. See also Roane, Spencer

Hampden-Sydney College, 78, 108

happiness, 14, 205; indolence and, 32; pursuit of, 3, 16–17, 44, 58–59

Harrison, Benjamin, 92

Hartford Convention (1814–1815), 29

Hartz, Louis, 78

Harvard University, 63, 65, 67, 69, 77, 84, 88

Hayne, Robert, 182, 191

Heath, James, 78

Hemings, Sally, 3, 46

Henry, Patrick, 4, 11, 49, 148; Constitution, U. S., opposition to of, 134–137; slavery as evil and, 55

History and Present State of Virginia (Beverley), 36

Holcombe, James, 81

Holmes, George Frederick, 78, 80

Holmes, Oliver Wendell, 78

Hoover, Herbert, 219

Hopkins, George, 196

Hopkins, Mark, 73

hospitality, 15, 35, 125, 205

House of Representatives, U. S.: antislavery petitions and, 196–198, 201; Southern leverage in, 44–45

Hume, David, 113

Hunter, David, 140

Huston, James, 123

Illinois, 41–42

Illinois and Michigan Canal, 105

illiteracy, 9, 77. See also education

immigration, 205; Hamilton, Alexander and, 116; land value and, 21

Indiana, 90

indolence: happiness and, 32; Jefferson, Thomas and, 31–33; labor, value of and, 31, 32; slavery and, 31, 33, 34, 36–40; Southern youth and, 61–62; time, value of and, 32–33; wage-labor system and, 131; Washington, George and, 32–33

industrialization: agriculture and, 113, 115; Hamilton, Alexander and, 115, 116, 117, 137; Jefferson, Thomas and, 116–118, 119; North and, 12; slavery and, 124–125, 126–127; in Virginia, 9, 125–131; wage-slavery and, 126–131

internal improvements: Adams, John Quincy and, 87, 98; Bonus Bill of 1816 and, 94–97, 107, 111, 177; canals and, 90–101, 104–105; Constitution, U. S. and, 88, 95, 97, 100; Constitutional Convention (1787) and, 96; federal government and, 85–88, 94–98, 98–101, 107; funding for, 14; Jefferson, Thomas and, 85–88, 91–92, 97, 98, 111–112; Madison, James and, 85–88, 89, 91, 107; Monroe, James and, 98; national government and, 91; North and, 110; purpose of, 110; railroads and, 105–111; roads and, 14, 85–89, 91; states' rights and, 108–109;

internal improvements (*continued*)
   Survey Bill (1824) and, 96, 98–101;
   taxation and, 14; trade and, 104;
   turnpikes, 107; Washington, George
   and, 99, 111; West and, 98
Israel, 57

Jackson, Andrew, 127, 185; antislavery
   propaganda and, 194, 195; internal
   improvements and, 101;
   nullification and, 185
James Canal, 105, 106
Jefferson, Israel, 2
Jefferson, Martha Wayles Skelton, 18
Jefferson, Thomas, 4, 7, 8, 10, 11, 83;
   agrarian vision of, 5, 20, 27,
   111–112, 113, 132, 215;
   agricultural reform and, 23–26, 28;
   banking and, 121; biracial society
   and, 50; Bonus Bill of 1816 and,
   97; continual change and, 149–151,
   215; democracy and, 11, 151–152,
   159; economic diversification and,
   113–114, 116–117; education and,
   65, 66–68, 71–72, 73, 76; Election
   of 1800 and, 9; emancipation plan
   and, 46–48; equality and, 11, 17,
   46; financial problems of, 18, 23,
   27–28; happiness, pursuit of and, 3,
   16–17, 44, 58–59; indolence and,
   31–33; industrialization and,
   116–118, 119; internal
   improvements and, 85–88, 91–92,
   97, 98, 111–112; judicial tyranny
   and, 133–134, 143–144, 145, 146;
   Kentucky and Virginia Resolutions
   and, 179–187; labor, value of and,
   31; Lafayette, Marie Joseph Paul,
   Marquis de and, 1–3; legacy of,
   213, 215–216, 219, 220, 221, 223,
   224; Louisiana Purchase and, 20,
   45; *Marbury v. Madison* and,
   138–139; Marshall, John clash
   with, 133, 138–139, 143–144;
   master-slave relationship and,
   42–43; as minister to France, 2, 18;
   Missouri Compromise of 1820 and,
   43, 44, 66; Monticello, life at of,
   15–17, 18–19; nullification and,
   183; progress and, 113–114; public
   life of, 17–19; religious freedom
   and, 16, 153; retirement of, 17, 88;
   secession and, 29, 206–207;
   segregation and, 220; slave
   breeding and, 45–46; as slaveowner, 17; slavery and, 2–3, 37, 39,
   42–43, 46, 51, 55, 58–59; speech,
   freedom of and, 16, 195; states'
   rights and, 6; unalienable rights
   and, 3; Virginia, decline of and,
   28–29; Virginia, fleeing of and, 42;
   Virginia, University of and, 1–2,
   68–71, 83; Virginia Constitution,
   defects of and, 151; Virginia
   Constitutional Convention of
   1829–1830 and, 157, 158, 159;
   Virginia motto and, 31
Jesus Christ, slavery and, 52–53, 57
Johnson, Lyndon, 222
Judiciary Act of 1789, 140–141

Kanawha Republican, 75
Kansas, 207
Kefauver, Estes, 222
Kendall, Amos, 194
Kennedy, John Pendleton, 10, 35, 82,
   101, 112
Kentucky, 42
Kentucky and Virginia Resolutions,
   179–187, 180–182

Kercheval, Samuel, 150
Key, V. O., 218
Kilpatrick, James, 221
King, Rufus, 43
Knox, Alexander, 56

labor: child, 218; moral necessity to, 39; use of free, 40; value of, 31, 32; wage, 126–131
Lafayette, George Washington, 2, 65
Lafayette, Marie Joseph Paul, Marquis de, 49, 92, 169; ceremonial tour of United States of, 1–3; French Revolution and, 2; slavery and, 2, 3
land: accessibility of, 20, 216; agricultural reform and, 23–28; bankruptcy and, 22; debt and, 27–28; declining value of, 9, 18, 21–23, 118, 188; federal intervention in disputes over, 140; liberty and, 27; permanence and mystique of, 19, 21, 27, 29, 125, 132, 205; productivity of, 9; republican virtue and, 27, 29; slavery and, 45; theories of management of, 25; Virginia, decline of and, 9, 18, 21–23; vote, right to and, 20; Washington, George and, 21. See also agriculture; nostalgia; property; soil exhaustion
La Rochefoucauld-Liancourt, François, Duke de, 23
Larson, John Lauritz, 102–103
Lawrence, Abbott, 75
leadership: and Virginia, 4, 6, 11–12, 49–50, 55, 74–75, 108, 154, 159–160, 167, 189, 192, 209–211, 214–216, 222, 224
Lee, Henry, 206
Lee, Robert E., 63

Lee, Robert Edward "Roony," 63
Leigh, Benjamin Watkins, 10, 12, 160, 161, 195
Levasseur, Auguste, 2
Liberia, 49, 50
liberty. See freedom
Lincoln, Abraham, 42, 136; secession and, 70; slavery and, 203–204
literary associations, 78
Literary Fund, 72, 75
Liverpool, Lord (Robert Banks Jenkinson), 5
Locke, John, 131, 165
Longfellow, Henry Wadsworth, 78
Louisiana, 43, 48–49
Louisiana Purchase, 20, 45
Lowell, Mass., 127–128
Lowell Offering, 127
Loyalist Party, Loyalists, 140
Lynchburg Daily Virginian, 109
Lynchburg News, 214
Lytle, Andrew Nelson, 34, 35

Madison, Dolley, 155
Madison, James, 4, 11, 16, 38; agricultural reform and, 23, 26; antislavery propaganda and, 198–199; biracial society and, 50; Bonus Bill of 1816 and, 94–97, 107, 111; *Cohens v. Virginia* and, 145, 147–148; continual change and, 149–150; economic diversification and, 119, 132; education and, 72, 74–75, 76; financial problems of, 7, 28, 41; internal improvements and, 85–88, 89, 91, 107; judicial authority and, 145; Lafayette, Marquis de ceremonial tour and, 1, 3; majority rule and, 162–163, 186–187; *Marbury v. Madison* and, 139;

Madison, James *(continued)*
Missouri Compromise of 1820 and,
43–44; nationalism of, 11, 137, 148,
181–182, 184, 187, 190;
nullification and, 179–187; pro-
slavery arguments and, 59–60;
retirement of, 7–8; secession and,
29, 207, 208–212; slavery and, 26,
39, 49, 59, 193; slaves, condition of
and, 129; soil, cult of and, 118;
Southern culture, promotion of and,
78; state interposition and,
179–187; states' rights and, 6–7,
135–136, 181; Supreme Court, U.
S. and, 134, 147–148; tariff wars
and, 172–173, 175–176, 179–187,
186–190; trade policies of, 29;
Virginia, decline of and, 7; Virginia,
fleeing of and, 41; Virginia,
University of and, 69, 69–70;
Virginia Constitution, defects of
and, 151; Virginia Constitutional
Convention of 1829–1830 and,
151–152, 155, 156–157, 162–169;
Virginia slavery debate of
1831–1832 and, 50; Virginia
demography and, 48; Virginia
Ratifying Convention (1788) and,
135–136, 137; Virginia Resolutions
and, 179–187
Magnolia, 78
Maine, 85
majority rule: Madison and, 162–163,
186–187; representation and, 162;
tariff wars and, 186–187; taxation
and, 160; Virginia Constitutional
Convention of 1829–1830 and,
159–161, 162–163
manufacturing: agriculture and,
114–115; economic diversification

and, 114, 114–115; slavery and, 118;
trade and, 175–176; in Virginia, 12
Marbury, William, 138
Marbury v. Madison, 138–139
Marshall, John, 3, 4, 5, 6, 10, 49, 56, 82;
Adams, John appointment of, 138;
agricultural research and, 24; Bonus
Bill of 1816 and, 95; *Cohens v.
Virginia* and, 145–146; Constitution,
U. S. and, 11, 138; Jefferson, Thomas
clash with, 133, 138–139, 143–144;
judicial review and, 138–139;
Marbury v. Madison and, 138–139;
McCulloch v. Maryland and, 142;
nationalism of, 133, 143; public
education and, 75; Southern culture,
promotion of and, 78; Supreme
Court, U. S. interpretation of,
143–144; Virginia Constitutional
Convention of 1829–1830 and, 155,
156; Virginia Ratifying Convention
(1788) and, 145
Marshall, Thomas (nephew of John
Marshall), 124
Marshall, Thomas (son of John
Marshall), 37, 49
Martin, Denny, 140
Martin v. Hunter's Lessee, 141, 148
Maryland, 10, 172
Maryland Court of Appeals, 141
Mason, George, 4, 19, 140, 148, 171;
abolition of slavery and, 51;
Declaration of Rights of 1776 and,
153; federal judiciary and, 134;
internal improvements and, 96;
property, security of and, 193
Mason, James, 77
Massachusetts, 86, 154; banking in,
121; education in, 77; revolutionary
movement and, 4; trade in, 10

Massachusetts Institute of Technology (MIT), 110

materialism, 14, 21, 29, 80, 205

McCoy, Drew R., 117, 166

McCulloch v. Maryland, 141–144, 148, 171

McDowell, James, 50, 52, 75, 203

Mercer, Charles Fenton, 75

Miami Canal, 105

miscegenation, 46, 83

Mississippi, 45; constitution of, 154; trade in, 10

Missouri Compromise of 1820: Constitution, U. S. and, 201–202; demographic impact of, 48; education and, 66–67; Jefferson, Thomas and, 43, 44, 66; Madison, James and, 43–44; Monroe, James and, 43, 44; national government, power of and, 44; secession and, 48; slavery and, 43, 43–44, 201–202; states' rights and, 43, 44, 66

MIT. *See* Massachusetts Institute of Technology

modernization, 112, 115, 116. *See also* banking; industrialization

Monroe, James, 4, 5, 6, 9, 11, 145, 168, 169; Bonus Bill of 1816 and, 95; financial problems of, 28; internal improvements and, 98, 100; Lafayette, Marquis de ceremonial tour and, 3; Missouri Compromise of 1820 and, 43, 44; retirement of, 18; Sedition Act, 180; Virginia Constitutional Convention of 1829–1830 and, 155

Monticello, 26; Jefferson, Thomas life at, 15–17, 18–19; Lafayette, Marquis de ceremonial tour and, 1–2; as place of leisure, 32; slave auction at, 42; Virginia, decline of and, 8

Montpelier (Madison's estate), 7, 26, 168

Moore, Samuel McDowell, 37, 51–52

morality: civic, 3; of slavery, 3, 33, 40, 45, 129, 198; soil, cult of and, 20; unalienable rights and, 3

Morris, Gouverneur, 90, 91, 135, 206

Mount Vernon, 8, 26, 114

Mount Vernon Conference (1785), 93

National Association for the Advancement of Colored People (NAACP), 223

National Gazette (Madison's articles in), 137, 162, 164, 165, 166, 172

national government. *See* federal government

National Industrial Recovery Act (1933), 216

National Intelligencer, 175

nationalism: of Calhoun, John, 176; of Madison, James, 11, 137, 148; of Marshall, John, 133, 143; in North, 69; Story, Joseph and, 6; Washington and, 6, 65, 136

National Labor Relations Act (1935), 214

Nebraska, 207

New Deal, 213–215, 216–217, 219

New England: development in, 115; education in, 77; illiteracy in, 9

New Haven, Conn., 2

Newton, E. W., 75

New York, 9, 41, 90; industrialization in, 117–118; literature of, 78; suffrage in, 154

New York City, N. Y., 2

New York Commercial Advertiser, 90

New York Manumission Society, 131
New York Times, 219
Nicholas, Philip, 132
Nicholas, Wilson Cary, 121
Niles' Register, 155
Norfolk Southern Argus, 76
North: abolitionism, response to of,
    199–200; character of, 34; economic
    development in, 36, 120, 124;
    education in, 61–63, 65, 77;
    illiteracy in, 77; industrialization
    and, 12; internal improvements and,
    110; land productivity in, 9;
    literature of, 78; mentality of, 28,
    31–32, 33–34; nationalism of, 69;
    Southern dependency on, 33–34.
    See also Lowell, Mass.
North American Review, 144, 182, 185
North Carolina, 86, 134, 154
Northwest Ordinance (1787), 42
nostalgia, 11–12, 14, 19, 112, 125, 132,
    205, 210–211
Notes on the State of Virginia (Jefferson),
    19, 28–29, 37, 42–43, 46, 58, 114
nullification: *Brown v. Board of
    Education* and, 221; Calhoun, John
    and, 179, 185, 221; Constitution, U.
    S. and, 190; Jefferson, Thomas and,
    183; Madison, James and, 179–187;
    Ordinance of Nullification (1832)
    and, 184–186; states' rights and,
    108; tariff wars and, 108, 178,
    179–187, 184–187; Union and, 190

Office of Public Roads, 111
Ohio, 41
Old Dominion. *See* Virginia
Olmsted, Frederick Law, 8–9, 34, 35,
    83, 89
Onuf, Peter S., 46

Page, Logan Waller, 111
Panic of 1819, 102, 142
parochialism, 65
The Partisan Leader (Tucker), 204–206
Pate, Henry Clay, 108
Paulding, James Kirke, 7, 10, 130
Pendleton, Edmund, 4, 11
Pennsylvania: internal improvements
    and, 87; labor, value of and, 31; land
    value in, 9, 21; slavery, abolition of
    and, 22
Pennsylvania Portage and Canal
    System, 105
Peterson, Merrill D., 168
Philadelphia National Gazette, 192
Pierce, Franklin, 201
Poe, Edgar Allan, 82
Poinsett, Joel Roberts, 33–34
Poplar Forest plantation, 45
Potomac Canal, 91–93, 104, 105, 106
Potomac Canal Company, 93
Powell, Lewis, 3
press, freedom of. *See* censorship
Preston, James, 50
Preston, William, 51, 54
primogeniture, 20, 153
Princeton University, 65, 84
principles of '98, 182
property: education and, 160; fugitive
    slave, 193; government and
    protection of, 57; intangible
    property and, 165–166; pro-slavery
    arguments and, 56, 57, 60; right to,
    56; suffrage and, 157–161; vote,
    right to and, 154. *See also* land
pro-slavery advocates: Brown, John
    Thompson, 52–53; Dew, Thomas
    Roderick, 57–60, 78, 109, 188–189;
    Fitzhugh, George, 39, 78, 80, 81, 83,
    109, 129–130; Gholson, James,

52–54; Goode, William, 53, 56; Knox, Alexander, 56; Paulding, James Kirke, 130; Tyler, John, 39; Upshur, Abel, 39

pro-slavery arguments: Adams, John Quincy and, 59–60; equality and, 58; freedom and, 58, 81; justice and, 81; legitimization of, 55–60; Madison, James and, 59–60; property, right to and, 56, 60; republican virtue and, 58; slave insurrections and, 58–59; slavery, benevolence of and, 39, 58; slavery and class conflict and, 129–130; southern literature and, 80–83; Southern work ethic and, 40; states' rights and, 53; Virginia slavery debate of 1831–1832 and, 52–54, 55–60; wage-labor system and, 126–131; white laboring class and, 40

provincialism, 6, 12, 65, 70, 78, 83–84, 205. *See also* nostalgia

public education. *See* education

public works. *See* internal improvements

Quakers, 40, 54, 201

race-mixing, 46, 83

railroads, 105–111; Baltimore and Ohio Railroad, 106, 110; canals and, 106; Covington and Ohio Railroad, 109; opposition to development of, 106; Southern Railroad Convention (1851) and, 108. *See also* internal improvements

Randolph, Edmund, 4

Randolph, Jane, 56

Randolph, John, of Roanoke, 11, 21, 38, 78; bankruptcy law and, 22;

education and, 73–74; financial problems of, 23; internal improvements and, 98–100; Southern way of life and, 35; Survey Bill (1824) and, 98–101; tariff wars and, 173; Virginia, decline of and, 10; Virginia Constitutional Convention of 1829–1830 and, 156, 158–159, 160–161, 163, 168

Randolph, Judith, 38

Randolph, Martha Jefferson, 42, 56

Randolph, Mary Jefferson, 42

Randolph, Peyton, 4

Randolph, Richard, 10

Randolph, Thomas Jefferson, 49, 51, 52, 54, 56

Randolph, Thomas Mann, 22

Ransom, John Crowe, 34–35

reapportionment bill of 1811, 91

Reflections on the Revolution in France (Burke), 158

Reform Act of 1832, British, 56

religion: education and, 67–69; freedom of, 16, 153; Virginia, University of and, 68–69

"Report on Manufactures" (Hamilton), 115, 172

"Report on the Alien and Sedition Acts" (Madison), 221

representation: majority rule and, 162; three-fifths rule and, 160, 163–164, 167, 193; Virginia Constitutional Convention of 1829–1830 and, 156–164, 167; in Virginia House of Delegates, 163

Republican Party, Republicans: federal government and, 116; principles of, 69; states' rights and, 69, 116; Virginia presidential monopoly and, 5

"Review of the Debate in the Virginia
    Legislature" (Dew), 57
Rhode Island, 134
Richmond City Council, 84
Richmond Enquirer, 40, 49, 54, 56, 74,
    83, 87, 97, 101, 102–103, 108, 120,
    122, 123, 132, 142–143, 156, 162,
    176, 186, 187, 191, 192, 199, 200
Richmond News Leader, 221
Richmond Society for Promoting
    Agriculture, 24
Richmond Times-Dispatch, 215, 219
Richmond Whig, 192
rights: of slaves, 47, 50, 51–52;
    unalienable, 3, 165–166. *See also*
    states' rights
Ritchie, Thomas, 87, 97, 143, 147,148,
    176, 202
Rivanna River, 92
Rives, William Cabell, 212
Rives, William M., 74, 75
roads, 85–89, 107, 176–178; Bonus Bill
    of 1816 and, 94–98; funding for, 14;
    Survey Bill (1824) and, 98–101. *See
    also* internal improvements
Roane, Spencer, 11, 134, 138, 146,
    148; Missouri Compromise of 1820
    and, 48; nullification and, 185;
    pseudonyms of, 143; secession and,
    48; slavery, spread of and, 48;
    Supreme Court, U. S. and, 140, 142
Roane, William Henry, 49, 51
Robinson, Joan, 124
Rogers, William Barton, 110
Roosevelt, Franklin D.: Jefferson and,
    215; New Deal and, 213–215,
    216–217, 219; popularity of, 219;
    South and, 216, 219
Rothery, Agnes, 217
Ruffin, Edmund, 23, 25, 78

Rumsey, James, 93
Rush, Benjamin, 113

Sabato, Larry, 218
Scottish Enlightenment, 66
secession: abolitionism and, 206–207;
    Jefferson, Thomas and, 29, 206–207;
    Lincoln, Abraham and, 70;
    Madison, James and, 29, 207,
    208–212; Missouri Compromise of
    1820 and, 48; Roane, Spencer and,
    48; slavery and, 206–212; states'
    rights and, 70; tariff wars and, 178,
    185, 186, 189, 197; Virginia and,
    206–212; Washington, George and,
    207. *See also* Civil War
Second Bank of the United States, 56,
    94, 96, 121–122, 141–142, 143
Sedition Act of 1798, 179–180, 182
segregation, 220–224
Senate, U. S., 94, 187, 194–195, 198,
    222, 223; antislavery petitions and,
    198, 201; and tariffs, 174, 186
Seward, Frances, 8–9
Seward, William, 8, 208
Shell, John, 53
Simms, William Gilmore, 78
slave insurrections: John Brown's Raid,
    83–84; Nat Turner rebellion, 48–49,
    51; pro-slavery arguments and,
    58–59
slavery: agriculture and, 26;
    benevolence of, 39, 58, 80–82;
    capitalism and, 124; children and, 8;
    class conflict and, 129–130; in
    District of Columbia, 196–197;
    economic impact of, 40, 45, 52, 74;
    federal government and, 200–202;
    indolence and, 31, 33, 34, 36–40;
    industrialization and, 124–125,

126–129; Jesus Christ and, 52–53, 57; justice and, 81; labor, free and, 41; land value and, 22, 41, 45; master-slave relationship and, 42–43; Missouri Compromise of 1820 and, 43–44, 201–202; morality of, 3, 33, 40, 45, 129, 198; property, security of and, 74, 100, 193; secession and, 206–212; slave breeding and, 45, 47, 52; slave insurrections and, 48–49, 51, 83–84; slave trade and, 42, 45, 198; Southern work ethic and, 36–40; Supreme Court, U. S. and, 201; Union, preservation of and, 198; Virginia, decline of and, 41; Virginia, fleeing of and, 40–42; Virginia slavery debate of 1831–1832 and, 49–60, 198; Virginia demography and, 48–49; Virginia slavery debate of 1831–1832 and, 49–60, 198, 202; wage-slavery and, 126–131; work ethic and, 22, 33, 34, 37. *See also* abolitionism; pro-slavery advocates; pro-slavery arguments; slaves

slaves: breeding of, 45; colonization of, 3, 43, 47; deportation and, 46–47; deportation of, 3, 43, 46; dignity of, 3; education and, 54–55; education of, 76; emancipation of, 3, 45–48, 51–54; equality and, 46; as property, 45, 53, 57; rights of, 3, 47, 50; slavery, benevolence of and, 39; treatment of, 2, 129; Virginia slavery debate of 1831–1832 and, 54; work ethic of, 39. *See also* slavery

slave trade, 42

Smith, Howard, 222

Smith, Margaret Bayard, 19

Social Security Act (1935), 214

soil exhaustion: crop rotation and, 23–24, 26; farming methods and, 23; ignorance and, 27; Jefferson, Thomas and, 18; land value and, 23–28; tobacco and, 23–24, 25, 27, 28; Washington, George and, 23, 24. *See also* agriculture

"Solemn Declaration and Protest of the Commonwealth of Virginia" (Jefferson), 88

South: character of, 31, 33–34; dependency on the North of, 33–34; economic decline of, 33; education in, 66–68; hospitality in, 35; in House of Representatives, U. S., 44–45; literature of, 77–81, 80–83; mentality of, 28, 31–32, 33–34, 63; modernization in, 116; North vs., 2; poverty of, 35; slavery and, 13, 33; time, meaning of and, 34–35; work ethic in, 33

South Carolina, 33, 56; antislavery propaganda and, 191; Ordinance of Nullification (1832) of, 184–186

South Carolina, 56; College of, 66

Southern Literary Messenger, 76, 78, 82, 109

Southern Magazine, 78

Southern Manifesto (1956), 222

Southern Politics (Key), 218

Southern Quarterly Review, 78, 82

Southern Railroad Convention (1851), 108

Southern Review, 82

Southern Rights Association of Richmond, 84

speech, freedom of, 180, 195–196. *See also* Sedition Act of 1798

Stamp Act (1765), 113–114

Stanley, Tom, 221

state sovereignty: Constitution, U. S. and, 137, 141; defense of, 7; Supreme Court, U. S. and, 133, 134, 139–140, 141, 145, 207; tariff wars and, 176; Union and, 178; Virginia presidential monopoly and, 6

states' rights: banking and, 121; Constitution, U. S. and, 181; defense of, 6–7, 134–135; internal improvements and, 108–109; Jefferson, Thomas and, 6; Kentucky and Virginia Resolutions and, 180–182; Madison, James and, 6–7, 137; Missouri Compromise of 1820 and, 43, 44, 66; New Deal and, 217–218; nullification and, 108; pro-slavery arguments and, 53; Republican Party, Republicans and, 69, 116; secession and, 70; Supreme Court, U. S. and, 6, 145–148; tariff wars and, 173–174; Union and, 7; Virginia, University of and, 69, 70; Virginia presidential monopoly and, 6

Statute for Religious Freedom, Virginia (1777), 16

Story, Joseph, 6, 7, 141, 142

suffrage, 150; education and, 160; in New York, 154; property qualifications for, 157–161; in Virginia, 152; Virginia Constitutional Convention of 1829–1830 and, 157–161, 166–168. See also vote, right to

Summers, George, 39, 50, 52, 77

Supreme Court, U. S.: appellate jurisdiction of, 139–141; banking and, 141–142; Bonus Bill of 1816 and, 95; Brown v. Board of Education and, 220–221; Cohens v. Virginia and, 145–146, 148, 171; Constitution, U. S., interpretation of by, 133–134, 143–144; Dred Scott v. Sandford and, 3, 201–202; Fairfax's Devisee v. Hunter's Lessee and, 140–141; judicial review and, 138–139; judicial tyranny and, 133–134; Marbury v. Madison and, 138–139; Martin v. Hunter's Lessee and, 141, 148; McCulloch v. Maryland and, 141–144, 148, 171; slavery and, 201; state governments and, 134; state sovereignty and, 133, 134, 139–140, 141, 145, 207; states' rights and, 6, 145–148; Virginia, decline of and, 3

Survey Bill (1824), 96, 98–101

Swallow Barn (Kennedy), 35, 101, 112

Taney, Roger, 201–202

Tappan, Arthur and Lewis, 192

Tariff Act of 1816, 173, 176

Tariff Act of 1824, 174

Tariff Act of 1828 (Tariff of Abominations), 175, 176

Tariff of Abominations. See Tariff Act of 1828

tariff wars: Calhoun, John and, 175; Clay, Henry and, 176, 186; Compromise Tariff Bill (1833) and, 186; Constitution, U. S. and, 172, 173–174, 175–176, 177; federal government and, 171–172; Force Bill (1833) and, 186; Madison, James and, 173, 175–176, 179–187, 186–190; majority rule and,

186–187; national debt and, 176;
nullification and, 108, 178,
179–187; secession and, 178, 189;
Southern objection to, 173–174;
state interposition and, 177–178;
state sovereignty and, 176; Tariff
Act of 1816 and, 173, 176; Tariff
Act of 1824 and, 174; Tariff Act
of 1828 (Tariff of Abominations)
and, 175, 176

taxation: education and, 73–74, 128;
federal government and, 97;
internal improvements and, 14;
majority rule and, 160; public
education and, 9, 14, 72

Taylor, John, of Caroline, 21, 55, 61;
agricultural reform and, 23–26;
education and, 64; internal
improvements and, 100; slavery and,
129

Tazewell, John, 63

Tazewell, Littleton Waller, 63, 122,
158, 163; abolitionism and, 108,
199–200; abolition societies and,
192; education and, 160; Virginia
Constitutional Convention of
1829–1830 and, 156

Tennessee, 154

Tenth Amendment, 95–96, 137

Texas, 207

Thompson, John, 82

Thoreau, Henry David, 78, 81

three-fifths rule: attempt to abolish,
201; representation and, 160,
163–164, 167, 193; Southern
political leverage and, 45; Virginia
Constitutional Convention of
1829–1830 and, 160, 163–164,
167

Thurmond, Strom, 221

Ticknor, George, 68

tobacco, 23–24, 25, 27, 28, 54, 102

Tocqueville, Alexis de, 12, 33, 34, 36,
54

Tompkins, Daniel, 5

trade: canals and, 91; federal
government and regulation of,
171–172, 179; internal
improvements and, 104;
manufacturing and, 175–176;
Virginia, decline of and, 10

transportation: canals and, 90–101,
104–105; railroads and, 105–111;
roads and, 85–89; water, 104–105.
See also Bonus Bill; internal
improvements; tariff wars.

Travis, Joseph, 48

Tredegar Iron Works, 111, 125

Trist, Nicholas, 167, 184

Tucker, George, 10, 56, 70, 82, 173,
174, 202–203

Tucker, Henry St. George, 11, 39, 40,
51, 66

Tucker, Nathaniel Beverley, 10, 78, 82;
internal improvements and, 109;
The Partisan Leader of, 204–206

Tucker, St. George, 40

Turner, Nat, 48–49, 51

Tyler, John, 3, 11, 119; banking and,
122; slavery, defense of by, 39; tariff
wars and, 173, 186; Virginia
Constitutional Convention of
1829–1830 and, 156

Union: national university and, 64;
nullification and, 190; preservation
of, 198; secession and, 207,
209–210; state sovereignty and, 178;
states' rights and, 7. See also
nationalism

United States Post Office Department,
    191–192, 194–196
Upshur, Abel: slavery, defense of by,
    39, 129; Virginia Constitutional
    Convention of 1829–1830 and, 156,
    160–161, 167
urbanization, 14, 29, 82, 91, 114

Van Buren, Martin, 33, 156, 185, 201
Vermont, 154, 207
Virginia, University of, 56, 62, 68–71;
    faculty of, 2, 69; Jefferson, Thomas
    and, 1, 68–71, 83; Lafayette,
    Marquis de ceremonial tour and,
    1–2; religion and, 68–69;
    Republican values and, 69–70;
    Rotunda of, 1, 68; states' rights and,
    69, 70; Virginia slavery debate of
    1831–1832 and, 70; Virginia
    intellectual life and, 83
Virginia Agricultural Convention
    (1836), 25
Virginia Bill of Rights (1776), 4
Virginia Constitution (1776), 151
Virginia Constitution (1830), 167–168
Virginia Constitutional Convention of
    1829–1830, 77; delegates at,
    155–156; Jefferson, Thomas and,
    157, 158, 159; Madison, James and,
    151–152, 155, 156–157, 162–169;
    majority rule and, 159–161,
    162–163; Marshall, John and, 155,
    156; Monroe, James and, 155;
    Randolph, John, of Roanoke and,
    158–159, 160; representation and,
    156–164; suffrage and, 157–161,
    166–168; three-fifths rule and, 158,
    160, 163–164, 167; Virginia
    Constitution, defects of and,
    151–155

Virginia Court of Appeals, 48
Virginia debate of 1831–1832. See
    Virginia slavery debate of
    1831–1832
Virginia General Assembly, 102, 208;
    segregation and, 222
Virginia Historical and Philosophical
    Society, 78
Virginia House of Delegates, 10;
    antislavery petitions and, 196;
    banking and, 120, 121–122; internal
    improvements and, 102; land,
    accessibility of and, 20;
    representation in, 151, 163, 167;
    slavery debate of 1831–1832 in,
    49–60
Virginia Literary and Philosophical
    Society, 78
Virginia (Old Dominion): American
    Revolution and, 4; aristocracy of,
    10, 14; Confederate States of
    America and, 55, 212;
    Constitutional Convention (1787)
    and, 4; decline of, 3–4, 7–14, 28–29,
    48, 154; demography in, 9, 48–49,
    72, 91, 152, 203; economic decline
    in, 7, 9–10, 113, 103, 107, 118;
    education in, 9, 61–84, 220–224;
    First Continental Congress (1774)
    and, 4, 5; Great Seal of, 21;
    indolence and, 31–33, 34–36;
    industrialization in, 9, 125–131;
    intellectual life in, 83–84; land
    value in, 9, 21–23; leadership in, 4,
    6, 11–12, 49–50, 55, 74–75,
    159–160, 167, 189, 192, 209–211,
    214–216, 222, 224; life of leisure in,
    34–36, 36–40; literature of, 12;
    manufacturing in, 12; moral
    problems of, 7; motto of, 31;